8/98

CRAFTING A CLASS

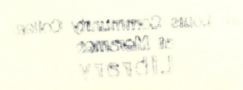

CRAFTING A CLASS

COLLEGE ADMISSIONS AND FINANCIAL AID, 1955–1994

Elizabeth A. Duffy
and
Idana Goldberg

PRINCETON UNIVERSITY PRESS   PRINCETON, NEW JERSEY

Library of Congress Cataloging-in-Publication Data
Duffy, Elizabeth A., 1966–
Crafting a class : college admissions and financial aid, 1955–1994
/ Elizabeth A. Duffy and Idana Goldberg.
p. cm.
Includes bibliographical references and index.
ISBN 0-691-01683-6 (cloth : alk. paper)
1. Universities and colleges—United States—Admission—
History—20th century—Case studies.   2. College attendance—United
States—History—20th century—Case studies.   3. Student aid—United
States—History—20th century—Case studies.   4.Universities and
colleges—Ohio—Admission—History—20th century.   5. College
attendance—Ohio—History—20th century.   6. Student aid—Ohio—
History—20th century.   7. Universities and colleges—Massachusetts—
Admission—History—20th century.   8. College
attendance—Massachusetts—History—20th century.   9. Student aid—
Massachusetts—History—20th century.   I. Goldberg, Idana,
1971–. II. Title.
LB2351.2.D84   1997
378.1′61′0973′09045—dc21   97-5645

Publication of this book has been aided by a grant from
The Andrew W. Mellon Foundation

This book has been composed in New Caledonia

Princeton University Press books are printed on acid-free paper
and meet the guidelines for permanence and durability of the
Committee on Production Guidelines for Book Longevity of the
Council on Library Resources

Printed in the United States of America

1   3   5   7   9   10   8   6   4   2

To our parents, who inspired us by their example

Contents

Figures and Tables

FIGURES

TABLE

Foreword

William G. Bowen and Harold T. Shapiro

ALTHOUGH today's liberal arts college is a distinctively American contribution to contemporary higher education, its roots go back not only to Colonial America but also to the British colleges and universities of the seventeenth and eighteenth centuries. Moreover, its formative attributes tell us much about the history of our country and the place of higher education within it. In the mid-nineteenth century, the traditional liberal arts college was typically small in scale, rural, privately controlled rather than publicly supervised, concerned with the development of character and piety no less than intellect, and rarely very comfortably off—often having struggled for survival. Today's liberal arts colleges still share many of these attributes.

Since the mid-nineteenth century, some of the early liberal arts colleges have evolved into private research universities, generally retaining their "colleges" within them. We have also seen the evolution of major universities with a technical emphasis from what were originally technical institutes; the establishment of great land grant universities and of other "comprehensive" institutions, frequently located in urban areas; and then the "filling out" of state systems of higher education, through the establishment of more layers of four-year institutions and, finally, the community college movement of the 1960s and 1970s. As a result, the traditional liberal arts college has a very different and far less dominant role within American higher education than it did in earlier periods. Yet these colleges continue to serve very important functions:

- They enroll substantial numbers of high-achieving students, including a disproportionate share of those who go on to graduate and professional schools;
- Their curricula, intimate communities, and opportunities for close interaction with faculty represent an educational philosophy that most of us would hate to see lost;
- More generally, they constitute part of the private sector in a system of higher education that works to retain considerable independence from current political pressures;
- Finally, they remain important "assets in being," with their libraries, laboratories, residence halls, faculty communities, devoted adherents in all walks of life, and valued ties to local communities.

In short, these unique institutions unquestionably matter.

In this book, which is the product of two years of intensive work, Elizabeth Duffy and Idana Goldberg study the experiences over the last 40 years of 16 liberal arts colleges in Ohio and Massachusetts in "crafting a class": recruiting, admitting, and enrolling successive cohorts of students. As the historical record they present makes abundantly clear, this is a highly complex process in which external forces interact with the inherited missions, present circumstances, and particular needs of individual institutions. Their study is based on the premise that to understand what has happened, why it happened, and what may lie ahead, there is no substitute for looking in detail at specific institutions that have had to confront defined problems and make actual choices. Aggregative statistics alone can take us only so far. The 16 institutions that agreed to participate in this study have the advantage of being similar enough—and yet different enough—to permit the kinds of close comparisons that truly inform. The group includes two of the most selective coeducational liberal arts colleges in the country, a group of highly respected women's colleges in Massachusetts, and very good colleges in the Midwest that nonetheless have "admit rates" (percentages of applicants offered admission) that range from 65 percent to 90 percent. Liberal arts colleges in all parts of the country (as well as other selective institutions, including major universities) will see the relevance of the lessons learned by observing how these colleges coped with dramatic fluctuations in applicant pools, decisions of powerful university "neighbors" to become coeducational, the impact of the civil rights movement, changes in the demographic profile of the college-age population, major shifts in federal financial aid policies, and the veritable sea of changes in modes of recruitment and the aggressive use of financial aid.

The decision by Duffy and Goldberg to focus on student populations, rather than on faculty development, curricula, administration, or institutional finance, is, in part, no more than a way of limiting the scope of the study. But it also reflects an important reality. As one commentator on an earlier draft of their manuscript put it: "These institutions live and die on their ability to recruit *enough* students, enough *good* students, and enough good students *who can pay.*" Obviously, curricula, faculty, location, finances, reputation, and many other internal factors affect the ability of colleges to meet their enrollment targets—but so do powerful external "waves" (economic, demographic, and sociopolitical) that wash over all institutions. As Duffy and Goldberg demonstrate, these external forces change much faster than established institutional strengths and weaknesses, which function as rough "constants," at least over intervals measured in decades. It is, then, the interplay between changes in the external environment and policy decisions made (and not made) by individual institutions that interests the authors.

Duffy and Goldberg also help the reader understand that how an institution fares—what range of options it has open to it as it confronts, say, new forms of competition for students engendered by increasing use of merit aid programs—depends greatly on both its initial "market position" and the behavior of its closest competitors. It is differences of this kind that explain what the authors refer to as "the Ohio merit wars," as well as the more restrained approach to the use of merit aid that still prevails in the Northeast. Similarly, their discussion of the ripple effects of the coeducation movement among formerly all-male Eastern colleges and universities in the late 1960s and early 1970s makes it clear that the consequences for women's colleges—and for colleges that were already coeducational—depended very much on how vulnerable each school was to rather sudden changes in its applicant pool. Easy as it is to exalt the importance of "mission," we are reminded again that the ability to insist on one principle or another also depends in no small degree on practical considerations such as the pulling power of the school and the size of its endowment.

In examining trends in applicant pools, admit rates, yields, enrollment, measures of quality, and outlays on financial aid, numbers plainly matter—a lot. Accordingly, Duffy and Goldberg began their work by laboriously collecting detailed data from each of the 16 participating institutions. But they did not content themselves with simply feeding the raw numbers into a standard statistical program that would quickly grind out "results." Rather, they treated their statistical data as indicators of questions to be asked, benchmarks, and reality checks. By moving forward to extensive searches of archival records and discussions with individuals who are or had been key decision makers at individual colleges, Duffy and Goldberg added a dimension of "thick description" to their work that is lacking in all too many efforts to explain empirical phenomena. What we have here is really a "bottoms-up" history. The aggregate statistical data are enriched with story lines told through memos, reports, and other materials written at the time decisions were made—often in the words of some of the chief protagonists. The result is a rich blend of data, quotations, and interpretations, all placed in the context of national developments and summaries of earlier studies of liberal arts colleges.

The product is highly readable as well as informative. Even experienced deans and faculty members at institutions of all kinds, not just at liberal arts colleges, will learn a great deal about the evolution of policies and practices. Certainly we did. For example, Duffy and Goldberg document carefully how the admissions process itself has been transformed from "early gatekeeping" to a part of a businesslike operation called "enrollment management" by some of its practitioners. Similarly, financial aid officers of even 25 years ago would have a hard time recognizing how their counterparts of today function. The authors also explain the penalties paid for holding on too long to established practice.

The blending of quantitative analysis and qualitative examination of records and memories permits the reader to understand what did not happen, as well as what did. Time and again, we encounter "facts" that ordinarily might seem bland—a good example is the extraordinary stability in the African American share of enrollments at these colleges from the early 1970s to the present day. But behind this rather monotonous line on a graph is a story of sharp shifts in recruitment strategies, sobering lessons learned about what is possible as distinct from what is desirable, and a clear warning for colleges about the danger of overly optimistic projections of future applicant pools as the country's demographic profile continues to change. No regression equation by itself could have captured this textured set of lessons beneath the surface of the numbers.

A word should also be said about "attitude." As many students of higher education have noted, institutional histories are of limited value because of the common tendency toward self-pleading. At the other end of the spectrum, many of us have become all too familiar with the "unloving critics" of higher education, who seem interested mainly in proving points that one suspects are not new to them. We would characterize the attitude revealed here as a combination of independence and empathy; Duffy and Goldberg respect the missions of the colleges that they have studied, and the ways in which dedicated professionals have tried to solve hard problems.

This study has no single plot line. It certainly does not conclude that these colleges are endangered, never mind doomed, or even that they will diminish in importance. On the contrary, the authors believe that these venerable places will continue to be able to attract a sufficient number of able students for whom they will be the preferred choice—which is hardly to suggest that nothing will change. One of the themes running through this book is the presence among the colleges of what the authors call "stratification" (revealed, for example, by substantial differences in average SAT scores). The evidence demonstrates that over these 40 years stratification, as judged by the preferences of many students, has increased. In short, the "distance" between the colleges that are—and have been—the most selective and those that are less selective has tended to grow. The ensuing dynamic is both interesting and instructive and it certainly raises major questions for the future.

First, has the process of "nationalizing" the competition for places in leading liberal arts colleges and the recruitment of students run its course? Whether the answer to that question is yes or no, what will be the long-term effects of this "nationalizing" phenomenon on the viability of colleges that once occupied niches of various kinds (religious as well as geographical)? The data reported here suggest that colleges that once could recruit confidently from their own "cachement basin" can no longer do so—at least not with the same confidence concerning yields. Much more information about colleges is now available to everyone; transportation is easier and sometimes even cheaper than it used to be; students and families are more mobile. One evident effect is a closer linking of the fortunes of schools in different locales and regions. Amherst College today recruits successfully all over the United States and abroad as well. As a result, any change in either circumstances or policies at Amherst will have at least second-order effects on a larger number of other schools that would have been much more insulated from Amherst 40 years ago.

When Duffy and Goldberg began their study, they elected to work with schools in Ohio and Massachusetts in part because they thought that the differences between the states (especially in the role of the public sector in higher education) might reveal interesting patterns. In fact, they find that state location *per se* no longer makes much difference. Much more important are differences in mission, reputation, cost, and other attributes of a college that have little if anything to do with its geographic location. The most general implication of this "nationalizing" process, it seems to us, is that society-wide trends must be expected to move through the entire system of higher education more rapidly than in the past, and perhaps to have especially powerful effects on the less strongly established institutions.

Second, what is the future of merit aid, awarded without reference to students' financial needs? Is it a good thing or a bad thing? In their final chapter, the authors acknowledge that they now have a more nuanced view of merit aid than they did when they began their study. At the very least, they now see the value to a particular college of a carefully crafted program of merit aid that enables them to increase the quality of their student bodies while simultaneously meeting enrollment targets and controlling financial aid outlays. But what are the spillover effects of such policies? Will the benefits to College A be offset by harmful effects on College B? An even larger question has to do with public benefits and costs. What are the relevant criteria for assessing whether the public good is advanced or set back by the spread of merit aid programs? Does the answer depend on how they are devised and implemented, and by what entity? Would the answer change if we were talking about nationally supported merit aid programs that were portable, rather than institutionally oriented programs? A related query is whether the data and stories recounted in this study foretell the end of need-based aid as it was developed and understood in the 1960s. These questions inevitably connect to federal and state policies, and they deserve the sustained attention of a wider set of scholars.

Third and last: Is there any likelihood that the overall excess supply of places in liberal arts colleges will diminish? Should it? Is this an issue of public policy? These questions are prompted by recognition that the competitive pressures besetting almost all of the colleges in this study (there are a few exceptions) derive at least in part from a chronic imbalance between supply and demand in this sector—an imbalance that affects, directly or indirectly, the vast majority of liberal arts colleges. Some time ago, a staff member at the Mellon Foundation asked the presidents of a number of leading liberal arts colleges if their colleges would be better off, educationally and financially, if it were possible to increase enrollment while maintaining quality and retaining present financial aid programs. The overwhelming response was "absolutely." As more and more colleges with excess places in the entering class have used tuition discounts in attempts to bid away candidates from institutions that are slightly more prestigious, the pressures generated by this endemic excess supply of places have moved from one level of colleges up to the next. In this respect, the market plainly works.

But in other respects, it does not. There is a fundamental disequilibrium in the system, which results in large part from the combination of (1) the great difficulty faced by colleges trying to "downsize," given both their high levels of fixed costs and the never-ending pressure to augment offerings; and (2) the lack of mechanisms in the nonprofit sector that would encourage (or sometimes even allow) institutions experiencing severe problems to merge with stronger institutions or to close normally, naturally, and peacefully. To be sure, the question of overall excess supply is not one that Duffy and Goldberg set out to address, and we list it at the close of this Foreword only to indicate that one mark of a good book is that it stimulates broader inquiries at the same time that it answers its own set of questions. *Crafting a Class* passes this test with flying colors.

Preface

WE THOUGHT long and hard about how to title this book. *Creating* a Class? *Recruiting* a Class? *Shaping* a Class? *Building* a Class? None of them seemed quite right. Then we hit upon *crafting*. On the one hand, the verb "to craft" connotes constraints—working with given raw materials and within rules and parameters. On the other hand, "to craft" allows for the exercise of judgment and implies the use of skill, ingenuity, and care. Such an interplay between external constraints and internal actions describes well the complex system of admissions and financial aid that has developed at selective colleges and universities in this country.

Liberal arts colleges have a deeply vested self-interest in enrolling a class of the desired quality and size. Their intimate environments and emphasis on broad learning require that colleges attract students with strong academic qualifications. Because they are highly dependent on tuition revenues, colleges must also meet their enrollment targets. These twin goals of class size and quality are what make liberal arts college admissions challenging.

It was impossible to study the admissions and financial aid histories of all the liberal arts colleges in the country, so we limited our study to the most selective colleges in Ohio and Massachusetts, two states with strong but distinct liberal arts college traditions. Ohio's colleges have been largely coeducational since the beginning of the century, while in Massachusetts there is a long legacy of single-sex education. The control of the higher education systems in Ohio and Massachusetts also differs. Ohio has a strong public college and university system that enrolls 72 percent of college students in the state. By contrast, private colleges and universities in Massachusetts enroll 68 percent of the state's postsecondary students.

We chose to begin with conditions in 1955, a point in time after the temporary bulge in applicants from the GI Bill but before the prolonged enrollment surge in the early 1960s when the first children of the baby boom entered college. The standards established during this period, which became known as the "Tidal Wave," have set much of the tone for admissions and financial aid ever since—too much so, in our view, since the 1960s were clearly an aberrational period.

METHODOLOGY

In the fall of 1994, we sent surveys to 17 of the 19 liberal arts colleges in Ohio and Massachusetts designated Baccalaureate I in the 1994 Carnegie

Classification.[1] All but one agreed to participate.[2] We asked for information for five-year intervals between 1955 and 1985 and then for each year from 1985 through 1994. (See Appendix A for copies of the survey forms.) We requested detailed data on the academic, geographic, and racial composition of applicants, admitted students, and enrolled students as well as enrollment data and statistics on institutional financial aid expenditures. The data that we sought—such as mean SAT scores, percentage of minority students, and institutional dollars spent on financial aid—seemed standard to us. However, what we consider to be basic information in 1996 has not always been seen as essential, or even as important enough to save. Thus, some of the data we requested was unavailable. Also, available information was not always consistent over time, either between institutions or within a single institution.

In order to fill in the holes in the data, resolve discrepancies, and get the stories behind the numbers, we visited all 16 liberal arts colleges in our study. At each college we met with current college administrators, including admissions and financial aid directors, registrars, and directors of institutional research. In addition, we spoke with former college officials who had long institutional memories. Many still lived in the town where the college was located, often just blocks from campus. To a person, the admissions and financial aid directors generously welcomed us into their homes and offices and recounted their experiences, explained the numbers, and pointed us toward relevant reports and materials. At the majority of the colleges we met with people whose tenures spanned the full period of our study.[3]

At each school we visited, we also spent time in the college archives. The archives ranged from fully-cataloged collections in well-appointed, oak-paneled rooms, to boxes of unsorted musty documents in dank basements. At two schools we were even offered surgical masks to combat the mold. (Fortunately neither of us has allergies!) In the archives we found copies of annual admissions and financial aid reports, correspondence between administrators, special college studies and reports, and back issues of student newspapers and alumni magazines. All of these materials were essential as we pieced together the admissions and financial aid histories of the colleges.

Although our study began as a data analysis project, the missing and inconsistent data together with the small sample size precluded any sophisticated statistical analysis. Instead, we have used the data we received from the colleges descriptively; the data have formed the framework upon which we have built our understanding of institutional histories. Trends in the data pointed us toward the questions to ask and the periods on which to focus. The data also allowed us to verify the archival record since reports and commentaries are often subjective. What emerged was a history of enrollment, admission, and financial aid that was informed by institutional data, rather than a statistical analysis of data reinforced by historical material.

EXTERNAL AND INTERNAL FACTORS

Prior to World War II, most liberal arts colleges were very small (enrolling fewer than 1,000 students) and the preserve of a homogeneous, white, upper-income elite. Admissions was not very competitive, federal student aid did not exist, and most colleges awarded only a limited number of scholarships to less affluent students as a reward for outstanding achievement. With the influx of students first from the GI Bill and subsequently from the baby boom, the process of both admissions and financial aid changed dramatically.

The 1960s represented a golden age for higher education. Beginning in the late 1950s and extending through the end of the 1960s, applications and enrollments swelled at colleges and universities across the United States. This so-called tidal wave of students allowed colleges to expand significantly their enrollments and simultaneously to improve their institutional profiles. In such an environment, the primary purpose of admissions became to *select* students from a surplus of highly qualified applicants. Because applicant pools were so strong academically, the colleges had the luxury of considering other factors such as ethnicity, socioeconomic status, and nonacademic traits as they crafted their classes. Efforts to attract the best students from all backgrounds were aided by a new federal program of financial aid and by a new system for calculating the financial need of students.

A sharp reversal of institutional fortunes occurred in the 1970s. The ubiquitous growth in size and quality in the 1960s had obscured a growing stratification in admissions among the colleges and a heightened competition for the best students. The move toward coeducation and continued growth of the public system in the late 1960s and early 1970s, coupled with a leveling off in the number of students attending college, brought these issues to the fore. Enrollments at all but the newly coeducational colleges in our study stabilized or declined, and student quality fell everywhere despite increased recruitment efforts. In part to help stem the enrollment losses at private institutions, both federal and institutional financial aid expenditures grew.

Since 1980, quality and enrollment concerns have predominated. In order to cope with unfavorable population trends, colleges have adopted business practices. Today, enrollment management supplements (and in some cases even supersedes) the traditional admissions process. An enrollment manager coordinates admissions, financial aid, retention, and institutional research in order to ensure that the college achieves its enrollment goals of quality and diversity and still realizes a positive net tuition revenue. Financial aid has become a tool with which to build a class. To that end, many colleges now award aid not only on the basis of financial need but also on the basis of academic merit regardless of financial need. Even those colleges that still have need-only financial aid policies generally package their awards to attract the top students.

All the colleges in our study felt the impact of the same broad trends. However, the quality, coed status, and location of each college determined how it adapted. The historical quality of a college's student body, as measured by SAT scores and high school class ranks, determined its ability to enroll a future class of the desired size and quality, to attract a diverse student body, and even to maintain a need-based aid policy. Similarly, a college's decision to become coed or not had immediate and continuing implications for its admissions situation and the quality of its student body. Conventional wisdom says that women's colleges were the hardest hit by the coeducation movement. Although many women's colleges did face greater competition than ever before, colleges that were already coed suffered just as significant losses of high-quality students, who had many new options. Finally, the location of a college affected a college's ability to craft a class, but not to the degree that we had anticipated. In recent years, the location of a college has been a reliable predictor of its use of merit aid and its success in enrolling students of particular ethnicities, but other outcomes have been driven more by a college's coed status and selectivity than by its geography.

STRUCTURE OF THE BOOK

This book is divided into three sections. Part I contains three chapters which focus on trends in enrollment and admissions. Chapter 1 examines when and why the institutions expanded their enrollments. In Chapter 2, we explore the changing policies, purposes, and priorities of the admissions office and its role in the life of the college. In Chapter 3 we consider the quality of matriculated students. We analyze not only SAT scores and class ranks, but also how the criteria used to define quality evolved.

In Part II, we turn to the institutions' responses to two major social forces—the women's movement and the civil rights movement. Chapter 4 explores the push toward coeducation in the late 1960s and early 1970s. We examine specifically why men's colleges were the first to make the momentous decision to become coed and what factors led many elite women's colleges, including those in our study, to remain single sex. We also examine how the men's schools became coeducational. Chapter 5 looks at the efforts of the colleges to recruit and enroll more minority students. We investigate the legacy of the civil rights movement, analyzing how the colleges' commitments to increased access and diversity differ today from the policies of the late 1960s and early 1970s.

Part III chronicles the evolution of financial aid. Chapter 6 summarizes aid policies and spending levels both at the institutions in our study and nationally from the mid-1950s to the present. The emphasis in Chapter 7 is on the use and impact of merit aid in the last decade.

The experiences of the colleges we studied demonstrate how decisions that are made at the institutional level reflect and respond to environmental changes. It is also clear that past decisions affect future choices. Although we focus in this study on just sixteen liberal arts colleges in two states, the operational trade-offs with which these colleges were confronted provide insights into institutional strategies that are relevant to all types of institutions.

Acknowledgments

WE WOULD like to thank our colleagues at The Andrew W. Mellon Foundation—William G. Bowen, Richard Ekman, Alice F. Emerson, Mimi McGrath, Kamla Motihar, Thomas I. Nygren, Sarah E. Turner, James Shulman, and Harriet Zuckerman—who read and commented on various drafts of this manuscript, as well as our other colleagues at the foundation, who, along with those mentioned above, supported us during the two years that we worked on this book. We would also like to thank Princeton University and the Mellon Foundation for inviting us to participate in the Conference on Higher Education at Princeton on March 21–23, 1996. The comments we received on the conference paper we presented helped us to write this book. Most of all, however, we would like to thank the 16 colleges that provided us with data and opened their archives to us and the many college administrators—both past and present—who shared their insights into the complex process of crafting a class. Although they are too numerous to mention individually here, they are listed in Appendix B. Many of the administrators are quoted in the book, and the ideas of all of them shaped our understanding of the evolution of admissions and financial aid over the last 40 years.

Part I

ENROLLMENT, ADMISSIONS, AND QUALITY

CHAPTER 1

Enrollment Pressures: Ebbs and Flows

> Generally speaking there is no "perfect" size of a college or university. . . .
> Members of each generation tend to think their institution was at its best size
> when they were there. And, perhaps it was. The "best" size clearly varies with
> the time and with what a college or university wishes to do and to be, and on
> what the consequences of a change would be.[1]

OVER THE course of the 40 years which our study spans, all of our colleges
grappled (more than once) with the question of what size they should be.
Two counter considerations framed their discussions. On the one hand,
there is a minimum enrollment level which enables a liberal arts college to
function effectively. Below some size a college can't afford to offer a reasonable variety of courses, attract distinguished faculty, or support its infra-
structure. On the other hand, beyond some size an institution may lose its
small-college character.

Liberal arts colleges tend to have small endowments and high expenditures per student. Therefore, they are extremely reliant on tuition revenue.
In order to maintain current operating levels, colleges must meet enrollment targets that are consistent with existing commitments. The ability of
a college to meet its enrollment target—given demographic trends and the
size and quality of its expected applicant pool—is perhaps more important
even than the target itself. Once a college has set an enrollment target,
deviations around that target cause revenues to change much faster than
costs, because budgetary commitments to faculty, curriculum, and facilities
must be made before final enrollment numbers are known.

Given the variability of entering class size, we concentrate throughout
this chapter on total undergraduate enrollment rather than first-year enrollment. When we refer to enrollment, we mean full-time undergraduate
enrollment. The few colleges in our study with graduate programs have
very modest graduate enrollments, and, except where noted, part-time enrollments at our schools were also insignificant.

In order to understand the enrollment histories at the colleges in our
study, we divided the 40 years that our study encompasses into three periods. The first period—the years between 1955 and 1970—was known as
the "Tidal Wave" since both applications and enrollments swelled at colleges and universities across the United States, including almost all of the
liberal arts colleges in our study. During this period, the rate at which

a college expanded seemed to depend most on its starting size. In the second period, the decade of the 1970s, the rapid growth rate that higher education had been experiencing leveled off and a stable "zero growth" period ensued. In addition, coeducation, a drop in college-going rates, and worsening economic conditions led to major shifts in enrollments not only between the different sectors of higher education but also among liberal arts colleges. The only colleges in our study that were able to expand significantly during this period were the men's colleges that became coeducational. The third period, which extends from 1980 through the present, saw a renewed emphasis by parents and the public first on quality and then on value. The most prestigious colleges were able to capitalize on these trends and maintain, or even moderately expand, their enrollments. Many of the other colleges in our study experienced declining enrollments either because they couldn't fill their classes with students of desired quality or because they purposefully reduced their class sizes in order to improve their class profile.

THE TIDAL WAVE (1955–1970)

After the veterans returned from fighting World War II and settled down to peace and prosperity, the country's birthrate exploded. As a result, between 1955 and 1970, the number of 18- to 24-year-olds (generally considered to be the college-age population) grew 60 percent, from 15 million to 24 million. Even more important, the high school graduation and college-going rates increased. (See Figures 1.1A and 1.1B.) In 1955, only 63 percent of 17-year-olds were high school graduates. In 1968, when the high school graduation rate peaked, 77 percent of 17-year-olds had earned high school diplomas. The absolute numbers of high school graduates approximately doubled between 1955 and 1969 from 1.4 million to 2.8 million. College enrollment rates also increased nearly 10 percentage points during the 1960s so that in 1968, when the college-going rate reached its peak, 55 percent of high school graduates were attending college.[2]

These demographic facts reflected a heightened sense among all Americans of the importance of education at both the high school and college levels. After World War II, the GI Bill opened up educational opportunities for millions of veterans, many of whom had previously not considered a college education. A decade later in 1957, the Russians launched *Sputnik I*, causing the United States to doubt its scientific and military capabilities. Shortly after, economists, most notably Theodore Schultz and Gary Becker, began to develop models of "human capital" that articulated why well-educated workers were essential to the country's economic strength and, thus, enabled policy makers to justify greater investments in

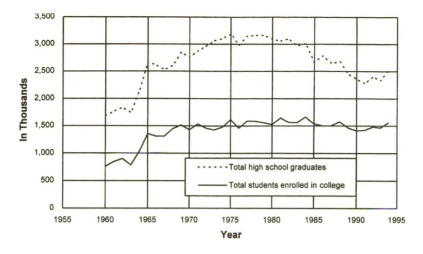

Figure 1.1A. Number of High School Graduates and Number of Students Enrolled in College (1960–1994).

Source: U.S. Department of Education, National Center for Education Statistics, *Digest of Education Statistics, 1995* (Washington, DC: U.S. Government Printing Office, 1995).

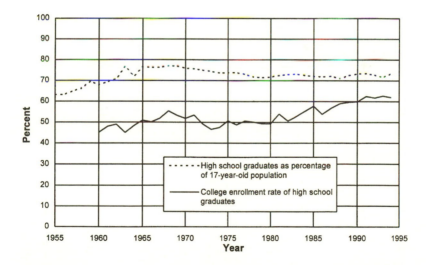

Figure 1.1B. High School Graduation Rate and College Enrollment Rate (1955–1994).

Source: U.S. Department of Education, National Center for Education Statistics, *Digest of Education Statistics, 1995* (Washington, DC: U.S. Government Printing Office, 1995).

higher education.[3] The concept that there was a social return to higher education, coupled with the "security fear" prompted by *Sputnik*, committed the United States to increasing the number of students graduating from high school and continuing to college. This national commitment to expanding the educational attainment of students coincided with the maturation of the first children of the baby boom, leaving colleges and universities overwhelmed by the sheer number of applications.

The tidal wave of students brought new pressures (and opportunities) for the colleges in our study to enlarge their student bodies. At the extremes, either colleges could maintain their same admissions standards and expand their enrollments to accommodate the increased number of applicants, or they could stay the same size and become far more selective. In reality, the sheer number of applicants precluded the first option. A 1956 staff paper entitled "Admissions Problems in a Time of Expanding Enrollments" described what would happen if Ohio Wesleyan continued its current admissions policies:

> If we start with the proposition that Ohio Wesleyan will maintain its present position in relation to the total number of applications received by its most directly competitive sister Ohio colleges, then we may expect an annual increase of at least 10 percent in applications received during the next decade. Under these conditions Ohio Wesleyan could reasonably look forward to a total of 2,319 applications in 1960–61 and 4,105 in 1966–67. The unmodified continuation of present practices would in turn lead to 1,948 approvals in 1960–61 and 3,448 in 1966–67. To state such a prospect is, of course, to affirm that we must find good ways to keep it from happening.[4]

Although no college in our study opened its door to all qualified applicants, many of them did expand. The colleges we studied grew by an average of 62 percent between 1955 and 1970. Such growth necessitated major capital investments. A 1955 report described what was required at Wheaton College, which at the time enrolled fewer than 550 students:

> In order to accommodate 750 students the College will need to erect within the next few years three additional dormitories. . . . A new dining room and kitchen will have to be provided . . . steps must be taken to erect a new classroom building. . . . Some other campus structures will need to be enlarged to accommodate the increased student body. These will include the library, the gymnasium and the science building.[5]

Because growth required substantial investments in classroom and dormitory buildings, there was often a delay—sometimes of nearly a decade—between the initial decision by trustees to expand and the actual admission of a larger class while a college first raised capital and then built new facilities. These delays would become highly problematic for some colleges in the late 1960s and early 1970s when the college-going population leveled off.

The major reason that colleges in our study chose to expand during the 1960s was financial. The trustees of Wheaton voted to increase the size of the college by 40 percent in 1955 because "the enlarged college will result in providing a sounder educational and economic unit."[6] The College of Holy Cross's 1962 decision to grow was also "made with the hope that increased tuition would help the financial status of the College."[7] For at least one of the colleges in our study, expansion was perceived as a way to solve recurring deficit problems. In 1965, Kenyon, which had had an operating deficit each year since World War II, decided to expand from 750 to approximately 1,250—a sizable expansion especially considering that the college had already grown 53 percent between 1955 and 1965. In explaining the decision, the treasurer of the college, Samuel Lord, wrote in the *Kenyon Alumni Bulletin*, "I believe that the indicated expansion of the student body without a corresponding increase in costs, in combination with the continuing growing success of our development efforts, will solve our financial problems—at least for the next decade."[8]

As shown in Figure 1.2, there was a strong inverse correlation between the size of the full-time undergraduate student body in 1955 and the extent of expansion over the next decade and a half.[9] In general, the smallest colleges increased their enrollments by the largest percentages, in order to benefit from economies of scale. Not only did the small colleges have the most to gain by growing, but they also had the least to lose. Liberal arts colleges have always valued their smallness as essential for forging close bonds between and among students and faculty. Those colleges that were the smallest to begin with could afford to expand significantly without worrying that they would sacrifice these relationships.

The three colleges that lie well below the trend line in Figure 1.2 grew less than would have been expected considering their starting sizes. These colleges were among the most competitive and wealthiest colleges both in our study and in the country. That the most prestigious and selective colleges and universities were limiting their expansion was recognized even at the time. In 1966, Richard Pearson, president of the College Board, wrote an article outlining ways for liberal arts colleges to increase their influence in the educational system. In it, he lamented, "The older, liberal colleges and universities have limited their expansion, for compelling reasons, to something on the order of 10 to 20 percent. Rather than expand, the liberal institutions have raised admissions standards to the point where they are denying admission to many students whom the schools identify as both able and well prepared."[10] In the epilogue to his often-cited *The American College and University: A History*, Frederick Rudolph explained just how unusual such behavior was:

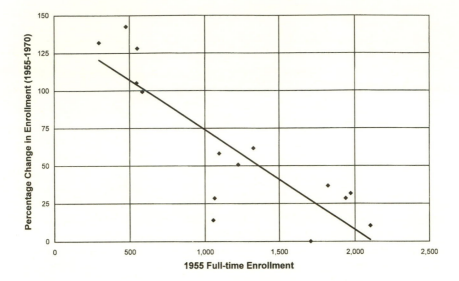

Figure 1.2. Relationship between 1955 Enrollment and Enrollment Growth (1955–1970).

The question of numbers was no question at all, except perhaps in the little quality colleges and Ivy League universities of the East, where the belief existed that a choice could be made between quantity and quality; here the admissions standards would go up faster and higher than the dormitories. Elsewhere, in characteristic American fashion the pursuit of quality and quantity would . . . be accepted as an inevitable challenge and as a public responsibility."[11]

An Obligation to Expand

Although the liberal arts colleges in our study might not have grown as much as other types of institutions, many of them did feel an obligation to do their part to accommodate the increasing numbers of college students nationwide. For example, a 1956 report of Wheaton's long-range planning committee noted, "The enlargement of the College will also enable Wheaton to make a modest contribution in furnishing increased educational opportunity for the 'tidal wave' of young people who will be seeking admission to institutions of higher learning within the next two decades."[12] Similarly, when the College of the Holy Cross decided to increase its size in 1962, it was in part because the college recognized its obligation, "'to do our share' to assist in the education explosion which had already begun across the nation."[13]

Many of the Ohio liberal arts colleges in our study also felt obliged to expand. In 1956, the Committee on the Expanding Population of the Ohio College Association commissioned a study on "Meeting Ohio's Needs in Higher Education." The Russell Report, as it came to be known, found:

> Most of the privately controlled institutions are giving thought to the question of the number of students they will be able to accommodate in the future. . . . In general, the privately controlled colleges and universities look forward to expansions that will amount in the next ten years to approximately a 65 percent increase over the 1955 enrollment levels. The increase in the period up to 1970 may be as much as 77 percent over the 1955 levels.[14]

Although private colleges in Ohio, including those in our study, did grow, many of them worried about the impact growth might have on their quality. Ohio Wesleyan, for example, believed that "The impending crisis is twofold. There is the *quantitative* problem of how to give all qualified applicants an opportunity to gain a college education; and there is the *qualitative* problem of how to maintain and raise the standards of education in colleges as this increased load is placed upon their facilities and resources."[15] Ohio Wesleyan's faculty were particularly concerned that the university not expand at the expense of quality. In 1955, 1956, and 1958, groups of faculty members urged President Flemming that "there should be no expansion of Ohio Wesleyan unless we can be assured that the quality of education it offers will not merely be maintained, but improved before such an expansion."[16] (As it turned out and as is described in Chapter 3, during the tidal wave, candidates to Ohio Wesleyan and the other colleges in our study presented higher qualifications than ever before.)

Perhaps the most radical response to the enrollment crisis among our colleges (and the strongest evidence that the pressure to expand was ubiquitous) was "The New College Plan." In 1958, with support from the Ford Foundation, four institutions in the Connecticut Valley of Massachusetts— Amherst, Mount Holyoke, Smith, and the University of Massachusetts— developed a plan to create a new private liberal arts college. A 1958 faculty committee report described the genesis of "The New College Plan":

> It is acknowledged on all sides that American higher education is facing a crisis and that if we are to continue "the pursuit of excellence" on which our society's growth, health, and safety depend, we shall have to bring to bear both great resources and great imagination. Many things will need to be done to meet the rapidly mounting demand which is the result not only of a drastic increase in the college age population but also of the steadily rising proportion of our young people who are seeking a college education. Amherst, Mount

Holyoke, Smith, and the University of Massachusetts are already engaged in exploring and carrying out measures which each can take individually to meet the coming challenge. This report proposes that the four institutions also make a contribution cooperatively by sponsoring a new departure in liberal education of the highest quality. . . . To sponsor such a pilot plant should be a particularly appropriate role for privately endowed colleges, since as they are presently constituted they cannot, for economic reasons, expand rapidly and still maintain the higher standards which are their distinctive contribution.[17]

Raising funds and working out the details for the new college proved complicated, but Hampshire College finally opened in 1971.

New Opportunities for Women

One factor that encouraged the creation of new coeducational colleges such as Hampshire and the expansion of many small women's colleges including Mount Holyoke and Wheaton, was the growing participation of women in higher education. Between 1955 and 1970, Wheaton grew by 105 percent and Mount Holyoke grew by 51 percent. Michael Robinson, an economics professor at Mount Holyoke who has carefully studied the college's history, maintains that "the driving force for the college prior to 1968 seems to be the tremendous increase in college attendance for women."[18] During the decade from 1955 to 1965, the number of female high school graduates nearly doubled, and the female college-going rate increased from less than 35 percent to more than 45 percent.[19] At the same time, opportunities for women outside traditional fields such as education expanded, prompting more women to pursue humanities and social science degrees. In a 1990 *Science* article, Sarah Turner and William G. Bowen examined trends in degrees conferred. They found that in the early to mid-1950s, many women majored in education, in part to meet the increasing demand for teachers caused by the baby boom and in part because education was one of the few fields open to them. By 1958, almost half of all of the BA degrees awarded to women were in education. Between 1958 and 1966 opportunities for women widened so many more chose to major in the humanities or, to a lesser degree, the social sciences.[20] Such trends clearly benefited women's (and coed) liberal arts colleges.

The increase in women pursuing liberal arts degrees, documented by Turner and Bowen, was part of a broader trend. In a 1995 article in *Change*, Joan Gilbert analyzed changes in the percentage of liberal arts degrees awarded since the early 1900s. During the twentieth century, the percentage of students pursuing liberal arts degrees has declined dramatically as both the number of postsecondary students and the variety of higher education institutions has expanded. The only exception to this general trend was the period between 1956 and 1970, when the percentage of liberal arts degrees increased at all types of institutions.[21]

The Expansion of Public Higher Education

Despite the increasing popularity of liberal arts degrees, the establishment of Hampshire, the findings of the Russell Report, and the conviction by Wheaton, Holy Cross, Ohio Wesleyan, and others that they had a duty to expand, the private sector in general, and our colleges in particular, did not grow nearly as much during the 1960s as the public sector did. The vast majority of the baby boom students were absorbed by state systems. In 1950, postsecondary enrollments were distributed evenly between the public and private sectors; by 1970 public colleges and universities enrolled about 75 percent of all students. Two developments account for this divergence between public and private enrollments. During the 1960s many state teachers colleges and universities expanded three- and four-fold to accommodate the new students.[22] At the same time, new institutions, particularly community colleges, regional universities, and additional branches of existing universities, were created to ensure that everyone had access to higher education.

The 1956 Russell Report estimated that if Ohio private institutions' enrollment forecasts proved true and no new private colleges were established, public enrollments would need to expand:

> Publicly controlled institutions will have to care for the remainder of the large increase in the number of students expected to enroll by 1965 and 1970. On this basis, it is estimated that the enrollments of the publicly controlled institutions by 1965 will be two and one-fourth times their enrollments in the autumn of 1955. By 1970, the publicly controlled institutions may enroll as many as four times the number of students that they had in the fall of 1955.

In 1963, Governor James A. Rhodes of Ohio ensured that the report's estimates would be met when the state created the Ohio Board of Regents. The Board developed a set of recommendations focused on expanding the availability of higher education in Ohio. Locating an institution of higher education within commuting distance of every Ohioan became a state priority.[23] Since 1970, Ohio public institutions have consistently enrolled 70 percent of all students in the state.

In Massachusetts, private institutions have always enrolled the majority of students. Between 1962 and 1968, enrollments in the private sector increased by almost a third. According to a study done by McKinsey and Company, two groups—(1) the liberal arts colleges with the highest expenditures per student and (2) Harvard and MIT—were the smallest contributors to this expansion with increases of 16 and 12 percent, respectively. The less selective four-year colleges and the other universities were principally responsible for the growth with expansions of 50 and 44 percent.[24]

Despite Massachusetts's traditional emphasis on private education, the state's public system underwent a transformation during the 1960s. Many community colleges were founded, teachers colleges became state colleges and were accredited to award bachelor's degrees in the arts and sciences, and regional universities were expanded and new ones created. Altogether, these developments bolstered public enrollments in Massachusetts from 16,000 in 1960 to more than 60,000 by the end of the decade.[25] In 1962, the public sector enrolled only 17 percent of students in the state; by 1968, 32 percent of all postsecondary students in Massachusetts attended public institutions.[26]

The result of these expansion patterns was to weaken considerably the relative role of the small liberal arts college. Whereas in 1955 liberal arts colleges accounted for nearly 40 percent of higher education institutions and enrolled 26 percent of all students nationwide, by 1970 private colleges made up only 24 percent of the higher education sector and enrolled only 7.6 percent of students.[27] As Rudolph explained, "The independent liberal arts college, traditionally 'the nucleus and backbone of American higher education,' was now challenged on the one side by the great university complexes and on the other side by the new community colleges which everywhere were answering an insistent demand for the collegiate experience."[28] This situation would be compounded in the 1970s by new challenges, most notably unfavorable demographic trends, lower returns to a college education, and reduced interest in liberal arts fields.

SHIFTING ENROLLMENTS (1970–1980)

Beginning in the late 1960s, the tidal wave of students ebbed. Although the absolute number of high school graduates continued to increase until 1975, a decline in the high school graduation rate (from 77 percent in 1968 to 73 percent in 1975) paralleled a decline in college enrollment rates. The college-going rate for high school graduates, which had peaked at 55 percent in 1968, declined to a low of 47 percent in 1973 and 1974. (See Figure 1.1B.)

The decline in college enrollment rates was most pronounced for males. The college-going rate for male high school graduates reached a high of 63 percent in 1968. Just five years later, in 1973, only 50 percent of male graduates enrolled in college. This decline has been attributed mainly to the abolishment of the draft after the Vietnam War. During the war, enroll-ment in college had provided a deferment.[29]

Despite the decreasing high school graduation and college-going rates, overall enrollment in higher education did not actually decline during the 1970s. Rather, the high rate of growth that colleges had become accus-tomed to in the 1960s subsided, falling from 4.0 to 1.7 percent annually.[30] The resulting "steady state" period was marked by enrollment shifts among types of institutions. In particular, a major shift occurred in the number of students who chose to attend two-year institutions rather than either pri-vate or public four-year institutions. In the late 1960s, the 2 million stu-dents enrolled at two-year colleges comprised only one-quarter of the total enrollment. By the mid-1970s, enrollments at two-year colleges had dou-bled and accounted for 35 percent of all enrollments.

In addition to the shift away from four-year institutions, the colleges in our study had to contend with a major social development—coeducation. During the late 1960s and early to mid-1970s, almost all of the men's institutions in this country and all but about 150 of the almost 300 women's colleges became coed. These changes completely altered the competitive landscape, even for colleges that had always been coed. It almost seemed as if no student was going where he or she used to go anymore.

Coeducation had a dramatic impact on the size of the schools in our study. Whereas in the earlier period changes in enrollment were correlated most with beginning enrollment, in this period, the coed status of institu-tions seemed to account best for enrollment growth (or lack of growth). Indeed, between 1970 and 1980, the newly coed colleges in our study grew by over 23 percent on average; the women's colleges expanded by about 9 percent on average; and the always coeducational colleges on aver-age actually declined in size by almost 3 percent.

Expansion at Men's Colleges

Between 1969 and 1980, all four of the all-male institutions in our study became coed, and at three of these institutions enrollments grew from 28 to 85 percent in order to accommodate new female students. To varying degrees these three schools used coeducation as a way to improve their financial positions by increasing their enrollments.

The impetus for Kenyon to become coeducational was in large part fi-nancial. As described in the last section, by the early 1960s, Kenyon faced a difficult financial situation. In 1964, examiners from the North Central Association of Colleges and Secondary Schools Commission on Colleges and Universities reviewed the college and concluded, "The paramount problem at Kenyon is financial."[31] In June 1965 Samuel Lord, treasurer of the college, wrote an article in the *Kenyon Alumni Bulletin*, examining this "paramount problem" in some detail and describing the administration's thinking and efforts toward a solution. Lord and other administrators realized that "the one remaining source of increased financial support—and probably our best route toward financial stability—is our student body itself. . . . Since it is clear that we cannot simply raise 'prices' and eliminate the deficit as a problem, we must consider a major expansion in the size of the student body—without a corresponding increase in instructional and other operating costs."[32] Noting the difficulties the college had been experiencing with recruitment and retention of men and recognizing that men's colleges no longer had a broad appeal, Kenyon decided that admitting women was the most reasonable way to expand.

The decision at Williams to become coed also was partially motivated by the college's desire to expand. The 1969 Final Report of the Committee on Coordinate Education at Williams enumerated five reasons for recommending that Williams become coed. The second reason concerned underlying pressures for expansion:

> It seems fairly clear that undergraduate liberal arts colleges will need to grow continuously in the years ahead, as they have in past years, in order to add to the range of studies that they offer and to include new fields of knowledge in their curriculum. . . . If growth in the years ahead seems to be a reasonable certainty, one can ask the question whether it is better to grow in student body size by adding more men or by introducing women to the student body.[33]

Williams decided to admit women, not only because administrators believed that coeducation would enhance the academic and social climate and aid recruiting, but also because, as described in more detail in Chapter 4, admitting women made financial sense. Williams enrolled its first class of women in 1972 and by 1974 had made the transition from a men's college of 1,200 students to a coeducational college of roughly 1,800 (1,200 men and 600 women).

Amherst admitted its first class of women relatively late, in 1976—seven years after Kenyon and four years after Williams. Nevertheless, many of the same financial and size considerations that had factored into Kenyon's and Williams's decisions influenced Amherst too. Like Williams, Amherst was in strong financial shape when it was first debating whether to become coeducational. As President Ward wrote in the *Amherst College Bulletin* in October 1972, "There are no immediate external pressures, beyond the pressure of principle involved in the question of coeducation itself, which force the College to admit women. There is no decline in the quality of applicants for admission to the College; there is no difficulty in attracting and keeping superior faculty; there is no financial problem which might suggest coeducation as a solution."[34] Just two years later, however, financial projections from the treasurer's office were much less rosy. The projected operating deficit in 1979/80 if the college remained a men's college of 1,300 students was $893,000 unless the college increased its 8.5/1 student/ faculty ratio to 10/1.[35] Faced with the choice of eliminating 20 or so of its 150 faculty or expanding the size of the college to 1,500, Amherst opted to expand and began admitting women in 1976.[36]

The only one of our four men's schools that went coed but did not expand was Holy Cross. When Holy Cross became coeducational in 1972, it maintained its class size, replacing 40 percent of the spaces formally reserved for men with women. Holy Cross did not increase the number of students, because most faculty and administrators thought that the college was already too large. In fact, in 1968 the college had discussed reducing enrollment from 2,400 to 1,800 by 1973 as a way of improving selectivity and quality. The authors of a paper that described those deliberations asserted, "[This paper] is not concerned with problems of coeducation since it assumes that a student population of 1,500 does not mean that there are 1,500 men plus several hundred girls. If the College should decide to become coeducational, the total number of students should not be a factor in the decision."[37] A 1969 Interim Report to the Faculty on Coeducation also recognized that the faculty opposed expansion and, therefore, presented statistics only for zero-growth options.[38]

Although Holy Cross did not grow when it became coed, it did not shrink either. In 1980 Holy Cross enrolled 2,513 students, only 15 more than it had enrolled in 1970. It is interesting to speculate what would have happened to Holy Cross's enrollment numbers had it not admitted women. Would the college have remained at 2,500 students or shrunk below 2,000 students as advocated by the faculty?

Moderate Growth at Women's Colleges

All of the women's colleges in our study also grew between 1970 and 1980, but at more modest rates, between 4 and 16 percent. The fact that they grew at all is somewhat surprising, because none of them went coed during this period, and they were experiencing increased competition from the newly coed colleges and universities. During the first few years of coeducation, the period Mary Ellen Ames, director of admission at Wellesley College, dubbed the "coed panic," some of the women's colleges experienced slight declines in enrollment (about 1 percent) as women rushed to apply to the colleges that had previously been closed to them. However, these modest declines did not persist.

The experiences of the women's colleges in our study were similar to those of women's colleges nationwide. In 1981, the Women's College Coalition reported that as a sector, those colleges that had decided to remain women's colleges experienced an enrollment increase of 25 percent during the 1970s.[39] The increasing numbers of women attending college undoubtedly helped sustain enrollments at women's colleges. Although the number of women who graduated from high school had historically been greater than the number of men, the participation of women in higher education had traditionally been lower. During the 1970s, the college enrollment rate for women reached a new high of almost 50 percent, and in 1975 the number of women high school graduates entering college surpassed the number of men. By 1979, there were more women than men enrolled in colleges and universities. The increasing numbers of women in higher education was related to many factors, including the women's movement of the late 1960s and early 1970s; the changing labor force participation of women, which saw women moving from traditional occupations like teaching into the broader labor pool of business and social sciences; and rising divorce rates and lower fertility, which both freed more women to pursue education and necessitated that they do so.[40]

Although the number of women attending college increased during the 1970s, the number of women with top scores actually declined. At the same time, the number of slots for high-scoring women almost doubled as many of the strongest men's colleges became coed. These trends were especially problematic for top women's colleges. Emily Wick, special assistant to the president for long-range planning at Mount Holyoke College, described their impact in a 1982 report:

> The number of women with scores of 700 or above dropped steadily and precipitously from 8,800 in 1967 to 4,800 in 1981. The number with scores of 600 or above peaked in 1971 at 51,000 and dropped to 21,900 by 1981. In this same time period approximately 11,000 places became available for women in the newly coeducational institutions in the COPHE and Twelve College Exchange groups. This is almost as many places as the approximately 12,000 places already existing in the sister colleges, Barnard, Bryn Mawr, Radcliffe, Mount Holyoke, Smith and Wellesley. Hindsight clearly shows that the newly coeducational institutions threw their recruiting lines into a pool which already was declining in its stock of new students of so-called "high ability." It is also very clear that this pool has not been replenished from the still increasing number of women who take the SAT tests. The prognostications of the 1970 Report of the Fact Finding Committee on Coeducation that the pool of women whose scores are at least 600 would increase by 30 percent by 1974, and that as much as 15 percent of each class should score 699 or above in the SAT turned out to be empty dreams.[41]

If the number of top women students was decreasing, why did the women's colleges in our study expand? Archival records suggest that much of the growth was unintentional. According to Smith's 1987 self-study, during the 1970s, "the size of each entering class had grown without any predetermined plan."[42] Similarly, Mary Ellen Ames explained why the increased enrollment at Wellesley in the 1970s was "partly a mistake":

> When Yale went coed in 1969–1970, they only wanted to take high quality women who had some college experience, so they decided to first accept transfers and they recruited at the women's colleges. Although they promised not to take more than ten students from any school, they took 40 from Wellesley. So, Wellesley had to make up for it by accepting larger classes. . . . If you keep adding students in the first year, obviously the total enrollment goes up. . . . By the mid 1970s we had established 550–600 as a good class size. Our financial people liked it as well because it brought in extra money, yet we didn't have to build new dorms.[43]

As Ames pointed out, expansion was not unwelcome. Like the other colleges in our study that expanded, the women's colleges, too, found it difficult to resist the financial incentive to enroll larger classes.

Three of the four women's schools in our study—Smith, Mount Holyoke, and Wellesley—established formal continuing education programs for older women during the 1970s, which also contributed to their enrollment growth, particularly of part-time students. Smith's program actually began in the late 1960s when a few dozen women inquired about finishing degrees that they had started at Smith. Smith had always had a generous readmissions policy, but it had allowed women to enroll only as full-time students. The few older women who returned full-time did better than they had as younger students, so Smith started allowing women to return on a part-time basis too.[44] In 1968, there were 15 to 20 such nontraditional-age students, and admissions was done on an ad hoc basis. In 1974, the program was formalized as the Ada Comstock Program in recognition of the fact that "over the last decade a growing number of women older than the average students and often able to pursue for personal or family reasons only a partial program each semester have been encouraged to enter Smith."[45] Thirty-three women enrolled that first semester; when enrollment peaked in the late 1980s, over 350 Ada Comstock scholars were on campus. Mount Holyoke and Wellesley also instituted special programs for nontraditional-age students, although their enrollments never reached Smith's level. Mount Holyoke capped its Francis Perkins program at about 150 students, and Wellesley's Davis Scholar program rarely enrolled more than 200 older women.

The women's colleges were not the only schools in our study to implement continuing education programs. Hiram established its Weekend College in 1977. The purpose of the program was twofold: to provide a liberal arts education to older students and to offset declining enrollments. In the

1977 alumni magazine article that announced the formation of the Weekend College, President Jagow outlined this dual rationale:

> We realized that Hiram College might be ideally suited to offer a discerning adult clientele precisely what they sought: a traditional—hard core if you will—education in a new format. Certainly it was never decreed that liberal arts learning should be undertaken only on weekdays by eighteen year olds. I believe that all colleges, not just the big universities, should use their physical facilities to benefit the adult community. Now is the time to do it, for there is a drop in the number of 18-year-olds, and this country has all these magnificent facilities for higher education. Let's use them since education for adults is the path of the future.[46]

Enrollments in Hiram's Weekend College—typically on the magnitude of 350 to 450 students—helped make up for the decline in its traditional-age population.[47]

Enrollment Losses at Coed Colleges

Hiram was not the only coed college in our study to suffer sustained enrollment losses during the 1970s. In the first half of the decade, at all but one of the seven coed colleges in our study, enrollment growth was modest, and in two cases enrollments actually fell, as college-going rates declined and single-sex institutions became coed. This trend continued into the second half of the 1970s when five of our colleges experienced falling enrollments, ranging from a mere 2 percent to 53 percent at Antioch after student strikes disrupted classes. Even the two coed colleges that expanded during this period grew by only 3 and 4 percent.

The experiences of the coed colleges in our study were more typical of what was happening in higher education than were the experiences of either the men's or the women's colleges. In the early 1970s, colleges and universities across the country struggled to fill their freshmen classes as total first-time freshmen enrollments at both private and public four-year colleges and universities declined. A 1974 article in *U.S. News and World Report* described their plight: "Declining enrollments are leaving empty seats in colleges throughout the country. Many schools are mounting 'hard sell' campaigns this spring to fill those seats. . . . College administrators say the admissions boom is a thing of the past as the last crop of youngsters from the post–World War II baby boom filters through the nation's high schools."[48] The National Association of College Admissions Counselors reported that "On May 1st an estimated 85 percent of all U.S. colleges and universities still were seeking freshmen and transfer applicants for the fall, 1972. Most of these institutions will be accepting applicants until opening day of the fall term."[49] At least one of the coed liberal arts colleges in our study was among that 85 percent:

> The picture looked a little glum on May 1st, the date the deposits were due. We were short of our original quota by about 90 men and 80 women, which even with our long waiting lists, seemed almost unattainable. . . . It is too early to get reports from other institutions on their fall enrollments, but we do know that nationally we were not alone, either in our decrease in applications, or in the percentage of withdrawals from the accepted group. The sketchy reports we have had indicate that the situation at many colleges is critical, that freshmen quotas were not filled, and that the prospects for the future do not look any brighter for another year.[50]

The expansion of many existing colleges and universities and the building of new ones during the 1960s compounded the problems presented by the declining growth rate. Expansion of facilities had been undertaken anticipating continuing increases in the college population. According to a 1975 Carnegie Foundation Report:

> Some private institutions in all categories are burdened by decisions to grow that were made in the 1950s and 1960s, often in response to government urging. They incurred substantial debt and planned buildings without secured funds for future maintenance and operation, or realistic plans for debt service. . . . The great public pressure put on institutions in the 1960s implied continuity of support for expansion and induced decisions about enrollments and research which, in retrospect, seem less than wise.[51]

Ironically, because of the time it took to raise capital and the inevitable delays involved with construction, many colleges (including a few of those in our study) were opening dorms even as their applicant pools were shrinking.

Because of the relationship between enrollment and tuition revenue, declining enrollments are particularly damaging for liberal arts colleges. Liberal arts colleges, which generally have modest endowments and receive minimal federal research funding, are extremely dependent on tuition revenues. Thus, even small declines in enrollment can have serious financial consequences, and large drops can be devastating, as evidenced by the experience of Antioch College in the early 1970s. In 1973, a notice at Antioch College calling upon students to attend a meeting to discuss the college's enrollment crisis succinctly described the implications of falling enrollments:

> What is the Enrollment Crisis? Simply this: This campus' budget is financed by students' tuition—a total of approximately 1,800 Full Tuition Equivalents is needed to maintain and finance our already tight budget. But—and here's the

crisis—applications to Antioch are down to 1/4 of last year's level, and at this rate we will have an entering class next year of only 400 students unless we do something. Take into account the number of students expected to graduate or withdraw from Antioch this year, we could possibly end up with as few as 1,400–1,500 Full Tuition equivalents next year. This would necessitate budget cuts somewhere in the neighborhood of one million dollars.[52]

Because of their small size, liberal arts colleges are less able to weather changes in enrollments than are universities; the loss of even a few students reduces tuition revenue proportionally a lot without an accompanying decrease in costs. The inescapable result is an even higher cost per student ratio.

The national economic circumstances of the early 1970s exacerbated the problems liberal arts colleges confronted. As Earl Cheit documented in his classic study, *The New Depression in Higher Education*, in the late 1960s and early 1970s, higher education was caught in a cost–income squeeze. Instead of providing additional tuition revenues, the expansion at many institutions during the previous decade had left them "undercapitalized, overextended, moving into enlarged areas of responsibility without permanent financing."[53] Costs at institutions, including faculty salaries, student services, and financial aid expenditures, rose sharply. At the same time, income growth declined. The increase in federal aid did not match the rise in the price of college, foundation support leveled off, and private support dropped.

Competition from the Public Sector

Cheit noted that liberal arts colleges were among those types of institutions most severely affected by the cost–income squeeze, in part because they faced tough competition from lower-cost public institutions. As tuition charges at private colleges continued to increase more rapidly than at public colleges, Cheit worried that soon students from middle-income families would not be able to attend private colleges. Many others echoed Cheit's concerns. For example, Father Edmund G. Ryan, executive vice president at Georgetown University, contended that "private colleges and universities are on 'the endangered species list' for the 1970s, at least."[54] Donald L. Pyke, coordinator of academic planning at the University of Southern California, also warned that private universities were in danger of being replaced by less expensive public colleges and universities.[55]

The colleges in our study were not immune from these national trends. Indeed, in the early 1970s the term "middle-income squeeze" began to appear in the admissions and financial aid reports of our colleges. Inflation and the rising costs of college seemed to be driving many middle-class families away from expensive private colleges and universities. As the gap between public and private tuition widened, competition from public institutions intensified. Although such competition was felt most in states, such as Ohio, with strong public higher education systems, the Massachusetts liberal arts colleges in our study were affected too, both because the Massachusetts state system was expanding[56] and because most of our Massachusetts colleges recruited nationally for students. As early as 1968, Clara Ludwig, the director of admissions at Mount Holyoke College, cited the growing competition from public universities as a cause of falling applicant numbers:

> A close analysis of the figures geographically shows that admission application numbers held at the same level for Connecticut and Massachusetts but were accompanied by a sharp rise in scholarship applications. This may point to the appeal of public institutions as one of the chief reasons for the applications change. In Connecticut and Massachusetts where we are relatively well-known and where our opportunities for financial aid are also understood and where public education has not had the long tradition of other states, our numbers held, but in areas further away where we are not so well-known, where state universities have high prestige, applications declined. . . . The appeal of public institutions with lower fees, large and diverse student bodies, and increasing standards of excellence is growing.[57]

As Cheit predicted, rising college costs in the 1970s compounded the competitive problem Ludwig described. In 1976, Mary Ellen Ames, explained:

> Another significant factor in the rapidly changing admissions field has been the effect that inflation has had on the colleges and on the applicants as well. The steadily rising costs of operating colleges has been reflected in increased fees for students. A side effect of the increased fees at the private colleges has been a shift of a large number of applicants to public institutions. This shift has also played a part in our decreased applicant pool and decreased yield.[58]

During the late 1960s and early 1970s, public institutions became more attractive to top students not only because of their low costs but also because of their increasingly strong academic programs. Some public colleges and universities even challenged the traditional strength of the liberal arts college—the small intimate community of scholars and students. A 1968 report considering the future of Holy Cross reported:

> We cannot simply assert that students will seek out Holy Cross in order to keep away from giant universities. The latter have already begun a highly competitive battle for the "individualistic student" by creating competitive small colleges within the university. The University of Michigan was swamped with

applicants for such a new college even before plans were completed for the first group of students to enter in 1967.[59]

Although students could get a traditional liberal arts education at universities such as Michigan, they could also take more vocational courses in business, education, engineering, and the like. This flexibility became important in the 1970s when interest in liberal arts waned. Beginning in 1970, there was a significant decline in the percentage of all degrees awarded in the liberal arts. This phenomenon was particularly noticeable after the substantial boom in liberal arts degrees in the 1960s, even though, as Gilbert argued in her *Change* article, what the decline represented was merely "a close return to the trajectory established over the past century."[60]

Labor market forces were largely responsible for the reversal. On the one hand, occupational opportunities expanded for some groups of students; for example, more women entered fields such as business, which had previously been closed to them.[61] On the other hand, the returns to education fell as an oversupply of college graduates flooded the job market, and it became more difficult for college graduates to find jobs commensurate with their educations. Between 1971 and 1979, the wage premium for college graduates at all experience levels declined from 61 to 48 percent.[62] As the wage differential fell and economic conditions in the country worsened, many students determined that a college education—and in particular a liberal arts education—was not the best investment.

Many of the liberal arts colleges in our study felt the impact of students' vocationalism on their enrollments. Van Halsey, director of admission at Hampshire College, for example, cautioned his president, "A burgeoning interest on the part of students in vocational pay-off for their money and their B.A. degree will continue to affect the applicant pool. The career counseling movement in secondary schools and the economic situation in the country will stimulate a sincere vocational interest on the part of students applying to Hampshire and other colleges."[63] Nationwide, many colleges and universities adapted their curricula to accommodate this growing vocational interest. At least in the short term, those institutions that could provide pre-professional education seemed to benefit. For example, Babson College, an undergraduate business college outside of Boston, saw applications nearly triple between 1970 and 1980. As a result, Babson was able to increase its enrollment by 12 percent. For the most part, the liberal arts colleges in our study maintained their traditional liberal arts curricula. The fact that they did not alter their curricula is consistent with Gilbert's finding that Liberal Arts I colleges retained their focus on liberal arts.

The Transfer Problem

Even for those colleges that succeeded in enrolling a first-year class of budgeted size, difficulties in maintaining total enrollments remained. During the 1970s, colleges became more aware that student attrition and transfers were factors that needed to be accounted for in the total enrollment picture. Students who began college at a particular institution no longer necessarily continued there. Mary Ellen Ames described the new college population in a 1972 article in the *Wellesley Alumnae Magazine*:

> The college population of today is a much more fluid one than ever before. College students may transfer to other colleges with greater ease, they may graduate in less than four years thus leaving places at the upperclass level for more transfers. Other students in the meantime are taking advantage of the exchange program and of the more flexible leave policies; thereby leaving places open.[64]

The attrition of students through transfer or dropout had powerful effects on enrollments. As a 1981 article in *The (Oberlin) Observer* explained, "Each person retained to graduation is one fewer that must be enrolled. Each enrolled student not needed represents approximately three who need not be admitted, four or five we need not recruit as applicants and forty initial inquiries that need not be generated."[65] Although the numbers varied according to a college's admit rate and yield, the principle remained the same. At Oberlin, attrition was mainly responsible for the increasing first-year class size during the seventies. When David L. Davis-Van Atta, Oberlin's director of institutional research, studied the increases, he found: "The sources of these rises are two: the trustee-mandated 50 student increase in Oberlin's class size and an increase in attrition. Except for the one year that the class size was increased, all rises in this line indicate equivalently increasing attrition."[66] When students in the upper classes left, a college needed to replace them by admitting a larger freshmen class the following year. The Retention Task Force at Ohio Wesleyan emphasized that "admissions and retention are really just two ends of the same continuum." Increasing the retention rate by even small amounts would significantly increase the total enrollment of the college. In addition the task force pointed out, "Increasing retention will allow us to be more selective in admissions *without* decreasing the total University size."[67]

Because retention of students was so crucial to enrollments, many institutions carefully studied why students left. In 1978, when student attrition reached 40 percent, Hampshire College devoted considerable time and resources to examining the problem. The task force concluded that "engagement, involvement and commitment were essential for retention," and so the college "concentrated its efforts on how these characteristics could be developed and sustained," given Hampshire's unique curriculum which encouraged independent work.[68] At Ohio Wesleyan, attrition of two groups was attributed to the academic environment at the college. The weakest group of students dropped out of the college because they could not meet the standards of the school, while the strongest group of students transferred because the classes were not stimulating enough.[69]

Often, there were no clear causes for student transfer or dropout. Kenyon, for example, found:

> Interestingly, requests for information about transfers flood the Admissions Office—about fifty letters every week of which there will be some 150 applications. Transfers have become a way of life; most transfer applications are made because it is vogue, rather than because of real dissatisfaction. When problems do get in the students' way, they fail to realize that they are likely to transfer their unhappiness with them, finding only new ground for old problems.[70]

One way that colleges tried to counter the effects of students transferring out of their institutions was to replace those students with transfers from other institutions. This solution was not as simple as it seemed, especially since those colleges that had the more severe attrition problems were often not as successful at attracting quality transfers. Colleges could not directly solicit transfer students from other institutions because that was not considered ethical. In addition, many transfer students needed financial aid, which colleges were often unable to provide, especially when their continuing students were often left unaided. Clara Ludwig, director of admissions at Mount Holyoke, recognized many of these problems:

> Two problems appear to dominate discussions of transfer candidates: the number who apply for aid and our limited funds, and the difficulty of evaluating college transcripts. . . . In any case, the transfer group never looks to us very strong, we have difficulty ferreting out their real reasons for the transfer, we have disappointedly few candidates from community colleges and so many in the total group need financial aid. It seems doubtful that Mount Holyoke will ever draw many transfer candidates. Much as we may think this an excellent place for a transfer, particularly one from a large public institution, our appeal seems very limited.[71]

Although bolstering enrollments was the primary reason for accepting transfers, it was not the only one. At Wheaton College, members of its planning committee recommended accepting transfer students as a way of correcting imbalances in departmental majors. "We have begun active recruitment of transfer students. Probably that effort will not make a sharp difference for a few years, but we look forward to the time when we can select students who have already established a field of interest."[72]

Even colleges such as Amherst, which had high retention rates, implemented transfer policies in the 1970s to meet other institutional goals. Until the early 1970s, Amherst rarely accepted transfer students; since the college denied admission to more than 75 percent of its applicants, most of whom Amherst acknowledged were qualified, the college felt it was unfair to admit transfers. Moreover, because it had such a high retention rate, in order to make room for transfers Amherst would have had to reduce the size of the freshmen class—making admission even more competitive. Nevertheless, in 1972 Amherst tripled the number of transfer students it would admit. A 1972 report explained the change:

> Amherst has adopted this new policy because we value diversity in our student body. We find among the transfer applicants socio-economic backgrounds, age levels, life experiences, levels of motivation and academic interests which at the present time are under-represented in our freshmen applicants. Because the kind of diversity we seek is most often found there, first priority is given to applicants who are graduates of junior or community colleges.[73]

Amherst set aside financial aid funds to enable students with financial need to attend. Other colleges also gave preference in their transfer policies to students from junior or community colleges. These commitments to enrolling diverse groups of students coincided with the movement in the 1970s to increase access for disadvantaged students to higher education, which is discussed in detail in Chapter 5.

If the 1960s were marked by the tidal wave of new students, then the 1970s should be remembered as the decade of enrollment shifts. During the 1970s enrollments shifted from four-year to two-year institutions, from private to public colleges and universities, and from single-sex to coeducational environments. Even students already enrolled at institutions often moved as they transferred and participated in college exchanges in record numbers. The result for our colleges was a difficult decade. Many feared that the 1980s would be even worse.

QUALITY CONCERNS (1980–1994)

Beginning in the late 1970s, the absolute number of 18- to 19-year-olds in the country began to decline, and projections indicated that their number would fall at least 25 percent by the mid-1990s. Most people expected that this demographic slump would be disastrous for higher education institutions, many of which were still reeling from the 1970s. In 1984, Mary

Ellen Ames reported, "A predicted result is that 10 to 30 percent of the 3,100 colleges in the United States will close by 1995."[74]

The demographic declines were expected to be especially detrimental to liberal arts colleges, because most liberal arts colleges were located in and drew their students from the areas of the country with the largest predicted declines in numbers of high school graduates, namely the Midwest, the Middle Atlantic, and New England. The 13 states expected to be hardest hit (in order of the anticipated percentage decrease in high school graduates between 1979 and 1994) were as follows: Rhode Island (49 percent), Connecticut (43), Massachusetts (43), New York (43), New Jersey (39), Pennsylvania (39), Michigan (36), Minnesota (35), Illinois (34), Iowa (34), Ohio (34), Wisconsin (34) and Indiana (30).[75] Not only were these 13 states the major feeder states to the colleges in our study, but in the early 1980s these states encompassed 51 percent of all private four-year colleges. To make matters worse, families from those segments of the population that were expected to grow—minority and low-income—and families living in those parts of the country that were expanding—the West and the South—had not traditionally sent their children to liberal arts colleges in large numbers.

The colleges we studied were well aware of both the dire demographic predictions and their particular predicaments. An interim report of Williams's Committee on Priorities and Resources for the 1980s, for example, noted:

> The decline in the college-age population is severe from now to 1985. Following some recovery in the late 1980s, there is further decline to the 1990s. This major factor is unprecedented in U.S. history. Further, the migration of the U.S.'s population away from the northeast and Midwest will result in even larger reductions in the number of eighteen-year-olds in Williams' traditional recruiting area, and the decline could be as much as 30 percent or more in those areas.[76]

A 1987 letter from David Davis-Van Atta to Richard F. Boyden, director of admissions at Denison, described similar market forecasts for those states from which Denison drew the majority of its applicants: "The primary market shows uninterrupted shrinkage . . . [it] will sink to a minimum significantly below current levels and practically speaking will remain at its lowest level through the middle of the next decade."[77]

Fortunately for the colleges in our study, the demographic bomb did not hit, at least not to the extent that had been generally predicted. As Paul E. Harrington and Andrew M. Sum, both of the Center for Labor Market Studies at Northeastern University, concluded in 1988, "The 'worst case scenario' for declining enrollments has simply failed to materialize."[78] Although the number of high school graduates did decline 26 percent between 1978 and 1993, the number of students enrolled in college fell by only 8 percent, because the college-going rate rose to nearly 60 percent in the late 1980s. (See Figures 1.1A and 1.1B.)

The increase in the college-going rate can be at least partially attributed to an increasing wage differential between college and high school graduates, which prompted more high school graduates to enroll in college. The wage premium for college graduates, which had declined in the 1970s, rebounded in the 1980s. In a 1989 article, Kevin Murphy and Finis Welch explained the trend in wage premiums:

> The erosion in the economic incentives to attend college that was experienced in the 1970s seems to have been the predictable consequence of a phenomenal increase in numbers of college graduates that coincided with the entry of the baby boomers into the job market. The subsequent erosion in returns to schooling appears in retrospect to have been a temporary break in a general pattern of increasing returns.[79]

From 1979 to 1986, the earnings differential for young workers expanded from 32 percent to about 70 percent, and the differential for experienced workers increased from 48 to 67 percent. By 1986 college/high school earnings differentials were larger than ever. Murphy and Welch attributed the enormous rise in the wage differential during the 1980s to the increased demand for college-educated workers as employment shifted from goods-producing industries to service-producing industries and the educational intensity of production in all industries rose.

During the decade of the eighties and the first half of the nineties, the colleges experienced level and declining enrollments. Unlike earlier periods, when expansion was common, during this period, enrollment reductions were more typical. Between 1980 and 1994, half of the colleges in our study experienced a net decline in their full-time enrollments; in fact, enrollments at two of the colleges declined by more than 19 percent. Even among those colleges that did not reduce their enrollments, most expanded only modestly; only two of our colleges expanded by more than 10 percent. The college that expanded the most did so by becoming coed. Wheaton decided to become coeducational in 1988 after its enrollments had declined 11 percent between 1980 and 1987 and administrators realized that its survival as a quality liberal arts college depended upon expanding its pool of applicants. Coeducation has allowed Wheaton to recoup its enrollment losses so that it now enrolls more students than at any other point in its history; its quality has begun to improve as well.

Michael O'Keefe, former president of the Consortium for the Advancement of Private Higher Education (CAPHE), examined factors correlated with enrollment growth at private colleges and universities between 1978 and 1987. He found: "The data confirm the conventional wisdom: a competitive admissions position has been an advantage in the 1980s. The surprise is that the obverse is not true; lower selectivity, *by itself,* did not imply a decline in enrollments; more than half such colleges have had increases, in some cases spectacularly large."[80]

The colleges in our study behaved much as O'Keefe's findings would suggest. As shown in Figure 1.3, during the 1980s and early 1990s, with the exception of the two schools indicated by the open squares, there was a strong correlation between growth and starting SAT scores among our colleges. On the one hand, colleges with relatively high starting SAT scores were able to maintain and even modestly expand their enrollments. On the other hand, many schools with relatively low SAT scores experienced declining enrollments. The two schools on the left of the figure that lie considerably above the trend line are consistent with O'Keefe's finding that lower selectivity, by itself, did not imply a decline in enrollments. As mentioned above, one of the schools increased its enrollments by becoming coed; the other is a Christian college that merged with another small Christian college in 1985.

Given that eight of the colleges we studied experienced a net decline in their full-time enrollments between 1980 and 1994, it's important to understand why. Were the declines the result of the major demographic trends described above? Or did they reflect institutional decisions and priorities? The answer is both.

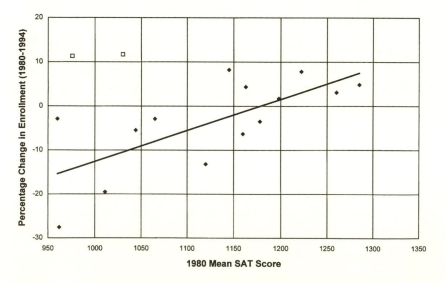

Figure 1.3. Relationship between 1980 Mean Combined SAT Score and Enrollment Growth (1980–1994).

The enrollment experiences of the colleges in our study during the 1980s and early 1990s closely matched trends in the college-going population. In the first half of 1980, the number of 18- to 24-years-olds in this country fell sharply. Between 1980 and 1985 enrollments at the colleges we studied fell an average of 6 percent. Moreover, during this period all but six of the colleges declined in size. In the late 1980s, there was a small recovery in the number of 18- to 22-year-olds, which is also reflected in the experiences of the colleges. Between 1985 and 1990, enrollments at the colleges in our study rose an average of 9 percent and only four fell in size, two by just 1 percent. In the early 1990s, the college population declined again. During this last period, nine of the sixteen colleges became smaller, four by more than 10 percent. On average, the colleges became 3 percent smaller between 1990 and 1994.

Enrollment Strategies

Demographics clearly drove the enrollment patterns at the colleges we studied in the 1980s and 1990s, but institutional decisions had a part, too. Perhaps the best way to understand the role the colleges themselves played is to consider the options available in the early 1980s in light of the predicted decline in the traditional college-age population. In 1983, Thomas Wenzlau, president of Ohio Wesleyan, wrote an article entitled "The Outlook for Liberal-Arts Colleges" in which he described the situation confronting colleges and outlined three possible responses:

All of higher education is facing a major decline in the size of the traditional market—the segment of the population eighteen through twenty-two years old. Every college and university is seeking ways to offset the potential negative effects of the coming decline in enrollment. Three general actions are possible for these institutions: 1) they may seek new and different sources of additional students; 2) they may lower tuition and fees in order to attract a larger number of students from existing and new markets; and 3) they may reduce their size or capacity in accordance with the decreasing demand for services.[81]

To a limited extent, the liberal arts colleges in our study pursued Wenzlau's first option. As described in the preceding section, during the 1970s, three of the women's colleges and one of the coed colleges in our study introduced programs for nontraditional-age students at least in part to bolster their enrollments. Although all four programs continue to this day, the three women's colleges curtailed their continuing education enrollments in the 1980s, because the financial aid budgets for these students had grown very high and because the colleges worried that enrolling too many older students would compromise their reputations as high-quality, traditional liberal arts colleges. Some of our colleges also tried to recruit more international students, to limited degrees and with varying success.

Wenzlau's second option—reducing tuition to attract more students—was not aggressively pursued by the colleges in our study. As described in Chapter 6, during the 1980s, high tuition came to be associated with high quality, and all of the colleges raised their tuition at unprecedented rates. In such a climate, colleges worried that reducing tuition would signal a drop in quality. Although their fears may have been exaggerated, when one of the colleges held its tuition steady rather than increase it at the same rate as its competitors, its applications dropped.

For the most part, the colleges seemed to have adopted Wenzlau's third course of action; when necessary they reduced their enrollments in order to maintain their academic standards. During the 1980s most, if not all, of the colleges conducted self-studies, which explored the declining demographic trends and the trade-off between enrollment and quality. Ohio Wesleyan, for example, formed a Committee on a Smaller College in 1982 to plan for a smaller college "with the dual objective of strengthening our programs and improving the quality of our students."[82] Similarly, a 1982 Mount Holyoke strategic planning document began with the questions:

> What is the probability that Mount Holyoke can maintain the present quality, as well as the present size, of the student body as the number of qualified women high school graduates drops along with the decrease in the cohort of eighteen year olds? Do we believe that maintaining the quality of the student body is as important, less important or more important than maintaining the size of the student body?[83]

In general, during the 1980s the colleges became more savvy about quality/enrollment trade-offs, and admissions officers adopted the attitude: "Manage enrollment rather than let enrollment manage you."[84] Some of the colleges were prepared to—but never actually had to—reduce their enrollments during the 1980s to maintain their quality. In 1980, for instance, the admissions director at Oberlin advised his board of trustees:

> We must continue to monitor the interplay of application numbers and quality and yield projections and face squarely the possibility, and I underline possibility, of a slightly reduced enrollment for a few years. . . . If, however, we encounter, at some point down the road (and we are not there now), the choice between maintaining quality and filling unrealistic enrollment quotas, I hope we will be willing to bite the institutional bullet and opt for quality. For once admissions standards are seriously compromised, they are rarely, if ever, recovered."[85]

Other colleges including Smith, bit the proverbial bullet: "In 1983, at a time when enrollments nationally were declining, an important decision was made to decrease the size of the freshmen class by 10 percent in order to maintain the college's high academic standards. . . . As a result, Smith will be entering its strongest freshmen class in 5 years this coming fall."[86]

Even when the proposed enrollment reductions were too modest to improve a class's academic profile, administrators believed that curtailing enrollments would send a strong signal to high school guidance counselors that the institution was committed to quality. In 1980, for example, the Admissions and Financial Aid Committee at Ohio Wesleyan recommended that the size of the first-year class be reduced by 25 students to 675. Although the committee acknowledged that this reduction would not have "any immediate impact on the profile of the incoming class," the committee hoped that "in tightening the admissions standards even this small amount we will show the thousands of high school counselors with whom we are in some contact, that Ohio Wesleyan is serious about raising the quality of the students it admits." In fact, the committee made its recommendation conditional "on a firm commitment on the part of the administration to engage a 'PR' campaign to let these various counselors know for certain that we have 'turned the corner' so to speak and are unwilling to accept many of those students which we might have accepted in the past."[87]

Wenzlau probably would have been surprised by how many of the colleges limited their enrollments rather than suffer further quality declines. As a college president, Wenzlau understood well how difficult it was for a college to restrict enrollment. Toward the end of his paper, he wrote:

> For most liberal arts colleges, size-reduction options are a series of Hobson's choices. Past growth in size or in resources has permitted increased specialization and professionalism in both academic and student-services areas. To reverse the process demands more versatility among faculty members and staff in order that more functions can be performed by fewer persons—a result not previously associated with enhanced quality.[88]

Some of the colleges we studied tried to put a good spin on bad circumstances. At the end of the 1982 Mount Holyoke study cited above, Emily Wick concluded:

> Perhaps the pressure generated by an expectation that smaller classes will be necessary is exactly what is needed to bring about fundamental reevaluation of activities across the campus in every department and office in the College. It may provide the push needed to bring about a curriculum evaluation that is not a perfunctory academic exercise. It should, in fact, put the fear of God and the devil in all of us![89]

Although by the end of the 1980s it was clear that the college population would not decrease to the extent predicted, one legacy of the 1980s seems to be a keen awareness of both the possibility and the difficulty of restricting enrollments in order to maintain quality. Self-studies and strategic plans from the 1990s, like those from the 1980s, are peppered with references to the size/quality trade-off. For example, the authors of the Long Range Plan for Denison University, 1991/95 wrote, "It is important to keep tough admissions standards, even if this means smaller enrollments for a few years. Academically motivated students will not be attracted to Denison if they think they will meet few students here like themselves."[90] Similarly, the Report of the Committee for Wellesley in the Nineties concluded, "A slight reduction in the size of the student body for a year or two would be a preferable alternative to the reduction of the quality of a class. However, any reduction in the size of the student body over a longer period of time would have a strongly negative effect on the curriculum that could be offered."[91] In the short term, some of the colleges in our study have been willing to weather budgetary pressures in order to preserve their academic standards. For example, at Kenyon in 1993:

> Administrators discovered . . . a market that simply didn't produce enough high quality students who wanted to spend four years in Gambier. The choice was to enroll . . . students whose academic credentials were lower than established standards or to maintain high selectivity criteria and reduce the Kenyon operating budget to reflect reduced income. Agreeing with Anderson [the dean of admissions] that the decision was obvious—lowering standards could only impair the College's academic reputation—President Philip H. Jordan, Jr. enlisted offices across the campus to submit ideas to trim spending in ways that would affect Kenyon's academic mission as little as possible.[92]

This difficult choice is likely to continue to confront all but the most selective liberal arts colleges as the 1990s unfold.

At a recent conference on higher education at Princeton University, David Breneman, dean of the School of Education at the University of Virginia, recalled, "I remember well discussing the economics of the small college with Joe Kershaw, then Provost of Williams, for he had concluded that enrollment growth was essential. . . . His general—if tongue in cheek—prescription for financial stability in the small college was to increase enrollments by 25 students per year, forever."[93] To some extent, the colleges in our study have followed Kershaw's prescription. Over the period 1955 through 1994, the colleges grew an average of 73 percent. This growth, however, was neither steady nor continuous. Rather, as we have seen, enrollment experiences varied considerably during the three subperiods of the study, depending on demographics, returns to education, and other societal factors. Between 1955 and 1970, the colleges expanded at an average rate of 62 percent. Enrollment growth then slowed considerably in the

1970s to an average rate of only 5 percent, and between 1980 and 1994 enrollments actually declined by an average of 2 percent.

Just as the enrollment trends of the colleges varied by subperiod, so too they varied by college. At the extremes, during the entire period 1955 through 1994, one college declined 14 percent in size, while three other colleges expanded their enrollments 1.4, 2.2, and 2.9 times. During each subperiod, different types of colleges grew the most. Small colleges expanded relatively the most during the tidal wave. In the 1970s, men's colleges that went coed grew much more than either their women's college or their always-coed counterparts; and during the 1980s and early 1990s, the most prestigious colleges have been best able to weather the population declines.

Although a few of our colleges experienced continuous growth, most had erratic enrollment patterns, with increases and decreases, both planned and unplanned. Planned enrollment increases were usually prompted by either the need or the desire to increase tuition revenue. The growth of the colleges we studied reflected pressures to offer more specialized courses, build better facilities (such as state-of-the-art science and foreign language labs), reduce faculty teaching loads, and provide more non-academic services to students. All of these changes required money to create and sustain them, which for liberal arts colleges translates into more tuition-paying bodies.

Notwithstanding Kershaw's prescription and the multiple pressures to become more like small research universities, expansion has not always been the best course for the colleges in our study. Since 1980 some of the colleges have deliberately decreased their entering class size in order to preserve or enhance their class profiles. Except for periods of intense growth, like the tidal wave, there has always been a size/quality trade-off evident in enrollment decisions. This interplay between size and quality has become increasingly important over the last 15 years as admissions situations have worsened, and it has become more difficult to enroll a class of the desired size and quality.

CHAPTER 2

The Admissions Process

IN A 1959 article entitled "The National Scene" Eugene Wilson, dean of admissions at Amherst, described three stages of admissions: *stage 1*—warm body, good check; *stage 2*—only the qualified; and *stage 3*—many called, few chosen.[1] Five years later, Noel Baker, director of admissions at Hiram, outlined a similar hierarchy: "It is the practice of mass application to college that has developed the practice of *open admission* which grants admission on the basis of simple fulfillment of minimum stated requirements; *selective admission* which amounts to not much more than the rejection of the unfit; and *competitive admission* where the choice is between highly qualified candidates."[2] Although both Wilson and Baker believed that colleges passed sequentially through these stages, the admissions histories of the colleges in our study suggest that the hierarchy is more complicated and fluid, with schools moving back and forth among the categories. Such movements seem to depend mostly on national demographic and social trends, but also on institutional priorities and policies.

In this chapter, we explore how the process of admissions has changed at the colleges in our study over the last 40 years as they have traversed Wilson's and Baker's categories. We pay particular attention to trends in three factors: applications, admit rates, and yields. The number and character of applications a college receives determines its ability to enroll a class that meets institutional priorities of size, quality, and diversity. The admit rate, or selectivity, of a college is defined as the percentage of applicants admitted.[3] A smaller applicant pool necessitates the admission of a greater percentage of the applicants and, therefore, constrains a college's ability to determine the specific class composition. Finally, yield is defined as the percentage of admitted students who enroll. A low yield adversely affects the admit rate, because the lower its yield, the more students a college must admit to reach its targeted class size.

For the purposes of this chapter, we have grouped ten of the colleges into three categories, and we examine the particular admissions experiences of these groups in relation to the average experiences of all sixteen colleges in our study. The three groups we established are (1) Amherst-Williams, as representative of the most selective formerly men's colleges; (2) a set of women's colleges, which is comprised of the three colleges in our study that are still women's colleges—Mount Holyoke, Smith, and Wellesley; and (3) the Ohio Five, which includes the five most selective

Ohio liberal arts colleges—Denison, Kenyon, Oberlin, Ohio Wesleyan, and the College of Wooster. While we will also discuss the experiences of the other six colleges, and they are included in the average, each is idiosyncratic and could not be grouped easily with any of the others.

EARLY GATEKEEPING (PRE-1955)

Prior to the post–World War II baby boom, liberal arts college admissions officers were gatekeepers, letting in many, if not most, of the students who came knocking at their doors. As long as they could find enough qualified applicants to fill the entering class, the admissions officers of old were doing all right. The situation at Denison in 1951 described by Charlotte Weeks, secretary of the Admissions Committee, was typical:

> We have just about reached a perfect balance in the number of applications (women!) we can accept and the number we receive—so there should be no more loud mourning in the land over rejections! In fact as far as the men are concerned, we would only be too happy to receive as many applications as we could accept. This year we could easily have accommodated at least another seventy-five freshmen in Curtis Hall. The smaller number of high school graduates coupled with the Korean War and our failure to secure an ROTC unit decimated the ranks of freshmen men as effectively as the plague![4]

Until the 1950s, admissions staffs typically consisted of one professional and possibly a secretary to take care of clerical work. Often, a dean would split responsibilities between admissions and some other aspect of administration or teaching. Colleges could function effectively with such a simple admissions structure, because students tended to apply only to their first-choice college, and they were usually accepted. A close collaboration between admissions officers and guidance counselors also facilitated such modest staffing. Admissions officers visited selected high schools, interviewed candidates for admissions, and then usually offered admission to students on the spot. Philip Smith, dean of admissions at Williams College, recounted a visit as an admissions officer in the late 1950s. After he interviewed the students, Smith sat down with eight teachers; he was given a pat on the back and a Scotch, and was expected to offer admission to all the candidates right then.[5]

INSTITUTIONAL UTOPIA (1955–1965)

College admissions changed dramatically when the baby boom generation began to apply to college. In 1956, Benjamin Fletcher Wright, president of Smith College, reported to his board of trustees, "Last year I discussed the much talked about 'tidal wave' of students now in elementary schools who will soon be pressing for admission to the colleges. Not even the astronomers can predict how high this tide will rise, for the birth rate which began to go up after 1940 is still high. The word 'tidal' is therefore misleadingly inappropriate—this so-called tide shows no signs of ebbing."[6] Wright's concerns were warranted. Between 1955 and 1965, applications increased an average of 69 percent at the liberal arts colleges in our study—increases which ranged from 11 percent to close to 150 percent.

More meaningful than the absolute increase in applications is the ratio of applications to entering class size. Figure 2.1 shows this ratio for the colleges over the entire length of our study. During the period between 1955 and 1965, all three groups increased their applicant-to-size ratios. Nevertheless, we begin to discern the stratification in admissions that would widen over the subsequent three decades. On average, the number of applications per place increased from 3.4 to 4.1. While the women's colleges ratio rose from 3.8 to 4.3 and the Ohio Five ratio increased from 2.4 to 3.4, the Amherst-Williams ratio swelled from 4.5 to 6.7 applications per place in the first-year class. The different sizes of the freshmen class accounted for this distribution. As discussed in Chapter 1, the women's colleges were on average larger than their male or coed counterparts during the 1950s and 1960s. Moreover, while the colleges in the Ohio Five group for the most part expanded significantly during this period, Amherst and Williams deliberately maintained their small sizes.

Although the influx of applicants would today seem like a blessing, the

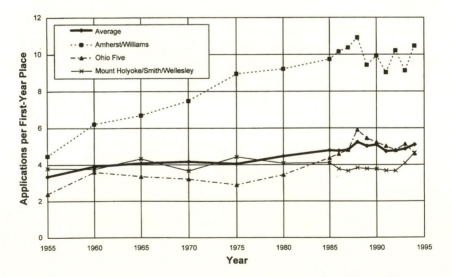

Figure 2.1. Applications per First-Year Place by Group (1955–1994).

"gatekeepers" of the 1950s were unsure how to deal with the application boom. As Rudolph wrote in 1960, "The spectre of numbers . . . was real. For the first time in history, American institutions of higher learning experienced prosperity and called it a problem."[7] On the positive side, the flood of applicants provided new opportunities for the colleges to expand their enrollments and increase the quality of their entering classes (as described in Chapters 1 and 3). On the negative side, colleges began to compete fiercely with each other for the best students. In 1957, a memo to Kenyon's Alumni Admissions Committee alluded to both the upside and the downside: "For the first time in Kenyon's history we closed enrollment three months in advance of the opening of the College because of the surplus of applications. For the first time we cut back on the size of the entering class because Kenyon's enrollment was at capacity." However, the memo also stressed, "If there is just one fact that I would like to really get across to you, it would be that colleges are fighting harder than ever, with no holds barred for top flight candidates."[8]

The increase in applications brought about by the tidal wave had profound implications for the admissions process. In 1959, Eugene Wilson characterized the new era in admissions:

> For generations prior to the last war the central problem of admissions at Amherst and similar institutions had been one of *recruitment*—finding enough qualified candidates to fill each entering class. Since 1946, however, the central problem of admissions has increasingly been one of *selection*—picking the "best" candidates from a great excess of qualified applicants.[9]

The need to choose among many students led to the concept of *selectivity* and the idea that the percentage of students admitted to a college was an appropriate measure of its standing. The College Board's decision to publish its first handbook in 1959 reinforced this new attitude. Previously, the number of applications and the number of students admitted by a college were closely guarded secrets. Once admissions statistics became public, however, they came to signify a college's quality.

The Specter of Multiple Applications

As the admissions standards at most selective liberal arts colleges became more rigorous, parents and children became concerned about the prospects for admissions. In 1961, Ambrose J. De Flumere, director of admission at Hiram College, noted "the growing hysteria over getting into college."[10] In order to ensure that they were admitted somewhere, students began to file several applications. These multiple applications overwhelmed admissions offices. Mary Chase, the admissions director at

Wellesley, described their impact: "The preparation of these applications has already created a clerical breakdown in some schools which have neither the staff to prepare records, nor funds to pay clerks if they are available. These multiple applications add to the harassment of the already burdened admission staff."[11] Admissions officers could no longer function with part-time directors and tiny staffs. In 1961, Barbara Ziegler, the admissions director at Wheaton, explained to her president that she would have to stop performing extra-admissions activities, such as advising, registering, and room assignments: ". . . the situation will become increasingly tight each year for some time in the future. It is for this reason that I find myself stating that in the future I believe we will have to limit our activities to those which are purely admission procedures."[12]

As the numbers of applicants increased and students began to file multiple applications, the process of assembling a first-year class became more complex. Prior to 1951, the College Board required each applicant to indicate her or his top one or two choices. Thus, colleges were reasonably certain that a student would enroll if admitted. When this practice was discontinued in 1951, admissions directors faced a great deal of uncertainty; they could no longer be sure who would enroll. The "plague of multiple applications" took the final decision regarding the composition of the class out of admissions directors' hands. According to Wilson, "No longer does an admission committee select an entering class. To-day [sic] the admission committee selects candidates who by their 'yeas' and 'nays' determine the composition of the entering class."[13] Smith's 1956 President's Report elaborated on this change: "This present system . . . does not give the college complete freedom of choice relative to the make-up of the freshmen class. The final decision to accept or reject remains with the successful applicant for admission. . . . This is indeed a change from the old system where the student applied to the college of her choice and, if admitted, entered that college without further discussion or consideration."[14]

Unsure how many admitted students would enroll, college admissions officers were forced to play what Reverend Miles L. Fay, dean of admissions at Holy Cross, called "an educator's blind man's bluff" in order to enroll a class of the desired size:

> One of the most formidable admissions problems found in the wake of the much publicized "tidal wave" is the chimera of over-acceptance resulting from the Medusa of multiple applications injecting its sting everywhere. In the panic they face, even very good students apply to several different colleges, in the hope either that the school of their first choice will accept them, or that some one of the colleges will offer lucrative scholarships and/or financial aid. For a selfish security, this brand of student often times will not inform, until a

very late date, if at all, the colleges of his earlier acceptances that he will be matriculating elsewhere. . . . To allow for this as best they can, and to plan early to offset the later announced withdrawals, colleges everywhere, even the very best of them, partake perforce in a sheer guessing game of over-acceptance, which too often eventuates as an educator's "blind man's bluff". . . . According to an egregiously oversimplified rule of thumb, a guiding norm is said to be, "Capacity plus one-third."[15]

A Uniform Notification Date

The difficulty admissions directors faced in determining who would enroll was a result of both multiple applications and the lack of a uniform notification date. As competition for the best students increased, less selective colleges began to inform candidates of their acceptances earlier and earlier in the year. Although this practice sometimes hurt the yields at those schools with reply dates later in the year, it also sometimes inflated their yields. In 1955, Amherst sought a class of 250 but got 306. Amherst missed its target because it "failed to take into account the growing practice of early acceptances by other institutions which reduced the number of no-shows in the acceptance list."[16]

Despite the problems that the lack of uniformity created, colleges and universities were initially reluctant to adopt a uniform date. Daniel D. Test, Jr., the headmaster of a private school in Pennsylvania, sent letters to 112 colleges and universities in 1959 suggesting an earlier and perhaps uniform notification date as a way to mitigate the competition for students. He discovered that while many colleges "recognized and identified with the problem of the chaotic situation of college admissions . . . they indicated little hope of altering the situation. Most were willing to change if other institutions would do likewise, but none was optimistic that any uniform agreements could be made or successfully maintained." Their reasons varied according to their geographic and admissions situations. Test found, for example, that "the Midwestern colleges . . . seem to be under considerable pressure for college admission and seem to still have room for students. . . . Their practice tends to be to accept qualified students as the applicants' credentials are satisfactorily completed."[17] Among our colleges, both Ohio Wesleyan and the College of Wooster maintained rolling admissions policies through the early 1960s.

Just two years after Test sent his letter, many selective colleges and universities did agree to use January 1 as an application deadline, to notify applicants in the middle of April, and to require responses by May 1. The colleges seemed to have concluded that the benefits of uniform dates outweighed the risks. Williams, for example, worried that by adopting uniform dates it would lose students that it formerly enrolled by preempting Ivy League universities, but it also recognized that such uniform arrangements would eliminate most of its late withdrawals.[18]

The Introduction of Early Decision

Besides agreeing to institute uniform admissions deadlines, colleges tried various other methods during the 1950s and early 1960s to counter multiple applications and reduce their uncertainty. In the early 1950s many colleges began to charge application fees of $5 to $10. These fees were intended to dissuade "shoppers" and "acceptance letter collectors."[19] In the mid-1950s, colleges also started giving early verbal and written assessments of candidates' qualifications. Fred Copeland, director of admissions at Williams, first described this practice in his 1955 Admissions Report: "This year, Yale, and to some extent Harvard, gave early verbal and written guarantees to many top candidates in an attempt to reduce unnecessary 'safety measure' applications. . . . It seems to me that the practice is going to become more prevalent and that 'early acceptances' will become the rule rather than the exception; the problem will be not to let it go too far."[20]

The Seven Sisters formalized these "early encouragement/discouragement" practices in 1959 when they introduced early decision. Under this new program, the Seven Sisters encouraged well-qualified applicants who had a strong preference to apply to their first-choice college in the fall of their senior year. Early decision candidates were notified in December whether they were accepted, deferred, or rejected. Those who were accepted agreed to enroll. Those who were deferred or rejected still had time to file additional applications. The program was "intended primarily for the applicant who really needs only one application, but who is currently unwilling to wait until May for a decision without having one or more 'insurance applications.'"[21] In the first year of the program, the Seven Sisters admitted between 20 and 30 percent of their classes early. In 1959, Wellesley reported that early decision had produced a "heartening decline" in applications from the previous year, because "many applicants who preferred other colleges and who in other years would have appeared as Wellesley applicants simply did not file applications as they were successful candidates under the single application plan at the colleges of their choice."[22]

The success of the Seven Sisters' early decision plan, combined with pressure from students who didn't want to wait until late spring to decide where they would attend college, prompted many of the more selective coed and all-male colleges to implement similar policies during the early 1960s. Oberlin administrators initially rejected the idea of early decision,

but after many of their applicants complained that they had already received decisions from other colleges, Oberlin agreed to institute its own plan in 1961. Amherst adopted an early decision plan in 1962 "to minimize the uncertainties created by multiple applications. It followed earlier failures to control the problem by requiring successful applicants to make a deposit before Harvard, Yale or Princeton had informed their applicants of acceptance."[23] Williams followed suit in 1964. By 1965, some of these colleges were taking high percentages of their class under early decision; Amherst was accepting close to 60 percent, Oberlin 43 percent, and Wellesley 39 percent.

The introduction of early decision at some of the colleges, as well as the rise in applications at all of them, led to changes in yields. Figure 2.2 shows the yields for our three groups of colleges. In 1955, the yields at all the colleges were between 41 and 71 percent, with an average of 55 percent, and the averages for the three groups were clustered even more, between 52 and 58 percent. In 1965, the average yield had increased only slightly to 59 percent, but the range of yields among the colleges had widened appreciably. Unlike applications and admit rates, which generally moved in the same direction at all of the colleges in our study during the decade from 1955 to 1965, yields moved in two directions. All but one of the Massachusetts colleges benefited from improving yields of between 7 and 23 percentage points. Among the groups, the women's colleges and Amherst-Williams saw improvements in yield of 11 and 17 points, respec-

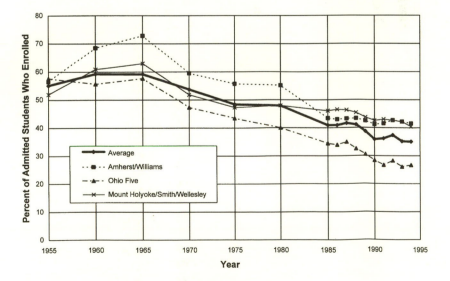

Figure 2.2. Yield by Group (1955–1994).

tively. At the same time, all except one of the Ohio colleges suffered declines in yield ranging from 2 to 8 points, and the yield of the Ohio Five group fell to 56 percent in 1960 before rebounding to 58 percent in 1965, exactly where it had started in 1955. Significantly, whereas the Ohio Five had the highest yield among the groups in 1955, it had the lowest yield in 1960 and 1965.

Those colleges at which yields declined most were also those colleges at which the rate of application increase had been the highest. Although they had expanded their application pools, these colleges were still among the least selective in our study. Their applicant numbers were undoubtedly bolstered by students sending out multiple applications. Not surprisingly, when students received multiple acceptances, the yields at less prestigious schools suffered most. The increases in yield at the other two groups of colleges were probably related to early decision. All of the colleges that experienced improved yields had instituted formal early decision programs. These programs increased yields because they enabled colleges to "lock in" a significant part of their classes at 100 percent yield.

Regardless of what happened to their yields, almost all of the colleges we studied became more selective in the early 1960s. As administrators at Kenyon College realized, "No longer need we attempt to interest a boy for numbers' sake. But let's pick the ones who will make their mark at Kenyon and later in the world and as Kenyon Alumni."[24] During this decade, the colleges were able to boast admit rates that had dropped between 10 and 35 percentage points. Whereas in 1955, only three colleges admitted *less* than half of their applicants, in 1965, only five colleges admitted *more* than 50 percent of their applicants. Four of the colleges became so selective that they were able to admit less than one-third of their applicant pools. Figure 2.3 shows the admit rates for the three groups. The average admit rate dropped 11 points during this decade from 59 to 48 percent. Although above average, the Ohio Five group dropped 14 points to reach an admit rate of 56 percent. The women's colleges group fell 14 points to 38 percent, and Amherst-Williams improved their selectivity by 19 points so that they were admitting only 21 percent of their applicants by 1965.

New Yardsticks

In order to exercise this selectivity and choose among the growing number of applicants washed up by the tidal wave, colleges had to define admission criteria. One consequence of the baby boom was an improvement in the academic qualifications presented by applicants at colleges and universities across the country. This increase in academic quality (which is discussed in more detail in Chapter 3) enabled admissions directors to tighten aca-

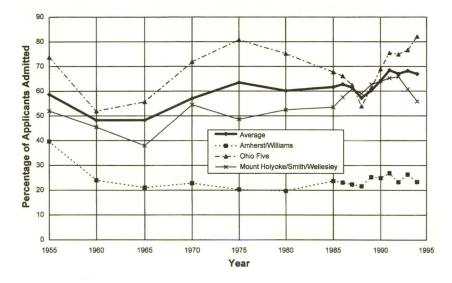

Figure 2.3. Admit Rate by Group (1955–1994).

demic requirements. As admissions standards rose, there was a growing concern among college administrators that too much emphasis was being placed on standardized test scores and high school grades. Vernon Alden, president of Ohio University, suggested that admissions officers needed to "find additional yardsticks to measure potential college students."[25] Many already were. In 1959, for example, a spokesperson from the University of Chicago told a reporter from the *New York Times*, "We . . . have asked ourselves if beauty and brawn do not deserve a place on our campus as well as brains. . . . The ordinary American boy who will only make a million in later life, the ordinary girl, who wants a husband as well as a diploma, are as welcome here as the Quiz Kid."[26]

The admissions directors at the liberal arts colleges in our study also increasingly looked to define the "other" that made a class interesting. It wasn't enough for an applicant just to have high test scores. According to President Wright:

> Smith doesn't want, any more than Harvard or Yale or Princeton wants, a freshmen class made up only of the precocious, any more than it desires one consisting exclusively of social butterflies or robust athletes. But then no one of these categories is exclusive and there is a reassuring proportion of students who combine the qualities which would be listed by almost any of us as those which are most desirable in a college population. . . . In addition to the essential academic preparation . . . we need to know as much as we can about her

seriousness of purpose, her staying power, her capacity for intellectual and moral development.[27]

In the early 1960s, the administration at Williams College faced pressure from its board of trustees to broaden its admission criteria. As the academic qualifications of Williams students improved, the board feared that the college was cutting out too much of its natural market; the board was concerned that when the next depression in higher education hit, Williams would be left with too few applications. In 1962, with support from the Ford Foundation, Williams instituted the "Ten Percent Program."[28] Under this program, Williams agreed to accept approximately 10 percent of each entering class "on the basis of criteria different from the prevailing quantitative indices."[29] In particular, Williams favored students with a special flair or forte, demonstrated leadership strengths, and enthusiastic teacher recommendations, as well as students with high class ranks but mediocre scores, or vice versa.

Even colleges that did not formalize admissions policies that looked beyond test scores acknowledged the desirability of using nonacademic qualities and choosing students from diverse backgrounds. In 1963, Bruce Haywood, provost at Kenyon, stressed, "our need now is to have a larger number of applicants of quality so that we can give our attention to the equally important matters of motivation, adaptability, originality, and personality as we select our candidates."[30] Wheaton's 1963 Long Range Planning Commission asserted, "We think it is important for an undergraduate body to maintain as much heterogeneity as possible. . . . For that reason we expect that Wheaton will be seeking more students whose backgrounds (geographic, ethnic or socioeconomic) are now sparsely represented in the college."[31] In general, admissions directors sought to extend the geographic distribution, increase the public secondary school representation, and expand the talent base of their students.

Broadened Pools

Such goals couldn't be realized unless admissions offices adapted their practices. Colleges could no longer maintain the same degree of personal relations with high schools as they had previously when many of their students came from relatively few feeder schools. Admissions counselors, however, also could not expect the diverse students they wanted to enroll simply to appear; they needed to go out and find them.

In the 1950s and 1960s, "going out and finding them" meant visiting high schools. Prior to the tidal wave era, if they made high school visits at all, colleges predominantly visited high schools in their region. Thus, colleges attracted students mainly from nearby. While data in the earliest years for the geographic distribution of our students are scarce, it appears that the colleges in our study enrolled students mostly from their region. For example, for the three schools in Ohio for which we have data in 1955, one enrolled 53 percent and the two others enrolled 72 percent of their students from the Midwest region. Similarly, all six of the Massachusetts schools for which we have data enrolled more than 60 percent of their students from the New England and Middle Atlantic states combined.

Beginning in the early to mid-1950s, many of the colleges visited more high schools over a wider geographic area. Some, like the College of Wooster, expanded their staffs by hiring someone charged specifically with making high school visits. Other colleges began to visit new territories. Even colleges such as Williams and Amherst, which did not need to recruit to the same degree as other colleges, expanded their geographical reach and visited new high schools. As early as 1953, Fred Copeland described changes in Williams's visitation program: "The list of school contacts was broadened markedly as the result of an expanded travel program on the part of the Admissions Director and his Assistant. This program included a trip to the West Coast which was the first such visit made by the Admission Office and enabled me to see schools and meet personnel, from many areas, with whom we have been dealing."[32] In a 1965 article entitled "Why Recruit," Walter A. Snickenberger, dean of admissions at Cornell, explained why selective institutions expanded and intensified their recruiting efforts even as they were turning away many qualified applicants: "To hold our position in the ranks of the great universities of the world, let alone to improve our position, we cannot afford to remain complacent or indifferent for, in fact, no university attracts all of the top youngsters it would like and certainly no university enrolls all of those it admits."[33] According to the O'Connell Report on admissions at Amherst, the selective admissions policy that developed after World War II "required extensive recruitment both to make Amherst's name nationally known and to draw applicants of outstanding intellectual promise from every socio-economic class and region of the country."[34] Amherst also had another reason for continuing its secondary school visits. Given Amherst's highly competitive admissions situation, many qualified students who applied were rejected. Dean Wilson worried that if Amherst didn't maintain close personal relationships with secondary school guidance counselors, they would start discouraging their best students from applying.[35]

When admissions directors expanded their travel itineraries, the proportions of students from different regions began to change. For the Massachusetts colleges, the most pronounced change from 1955 to 1965 was an increase in the proportion of students enrolled from southern and western states with corresponding declines in the percentages of students from other regions of the country, most notably from the Middle Atlantic states. For the six Massachusetts colleges for which we have information in both 1955 and 1965, the average percentage of students from the South increased from 9 to 12 percent, and the average from the West increased from 3 to 7 percent. The Ohio colleges were much less successful at enrolling students from the western states during this period. In 1957, Robert Jackson, director of admissions at Oberlin, even proposed that Oberlin institute two different admissions deadlines—an early one in February for easterners and a late one in May for westerners—in order to encourage more applicants from the West and to discourage some of the applicants from the East.[36]

While the number of students from the Middle Atlantic and New England states declined at the Massachusetts colleges between 1955 and 1965, representation of students from those regions increased at the colleges in Ohio. Ohio Wesleyan reported that a "significant increase in out-of-state enrollment came between 1953 and 1958."[37] Jackson explained why the numbers of students at Oberlin from Ohio and from New York were so close in 1961:

> We have an appeal to the eastern students as a school to which they can come with status approval. After the war when the pressure for places in college increased many eastern students turned to the mid-west since they could no longer be accommodated in the eastern colleges, and this trend to the mid-west and especially to Oberlin has continued. Also as our national reputation has increased we have lost some of our appeal to Ohio residents.[38]

The trends that Oberlin described were experienced to varying degrees by the other Ohio liberal arts colleges in our study. Although not all the Ohio colleges were able to attract as many students from the Middle Atlantic states as Oberlin was, most of them did report gains in their Middle Atlantic enrollments and corresponding declines in their instate and Midwest proportions. Earlier, some Ohio colleges had attributed losses of midwestern students to competition from eastern colleges. In 1954, for example, Kenyon administrators voiced concern over "the keen competition for outstanding talents":

> Middle western schools are now obliged to compete not only among themselves but with the great institutions of the East. About ten years ago the seaboard colleges decided to make a drive for national representation. Many of them have enormous prestige; they have the glamor of being far away; they have vast scholarship funds. Will the young man from Bucyrus accept a $600 scholarship from Kenyon when Harvard offers him $1,400? Will the brilliant student and star quarterback from Cleveland come to Kenyon to play football when Yale also makes him an offer? (Well, probably he won't go to Yale either,

this particular boy. He'll get an athletic scholarship to a state university and graduate a rich man.) Competition is so intense, in fact, that even state universities now send their representatives on far-flung trips (of course at the taxpayers' expense).[39]

While the eastern schools may have attracted some of the top students from the Midwest, the overall evidence from 1955 to 1965 is not consistent with Kenyon's analysis. The proportion of students from the Midwest at the Massachusetts colleges did not increase between 1955 and 1965. Instead, we suspect that the competition for Ohio and midwestern students came primarily from the state universities in the Midwest that were rapidly expanding during this period.

The geographic shifts described above coincided with changes in the private and public high school distributions at our colleges.[40] In the years before the baby boom students reached college age, the liberal arts colleges in New England enrolled students predominantly from private schools while midwestern colleges enrolled mainly students from public high schools. This difference was likely due to the admissions officers' limited geographic reach and the long-term relationships they had with school guidance counselors. Five of the liberal arts colleges in Massachusetts for which we have secondary school data in 1955 enrolled over 40 percent of their students from private schools, and three of them enrolled closer to 60 percent. In Ohio, the situation was the obverse. In 1955 and in 1960, the five Ohio colleges for which we have data enrolled between 75 and 90 percent of their students from public high schools. As part of their new emphasis on diversifying their student bodies, all five of the Massachusetts colleges made commitments to increase the representation of students from public high schools. Moreover, as the Massachusetts admissions directors recruited in regions beyond New England, they increasingly drew students from public high schools. By 1965, the percentage of public school graduates enrolled in the first-year classes at the five Massachusetts colleges had risen to between 58 and 65 percent.

Admissions officers have always carefully considered applications from alumni children. At many of the colleges, prior to the tidal wave all alumni children who could demonstrate a minimum level of ability were admitted. In 1959 Williams decided to continue "with the policy of making the final decision on the basis of whether or not the boy gave sufficient evidence that he could keep up with the pace and competition in order to receive his degree in four years. We realize that such a policy means some of this group will be the weakest members of the class."[41] As the competition for admission became tougher, colleges reconsidered and often reformulated policies that gave special consideration to alumni children. In 1961, De Flumere at Hiram asserted, "Another of the by-products is the concern of college graduates that their children will experience greater difficulty in getting into college than they did, even at their alma maters."[42] Eugene Wilson warned Amherst alumni, "What these changes in admissions mean is that the wise Amherst alumnus will not teach his boy to say 'Amherst' before he says 'mother.' Instead of putting an Amherst pennant over the crib, he will place five pennants of different colleges . . . and talk to his son about getting an education rather than an 'Amherst education.'"[43] Wilson's warning became especially relevant in 1966 when Amherst tightened its legacy policy and began admitting only those alumni sons who presented "total records of achievement that approximate other accepted candidates."[44] Even with the stricter alumni standards, the admit rate for legacies was generally between 60 and 85 percent, a rate as much as three times as high as the regular admit rate for some colleges. The yield on legacies, however, could also be twice as high as the overall yield for a class, thus making legacies a safe bet for admission during a time of uncertainty.

REDOUBLED RECRUITING (1965–1980)

By the middle of the 1960s, the liberal arts colleges had set new standards for themselves in terms of the quality and talent of their student bodies. They had all experienced the luxury of being able to choose the best candidates from strong pools. This experience was to spoil admissions directors who were largely unprepared for the changes in admissions that the late 1960s and 1970s ushered in and for the struggles they would face to maintain the admissions standards they had established. The leveling off of college-going rates, described in Chapter 1, left admissions directors at many colleges scrambling to increase their applicant pools in order to minimize selectivity losses. At the same time, the move to coeducation in the late 1960s and early 1970s completely altered the admissions landscape.

The average admit rate at the colleges increased from 48 percent in 1965 to 64 percent in 1975 before recovering slightly to 60 percent in 1980 (Figure 2.3). Both the women's college group and the Ohio Five became much less selective between 1965 and 1970. The women's college group recouped some of its selectivity losses in the early 1970s, ending the decade with an average admit rate of 52 percent. The Ohio Five, on the other hand, continued to accept a greater percentage of applicants through 1975, when the average admit rate reached 81 percent. Amherst-Williams, which already had a much lower admit rate in 1965, became even more selective over the period, so that by 1980 the two schools were accepting on average only 20 percent of the students who applied.

Looking at the admit rates of individual colleges is also instructive. All of the colleges, except for the men's colleges that became coed, experienced declines in their selectivity between 1965 and 1980. In 1965 only five colleges needed to accept more than 60 percent of their applicants; the rest admitted less than 50 percent. By 1980, however, 10 of the colleges in our study had admit rates greater than 50 percent. In fact, only three of the men's colleges and the most prestigious women's college were able to reject more applicants than they admitted.

The range in our colleges' admit rates led to a stratification of the overall admissions picture. By the end of the 1970s, there were very few colleges and universities left in the country that still had the luxury of surplus applicants. In 1979, Philip Smith acknowledged what a unique position Williams was in:

> Williams is among a handful of the very strongest academic institutions which increased their competitive admissions picture in the past year. Working against a national trend of fewer students, lower scores, more vocational interest for students and significantly higher costs for private institutions, a select group of prestigious institutions, will in my opinion continue to buck the national trends. Students, and their parents, will continue to be attracted to academic quality. A recently published college guide referred to "The Ancient Eight": Harvard, Princeton, Yale, Dartmouth, Brown, Williams, Amherst and Wesleyan. Our future is linked with this group, all of which should continue to show strength in admissions for the near term future.[45]

Falling Yields

Another important factor in the loss of selectivity was the declining yields which all of the colleges in our study experienced between 1965 and 1980. The impact of this decline in yield cannot be overstated. As David L. Davis-Van Atta, director of institutional research at Oberlin, explained in 1980, "If there is a culprit to be sighted among the lines of these charts, it must be the yield line. No other force but the declining yield has so powerful and inexorable an effect upon an admissions process. Even small declines in the yield must be countered by dramatic increases in the admit ratio, especially when the yield is already low."[46] A hypothetical example is illustrative. If College X has an applicant pool of 500 students, wants to enroll 100 students, and expects a yield of 25 percent, it must admit 400 students, or 80 percent of its applicants, to ensure that it meets its target. College Y, on the other hand, that has the same number of applicants and same enrollment target but an expected yield of 50 percent, needs to admit only 200 students, or 40 percent of its applicants. In this example, a 25 percentage point difference in yield necessitates a 40 percentage point difference in selectivity.

In 1965 the average yield at the colleges began to fall precipitously (Figure 2.2). Prior to 1970, most of the colleges had yields between 50 and 80 percent, averaging 59 percent. By 1970, with the exception of the brand-new Hampshire College, which had a 96 percent yield, the range of yields had shifted to between 42 and 62 percent and by 1975, most of the colleges had yields between 40 and 50 percent. In 1980 the yields averaged 48 percent. Even more striking perhaps than the 11 point drop in average yield between 1965 and 1980 is the fact that only two colleges had higher yields in 1980 than the average yield for all the colleges in 1965.[47]

The dramatic drop in yields at the colleges we studied, and more generally, during the 1970s was due to many factors. As noted above, the number of high school graduates attending college began to level off in 1968, so colleges began to compete more fiercely for the best students. In addition, in the late 1960s and early 1970s, many colleges broadened their recruitment efforts to target applicants from minority groups, less well-known public schools, and areas of the country outside their traditional geographic reach. Although colleges increased their numbers of applicants as they developed new applicant pools, yields fell since many of the students from the new pools did not necessarily have a strong commitment to attending the colleges that were recruiting them. During the late 1960s and 1970s those colleges in our study with the most well-defined missions and, therefore, the most focused applicant pools, were able to maintain their yields best. For example, Gordon College, a Christian liberal arts college, had yields in excess of 60 percent throughout the 1970s; and although Hampshire's yield fell from its first-year height, it was still 72 percent in 1980, suggesting that its alternative education program appealed to a distinct group of applicants.

Another development that explains the falling yields is the reduction in early acceptances. In 1980 Carl Bewig, the admissions director at Oberlin, attributed Oberlin's drop in yield to the decline in early decision candidates: "A serious reduction in the number of early decision applicants three years ago, which loss we have not recovered, has been a major contributing factor to the yield problem."[48] By the late 1970s, the use of early decision programs had begun to wane. Whereas in the mid-1960s, enrolling 40 percent of a class early was not uncommon for a college, by the late 1970s early decision programs generally accounted for less than a quarter of the enrollments at the schools in our study.

Efforts to Bolster Yields

As in earlier periods, early decision programs were used in the late 1960s and 1970s to try to ensure the composition and size of the first-year class.

In his 1977 report to secondary school counselors, Dean of Admissions Edward Wall explained that Amherst's early decision program "serves as the foundation of the class. The holes will be filled in later under regular admission."[49] More specifically, early decision provided Amherst with a way to combat its losses to its three top competitors. "So long as Harvard, Yale and Princeton refuse to accept the concept of Early Decision, we feel that we have no other choice," wrote Wall. "This may not be fair but how can we possibly be fair under the circumstances?" After a decrease in the size of the 1971 entering class, the admissions director at Denison looked for ways to stave off further declines the following year. "Hopefully, by offering greater flexibility in the criteria used for the selection of early-consideration candidates, we can expand the numbers in that group," suggested Burton Dunfield. "The probability of retaining an accepted early-consideration candidate is almost twice that for a regular acceptee. This might reduce substantially the number of regular acceptees required to fill the class, thus making it possible to obtain a high-quality group in spite of a smaller total pool."[50]

Despite Dunfield's optimism, Denison, like most of our colleges, found that as the 1970s progressed it received fewer early applications. In 1965, Denison enrolled 32 percent of its class through its early consideration program, a variant on early decision. This percentage fell over the next decade so that in 1970 the college enrolled only 23 percent early, and by 1975 only 12 percent. Other colleges faced similar reductions in the number of candidates for early decision and the percentage of their classes they were able to enroll early. Early decision fell out of favor, in part because of the buyer's market of the late 1970s—students seemed more reluctant to commit to schools early. In 1977, Williams noted "a growing trend to delay a final decision on the college choice until mid-April after all options are in hand."[51]

For at least one college in our study, however, the decline in early decision slots in the late 1970s was supply, not demand, driven. In 1978 Amherst decided to reduce the number of candidates accepted under early decision to no more than one-third of the entering class, down from 50 percent or more in earlier years, "in the spirit of 'equal access' and in an effort to ensure more diversity within the entering class and to make our admission process more equitable and flexible."[52] Amherst had found that "By taking nearly half the class under Early Decision, we simply ran out of room."[53]

As the number of students willing to commit themselves through early decision programs diminished, colleges tried other ways to bolster their yields and to attract top students. In a return to the early encouragement policies of the 1950s, in 1973/74 Wellesley instituted early evaluation, a nonbinding program that had an application deadline earlier than the regular deadline but later than early decision. The *Wellesley Alumnae Magazine* reported that in the program's first year 750 applicants requested to be rated. An A rating meant the candidate was very likely to be accepted in the spring; a B rating meant she was a realistic applicant if there were space; and a C rating indicated there was only a slight chance and the applicant should make plans to attend another college. The early evaluation system not only gave students an early assessment of where they stood, it also gave Wellesley extra time to target the A candidates.[54]

In the early 1970s, Williams added an "early write" program to its yield repertoire. Under this program, Williams notified the best applicants in its regular pool that they had been accepted in February. Philip Smith articulated the "Three Little Pig Theory" behind early write: "You have to get to the fair before the big bad wolf who is Harvard."[55] One of the major benefits of Williams' early write program, like Wellesley's early evaluation program, was that it gave the college more time to woo the best students it admitted. In February 1972, Williams invited the first early write candidates to campus. Of the 31 students who visited, 21 accepted Williams's offer, a much higher yield than Admissions Director Copeland anticipated, given that "most had offers of acceptance from our major competitors."[56]

Applicant Trends

By at least one measure—the number of applications—the various efforts by the colleges we studied to augment their applicant pools were successful. As shown in Figure 2.4, between 1965 and 1980 applications to the colleges rose slightly from an average of 1,757 to an average of 2,110. Although all three of the college groups experienced net gains in applications, the extent and timing of those gains differed considerably.

The women's college group began to feel the effects of coeducation between 1969 and 1971 during what was termed "the coed panic" when many women seized the opportunity to attend prestigious, newly coed Ivy League institutions. Between 1965, the height of the baby boom, and 1970, after the initial Ivy League schools became coed, applications at all of the women's colleges in our study declined between 6 and 34 percent. Not only did applications decline, but losses of admitted students to the newly coed colleges increased. In 1972 Mount Holyoke noted, "Of those who are entering other colleges, there is a decline in the number going to women's colleges, from 44 percent last year compared to 35 percent this year. Although Smith and Wellesley continue to draw off the largest numbers (over 1/4 of all our ghosts choose one of those institutions), we lost 23 students to Brown, which was more than we lost to Vassar, Radcliffe, Bryn

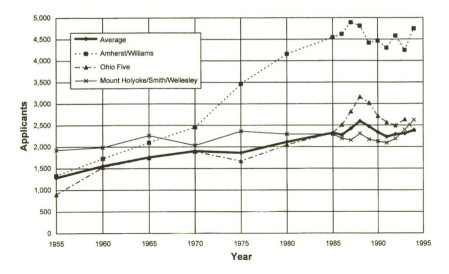

Figure 2.4. Applications by Group (1955–1994).

Mawr or Barnard. Of the other coed places, we lost 19 to Yale and 15 to Princeton."[57]

The women's colleges were the only colleges that faced application declines between 1965 and 1970. Among the formerly men's colleges, one had already become coeducational by 1970, resulting in a 96 percent increase in applications. The other men's colleges and the coeducational colleges continued the modest application increases they had been experiencing since the mid-1950s. The average number of applications at Amherst-Williams, for example, grew from 2,096 to 2,454 between 1965 and 1970, and the average for the Ohio Five increased from 1,744 to 1,892 in the last half of the 1960s.

In the first half of the 1970s, the application situations changed dramatically. At all but one of the women's colleges, applications increased from 10 to 20 percent and returned to the level before the coed panic. Two more of the men's colleges became coed during these five years, and their applications grew by 48 and 90 percent. Meanwhile, applications declined between 11 and 36 percent at all but one of the coeducational colleges, and at that college applications plummeted 70 percent as a result of campus strikes and student protests. The coeducational colleges, like the majority of colleges in the country, were affected by the declining college-going rate and competition from the public sector. They also faced more intense competition from other liberal arts colleges since their potential applicants had many more coeducational options. According to a report delivered to the Oberlin Board of Trustees, "Oberlin's loss of coeducational distinctiveness and corresponding lion's share of that particular college bound market have necessitated a redoubling of our efforts to identify, nurture and enroll the same slice of the pie that now has more institutions hungering after it."[58]

The Importance of Recruitment

In the 1970s, recruitment techniques, which had previously been used as a way to supplement applications to ensure the best possible choices, became imperative for all schools. Even for the newly coed colleges whose applicant pools became more robust, recruitment was necessary to increase their visibility in new markets. Although they were actively engaged in trying to attract new students, some of the colleges were hesitant to admit that they were recruiting, since the term had negative connotations for colleges accustomed to an oversupply of students. Mary Ellen Ames, director of admissions at Wellesley, insisted, "We like to say 'school visiting' although at times we have called it a recruitment program, for lack of a better word. When you think about it, we are not recruiting in the usual sense of the word. That word is most often associated with the raising of troops! We want to restore and replenish our student body, and in that sense you might call it recruiting, but 'school visiting' gives a clearer picture of what we are really doing."[59] Recruitment of students became very aggressive in all sectors of private higher education, not merely at the liberal arts colleges in our study. A 1974 article in *U.S. News and World Report* reported that "Colleges with sagging enrollments and financial worries are resorting more and more to 'head hunting.'"[60]

Those colleges that failed to recruit aggressively suffered more than their counterparts that did intensify their recruiting. During the 1960s, Wheaton, like most other liberal arts colleges, had the strongest admissions picture in its history and was able to admit less than half of its applicants. By some accounts, President Prentice thought that it was "immoral" to recruit more students than the college could take, so while Wheaton's competitors strengthened and expanded their applicant pools and increased their selectivity, Wheaton disbanded its high school visiting program. In a study prepared for Wheaton in 1971, the Barton-Gillet Company found:

> Wheaton has certainly not been alone in its reluctance to recruit aggressively, but in Wheaton's case this attitude has caused a clear attenuation of attitudes and agencies that could be of great use. It is not germane to discuss here if the policy of discontinuing admission visits to high schools a number of years back

was justified. What is germane is the lack of momentum which admission and recruiting has suffered in doing this. One practical example will suffice to indicate what is meant: Normally colleges visit a number of high schools each year, varying their lists in response to applications, to the reception they receive, changing neighborhoods, and so on. Wheaton has no such back log of information on which to rely and as a result a number of the high schools that admissions officers are now visiting are essentially unsuitable for Wheaton's purpose. Counselors have been visiting too few schools and the pattern of schools visited seems somewhat helter-skelter.[61]

The major consequence of Wheaton's failure to recruit was that during a time when applications dropped generally, Wheaton's applicant pool shriveled. By 1970 Wheaton's applications had fallen 34 percent, and by 1975 they were 44 percent lower than the 1965 high. As a result, Wheaton was forced to admit close to 80 percent of its applicants.

If Wheaton was relatively late in embracing recruiting, the rest of the women's colleges in our study were among the first to adopt aggressive recruiting strategies. According to Mary Ellen Ames, the coed panic of the late 1960s and early 1970s made the Seven Sisters realize that their system of cooperative recruitment wasn't working well enough, and so they all became more actively involved in recruiting for their own institutions. Beginning in 1970, for example, both Wellesley and Smith instituted intensive recruitment programs which included greatly increased high school visiting, more contacts with guidance counselors on and off the campus, greater participation in college fairs and college nights, and an Open Campus Day for accepted candidates. The admissions offices also increased personal correspondence and follow-up mailings, made more use of very active volunteer student admission programs, and solicited help from alumnae admission representatives. Ames believes that these new recruitment activities were in large part the reason that applications at most of the women's colleges recovered quickly after the initial coed panic.[62]

The Student Search Service and the Common Application

The major new development in recruitment at all the schools during the 1970s was an emphasis on unsolicited contact with prospective students. The College Board began offering the Student Search Service (SSS) in 1970 through which colleges and universities could buy the names and addresses of prospective students. Direct mail quickly became a staple of all admissions offices. Smith's 1976 Admissions Report noted that the admissions staff responded to, sent mail to, and processed information on between 9,000 and 12,000 inquiries per year. This total included 6,000

names procured from the SSS, 700 names of National Achievement final-
ists, 2,000 names submitted by traveling admissions representatives, and
400 students who had requested that their College Board scores be sent to
Smith.[63]

Initially names could be bought from SSS based on SAT scores and
gender, but gradually the service expanded to include divisions by ethnicity
and geographic region as well. Thus, colleges could target particular types
of students, who for various reasons were not in their traditional applicant
pools. Wellesley took full advantage of the tailoring options. For example,
in 1977 Wellesley ran a search for the top female science students and
then sent them an article about its Science Center.[64]

Williams also targeted its searches to achieve institutional priorities,
sending mailings to black students and candidates east of the Mississippi
with high College Board scores.[65] The major reason that Williams and
other colleges expanded their use of the SSS was that it apparently
worked. In 1983, Williams credited the SSS for its role in enrolling some
of its best students:

> Using the Student Search Service ... we contacted 5,000 students. ... Of
> those that responded by card, 265 applied to Williams. This represented 6.7
> percent of the total applicant pool. Of those who applied, 204 were accepted
> (76.9 percent). It is interesting to compare this acceptance rate to 28.4 percent
> overall acceptance rate as it provides some insight into just how specialized
> and academically talented this segment of our applicant pool is. Of those
> search students offered admissions 67 enrolled. This represents 13.1 percent
> of the class. The student search clearly is an increasingly important facet of
> our admissions efforts, and the statistics provided above demonstrate that, if
> anything, we should be increasing and refining our search activities, and for
> the class of 1988 we are doing just that.[66]

As colleges increasingly used direct mail, top students were bombarded
with material from hundreds of colleges. Since most prospective students
identified through a search knew little or nothing about a college, it became crucial that a student's first impression of the college be a memora-
ble one. In a 1977 admissions report, Philip Smith asserted that "any mail-
ing must be extremely well done in order to get past a prospective
applicant's mailbox."[67] Colleges hired design teams to create glossy and
colorful admissions brochures that presented carefully crafted images of
the college. Colleges also began to produce specialized publications featur-
ing specific aspects of college life, including minority experiences, athletics, and religious life. The creation of these materials became part of the
increasingly complicated machinery of the admissions office.

Another strategy admissions officers began to employ to augment their
applicant pools was the use of the common application. In 1974, Edward

Wall announced to secondary school counselors, "Amherst will be part of an experiment which we and the fourteen other participating colleges feel could lead to a major breakthrough in the admissions process at selective colleges. As a result, both students and college counselors should be spared hours of time and effort as well as acute cases of writer's cramp! . . . Students can fill out one form and photocopy it."[68] The next year Wall recounted how use of the common application had expanded:

> For the second consecutive year, Amherst will be a "hard core" member of the Common Application experiment. That is, we shall be using the Common Application format *exclusively*, with an Amherst College masthead. Last year there were six "hard core" colleges. As of August 6, there were 18. Last year there were 15 colleges involved in the experiment. This year there are 80! Last year there were 30 high schools participating. This year there are better than 300! Our ultimate goal—universal use of the Common Application—appears to be just around the corner.[69]

Considering that for years colleges had been complaining about the submission of multiple applications, at first it seems puzzling that so many colleges embraced the common application, which would easily increase the number of applications filed per student. However, the adoption of the common application can be seen as an indication of a shift in attitude toward multiple applications and perhaps of resignation regarding the new admissions reality. In the 1970s, admissions officers tried to get as many applications as possible so that their selectivity would improve and so that they would have a greater chance of enrolling the type of class they wanted. Even those colleges that received far more applicants than they could admit recognized the potential of the common application to reach students who were not generally in their applicant pools, such as minority students.[70]

Geographic Shifts

As in the earlier period, the primary way that our colleges expanded their applicant pools in the 1970s was by changing the geographic focus of their recruitment efforts. During the 1970s, the Ohio colleges had differing responses to students from instate. Some colleges focused their attention on enrolling students from outside Ohio as a way of broadening their reach, while others focused on students from Ohio and the Midwest in order to strengthen their home markets. At the beginning of the decade, Denison and Ohio Wesleyan enrolled 40 and 37 percent of their students from Ohio, respectively. By 1970, both enrolled only 27 percent of their students from instate and had increased their representations from New England and, in Ohio Wesleyan's case, from the western states too.

Kenyon had always drawn its students less heavily from Ohio than some of its counterparts. In the late 1960s, Bruce Haywood at Kenyon realized, "We're playing in the wrong ball park when we recruit eastern students who apply here as their fourth choice. . . . The time has come . . . when we can no longer drive a 1948 Ford on a 1967 turnpike." Instead Kenyon decided that the "emphasis of the new admissions thrust will be shifted from eastern prep schools to the Midwest."[71] Despite this new emphasis, five years later, the percentages of students from the various areas of the country remained virtually unchanged, prompting John Kushan, the director of admissions, to broaden his sights even further:

> About 85 percent of the student population comes from East of the Mississippi River, with Ohio contributing about 25–30 percent of the students. . . . We do not try, in a student population as small as ours, for a wide geographic spread, but we very definitely would like to draw more heavily from states West of Ohio. We cannot become too dependent on any one area for students. In the past two years we have noticed an increase in the number of students from the South and we hope this continues to grow. We welcome applicants from any area.[72]

Oberlin was another Ohio college that by 1970 enrolled more students from the Middle Atlantic states than it did from the midwestern states. At the beginning of the decade, Oberlin also decided to shift some of its recruitment priorities to Ohio. Because its reputation was better on the East Coast than in Ohio, Oberlin recognized "the need for an all out effort in the home region to present the positive advantages of attending Ohio's leading institution of higher education." Oberlin also felt that as an Ohio school it had a responsibility to educate youth from Ohio. More pragmatically, Oberlin realized that it could not afford to let its reputation slip among those students who should be its natural constituency.[73] Despite its efforts, Oberlin, like Kenyon, was unable to increase its representation from Ohio. In fact, during the 1970s, Oberlin's overall enrollment from the Midwest declined while its enrollment from the New England states doubled.

Public/Private High School Trends

During the tidal wave one of the priorities of admissions directors at some of the Massachusetts colleges had been to democratize admissions by enrolling more students from public high schools. Nevertheless, the most prestigious colleges had strong connections to independent and private schools in New England and the Middle Atlantic states, which admissions directors worked hard to preserve. In his 1976 Admissions Report, Philip Smith described the tension colleges such as Williams confronted:

> As Williams has become more selective in the past four or five years, independent schools have had the feeling that they were getting "pinched" more than they should be in our competition. This feeling has been particularly prevalent in the male schools. . . . I am not sure that this is a problem which has a solution. It is a fact that the number of male students we are accepting is 50 smaller than five years ago, and it is also true that the competition has increased greatly in that period for a smaller number of male spaces. The increase in our applicant pool has come largely from the high school and day school applicants, though we are receiving substantially larger numbers of applicants from Exeter, Andover and Hotchkiss than we have received in the past—and we are also accepting larger numbers from these schools than we have in the past ten years or more. . . . I feel confident in continuing to assure independent school people that Williams does not have a bias against their graduates. And I am also comfortable with the position that we do not have a bias in their favor. My feeling is that this will be a problem which will linger and which may fester in a few locations.[74]

Other Massachusetts colleges also continued to see an increase in the percentage of students enrolled from public schools. By 1978, for example, Hampshire was enrolling 70 percent of its students from public high schools, up from 50 percent when the college first opened.[75]

All of the more selective coed colleges in the Midwest experienced the opposite shift during the 1970s and began to enroll significantly more students from private schools. Of the four always-coed colleges in the Ohio Five, one increased its percentage of private school students from 11 to 30 percent, another from 24 to 39 percent, the third from 17 to 27 percent, and the fourth from less than 20 to 38 percent. These shifts were accompanied at all four colleges by an increase in the number of students from the New England area. This trend was most probably a result of changes in admissions at many of the liberal arts colleges in the Northeast. As the quote above from Williams demonstrates, it became more difficult for male students from the private prep schools in the Northeast to be admitted to the most selective liberal arts colleges in their region. As a result of coeducation, applications at the most prestigious liberal arts colleges increased and admissions standards became even more stringent. At the same time, the formerly men's colleges were accepting slightly fewer men than they had before, despite promises to the contrary. A third contributing factor was that the northeastern colleges were particularly successful in their attempts to expand their applicant pools and increase their national reach and began to enroll larger percentages of students from the West and South than before. All of these factors led to a surplus of male private school graduates, many of whom applied to quality liberal arts colleges in the Midwest, where it was easier to be admitted.

A More Complicated Job

As a result of the new innovations and responsibilities brought about by the admissions situation in the 1970s, the job of admissions director became much more complicated. Ames at Wellesley explained, "I feel that I'm a ring master of a seven ring circus all the time. . . . It's an exciting job, a real challenge, a constantly moving scene, with constant change and pulls from all directions."[76] In order to deal with this complexity, the staff at all of our liberal arts colleges increased markedly. Carl Bewig described some of the changes in the running of the admissions office:

> When I arrived back in Oberlin in 1968 to take up my duties as Assistant Director of Admissions, I joined a staff of four white males whose principal activity, as was altogether appropriate for that era, was the evaluation of candidates for admissions and determining, in 60 percent of the cases, who would NOT be admitted. Recruitment efforts were minimal, but certainly adequate for the times; direct, unsolicited contact of prospective students was unheard of; and the involvement of persons outside the professional admissions staff in our enterprise was just being developed. . . . Today's admissions staff numbers nine persons, whose work is supplemented by two ethnic counselors, four senior interns, and a cadre of hundreds of students, scores of faculty, and thousands of alumni volunteers. . . . While deliberations on the admissibility of candidates continue to occupy much of our time, our primary undertakings are in the area of recruitment.[77]

Williams also expanded its staff, from 9 to 13 people, and the admissions office bought its first computer in 1974 in order to cope with the large volume of applications.[78]

Part of what made admissions offices more complicated during the late 1960s and 1970s was the demands put on them to enroll different types of students. In 1978, Peter Wells, a teacher and dean at a private high school in New Haven, Connecticut, commented sardonically, "The admissions committee creates a class. Functioning on the supposition that a university needs many specialized people to make up its rich life—oboists, Slavonic choristers, computer wizards, lethal linebackers, barrel-jumping tricyclists, etc., etc.—the committee finds the people to fill the slots." He added that the committee is "under fierce pressure to admit alumni children, rich children, alumni children, minority children, alumni children, bright children, and in any event fill the school with a large enough percentage of paying customers to keep the school in business. More and more colleges express concern or are frankly desperate about this last item as population figures decline."[79]

More members of the college became involved in admissions as the functions of the admissions office shifted to accommodate new priorities and programs. Faculty, students, and alumni met prospective students, read files, and even made admissions decisions. At Oberlin, Carl Bewig attributed this greater involvement to the student protests of the 1960s: "The traditional bailiwicks of students, faculty and administration were profoundly jostled during the turmoil of the 1960s on college campuses . . . it was only natural for the Admissions Office to begin to incorporate other elements of the campus community into its operation." As a result, he continued, "In the past several years, due to the increased involvement of students, faculty, alumni and other administrators in the admissions process, the Oberlin Admissions Office has become more visible and controversial than ever before."[80]

THE ADMISSIONS MARKET (1980–1994)

As higher education entered the 1980s, the job of the admissions director didn't look like it was going to get any easier. Between 1979 and the mid-1990s, the absolute number of 18-year-olds was projected to decline 26 percent. A 1984 article by Jonathan Harr in the *New England Monthly* described the situation that the decline in the college age population had precipitated:

> In a word, the seller's market for America's colleges has closed down. For the Elite schools in New England, this means that the quality of their primary product (education) and its marketable equivalent (reputation) is at peril: There are only so many good kids to go around and too many schools who want them. This circumstance has forced colleges to arm themselves with new and unsettling weapons—aggressive marketing techniques, hard-sell persuasion, even offers of large scholarships to students who don't have money worries.[81]

Harr's war analogy seemed appropriate given the intense competition that ensued as colleges vied for the diminishing number of top-quality students. In 1978, Humphrey Doermann wrote an article for the College Board called "The Future Market for College Education." In it, he warned, "if colleges manage only to compete aggressively with each other for a larger share of a shrinking pool, the total system will be in disarray 15 years from now."[82] Many other educators also feared that the competition for students would lead to breakdowns in the congenial relationships colleges had always shared. Ames at Wellesley, for one, worried, "Unfortunately, there are signs that point to the real beginnings of cut-throat competition. College admissions and financial aid conventions, honored since the early fifties, are breaking down. There is outright buying or bribing of top candidates, preferential packaging in financial aid awards, disregard of the candidate's reply date, requirement of large deposits to retain a place—such practices are becoming more and more prevalent."[83] Dean Whitla, director of the Office of Institutional Research and Evaluation at Harvard University, also expressed concern that the traditional consensus in financial aid and admissions policies was being eroded in "the tournament for students."[84]

Liberal arts colleges used increasingly sophisticated techniques to "win" this tournament. The role of recruitment in the admissions process became firmly entrenched. A 1994 article in Kenyon's alumni magazine described the "courtship ritual":

Not too long ago . . . the phrase "college admissions" scarcely existed. Today, however, that innocent sounding phrase describes not merely a process but an industry. The courtship between colleges and prospective students, always subject to new complications, focuses the attention of several millions of Americans every year—from students just hoping to be accepted to entrepreneurs looking to make a buck on those same hopes. . . . The stakes are high: Students and their families increasingly see college, and more particularly the "right" college, as vital to professional and personal satisfaction. Tuition increases have made college choice a $100,000 question. At the same time, colleges compete against one another to remain fully enrolled while the number of high school graduates has declined over the last two decades. . . . For better or for worse, says John W. Anderson [dean of admissions] . . . "the simple days of college admissions are gone for good." The fundamentals are the same. Students want only the best colleges. Colleges want only the best students. It's a courtship dance. The steps though are increasingly complex. . . . In an era of high-profile advertising among colleges, Kenyon has had to raise its voice higher even to be heard among the crowd.[85]

As part of the admissions ritual, colleges made even more use of direct mail than they had in the 1970s. Admissions offices developed innovative, glossy publications dealing with various aspects of the collegiate experience, and they produced videos of the campus to send to prospective students and their parents. Colleges also tried to give their admissions activities a more personal touch, answering inquiries directly, and using faculty and alumni to contact prospective students. At times, these efforts have reached absurd extremes. One college in the Great Lakes College Association has staff members personally call every one of its 25,000 inquiries. "Recruiting is frightful. We are driven to distraction," said one admissions director we interviewed, who had just the day before called a prospective student: "The kid was only 13!"

Such personal touches not only distract admissions deans, they also cost money. Today, a college video can cost $80,000 to $100,000. The admissions director at one liberal arts college told us that in 1994, his college spent in excess of $200,000 on publications, despite the fact that the college is "not particularly publication rich." In 1980 Carl Bewig explained one ramification of such high levels of spending: "Ours is a half-million dollar a year operation which costs out to about $555 for each of the approximately 900 new students we will enroll at Oberlin during the next year. In other words one-tenth of their tuition will have been spent getting them here!"[86] Oberlin's expenditures were not out of line. In 1983, Thomas Wenzlau, president of Ohio Wesleyan, reported, "The cost of getting a student to college is already high and will probably continue to increase rapidly. Outlays in excess of $1,000 for each student recruited are not unusual."[87]

Corporate Practices

As we have seen, in the 1960s colleges increased their recruitment efforts primarily by expanding school visits. In the 1970s, colleges embraced direct mail. The most significant recruitment change during the 1980s and 1990s has been the adoption of business techniques and language. In his book, *Academic Strategy: The Management Revolution in American Higher Education*, George Keller applied approaches common in corporate America to the management of higher education. In order to plan for future exigencies, Keller argued that college administrators needed to become more like managers and strategic planners. Keller believed that colleges should focus on improving their quality, since in the new academic marketplace quality would be a necessary condition for survival.[88]

In admissions, perhaps the most direct evidence that colleges had embraced industry practices was the increasing use of market research firms. During the 1980s and early 1990s, nearly all of the colleges in our study hired marketing and consulting firms such as George Dehne, Jan Krukowski, and Maguire to help them analyze their admissions and enrollment prospects. These firms gathered and analyzed information not only on enrolled students but also on potential applicants and admitted students who chose to go elsewhere, in order to understand better an institution's reputation and market position.

Another indication of higher education's adoption of corporate principles was the creation of enrollment management positions. Until the 1960s most heads of admissions offices were called "directors." Then, as the importance of admissions to the educational environment of an institution was recognized, "dean" became the favored title. In 1972, for example, Oberlin created a dean of admissions position because the admissions office was "now recognized as one of the most important agencies of the college for projecting to potential students an accurate picture of Oberlin."[89] The subsequent switch to "enrollment manager" in the 1980s reflected a growing recognition of the impact of admissions and enrollment on the financial as well as the academic health of an institution. The task of an enrollment manager was to build a class of the appropriate size as budgeted by the institution while at the same time producing a student body of desired quality and diversity. An enrollment manager generally oversaw all aspects of enrollment including admissions, financial aid, retention, transfers, institutional research, and in a few cases even alumni affairs. Such "bottom-line" focus—on getting a class—and broad responsibilities were relatively new to admissions offices.

With the creation of enrollment management positions, institutional research assumed a primary position in the admissions process. Colleges first established institutional research offices in the 1970s when they began to use statistical data for budgeting and enrollment purposes. According to Samuel Carrier, provost at Oberlin, and David L. Davis-Van Atta, director of institutional research there, "Institutional Research should have as its main goal in the enrollment management program simply this—to provide the information and understanding necessary to influence the processes controlling both the number and characteristics of the student body."[90]

From the point of view of institutional research and enrollment management, the college selection process involves three stages: the inquiry stage, the application stage, and the enrollment stage. At each stage, institutional researchers can determine the characteristics of those groups of students most likely to be interested in the institution. Such information enables admissions counselors to allocate their resources and energies most efficiently. Institutional research became even more important in the late 1980s and early 1990s when schools used sophisticated modeling to package financial aid awards and developed merit aid programs. (Those programs are described in detail in Chapter 7.)

Some colleges have utilized the information they received from marketing analysis and institutional research to engage in longer term repositioning of their colleges. Analysis of matriculants and nonmatriculants helped those colleges pinpoint which aspects of their overall reputation and image had the strongest effects on students' enrollment decisions. For example, after considerable analysis, administrators at Oberlin realized, "Although making Oberlin's cost more attractive does have a positive effect on yield, turning attention to academic reputation and social life provides a larger return. The difficulty lies in how to affect these ratings. Cost is easy (although expensive) to change. Academic reputation and social life are more difficult."[91]

The Application Roller Coaster

The surprise in the 1980s was that for many colleges and universities in America, including most of those in our study, applications increased despite the decline in the number of 18-year-olds. Although the number of high school graduates did decline as expected, college enrollment rates increased significantly throughout the 1980s and 1990s. In 1980, 50 percent of high school graduates enrolled in college. By 1985 this percentage had increased to 58 percent, and in the early 1990s it reached 62 percent. According to Robert Zemsky, director of the Institute for Research on Higher Education at the University of Pennsylvania, "The real history of the late 1970s through the first half of the 1980s is the assiduousness with which this industry doubled its market potential principally by marketing itself."[92] Indeed, many admissions officers credit the new admissions techniques and marketing analysis with helping them to weather the dismal demographic trends of the 1980s.

A 1980 COFHE report examined population trends to determine how the applicant pools of COFHE member colleges would be affected. The report projected applicant declines by 1994 ranging from 30 to 35 percent for the five colleges in our study that were also members of COFHE.[93] Yet, at all of these colleges (except one), applications actually increased through the 1980s and early 1990s. On average, application growth continued through the late 1980s for all the colleges in our study (see the bold line in Figure 2.4).

As usual, however, the application growth was not uniform. In general, colleges that marketed aggressively were able to expand their applicant pools most. The College of Wooster, for example, doubled its applications between 1980 and 1988/89. The new admissions director was not content to accept as high a percent of students as the college had in the past and therefore made a concerted effort to recruit more students. Likewise, applications at Oberlin compounded 10 percent annually during the mid-1980s as a result of a deliberate policy: The college increased its direct mail from 35,000 pieces to 110,000 and "went more national" with recruitment. The colleges in the Ohio Five group were particularly successful during the period from 1980 to 1988 at increasing their applicant pools. In 1980, the Ohio Five received an average of only 2,000 applications, by 1988, the average was close to 3,200.

Among the colleges in our study, the women's schools experienced the most modest growth in applications during the 1980s and early 1990s. The women's college group actually experienced a decline in the number of applications received between 1980 and the late 1980s before seeing a resurgence during the 1990s. At Smith, applications increased less than 10 percent over the entire period, and at Wellesley applications remained fairly stable until the 1990s when they shot up, most likely as a result of a successful fund-raising campaign and the so-called "Hillary factor"— increased name recognition after Hillary Rodham Clinton, a Wellesley alumna, became the First Lady. Mount Holyoke suffered applicant losses in the mid- to late 1980s at least in part because of its passive approach to recruitment at a time when vigorous recruiting was a must. During the 1980s, the college became "virtually invisible in our own backyard," foregoing visits to many schools in New England and the Middle Atlantic states that had traditionally sent students to Mount Holyoke. In fact, when Mount Holyoke's new admissions director visited Stuyvesant high school in New York City in 1992, one guidance counselor asked her, "Where have you been?"[94] Like Wheaton in the 1970s, Mount Holyoke learned the hard way how essential recruiting had become. Applications to Mount Holyoke declined 27 percent in the second half of the 1980s even as applications to the other women's colleges in our study were fairly steady. In the early 1990s, Mount Holyoke hired a new admissions director and began to recruit students aggressively. The college finally recognized "Today, at Mount Holyoke and everywhere else, students are recruited: an arduous, year-round, and long-term endeavor. If, in the golden age of Mount Holyoke's unknown and unrecorded past, matriculants simply appeared on our doorstep with sharpened pencils in hand, those days are forever gone."[95]

The application increases at the liberal arts colleges in our study were to some degree illusory since they resulted from students' filing multiple applications rather than from an actual increase in the number of students interested in attending these colleges. In 1982, Emily Wick, special assistant to the president for long range planning at Mount Holyoke, warned: "Application figures lull colleges into complacency about the admission situation. They can be deceiving."[96] One year later, Henry Bedford, the dean of admissions at Amherst, reiterated Wick's warning: "Application statistics may mislead. Not long ago, many believed that selective colleges where the number of applications apparently increased as the college-bound population declined, were insulated from national demographic change. It now seems evident that this statistical artifact resulted from an increase in the number of applications filed by each candidate, rather than from an increase in the number of individuals actually seeking admission."[97] Gary Williams, president of the National Association of College Admissions Counselors (NACAC), speculated that "as a result of the increased unpredictability of who will get into what college, pupils are applying to more schools than ever before."[98]

Wick's and Bedford's interpretations are supported by a study of multiple applications first conducted by Dean Whitla and his colleagues at Harvard in 1967, then repeated in the 1980s. Using data from 43 colleges and universities, Whitla plotted applications against selectivity. He found that "The relationship is pronounced; if one is interested in a highly selective college one takes care to file his credentials in numerous places."[99] Another important finding of the study was that the higher an applicant's SAT verbal score the more applications she filed. Whitla concluded, "These findings tend to refute some of the more common mythology about the multiple application syndrome, that it is the student who can ill afford psychologically or financially to make multiple applications who actually does make many college applications. These data . . . say just the opposite, that it is the more talented student, coming from a more privileged background who tends to make the larger number of applications."[100] Since, the traditional pool of students for the colleges in our study consisted of such highly talented students, the colleges were strongly affected by the multiple application phenomenon.

Further Yield Losses

Not surprisingly, as their overlap applications increased, the yields at the colleges fell. By 1985, the yields at the colleges in our study ranged from 30 to 50 percent, with the majority of schools enrolling only 40 percent of those students whom they admitted. In 1985, the yields at all of the colleges converged after the yields at Amherst-Williams, which had consistently been at least 10 percentage points higher than those of the other colleges, dropped 12 percentage points between 1980 and 1985 (see Figure 2.2). There are several possible explanations. In 1982, Amherst pledged to reduce the number of applicants accepted under early decision, which had reached as high as 40 to 50 percent, to no more than a third of the class. A second possibility is that the dramatic decline in yield at these two colleges is related to the *U.S. News and World Report* rankings described in more detail below. Amherst and Williams have consistently ranked among the top three liberal arts colleges nationwide. Although their high rankings have undoubtedly resulted in an increase in applications from students across the nation interested in attending a top school, applications from students who live farther away or who may also be applying to top universities have probably depressed their yields since these students are less likely to attend.

After 1985, the yields at Amherst-Williams stabilized, but at the other colleges they continued to fall through the second half of the 1980s. By the late 1980s, only one college had a yield near 50 percent; the rest fell to between 24 and 45 percent. During the 1990s, the yields have stabilized. In general, the more selective colleges and those colleges with unique market niches have the strongest yields. The women's colleges, for example, have yields near or above 40 percent, and since 1989 Gordon has had yields over 50 percent, much higher than any other school in our study. The Ohio Five have consistently had the lowest yields. When they expanded their applicant pools in the 1980s, their yields fell. Clearly, a bigger applicant pool does not necessarily mean a more committed one.

The eventual stabilization of yields was the result of concerted efforts by the colleges to enroll the students they had admitted. In the 1980s, the colleges in our study and others began holding open houses and weekends on campus for admitted students, and a few institutions even rented catering halls in large cities and invited prospective students to banquet dinners or "yield parties" as they were dubbed by admissions officers. In addition, the colleges also encouraged faculty and alumni to write personal letters to top candidates and, perhaps most important, they used their sophisticated marketing models to allocate and package efficiently their limited financial aid dollars.

The colleges have also tried to bolster their yields by implementing or refining early decision programs. In *Alma Mater*, P. F. Kluge described early decision applicants as "fish jumping into the boat."[101] To ensure that the College of Wooster caught its fair share of such fish, one of the first things that Hayden Schilling did when he became admissions director in 1983 was to institute an early decision program. Although Schilling did not expect to enroll a lot of students early, he felt the presence of an early decision program was important, "because all of the most selective schools had them."[102] More recently, some of the colleges in our study, including Amherst, have instituted second rounds of early decision as a way to broaden the public school and minority representation among their early admits. In 1995, Holy Cross began a rolling early decision program; students who submit an application before January 15 will be notified within two weeks whether they have been accepted. At the same time that our colleges have expanded their early decision programs, so too have the most prestigious universities. In the winter of 1995, Stanford announced plans to offer an early decision option for the first time,[103] and shortly thereafter both Yale and Princeton changed their nonbinding early action programs to binding early decision programs. In 1996, the first year that these programs went into effect, Stanford accepted 36 percent of its first-year class early, Yale 31 percent, and Princeton 49 percent.[104]

Widened Stratification

Since yields were lower than ever before, even with the increases in applications described above, most of the colleges we studied became less rather than more selective between 1980 and 1994. In 1980, a third of the colleges had admit rates below 50 percent, a third between 50 and 70 percent, and a third over 70 percent. By 1994, there were four colleges with admit rates below 50 percent, two between 50 and 70 percent, and ten over 70 percent. Looking just at 1980 and 1994 obscures the real, but short-lived, improvements in admit rates that many of the colleges were able to achieve in the late 1980s through a combination of intensified recruiting and careful monitoring of first-year class size. In 1988, after 13 years of steadily improving selectivity, the Ohio Five colleges were able to reach what was an almost all-time low admit rate of 54 percent (see Figure 2.3). When applications and yields fell again in the late 1980s and early 1990s, the less selective colleges suffered the most. By 1994, the Ohio Five group was admitting a greater percentage of its applicants than ever before, and the stratification that had first developed in the mid-1960s widened. In 1994, Amherst-Williams could admit less than 30 percent of the students who applied, while seven of the colleges—nearly half of our sample—had to accept more than 80 percent of their applicant pools. When Gary Williams explained in 1987 that "competition to get into college today is tougher than it has ever been," he was referring to colleges such as Amherst and Williams, and the handful of institutions like them who still had competitive admissions.[105]

Differences in applications per enrolled student also testify to the growing stratification of the colleges in our study. In 1988, five of the colleges received more than 4,000 applications, but their applicants per student varied appreciably (see Figure 2.1). Amherst and Williams retained the most leeway in choosing their first-year classes, because during the last ten years they received between nine and twelve applications for each place that needed to be filled. Even those colleges that were able to attract more than 4,000 applications were more constrained, because they had only between five and seven applications per place. Five to seven applicants may not sound that much different than nine to twelve applicants, but when we take into account the fact that these colleges also had lower yields than Amherst and Williams, it becomes even more apparent that Amherst and Williams are in an admissions class by themselves. It is interesting to note that in the mid-1980s the number of applicants per place at the women's colleges fell below the corresponding ratio at the Ohio Five colleges for the first time. Because the women's colleges had higher yields, however, they remained relatively more selective.

The hierarchy among the colleges reflected in admit rates, applications per enrolled student, and overall admissions situations reflects an increasing concern with status and prestige. In 1984, Whitla from Harvard described a two-tier pattern of admissions. Second-tier schools relaxed their admissions requirements to meet their budget-driven enrollment targets, so it was very easy for students to be admitted. At top-tier schools, the competition to get in was stronger than ever.[106] For elite schools, the 1980–1994 period was comparable to the tidal wave; these colleges could select the most outstanding students from among a surplus of quality applicants. Philip Smith dubbed this phenomenon "the Mercedes syndrome" to explain why applications from high-ability students to the most prestigious and selective schools continued to increase despite the demographic decline. This theory suggests that as college costs continued to rise, parents were more willing to pay tens of thousands of dollars to the most prestigious institutions.[107]

U.S. News and World Report Ranking

In 1983 *U.S. News and World Report* first published its annual college rankings, which purported to help students choose the best college but which were considered by students and their families to be a measure of an institution's quality and prestige. Over the years the components of the rating system have been modified slightly. When *U.S. News* began conducting the survey, it was a subjective survey of college presidents. The presidents were asked to select the 10 schools in their own category that provided the best undergraduate education based on a variety of measures of resources, selectivity, and faculty quality. This biennial survey was repeated in 1985 and again in 1987. In 1988, the editors made two major changes to the survey, which were designed to give the rankings more validity. First, the editors included academic deans and admissions officers as respondents to the opinion part of the survey, since they were the officials most involved with the recruitment and education of students. Second, the survey incorporated so-called objective data. One new measure that they used—student selectivity—was a composite of the acceptance rate, mean SAT scores, and high school rankings of enrolled students. Another measure described faculty quality based on the percentage of full-time professors with a Ph.D., the student to faculty ratio, the per student instructional budget, and faculty salaries. A final category encompassed institutional financial statistics such as endowment per student and library budget per student.

U.S. News capitalized on anxious parents and students who worried about how to determine if a college was really as good as it claimed. The editors of the magazine made it easy for prospective students by simplifying all the variables into one composite number. Americans, who had become increasingly concerned with perceived value, could consult the rankings to find out how a college had fared. According to an article in Kenyon's alumni magazine, "*U.S. News and World Report's* college rankings are a major coup. It is a brilliant business idea. A well-regarded magazine ranks institutions that for many represent one of the most important financial and educational investments they will ever make, institutions where a large portion of Americans spend four years of their life. . . . *U.S. News* then enjoys the benefits of selling an incredible amount of magazines."[108]

Where a college ended up in the rankings could strongly affect its admissions performance. In 1984, after Amherst was ranked the number one national liberal arts college, Dean Bedford ordered 25,000 copies of the *U.S. News Report* and sent them to applicants all over the country.[109] In 1990/91, applicants to the College of the Holy Cross dropped 11 percent from the previous year. At the same time, the quality of the students who chose to enroll fell precipitously. Admissions officials attributed these declines to national rankings. That year, Holy Cross fell off of the *U.S. News and World Report* Top 25 list and out of *Barron's* most selective colleges category because of misreported data. Kenyon also seemed to suffer when it slipped from the first to the second quartile of national liberal arts colleges. The *Kenyon Observer* reported in 1991: "Kenyon is one of the victims of the ranking system. In fact, the college's national standing has recently taken a beating at the hand of *U.S. News*."[110] When we visited Hiram College, administrators were anxious to see what the results of their 1994 designation as a national liberal arts college would do for their admissions situation. Hiram had gone from being ranked at the top of the regional liberal arts colleges to the bottom of the national liberal arts college category.

Although the *U.S. News* rankings are ostensibly based at least in part on objective data, it has become clear that such data can and have been manipulated.[111] Some schools, for example, include only fully completed applications whereas other colleges count any student who has returned an information card as an applicant. Similarly, many colleges neglect to include minorities, alumni children, athletes, or other specially recruited groups when they report their SAT scores, thus bolstering their mean test scores. The article in the Kenyon alumni magazine cited above decried the *U.S. News's* ranking practices, not only for the way colleges reported data but also for the weights given to various factors and the entire concept of ranking schools in numerical order:

> The *U.S. News* ranking put Kenyon and every other college between a rock and a hard place. The data which *U.S. News* and the Carnegie Foundation treats as gospel is not always what determines the quality of a college. Also the methods used by colleges, which report the data themselves is frequently flawed at best and corrupt at worst. Then there is the rather empty idea on the part of *U.S. News* of giving colleges an overall score and ranking them in

numerical order. In its own strange way, this attempt at defining an objective truth where there is none goes against much of what colleges are supposed to be about. . . . Unfortunately, a school's financial situation constitutes 20% of its ranking while student satisfaction accounts for only 5%. . . . Of course, the idea that selectivity determines 25% of a college's total value (which is exactly what *U.S. News* does) is probably even more vacuous than saying that financial resources account for 20% of a college's worth.[112]

Despite the ubiquitous complaints by college officials about the ranking system, most colleges and universities continue to report their data and participate in the study. As Kenyon administrators conceded in 1991, "The *U.S. News* college rankings have become and will remain one of a multitude of factors, whether valid or invalid, that contributes to a college's reputation. The rankings do exist and they are rather visible."[113] For the highly ranked colleges that benefit from the exposure there is no incentive not to participate. Those colleges that refuse to submit data to the magazine are penalized since the magazine ranks them without their data. In 1995, for example, Reed College fell from the second tier of national liberal arts colleges to the bottom after deciding not to participate in the rankings.[114]

Building a Class

Institutional priorities during this period varied according to a college's admissions situation. Williams from the NACAC felt that "as competition [among students for entrance to college] increases, the mainstays of admissions criteria—top grades, a strong academic background, high SAT scores and varied extracurricular activities—no longer guarantee acceptance."[115] Williams's analysis certainly held for the most prestigious colleges in our study that continued to receive applications from more well-qualified students than they could admit. At Amherst, for example, admissions officials could safely focus on other qualifications in addition to scholastic achievement:

> The College has both an institutional and an educational interest in attracting and retaining a student body with varied talents and interests and with diverse backgrounds and experiences. Thus Amherst will actively continue to seek and, without apology, to give some preference in admissions to students whose energy promises a significant contribution to important campus activities, to students whose background or heritage differs from that of most Amherst undergraduates and to students whose presence is likely to enrich the Amherst experience of others.[116]

For most of the colleges in our study, however, the main priority was to enroll enough students to meet budgeted enrollment targets. For those schools that were admitting over 85 percent of their applicants, admissions no longer consisted of a selection process but rather more closely resembled a rejection of the unqualified. One admissions director said that after the admissions staff reject those who absolutely cannot do the work, they practice what they call the "Love Potion #9" admissions strategy, after a song of that name from the 1960s: They hold their noses and scrape the bottom of the barrel just to fill their class. Another college that must admit more than 75 percent of its applicants to enroll a full class reads applications looking for students "who just can't make it here." An admissions director from one of the Ohio colleges was at a conference of admissions people from around the country when the question of wait list activity came up. He raised his hand and said, only half facetiously, "I'm from Ohio. What's a wait list?" Liberal arts colleges in Ohio are not in the position to have wait lists. John Anderson's description of the choice faced by the admissions committee at Kenyon perhaps best captures the situation at many of the liberal arts colleges in our study: "In picking through these applications, there's a tension between the desire for perfect students and the need to have a class."[117]

As in earlier periods, one way that the colleges tried to find more "perfect students" was to identify new geographic markets. According to Gary Craig, admissions director at Hiram, in 1986 Hiram purposefully searched for talented students outside of its traditional geographic market: "One thing we are doing this year to get more and better students is taking our President's Scholarship on the road to new areas. We have added the cities of Buffalo, Rochester, Pittsburgh, Toledo, Cincinnati, Dayton and Columbus, and we hope to get some good students from those areas."[118] The search for new geographic markets bore fruit for some of the colleges we studied. During the 1980s, students from the West and the South began to attend liberal arts colleges in Massachusetts and Ohio in greater numbers. While representation from each region increased in both states, for the most part, the Massachusetts schools attracted more students from the West, and the Ohio colleges enrolled proportionally more students from the South. These shifts coincided with a national change in the ease and affordability of travel. In the 1980s, air travel became less expensive and more of a way of life for Americans. Thus, students became more willing to attend school farther from home. Although this access to new markets can help, it may also hurt. R. Stanton Hales, president of the College of Wooster, believes that the greater affordability and ease of travel and the nationalization of competition for admission to liberal arts colleges have contributed to the stratification. Those schools at the top of hierarchy today have always been at the top. Until recently, however, most students, even top ones, opted to attend school near home. Thus, less prestigious colleges could compete effectively for local students with colleges farther away, even if they were of higher quality.[119]

The differing abilities of colleges to enroll children of alumni, like their ability to enroll students from farther distances, is yet another indication of stratification. At the top-tier schools, although legacies are admitted at 2½ times the rate of regular admits, admissions officials still reject more than half of the alumni sons and daughters who apply. These schools worry that they are rejecting too many alumni children. At the other colleges, admissions officials express the opposite concern—that they cannot find enough legacy children to apply. This situation is particularly pressing at the women's colleges. Although throughout the 1960s and 1970s, daughters of alumnae constituted between 8 and 15 percent of their classes, since the late 1980s enrollment of legacies has fallen below 5 percent. Admissions directors attribute this decline to the fact that many alumnae are now sending their daughters to the Ivy League, Little Ivy, or other prestigious formerly male colleges. For most of the always-coed colleges in our study, admitting legacy students at a higher rate than regular admits is not an attractive or realistic possibility, because their admit rates are already very high.

A Thankless Job

During the 1980s and early 1990s, admissions directors found it increasingly difficult to enroll a class of budgeted size let alone enroll students of high academic quality and diversity. Yet, college presidents continued to demand both. The declining number of college-aged students, increased competition, and pressure from administration—all contributed to making the job of the admissions director harder. One of the admissions directors we interviewed described the pressures admissions directors faced as "schizophrenic"; on the one hand, admissions directors are told to increase enrollment, while on the other hand they are told to increase the average SAT score and class rank of entering students. A recent article entitled "The Scramble to Get the New Class" reported that admissions directors are losing sleep over meeting enrollment goals as the driving principle has become "delivering bottom line net revenue."[120] Many admissions directors have recently found that these pressures can cost them their jobs. One admissions director confided, "There is a lot less job security and a lot more pressure even at the top schools where the numbers still look good. Every year they are called upon to do more with fewer resources. The pressure really takes its toll. There is a tendency for new presidents to come in and say there is an enrollment problem, let's get a new dean." In a

1994 editorial, "If the Numbers Don't Look Good, Dump the Dean," David Treadwell, president of a communications company specializing in the development of admissions materials, vividly rendered the pressure admissions officers confront:

> What has caused a situation in which admissions directors have become more expendable than old newspapers or losing football coaches—and are just as quickly discarded? The answer, in part, is pressure. All kinds: Fill the class. If you can do that, get better students. If you can get better students, be sure they can pay $100,000 for a four-year degree. And oh, yes, don't forget to enroll enough blacks and Indians and Asians. And get some basketball players who can read. And maintain a 50–50 sex split. And . . .[121]

In the next chapter we examine how the colleges in our study have coped with at least one of these pressures—the pressure to enroll high-quality students.

CHAPTER 3

Student Quality

THERE ARE many aspects of a college that contribute to its overall quality, including its faculty, its facilities, its curriculum, and its student body. Although each of these factors is essential, we focus here on only the last—the quality of the student body.

The quality of students that a liberal arts college is able to attract is of critical importance. Quality is important in and of itself, since liberal arts colleges both want and need to enroll students able to take advantage of the kinds of curricula, advising, and other programming which they offer. The quality of students also matters because it affects enrollment. Numerous studies have found that the academic standards of a college are a major factor that students consider when applying to college.[1] The presence of excellent students at a college encourages other excellent students to apply. Conversely, the absence of high-ability students may discourage high-ability students from applying. As early as 1959, the Committee on Admissions at Ohio Wesleyan worried that "Any slackening in efforts to raise academic standards and, concomitantly, the requirements for admission may have the effect of driving away good students who would like to come here. In this day few parents are going to be willing to pay the rather high expenses of an education at Ohio Wesleyan if they learn that our academic prestige is slipping."[2]

The interaction between quality and size works both ways. Just as quality affects the applicant pool, and thus the enrollment that can be generated, so too enrollment targets can affect quality. If a college has fewer good students in its applicant pool than its enrollment target, the college may have to lower its admissions standards and accept students with credentials below its desired class profile in order to fill a class.

Throughout this chapter, we use mean SATs as a proxy for the quality of the student body. Many people have criticized SATs for being biased against women, minorities, and students from low socioeconomic backgrounds[3] and for not measuring such important attributes as "motivation, desire to learn, creativity, imagination and intellectual curiosity."[4] Others, however, defend the use of SAT scores in admissions as a means of expanding rather than reducing opportunities for good students regardless of their backgrounds. Amherst's 1982 O'Connell Report on admissions, for example, noted:

College Entrance Examination Board tests (SAT's) promised at least partial escape from the class and racial prejudice (and after coeducation, sexual) necessarily embedded in the older ways elite colleges and universities had selected their students. These tests, by facilitating comparisons among otherwise very different individuals, were indispensable in selecting applicants from a national pool, especially given the polyglot nature of American culture and the variations in the qualities of its schools.[5]

Fred Hargadon, dean of admissions at Stanford and chairman of the College Entrance Examination Board, made a similar argument in a 1980 *New York Times* article. In response to charges that SATs have been a barrier to poor and minority students, Hargadon replied that the tests "enable colleges to reach out, and find students with talent and ability, regardless of their background, all across the country, in ways that otherwise would have been impossible."[6]

In the epilogue to *Hurdles: The Admissions Dilemma in American Higher Education*, Joseph Katz, professor of human development at the State University of New York at Stony Brook, summed up the advantages and disadvantages of SATs:

> The advantages of using prior grades and the Scholastic Aptitude Test (SAT) or the American College Test (ACT) or the Graduate Record Exam (GRE) are that they allow institutions to process hundreds of thousands of applicants while giving each individual the chance to be considered in the light of the impersonality of the test, regardless of social class, ethnic and racial origins, personal appearance or the prestige of the school she or he is graduating from. The tests, by themselves do not, of course, allow for the deficits that derive from one's background and upbringing. They are impartial not in regard to the past, but only in regard to the present. But at least one's present test scores have an influence independent of social class and ethnicity; students, in fact, have found their scores an entering wedge to institutions that might otherwise have been closed to them.[7]

While we acknowledge that SATs have biases and are limited in what they can measure, we nevertheless focus on mean SAT scores because they can be compared both across colleges and over time, and because, for better or worse, they are used by students, parents, and college counselors to select colleges and by colleges to evaluate students. Peter Wells, a private secondary school dean and critic of SAT scores, bemoaned the fact that "Whatever the imperfections of the test, I have yet to meet a college admissions officer who did not know the mean SAT score of the entering freshmen class, and few did not regard the mean as a reflection on them and their college."[8] The same could arguably be said of entering students and their parents.

Not only critics of SATs, but also many supporters of SATs, believe that high school class ranks are better predictors of college performance than SATs. Although we supplement our SAT data with class rank data, we do not focus on it for two reasons. First, the class rank data we have is incomplete. Many of the colleges in our study did not keep consistent information on high school class ranks. Moreover, in recent years, increasing numbers of both private and public high schools have stopped ranking students.[9] Second, even for those colleges for which we have complete class rank data, it's not always clear how to interpret trends. Unlike SAT scores, which are standardized, the meaning of class ranks differs among secondary schools. Thus, as the makeup of entering classes has changed at liberal arts colleges, their class rank statistics have changed too, often with little relationship to the underlying academic quality of the entering class. In a 1982 admissions report, Emily Wick, special assistant to the president, warned Mount Holyoke administrators about the difficulties of comparing class ranks over time:

> The fact that in 1956 as much as 24.4 percent of the entering class were below the top 20 percent of their high school classes, compared to roughly 14 percent in recent classes, suggests that these groups of applicants must have been quite different. When I asked [Admissions Director] Miss Ludwig about this she said that the groups are not directly comparable. They are like apples and oranges. In 1956 the nature of high school programs, and the nature of the population of test takers, made it reasonable to admit a relatively large proportion of students in the lower ranks of their high school classes. In the late 1970's and early 1980's the much greater size and diversity of the populations of high school students, and of the programs in which they participate, make the population of students in the lower ranks much weaker candidates. Miss Ludwig's opinion is based on her evaluation of virtually every application for admission submitted to Mount Holyoke from 1952 to June, 1981.[10]

We take Ludwig's and Wick's warnings seriously, and, thus, for the most part, we present class rank trends only over short periods of time.

In this chapter, we focus on changes in mean SAT scores—not on absolute levels. In 1960 (the first year for which we have SAT scores for most of the colleges), the mean SAT scores of the entering classes extended from 1092 to 1308. This range of levels is the result of the particular missions, histories, and circumstances of each college—all interesting subjects, but subjects well beyond the scope of our analysis. In order to interpret mean SAT trends, it's important to understand the evolving standards of admissions and changing uses and importance of SAT scores, so we begin at the turn of the century when the College Entrance Examination Board (CEEB) was established.

CHANGING ADMISSIONS STANDARDS (1900–1955)[11]

Until almost the twentieth century, every selective college administered its own admissions tests to prospective students. This system was inefficient, not only from the perspective of the students, some of whom had to take multiple tests, but also from the perspective of high schools that had to prepare their students for different tests. Moreover, the system limited a college's or university's applicant pool to those students, usually from relatively nearby, who could take the locally administered tests. Toward the end of the nineteenth century, a number of innovations were introduced not only to increase the efficiency of the system but also to broaden the base of applicants. The University of Michigan, for example, developed a certificate program whereby the university certified schools with acceptable academic programs. The university then guaranteed that any graduate of a certified secondary school recommended by the headmaster would be accepted by Michigan.

Although many midwestern and western schools adopted Michigan's certificate system, most eastern schools resisted it. Instead, in 1900, a group of selective private colleges and prep schools in the Northeast, led by Nicholas Murray Butler, the dean at Columbia University, founded the College Entrance Examination Board (CEEB) to promote a common high school curriculum by offering comprehensive tests for applicants to leading private colleges. Although the most selective institutions (e.g., Harvard, Yale, and Princeton) initially spurned this innovation, by 1915 they all recognized the CEEB tests.

The first CEEB tests were essay-type tests in traditional subjects such as Latin, history, and physics. Like the institutional admissions tests that they were designed to replace, these early achievement tests were intended to measure the academic preparation of students. Such a purpose was in keeping with the general philosophy of admissions at the time as described by Christopher Jencks and David Riesman in their 1960 book *The Academic Revolution*:

> A generation ago most colleges spoke about their admissions requirements as if they were based on intrinsic standards of "what every freshman should know." This was manifestly untrue, in the sense that colleges adjusted their standards over time to take account of improvement or deterioration in their market position. Different colleges also had different standards at any given time, according to what they thought they could demand without going bankrupt. Nonetheless, people mostly talked as if a college set its standards and then admitted all applicants who met them. If this led to expansion so much the better for everyone. To some extent the colleges even acted out this rhetoric.[12]

Columbia University, for one, certainly acted out the rhetoric. From 1901 through 1919, all applicants to Columbia were required to take either Columbia or CEEB entrance exams in English, math, science, modern languages, and ancient languages. The result was not only an increase in traditional (i.e., WASP) students but also an increase in students from immigrant and Jewish families. By 1919, the applicant pool at Columbia was so large and the entering class was so diverse that Columbia administrators developed a "new method" of admissions to screen applicants more efficiently. Under this new method, students who had taken at least 15 units of secondary work in selected subjects could take an exam of "mental alertness and power," adapted from the Army Alpha test during World War I. It was expected that "the average native American boy" would perform better on this test than students from either immigrant or Jewish families.[13]

In 1925, Carl Campbell Brigham, a professor of psychology at Princeton, led a CEEB committee that developed a multiple-choice test, similar to the Columbia test, that was supposed to measure intelligence rather than academic achievement. Despite, or perhaps because of, evidence that the test was culturally biased and therefore did not accurately measure native intelligence, the multiple-choice test survived and evolved into what we now know as the SAT. Until after World War II, colleges used SATs only modestly, in large part because most colleges and universities during this period were accepting the majority of their applicants. Those few institutions with robust applicant pools used SAT scores in the same way that they used the early achievement tests—as cutoff criteria for admissions. According to Jencks and Riesman, "It was in this context that students could speak of 'passing' or 'failing' their College Board exams (i.e., getting a score known to be acceptable or unacceptable to the college of their choice)."[14]

The influx of college applicants returning from World War II dramatically altered college admissions. Not only did college admissions become competitive, but the idea of aptitude testing in general and the SAT test in particular gained greater credence. Jencks and Riesman described this change:

> Until World War II most private colleges evaluated applicants in terms of their mastery of standard secondary school subject matter. But experience with war veterans strengthened the hand of reformers who argued that formal preparation for college was less relevant in predicting college performance than motivation and native intelligence. Educational research also helped raise serious questions about the traditional emphasis on mastery of particular subjects as a way of separating sheep from goats. Statistical studies showed that general verbal and mathematical ability tests predicted college grades better than did achievement tests in particular subjects. ... Almost all leading colleges ...

placed more emphasis on general aptitude tests and on rank in high school class, less on knowledge of specific subjects. Academic work prior to college came to be seen less as an end in itself and more as a litmus test of future academic performance.[15]

This change in attitude, coupled with stricter College Board regulations requiring member institutions to use the SAT test, prompted many more schools to require SAT scores. Many colleges, particularly those in the Midwest, did not require SAT scores until the late 1950s. Ohio Wesleyan, for example, did not ask all students to submit SAT scores until 1958, and Hiram only made the tests mandatory in the early 1960s. Ironically, in the late 1950s and 1960s as the SAT test became more widely used and the mean scores at all our colleges rose, the weight given to SAT scores by admissions officers diminished.

REACHING NEW HEIGHTS (1955–1965)

In the introduction to *American Higher Education in the 1960s*, E. I. F. Williams, editor of Kappa Delta Pi Publishers, wrote, "Never has the urge for greater quantity and quality of higher education been stronger, in both the United States and abroad, than it is today [1960]."[16] Although Williams worried that "there is a growing conflict between quantity and quality,"[17] not everyone believed that the two were mutually exclusive. In 1956 the Committee on Education Beyond the High School appointed by President Eisenhower concluded:

> If an unwelcome choice were required between preserving quality and expanding enrollments, then quality should be preferred, because it would do neither individuals nor the Nation any good to masquerade mass production of mediocrity under the guise of higher education. But the choice between quality and quantity is not mandatory. The Nation needs more of both. . . . The Committee does not agree with those who argue that, in order to preserve quality, colleges must sharply restrict enrollments to something like their present level by steadily boosting admission standards.[18]

The committee's conclusions would seem Pollyannish today, but in fact, during the decade from 1955 to 1965 it was possible to increase enrollments and raise quality simultaneously.

As described in Chapter 1, the colleges in our study grew between 1955 and 1965 at an average rate of 41 percent. At the same time all the colleges were able to improve substantially the quality of their entering classes. Unfortunately, we are missing too much data for 1955 to examine overall trends in SATs for the colleges between 1955 and 1965. It is striking, however, that for all but three of the twelve colleges for which we have data in the earliest years, their 1965 mean SAT scores were the highest that they have ever reported. Indeed, nine of the twelve colleges had mean SAT scores in excess of 1200, and five had scores above 1300.

The academic credentials of the students at many of the colleges in our study rose to such heights during the late 1950s and early to mid-1960s that admissions officers talked about reaching "plateaus" and expressed doubts that it was possible to improve any further. For example, in a letter to the president of Kenyon from the Admissions Committee, Provost Bruce Haywood wrote, "It is the opinion of the Committee that we may have already reached as high a level in terms of test scores and rank in class, as we can hope to reach. It would be unrealistic to imagine that we can go on improving the quality of our entering classes much farther."[19]

The universal increase in SAT scores at the colleges resulted in part from a redistribution of students. As the academic credentials of applicants improved, admission standards at the most selective colleges became more demanding. A prediction by an admissions report at Amherst in the late 1950s that "by 1965, an Amherst class as a whole will compare with the upper half of any class in the 30's"[20] was realized. The admissions director at Wellesley also noted: "As a matter of fact all that has really happened so far is that most of the bottom 1/5 of the class has been eliminated and the whole academic center of gravity has thus been raised. Recent classes represent considerably less 'range' than was formerly the case."[21]

The former "bottom of the class" at the most selective colleges became the new "top of the class" at other colleges, which contributed to the overall increase of mean SAT scores and the tightening of admission standards. In 1961, Ambrose J. De Flumere, director of admission at Hiram, cautioned, ". . . we must expect young people to jump over more and higher hurdles than we did before admission is granted at Hiram or any other college."[22] Gordon College also tightened its admissions standards as the SAT scores of its applicants rose. Prior to the tidal wave, any Gordon applicant with SAT scores above 950, who also met a number of other non-academic criteria, would be automatically admitted; those with scores below 950 would be reviewed by a committee. By 1969, Gordon College had decided that "Academic requirements should gradually be upgraded as the pool of applicants becomes larger. Because there is already evidence that applicants are presenting higher qualifications than we have had in the past, the Admissions Committee during 1969–1970 will review any applicant whose combined SAT scores total less than 1000."[23]

One measure of just how high admissions standards became during this period, was the unease about the rising standards expressed by some commentators on higher education. David McClelland, professor of psychology at Harvard University, faulted the selective colleges for their overemphasis on academic criteria. He believed that the colleges were sending the wrong message to students by saying, "We are interested in only one quality—the ability to take examinations and to get superior grades in school."[24] Rudolph reiterated this perception of college admissions. He characterized the 1950s as a period in which "Some small colleges unwilling or unable to cope with the challenge of numbers abandoned a commitment to the all-around boy which their genteel traditions encouraged and organized new programs and inaugurated new practices designed to facilitate the training of an intellectual elite."[25]

The admissions officers at many our colleges shared the sentiments and concerns of these commentators. Wheaton's 1963 long-range planning document assured readers, "We do not propose that Wheaton should set itself the task of educating only those students who would today fall in the upper half of a typical class."[26] Similarly, Fred Copeland, director of admissions at Williams, stressed, "We are well aware of the importance of basic aptitudes but we do not wish to over-emphasize their part in the assessment of a candidate's qualifications nor do we feel that we should strive to increase our class averages."[27] In her 1965 Admissions Report to the Faculty, Jane Sehmann, the director of admissions at Smith, stated:

> The Board of Admissions does not have as its objective the admission of students whose test scores set new test records each year. Actually, it would seem some sort of plateau will be reached in the testing area, for above certain score limits it is rather commonly agreed that shades of differences between high test scores are meaningless. Other more elusive but less measurable qualities will continue to command our attention and direct our search for new students."[28]

In general during the late 1950s and early to mid-1960s there was "a lowering of the 'status' of intelligence testing in the college world, with other measures of evaluating fitness for higher education growing in favor."[29] Colleges believed that it was increasingly necessary to weigh other factors in admissions besides standardized tests and class ranks. Paradoxically, it was the large number of high-quality, high-scoring applicants for relatively few spots that forced them to consider nonacademic factors. As early as 1956, Eugene Wilson, the dean of admission at Amherst, described the need for and use of a broader set of admissions criteria:

> As you know, the increased number of qualified applicants has brought on a slow but rapidly accelerating change in the methods of selection. No longer do we pick students largely by marks and test scores. Instead we look among our qualified candidates for applicants who will give us a class of broad diversification. In other words, the factors which control admission from a large number of well-qualified candidates are now geographical; school distribution; extra curricular achievement.[30]

A decade later, Williams expressed similar priorities: "Because of the high quality of the candidates the Committee spent an extraordinary amount of time in making its selections in an attempt to shape the class and to secure a good 'mix.' We also gave considerable thought to acquiring a 'happy but productive bottom quarter' and the special departmental needs including athletics."[31]

Even Harvard broadened its admissions criteria substantially in the late 1950s and 1960s. In a 1970 letter to Van Halsey, the director of admissions at Hampshire, Dean Whitla, the director of institutional research of Harvard, wrote: "For the Classes of '59, '64, '66, '68 the weight of the personal attributes factor increased markedly. During this ten-year period the number of applicants more than doubled and the SAT scores of the applicant group increased more than a hundred points. Hence the committee had much more freedom in the decision process and it chose to give more weight to the personal strengths of the students."[32]

The Ten Percent Program at Williams, which is discussed in Chapter 2, allowed for the admission of students whose academic qualifications were not as high as those of the rest of the class. The program was a formal acknowledgment that too much emphasis was being placed on test scores and that test scores and high school grades were not the only predictors of college success. When Williams instituted its 10 percent program in 1962, the supply of high-scoring students seemed unlimited. By the time the program officially ended in 1973, the admissions situation at even top schools like Williams had deteriorated.[33]

PLUMMETING CREDENTIALS AND INCREASED STRATIFICATION (1965–1980)

Between 1965 and 1980, the mean combined SAT scores for graduating seniors nationally fell 77 points, from 967 to 890.[34] More important, for tuition-dependent liberal arts colleges such as ours, which were accustomed to enrolling only the highest scoring test takers, the number of students with high scores whose families could afford private college tuition was limited. In 1969, working with figures provided by the College Entrance Examination Board, Humphrey Doermann, director of admissions at Harvard from 1961 to 1966, projected that only 124,000 members of the high school class of 1976 would score 550 and above on the verbal aptitude test and have family incomes of $25,000 or more.[35] The result for our colleges was a steep decline in their mean SAT scores. Between 1965 and 1980, the mean SAT scores at all the colleges in our study fell, in many cases by more than 100 points. Whereas, in the mid-1960s, administrators at many of these colleges had fretted that their mean SAT scores were too high, in the late 1960s and 1970s, they worried instead that their scores were too low. For example, in a 1977 letter to the faculty, President Robert Good of Denison wrote, "We are making every effort to reverse the recent trend that has seen a precipitous decline in average SAT's and class rank, just as we are making every effort to expand the number of applicants. If we cannot accomplish a turn-around in quality in the next year or two while holding to the present size of our student body, we certainly shall not be able to improve our quality once the pool of college-age students begins to shrink."[36]

As the SAT scores plummeted, concerns about the weight and validity of the SATs that had so dominated admissions reports in the early and mid-1960s disappeared, with a few notable exceptions. In 1969, Wellesley began "taking more chances on Board scores" in recognition of the fact that "SAT scores are not necessarily the best predictors of success."[37] Amherst also continued to look for the "something other" required for admissions. Dean Wall's response to a professor who wanted to admit only students of "demonstrated brilliance" explained why: "When 2,100 of our 2,400 applicants could, if we had room for them, do the work of the college quite well, we must, if we care about variety, and I think we do, look for scale tipping factors in the selection process."[38] One "scale-tipping" factor that Amherst, and most of the other colleges in our study, began considering in the wake of the civil rights movement of the late 1960s, was minority status. In 1969, an Amherst admissions committee reported, "The past year has witnessed an ever growing attack on marks, test scores and rank in class. The attackers claim that these are faulty measures of intellectual ability, especially for minority groups; that these measures enable colleges and universities to discriminate unfairly against economically disadvantaged students."[39] As described in Chapter 5, such concerns led the colleges in our study to institute minority recruitment and admissions programs of varying scope and breadth in the late 1960s.

Although all of the colleges in our study experienced falling SAT scores from the late 1960s through the 1970s, the extent to which scores fell differed considerably and seemed to depend on two factors: beginning SAT levels and coed status. The colleges with the highest mean SAT scores in 1965 tended to lose the least ground between 1965 and 1980, whereas the colleges with the lowest scores in 1965 experienced the largest SAT drops (Figure 3.1). Thus, there was a substantial increase in the SAT stratification among our schools. In 1965, the mean SAT scores ranged from 1050 to 1340, a difference of 290 points. By 1980, the scores ranged from 960 to 1285, a difference of 325 points.

Changes in distributions by class rank were equally dramatic. In 1965, the percentage of top-quintile students ranged from 54 percent to 95 percent at the 10 schools for which we have data. In 1980, the corresponding

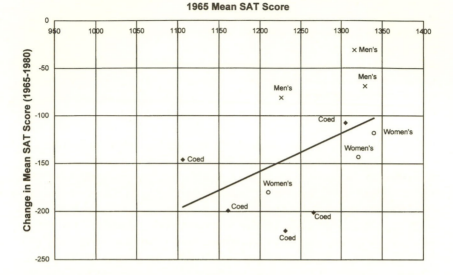

Figure 3.1. Relationship between 1965 Mean Combined SAT Score and Change in Score (1965–1980).

range was from 22 percent to 90 percent, reflecting again an increased stratification.

The Effect of Coeducation

It is important to note that all the men's schools in Figure 3.1 lie well above the trend line, which means that their SATs dropped less than would be expected given their starting SAT scores. As discussed in the next chapter on coeducation, one of the major reasons that the men's colleges started admitting women in the late 1960s and early 1970s was to ensure that they could continue to enroll high-quality male students. Williams's 1969 Committee on Coordinate Education and Related Questions, for example, reasoned: "If Williams wishes to continue to attract first-rate students and faculty, the trend for the decades ahead points to a community in which women are present."[40] That same year, the Interim Report to the Faculty on Coeducation at Holy Cross reached a similar conclusion.[41] Even the author of a dissenting report at Holy Cross conceded that many colleges expected top-quality men to be more attracted to coeducational environments: "Wesleyan, Franklin and Marshall, Union, and Trinity, as well as Princeton and Yale, are all banking heavily on the assumption that their change to coeducation will result in a marked improvement in the quality of their male applicants."[42]

It is impossible to tell what would have happened to the quality of students at the men's colleges had they remained all male. However, the fact that the SAT scores fell less than would be expected given their starting SAT levels is suggestive, as are the different admissions experiences in the early 1970s of two of the men's colleges in our study—one that was still all male and the other that had become coed. In 1972 and 1973, Amherst had fewer male applicants than either Bowdoin or Williams (both of which had recently gone coed), and in 1973 "200 young men who were interviewed by the [Amherst] staff and considered outstanding candidates for admission" did not apply. In a report to the faculty describing this situation, Edward Wall, dean of admissions at Amherst, attributed the situation to the college's remaining all male.[43] Whereas Amherst's initial decision to stay all male hurt its appeal, Kenyon's going coed made it more attractive. In 1974, five years after Kenyon went coed, John Kushan, director of admissions, reported, "Naturally the number of applications has increased because we receive applications from women now, but it has been gratifying to see the number of male applicants grow. Kenyon is now attractive to many men who previously shied away from a rural, all male environment."[44]

Coeducation had the opposite effect on the women's schools in our study. Mary Ellen Ames, director of admissions, described the result of coeducation on the Seven Sisters in a 1976 admissions report:

> The most telling effect of the changes Wellesley College experienced ... in the early 70's was not the drop in number of applicants, but the fact that we were now sharing our rather exclusive pool of top women applicants with a much larger group of top-quality institutions. Our competition was no longer chiefly the other Sisters, but had broadened to include at least 14 other colleges and universities, all of them offering an excellent academic education. On the other hand, the effect on our Brothers, the Ivies and the Small Ivies, was quite the opposite.[45]

Competition was especially fierce for women with high SAT scores whose families could afford the price of a private education. In a 1978 article in the *Wellesley Alumnae Magazine*, Ames described just how small the pool of top women applicants was relative to the number of available places:

> In 1978 there were only 12,500 young women among the over one million high school graduates taking these tests who had a score of 550 or better on the Verbal SAT and whose families have sufficient incomes to pay full costs at a COFHE institution. (Not many at all when you consider that Wellesley and the top 19 colleges listed as its top competitors have enrolled close to 10,000

young women this fall.) In 1984 the number of females in this same category will drop to 10,500. Fortunately for our colleges there are many more young women with Verbal scores of 550 and above but who come from families that will need financial assistance (48,000 in 1978; and 40,666 projected for 1984).[46]

One result of these trends was to depress the mean SAT scores at the women's colleges in our study relative to the scores at men's colleges that went coed. The mean SAT score at Wellesley/Smith fell from 1331 to 1200 between 1965 and 1980, a drop of 131 points. At the same time, the mean SAT score for Amherst/Williams declined from 1323 to 1273, a loss of only 50 points. Thus Wellesley/Smith, which had a slightly higher SAT average in 1965 than Amherst/Williams, had an average SAT score 73 points lower in 1980.

The trends in class rank for these colleges were even more pronounced. In 1955, 95 percent of entering Wellesley/Smith students and 81 percent of first-year Amherst/Williams students had graduated from the top quintile of their high school class. Whereas the percentage of top-quintile Wellesley/Smith students fell to 85 percent between 1965 and 1980, the comparable Amherst/Williams proportion rose to 90 percent.

The experience of coeducational colleges in the decade following the major push toward coeducation was remarkably similar to that of women's colleges. In a 1980 admissions report, Carl Bewig, director of admissions at Oberlin, echoed Ames's 1976 comment, "The most significant historical event to impact on the history of the college as far as admissions is concerned has been the move to coeducation at a majority of Oberlin's traditional competitors. Indeed, six of the top ten schools to which Oberlin lost accepted candidates in 1979 were single sex institutions a dozen years ago."[47] Coeducational colleges lost not only good female students but also good male students who formerly might have forgone an Ivy or Little Ivy education in favor of a coed experience, but who now didn't have to make that choice. Strikingly, the SAT scores of *both* the men and women at one coed college dropped by 88 points between 1970 and 1975.

By at least one measure—class ranks—the coed colleges suffered the most in the 1970s. Figure 3.2 shows the average percentage of top-quintile students at three types of institutions in 1965 and 1980—always-coed colleges, formerly men's colleges, and women's colleges.[48] The three coed colleges in our study for which we have complete data enrolled on average 64 percent top-quintile students in 1965—a level only 6 percent lower than the average for the men's colleges. Between 1965 and 1980, the percentage of top-quintile students fell 33 percentage points at the three coed colleges to a mean level of 31 percent. At the same time, the men's colleges actually increased their top-quintile proportions by 10 percentage points, so that in 1980 they enrolled an average of 80 percent top-quintile

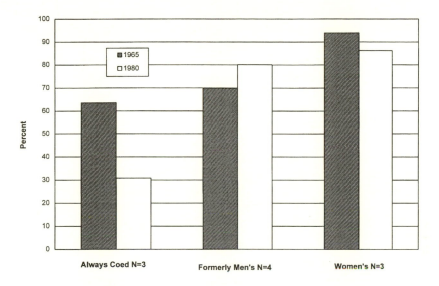

Figure 3.2. Percentage of Ranked Students in the Top Quintile of High School Class by Category (1965 and 1980).

students. Although the women's college class rank composite in Figure 3.2 also fell between 1965 and 1980, it started much higher and fell considerably less than the coed top-quintile composite.

The fact that many of the best all-male institutions went coed in the late 1960s and early 1970s should not necessarily have hurt already coeducational colleges. If the men's schools had maintained their enrollments, the new women they accepted would have filled slots formally reserved for men, thus requiring many males with top credentials to attend other institutions. But, like the men's schools in our study, most of the other high-quality men's institutions that went coed increased their enrollments rather than admit fewer males. These new spaces added pressure to a system in which there were already more openings than there were top students.

In 1982, Amherst conducted an elaborate admissions study. Among other issues, the O'Connell Report, as it came to be known, explored why the SAT composite of Amherst's entering class had deteriorated in the 1970s. Reviewing data on the SAT distributions of not only matriculants but also applicants and admits, Amherst concluded that "Changes in admission practices have not contributed to the decline in SAT scores in our applicant pool. The most evident reason for the deterioration in the quality of our applicant pool has been the nationwide decline in SAT scores. . . . Amherst's share of the better applicants has not declined."[49]

In 1980, Oberlin had conducted a similar study but reached very different conclusions. Between 1970 and 1973, Oberlin's mean SAT scores dropped dramatically, a development that Oberlin attributed to "the eastern selective colleges' and Ivy League schools' becoming coeducational." As the report explained, "Until the early 1970s, Oberlin was the only highest quality college boasting co-education. It easily commanded a very large and highest quality market. The co-education of Harvard, Yale et. al. decisively removed our exclusivity and began the SAT decline at Oberlin that has continued through nearly every year of the past decade."[50] Like Amherst's O'Connell Report, Oberlin's report examined SAT distributions as well as mean SATs. David L. Davis-Van Atta, the author of Oberlin's report, discovered not only a drop in "upper tail" students who had SAT verbal scores above 700, but also an increase in "lower tail" students with SAT verbal scores below 500. Davis-Van Atta found the "lower tail" gains both worrisome and difficult to explain. He posited:

> I believe the best answer to be that the institutional image of a college is not constant or certain. It is, especially now, in continuous revision, creation and re-creation among college-bound students. Each enrolled class begets the next year's applicant pool and losses of high quality students and the necessitated admission and enrollment of those of lesser academic prowess one year becomes a regenerative effect passing down and increasing from year to year. It is a very dangerous position for a college to be in, especially as we now face almost certain declines in our applicant pool, or, at best, maintenance of current levels.[51]

Oberlin was by no means the only coed college in our study to find itself in such a precarious position. In fact, the less prestigious coed colleges that had expanded their enrollments in the late 1960s suffered much more than Oberlin did. The experience of one of the coed colleges in our study is illustrative. In the early 1960s, Denison decided to increase its total enrollment to 2,000 students by 1971 and began to build new facilities. According to a 1962 planning document, this expansion was motivated by the college's desire to enroll a larger percentage of men and was based on the assumption that the number of high-quality men interested in attending the college would continue to increase throughout the decade. Although Denison essentially met its 1966 projections, it fell far short of its 1971 projections (see Table 3.1). As many of the top-quality liberal arts colleges went coed, Denison lost its competitive advantage. It became impossible to fill the new places and still maintain quality. As a result, the college's SAT scores fell by 220 points between 1965 and 1980, a considerable drop even during this period of declining SAT scores.[52]

The experience of another coeducational college in Ohio offers an interesting counterexample. In 1975, when its applications plummeted, Hiram

TABLE 3.1

First-Year Projections Made in 1962 versus Actual First-Year Numbers in 1966 and 1971, Denison University

	1961	1966			1971		
	Actual	Projected	Actual	Difference	Projected	Actual	Difference
Number of Applications	1647	2500	2035	−465	3000	1800	−1200
Number of Enrolled Students	465	503	487	−16	620	561	−59
Mean Combined SAT Score	1129	1210	1211	1	1270	1170	−100
Percent of Class Male	53%	56%	55%	−1%	59%	52%	−7%

Source: Profile of Denison University, 1952 to 1972, submitted on 27 February 1962, Table IV.

took nearly all—96 percent—of the students who applied. Although the college was able to maintain its enrollment, the mean SAT score at Hiram dropped precipitously—by a full 143 points from its 1965 high. At the same time, the percentage of enrolled students from the top quintile of their high school classes hit an all-time low of 39 percent. In subsequent years, as applications continued to decline, Hiram consciously chose to reduce enrollment and to accept a smaller percentage of students. Between 1975 and 1980, Hiram decreased the size of the entering first-year class by 14 percent. As a result, the college managed to stave off further declines in quality. By 1980 Hiram's top-quintile proportion had reached 46 percent, and by 1985 its mean SAT score had risen 60 points from its 1975 low.

The net effect of coeducation and the declining number of students with high SAT scores interested in attending private colleges was to increase substantially the stratification in students' academic qualifications among the schools we studied. In general, formerly all-male colleges that went coed were able to maintain their SAT levels and class rank percentages much better than either women's or always-coed colleges, and within these categories the less competitive schools fared least well of all. Moreover, how a college was positioned in 1980 would to a large extent determine its experience in the next period.

IMPROVING QUALITY AT THE TAILS (1980–1994)

As described in both the enrollment and admissions chapters, the 1980s began under the cloud of expected declines in college enrollments. All but a few of the liberal arts colleges in our study also entered the decade with academic profiles lower than they had been over the preceding 15 years. During the next 15 years, however, most of the colleges were able to improve both their mean SAT scores and their high school class rankings.

Figure 3.3 examines the relationship between changes in SAT scores between 1980 and 1993/94[53] and the mean SAT scores at the beginning of the period. As shown in the figure, two groups of colleges were able to increase their mean SAT scores over the decade and a half: those colleges with the best and those colleges with the worst SAT profiles at the beginning of the period. There were parallel improvements in the percentage of students enrolled from the highest ranks of their high school classes. The qualitative improvements at the two groups of schools are a result of different factors.

Capitalizing on Quality

The three schools with SAT scores above 1200 in Figure 3.3 are the most selective colleges in our study (as defined by mean SAT score and percentage of applicants admitted). On average, their mean SAT scores increased 41 points between 1980 and 1993/94. At the same time, the average percentage of top-decile students enrolled at these colleges rose from 74 percent in 1980 to 81 percent during the early 1990s.[54] Over 90 percent of students at these colleges now graduate in the top fifth of their high school classes.

During the 1980s and early 1990s, the most selective colleges capitalized on the general trend in America toward quality and prestige, which was

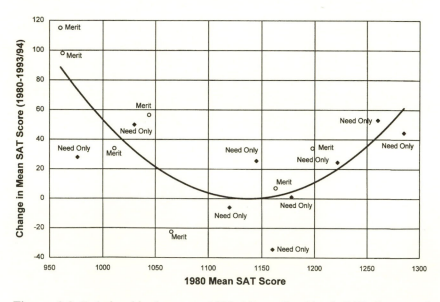

Figure 3.3 Relationship between 1980 Mean Combined SAT Score and Change in Score (1980–1993/94).

discussed in the preceding chapter. Concurrent with the emphasis on quality came an increasing concentration of the most academically qualified students at the most selective colleges and universities. Philip J. Cook and Robert H. Frank, professors of economics and public policy at Duke University and Cornell University, respectively, documented this growing concentration. In 1970, 32 percent of the 12,879 students who scored above 700 on the verbal SAT matriculated at one of the 33 colleges and universities that *Barron's Guide to Colleges* listed as "most competitive."[55] Cook and Frank estimated that in 1989 almost 43 percent of the 9,510 students who scored above 700 on the verbal SAT attended those same 33 colleges and universities. What is striking is that in both years, the 33 "most competitive" schools enrolled only 2.4 percent of all test takers.[56]

Another trend that has contributed to the ability of the most prestigious institutions to continue to enroll the highest quality students is the growing importance placed on the rankings of colleges by guidebooks and magazines. Nearly every guidebook and survey includes the mean SAT score in its quality calculation. Whereas in earlier periods, SAT scores were primarily considered to be predictors of students' performance, they are increasingly seen by students, their parents, and the general public as indicators of a college's quality and prestige. According to a study done by Randall Chapman and Rex Jackson, students tend to choose colleges with reported SAT means that are within the range or higher than their own scores.[57] Thus, again as described in the last chapter, many schools "massage" their mean SAT scores (for example, by excluding the verbal scores of foreign students, or the combined scores of underperforming groups such as recruited athletes) in order to bolster their means. The most competitive colleges in our study have a very different incentive to omit certain scores. According to Philip Smith, Williams's reported mean, which includes all students, is over 100 points lower than the mean SAT score for students admitted to Williams entirely on the basis of academic merit. Smith worries that many students with scores near Williams's reported mean will apply and be discouraged when they are not accepted.[58]

Successful Strategies

Besides the most selective colleges, the other colleges in our study that have been successful at improving their class profiles over the last decade and a half are those that had the lowest mean SAT scores in 1980. As described in Chapter 1, one strategy that these colleges have pursued to maintain their quality has been to reduce their enrollments, thereby eliminating the lower scoring bottom of their classes. At least on the surface, that strategy seems to have worked. All but one of the five colleges with

1980 mean SAT scores below 1050 for which we have class rank information have been able to decrease the proportion of students from below the third quintile who matriculated. The average change for all five colleges between 1980 and the 1990s was a reduction of 11 percentage points; one college, whose enrollment fell by 40 percent before rebounding for a net reduction of 28 percent, reduced its lower quintile proportion by 25 percentage points.

A second strategy some of the colleges have used to attract and then enroll high-ability students has been to institute merit aid programs. One college described why it began to award merit scholarships: "As to the academic quality of the student body, members of the faculty have continuously deplored what was felt to be a decline in the ability of entering freshmen. SAT scores dropped [100 points between 1969/70 and 1979/80] . . . and class rank of entering freshmen was also lower. . . . One effort made to reverse the apparent decline in quality of admitted students, was the establishment of a system of merit scholarships."[59]

A close examination of Figure 3.3 suggests that merit aid programs are effective in enhancing class quality, at least in the short term. Five of the six colleges in the two left-most quadrants of Figure 3.3 have been able to increase their SAT scores by 28 points to almost 120 points at least in part by introducing merit aid programs.[60] In fact, these colleges were the first among the schools we studied to implement merit programs, and they now have the biggest programs as measured both by institutional dollars spent on merit aid and the number of students receiving merit awards. Significantly, the three colleges in Figure 3.3 that experienced declining SAT scores between 1980 and 1994 had the following characteristics: average to below-average mean SAT scores in 1980; no merit awards; or very modest merit grants. The two other colleges in Figure 3.3 offering merit aid had relatively high SAT scores to begin with. They, too, have been able to improve their scores more than most colleges that had similar starting SAT scores but that did not institute merit aid programs.

As might be expected, trends in class rank are even more pronounced than trends in mean SAT scores, because merit aid programs are targeted at top students. Figure 3.4 shows changes at the merit aid colleges in the percentage of ranked entering students who graduated from the first quintile of their high school classes. Between 1980 and the early 1990s, every college except one improved its share of first-quintile students—from 9 to 29 percentage points. Merit E, the only college in Figure 3.4 that did not experience a gain in top-quintile students, had the least room to improve, because in 1980 it already enrolled more than 80 percent of its students from the top quintile.

A byproduct of merit aid that some of the colleges have experienced is a bimodal distribution in student quality. By offering merit awards, colleges

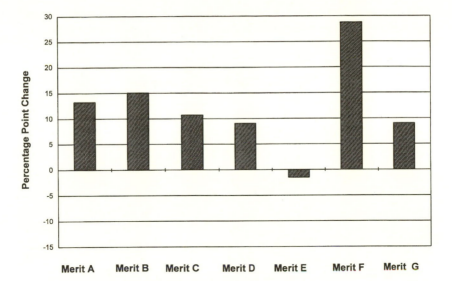

Figure 3.4. Change in Percentage of Students Enrolled from Top Quintile of High School Class (1980–1994), Colleges with Merit Aid.

are able to attract top students, but because their applicant pools are shallow they must still admit some students from the third quintile and below. As would be expected, the yields on students from the lower quintiles are relatively high, but so too are the yields on the top students who are offered merit awards. The result for a few colleges has been an increase in both top-decile and third-quintile and below students and a loss of students in-between. Such a distribution can lead to tensions and make it difficult for professors to teach classes since the ability levels of their students are polarized. The colleges are aware of the problem and in the past few years have successfully countered this trend by offering incentives to students with good as well as great credentials. Michele Myers, president of Denison, recently reported to her trustees on the progress Denison has made in this regard: "[There has been] a huge shift in the qualitative center of the gravity of the class. We no longer are getting a bimodal distribution of students. They are well represented in the middle categories as well as the best categories, and only very few of them are at the bottom of the range. It is a major gain for us."[61]

It is important to note that although there is a clear difference between those colleges who enroll a very high percentage of top-decile students—upward of 80 percent—and the rest who enroll between 20 and 60 percent from the top decile, all of the colleges in our study attract high-ability students. All but four of the colleges enroll more than 50 percent of their students from the top fifth of their class, and only four colleges enroll more than a quarter of their class from the third quintile and below.

Applicant and Admit Trends

Although ultimately a college cares most about the quality of its enrolled students, the composition of its applicant pool determines how easily it can enroll top students. Strikingly, seven of the twelve colleges for which we have class rank data on both applicants and admitted students, admit more than 90 percent of the top-decile students who apply; and at four of the seven schools, the admit rate of top-decile students is virtually 100 percent. In contrast, at the most selective colleges in our study, the admit rates for students from the top tenth of their classes more closely resemble their overall admit rates. Clearly, the applicant pools at the most selective colleges contain many more students from the upper ranks than do the applicant pools at the less selective colleges. Thus, even if they do succeed in enrolling a high percentage of top-ranked students, the less selective colleges have little leeway in choosing their class with an eye to other factors deemed desirable, such as ethnic and geographic diversity, special talents, or strong character.

A similar difference is evident in the mean SAT profiles of applicants. All of the colleges in our study admit a class with higher SAT scores than the one they ultimately enroll, which shows that everything is relative; all of the colleges in our study lose some of their "best applicants" to other colleges. In the hierarchy of colleges, and in the age of multiple applications, there is always another institution that will attract the very best students (even Harvard has "only" a 75 percent yield). Although all the colleges in our study lose some of their ablest students, how many they lose varies considerably. At the Ohio colleges, while the enrolled students for the most part still have stronger profiles than the applicants, this difference has been steadily declining over the last 10 years. In fact, in some years the enrolled students at a few colleges have had lower SAT profiles than the applicants. At all except one of our Massachusetts colleges, for the last 10 years the mean SAT scores of enrolled students has been 20 to 60 points higher than that for the applicant pool—a sign that these colleges are enrolling the better applicants in their pools. In a 1992 admission report, director Tom Parker described the increasing quality of Williams's applicant pool:

> In the applicant pool for the class of 1983, there were 2,353 students with Verbal SAT scores below 600. In this year's applicant pool, there were only 1,418. We have decreased this segment of the applicant pool by close to 1,000

students. We have successfully replaced them with more able students. Iron-ically, however, the 1,000 or so students we've lost once represented "our natural constituency" those who sought us out rather than those we recruited. My concern here is more of a question. Is this a phenomenon we should be worried about?[62]

Having a robust and high-quality applicant pool apparently does not mean that your worries are over—they're just different.

ARE THE ADVANCES SUSTAINABLE?
(THE LATE 1990s AND BEYOND)

Despite the fact that most of the colleges in our study have been able to improve the academic quality of their student bodies, not all have been successful—and successes have not come without struggles and in some cases a tremendous financial toll. Of course, the top colleges will continue to enroll their share of the most talented students. The other colleges—those below them in the competitive hierarchy—have more reasons to be concerned. George Dehne, an educational consultant, gave the keynote address at a recent meeting of the Annapolis group, an informal associa-tion of 50 or so top liberal arts colleges. His remarks were not very consol-ing. Dehne cautioned that because the price of colleges has outpaced the increases in incomes of Americans, fewer families can afford to send their children to a private college. He estimated that there are only about 80,000 students with SAT scores above 1000 and family incomes of more than $70,000. In addition, Dehne noted that private colleges are faced with competitive pressure from public colleges and universities, and not just for financially needy students. For example, Dehne cited one mid-western school that lost 30 students—28 of whom were no need—to Miami University in Ohio.[63]

After the steep declines of the 1980s and early 1990s, the size of the college-age population has begun to turn around. Nevertheless, educators are aware that the projected population increases may not benefit liberal arts colleges. A 1994 article in the Kenyon alumni magazine reported, "[Dean of Admissions] John Anderson isn't complacent about the years ahead though. Population charts indicate that the number of graduating high schools students is about to rise, but students from affluent families, traditionally a vital Kenyon constituency, will not be increasing appreciably in numbers."[64] Even more important, the numbers of high-ability and well-prepared students remain very small. In a recent study, the National Cen-ter for Education Statistics found that among a representative sample of 7,000 college-bound high school seniors who graduated in 1992, only 5.9

percent met all five admission criteria that the researchers chose as representative of admission criteria at highly selective colleges and universities. The criteria included: (1) GPA of 3.5 or higher; (2) SAT of 1100 or higher; (3) took four credits in english, three in math, three in science, and two in foreign language while in high school; (4) received positive teacher recommendation; and (5) participated in two or more extracurricular activities. When they lowered the SAT cutoff to 950 and the GPA to 3.0, 14.3 percent of the sample met all five requirements.[65]

These discouraging demographic trends notwithstanding, in the 1990s many of the liberal arts colleges in our study have reaffirmed their commitment to improving their quality and the diversity of their students. The Plan for Smith 2000 calls for the college to "maintain a large and diverse student body of high aspiration and exceptional ability. Our strategic agenda must therefore have as one of its highest priorities a vigorous admission campaign which will allow us to preserve the size, enhance the quality and increase the diversity of our student body."[66] At Wellesley, quality is also of central importance. The Report of the Committee for Wellesley in the Nineties stressed, "Our first recommendation is thus that the maintenance of the academic excellence of the Wellesley student body is central to the entire mission of the College. Our planning efforts must begin with that principle."[67]

Colleges are at least realistic about the admissions situations they face, even if they are somewhat optimistic about what they hope to accomplish. A strategic working paper at Kenyon acknowledged, "The environment for the 1990s for Kenyon is and will be demanding and competitive. We will, until the mid decade, compete for qualified students as their numbers decline and throughout the decade compete for students in a population that is growing more diverse, with minorities increasing steadily as a proportion of the whole." Nevertheless, Kenyon's goals for the future are similar to Smith's and Wellesley's goals: "Improvement in quality is the paramount purpose and goal of the College in the strategic plan for the 1990s. . . ."[68]

Kenyon set out detailed objectives that it hoped to accomplish in order to enroll "a student body of the highest quality which includes a mix of academic and non-academic qualities." The college plans to increase the percentage and number of entering students who are in the top tenth of their high school class and raise the middle 50 percent range of SAT and ACT scores. The college also wants to enroll students who have won external recognition, have taken the most challenging academic programs in high school, have been rated highly by teachers and counselors, have high writing and math skills, and have demonstrated leadership abilities. In order to help the college achieve its admissions goals, administrators intend to provide additional funding for financial aid and merit awards.[69]

Substitute the name of almost any of the colleges in our study for "Kenyon" in the preceding paragraph and the statement of intentions would hold true. As the twenty-first century approaches, all of the colleges hope to improve the SAT scores, high school rankings, and overall academic and nonacademic achievements of their students. With fewer such students available, the challenge is evident.

How has the quality of the students at our colleges changed during the past 40 years? By some measures very little, but by other measures a lot.

There has always been a hierarchy of SAT scores among the liberal arts colleges we studied, and the ordering in the hierarchy has remained amazingly constant over the last 40 years. When we rank ordered our colleges by their mean SAT scores in 1960 and then again by their mean SAT scores in 1994, only one school had either fallen or risen more than one place, and that school fell only two positions.

What has changed is the range of the hierarchy. Before the baby boom, scores at the colleges ranged from a low of 980 to a high of 1218—a difference of 238 points. Between 1955 and 1965, mean SAT scores increased to all time highs, and the range of means widened—in 1965, the spread was 290 points, from 1050 to 1340. As the tidal wave ebbed and the college-going rate declined, scores at all the colleges fell. But they did not fall equally. In general, the all-male schools that went coed were best able to maintain their SAT means, while the less competitive schools, whether coed or women's, experienced the largest SAT declines. The result of these trends was an increasing stratification that has continued through today. From 1980 to 1994, concerns about quality seem to have driven SAT levels. On the one hand, scores at the highest quality colleges have increased as top students vie for spots at the "best" schools. On the other hand, the less competitive colleges, particularly those in Ohio, have improved their class profiles by constricting their enrollments and implementing merit aid programs. Even so, the SAT scores at our schools now range from 992 to 1331—a spread of 339 points.

The quality of the students at the colleges today, as measured by SAT scores and high school standings, is higher than in the period before the tidal wave. In 1986, Philip Smith noted that at Williams, "Applications are up. For the Class of 1979, they totaled 4,410. Last year we received 6 percent more—4,686. Even more impressive than the numbers, however, is the academic quality of the applicant pool. I find it a little intimidating that all 4,686 members of that group averaged more than 50 points higher on the verbal Scholastic Aptitude Tests than did my entering class in 1951!"[70] While few of the colleges in our study have had as dramatic or as sustained improvements as Williams, all the schools for which we have data have improved their class profiles since the 1950s.

Although the quality of students at these colleges is by some measures better today than it was in the 1950s, by those same measures the quality is not as high today as it was right after the tidal wave. For the colleges in our study, and many other higher education institutions, the mid-1960s represented the height of student quality. SAT scores and class rankings reached all time highs. Today, only one college in our study has a mean SAT score higher than its 1965 reported score; the rest have seen declines in their mean scores ranging from 16 to 200 points.

In a 1995 article about women's colleges, the *Chronicle of Higher Education* compared 1968 SAT scores and class rankings with 1994 scores to show how the quality of students at women's colleges has declined significantly over 25 years. The author concluded that the most qualified women were losing interest in women's colleges.[71] What the article failed to point out is that almost all liberal arts colleges have lost ground since the late 1960s. Figure 3.5 shows the 1965 and 1993/94 average mean SAT scores for the three types of colleges in our study—always coed, formerly men's, and women's. The mean score has dropped on average 21 points at the formerly men's schools, 94 points at the women's (or in the case of Wheaton, formerly women's) colleges, and 110 points at the always-coed colleges. Thus, the women's colleges have fared worse than their men's counterparts but better than their coed peers.

The trends in class rank over this same period are consistent with the SAT trends. Of the 13 colleges for which we have data, eight colleges—six

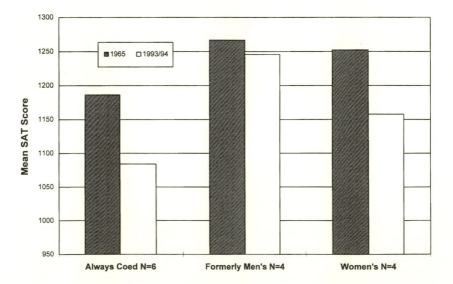

Figure 3.5. Mean Combined SAT Score by Category (1965 and 1993/94).

coed colleges and two women's colleges—enrolled markedly fewer students from the top quintile and/or top decile during the early 1990s than they did in 1965, even though their private school enrollments remained steady or declined over the period. Only three colleges have been able to improve class rankings since 1965, and all are formerly men's colleges that went coed in the 1970s. Two other colleges—the fourth formerly men's college and the top women's college—have been able to maintain their representation of top-quintile students.

The Experience of One College

Perhaps the best way to summarize not only this chapter but also Part I more broadly is to look closely at the experience of one school between 1955 and 1994. Figure 3.6 shows the mean SAT scores for the applicants, admits, and enrolled students at one of the Massachusetts colleges in our study. From 1955 to 1965, the mean SAT scores of all three populations increased dramatically as the tidal wave of baby boom students entered college. During this period, the college admitted, and was able to enroll, the top tier of its applicant pool as evidenced by the near congruence of the enrolled-student and admit lines, and their position well above the applicant line.

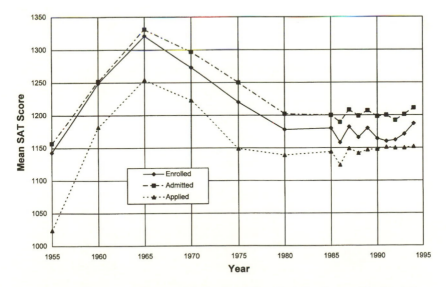

Figure 3.6. Mean Combined SAT Score of Enrolled Students, Admitted Students, and Applicants (1955–1994), Case Study.

Beginning in 1965 and continuing through 1980, the SAT scores of all three populations fell substantially. The widening gap in Figure 3.6 between the enrolled-student and admit lines is indicative of the sharp drop in yields experienced by all the colleges in our study during the 1970s as enrollments shifted among liberal arts colleges and between the different sectors of higher education as a result of coeducation, declining returns to college, and inflationary trends. As its yield dropped, the college was forced to reach further down into its applicant pool, so the mean SAT scores for the college's applicants and admitted students began to converge. One way to measure the effect of the decline in yield is to consider what would have happened if the relative relationships between the applicant, admit, and enrolled-student SAT scores had remained as they were in 1965. Between 1965 and 1980, the mean SAT scores of the college's applicant pool fell by 115 points. Had the enrolled student SAT scores dropped only that much, the college's mean SAT score in 1980 would have been 1206 rather than 1178, a small but nontrivial difference of 28 points.

The most remarkable feature of the 1980 to 1994 landscape is its flatness. Although the college experienced a problem enrolling its strongest admits in the late 1980s and early 1990s, in recent years it has been able to rectify that situation and reestablish the relationship between its applicant, admit, and yield scores that has persisted since 1980. The flatness of the curves might be thought to imply that this college has been passively accepting students during the last decade, but we know from our archival research and interviews that the admissions and financial aid offices at this college, and at the other liberal arts colleges in our study, have been busier than ever in the last decade trying to build classes of the size and quality mandated by their trustees. The flatness of the curves, in the face of these efforts, reminds us of a quotation from a 1959 admissions report: "Admissions work is not unlike the world of 'Alice in Wonderland' where 'one must keep running in order to stay in place.'"[72]

Although it may seem to our colleges (and to their critics) that they have stayed in one place, in many ways they have changed dramatically over the last 40 years. In Part II we examine in more detail two of the more radical changes—coeducation and minority recruitment.

Part II

RESPONSES TO SOCIAL FORCES

CHAPTER 4

The Coeducation Movement

IN 1955, four of the colleges in our study were men's colleges, four were women's, and eight were coeducational. By 1994, all were coeducational except three, which were still women's colleges. Faced with financial, competitive, social, and educational pressures to go coed, the four men's colleges started admitting women between 1969 and 1976. Although our women's colleges confronted similar pressures, all initially remained single sex. In fact, the only women's college in our study to become coed did not begin accepting men until 1987. In this chapter, we examine why the men's and women's schools responded so differently to the pressures to go coed in the late 1960s and early 1970s. We also explore how the colleges became coeducational. Before we examine either issue, however, we set the stage by reviewing the early history of higher education for men and women in this country.

EARLY FOUNDATIONS

Beginning with the founding of Harvard in 1636, America demonstrated a commitment to the values of higher education and religious piety. By the end of the Colonial period, there were 9 colleges in the 13 colonies, and more were founded in the aftermath of the American Revolution. When Williams College received its charter in 1793, it became the 21st institution of higher education established in the United States.

Higher education in America was transformed during the nineteenth century. In the decades before the Civil War, America experienced a college boom as new colleges sprung up all over the country and existing institutions expanded. The earliest colleges in New England and in the Midwest provided religious training for men who would enter professional vocations. Since at that time most of the professions, such as law, medicine, and the ministry, excluded women, the colleges enrolled only men. In 1821 a group of Congregationalist and lay leaders established Amherst in the Connecticut Valley of Massachusetts to counter the Unitarian emphasis of Harvard. Many of the founders of the colleges in the Midwest and West were religious missionaries who came from the Northeast; thus, the colleges they built emulated the small New England liberal arts colleges. Many of the colleges in our study were established by congregations in the early to mid-1800s. For example, Kenyon was founded by Episcopal Bishop Philander Chase in 1825, Denison began as a Baptist religious seminary in 1831, and Ohio Wesleyan was established by the Methodist church in 1842.[1]

Until the nineteenth century, there had been a deeply rooted prejudice against the serious education of women. This opposition rested on two contradictory premises: first, that women were dangerous when educated, and second, that women were not capable of being educated.[2]

The history of higher education for women grew out of two sources— female seminaries in the East and coeducational colleges in the Midwest. During the first half of the nineteenth century, a number of female seminaries were established, including Wheaton in 1834 and Mount Holyoke in 1837. Many of these seminaries evolved into four-year colleges.

Coeducation had its roots in the Midwest. Although a few women's schools were established in the new frontier, by the late 1800s most women college students in the Midwest attended coed schools. In 1837 Oberlin College matriculated women in its regular college course, becoming the first coeducational college in the country. Coeducation was favored in the Midwest for ideological as well as practical reasons. According to Gail Griffin, "the rigid roles and delicate concepts of feminism were hard to sustain against the demands of frontier life."[3] Similarly, Frederick Rudolph wrote, "The Western woman was not a thing apart. . . . She was a person in her own right who had commanded the respect of her menfolk by assuming responsibility and working hard."[4] Rudolph argued that the strength of the state systems in the midwestern and western states also favored coeducation. As the state universities expanded into large popular institutions, "it was to be expected that women be included."[5] Churches and communities also found it economically infeasible to establish separate men's and women's schools. In fact, the newer midwestern schools often needed women's tuition to supplement their relatively small endowments.[6]

At the same time that coed colleges were established in the Midwest, various types of women's institutions were founded in the Northeast and South. Some of these colleges were essentially finishing schools, built on the premise that women inhabited a separate sphere that required a separate education in the domestic arts. Others, however, most notably the seven independent schools that were founded in the mid- to late 1800s in the Northeast, which would later become known as the "Seven Sisters," represented a break in the traditional pattern of education for women. These colleges aimed to provide quality education for women equivalent to the educational opportunities that men received at Ivy League colleges and other independent men's liberal arts colleges. Roberta Frankfort described such schools as "place[s] where women's convictions and intellect might be strengthened without the interference of hostile forces."[7]

Three of the four women's colleges in our study were among the Seven Sisters, and all four embodied these goals. Mary Lyon, Mount Holyoke's founder, challenged her students to "Go where no one else will go, do what no one else will do."[8] Henry Durant established Wellesley in 1871 to provide a highly academic Christian education to women that would enable them to challenge society's "slavery of women."[9] Sophia Smith, the first benefactor of Smith College, pledged in her will "the establishment and maintenance of an Institution for the higher education of young women, with the design to furnish for my own sex means and facilities for education equal to those which are afforded now in our Colleges to young men."[10] When it first opened, Wheaton had the same curriculum and texts as Harvard.

Toward the end of the nineteenth century, many men's colleges decided to become coeducational. Colby College in Maine became the first previously all-male college to admit women when it accepted Mary Low in 1871. Denison, Ohio Wesleyan, the College of Wooster, and Hiram were among the men's colleges in Ohio that merged with sister seminaries or began admitting women near the turn of the century. By 1900, 70 percent of the nation's colleges and universities admitted both men and women. These developments led Nicholas Murray Butler, president of Columbia University, to declare, "Coeducation is a dead issue. The American people have decided in its favor."[11] Administrators at both Amherst and Williams discussed admitting women in the 1870s. Amherst even established a special scholarship for the first group of entering women. Nonetheless, both colleges remained all male, as did Kenyon College. The College of the Holy Cross, which had been founded by the Jesuit order of the Catholic Church, remained a secondary school and religious seminary for men only.

The education of women during the late 1800s at many of the coeducational colleges differed from that at the Seven Sisters since at the coed schools "women tended to preserve the relationships that prevailed in their home environments."[12] Despite Oberlin's status as the first coeducational college, women students occupied a secondary position. Lucy Stone, a graduate of Oberlin and a prominent suffragist in the post–Civil War era, described her alma mater's attitude toward female students: "Washing the men's clothes, caring for their rooms, serving them at table, listening to their orations but remaining respectfully silent in public assemblages, the Oberlin 'co-eds' were being prepared for intelligent motherhood and subservient wifehood."[13] Stone refused to prepare a commencement speech, because a male classmate would have had to read it since she and her female classmates were not allowed to give public addresses.

Mary Low graduated at the top of her class too, but the honor of giving Colby's class of 1875 valedictory address went to the second-ranked student, a man. The success of the first women students at Colby prompted the college to establish a separate coordinate college for women in 1890. A recent article in Colby's alumni magazine described what such a system entailed: "During this period [the late 1800s and early 1900s] the barriers separating male and female students at Colby were literal. Women could not compete for class standing or academic prizes, alongside men. Access to faculty was equal, but facilities were not, and men dominated student government and other leadership positions and were privileged with many more extracurricular opportunities."[14]

In contrast, a student at Mount Holyoke in the nineteenth century wrote home that the institution wanted to produce "hard marble" women.[15] The Seven Sister colleges trained women to use their minds and fulfill their intellectual potential. R. Clark Seelye, president of Smith, summed up the role of the women's college during the late nineteenth century: "The college is not intended to fit woman for any particular sphere or profession but to develop by the most carefully devised means all her intellectual capacities so that she may be a more perfect woman in any position."[16] This emphasis on and support of women's intellectual accomplishments and personal growth would continue to distinguish the leading women's colleges even when coeducational colleges abandoned their overt preferences for male students.

By the middle of the twentieth century, contrary to Butler's prediction, the elite men's and women's colleges were flourishing with a growing number of applicants. Particularly during the tidal wave period, the rising qualifications of applicants at both men's and women's colleges made the question of coeducation moot. In the late 1960s and early 1970s, however, the situation changed. Students' involvement in the civil rights movement, the women's movement, and Vietnam protests, along with the increasing heterogeneity on college campuses, ushered in a new era. The changing pattern of relationships between the sexes and the greater participation of women in the workforce and society led colleges to reexamine the premises of single-sex education.

In the late 1960s and early 1970s, there was a dramatic shift by single-sex colleges toward coeducation. In 1960, there were 298 women's colleges in the United States. In 1972, only half of these colleges were still women's colleges: One hundred nineteen schools had gone coed and 33 schools had merged or closed. Men's colleges became even rarer. Whereas in 1960 there were 261 men's colleges, by 1972 only 101 single-sex men's schools remained, most of which were religious seminaries.

Much of what has been written about the move toward coeducation in the 1960s and 1970s, and its ramifications for higher education, takes the perspective of women's colleges, as if those institutions were at the center of the coeducation movement. A more accurate portrayal would focus on the all-male schools, for it was the concerns of these institutions and their male students that dominated the discussions and decisions during the period. Examining the deliberations of the men's colleges in our study that became coed elucidates the complex motivations and circumstances that led colleges to make what many would later describe as the most significant decision in their histories. The women's colleges in our study faced similar circumstances. Yet, all four chose to remain single sex during the move to coeducation in the late 1960s and 1970s. Wheaton College didn't decide to become a college for women and men until 1987. After exploring the decisions by the men's colleges in our study to become coed, we investigate the factors that led all four women's colleges initially to remain single sex and then discuss how those factors relate to Wheaton's decision to become coed in the late 1980s.

COEDUCATION AT THE MEN'S COLLEGES

Princeton University was one of the first elite men's colleges to seriously consider admitting women to its undergraduate program. In 1967, Princeton undertook a 16-month desirability and feasibility study of coeducation that included a detailed financial analysis and a nationwide survey of alumni groups. The resulting Patterson Report stressed the positive impact coeducation would have on the institution and was used as a handbook on coeducation by many men's colleges.

Three of the four men's colleges in our study became coed between 1969 and 1971. In the mid- to late 1960s, faced with financial problems and a need to expand, Kenyon decided that the best solution would be to admit women to a newly created coordinate college. Kenyon admitted its first group of female students in the fall of 1969. In 1967, the Educational Policy Committee at the College of the Holy Cross created an ad hoc committee to study whether the college should become coeducational. At a meeting in May 1968, a large majority of the Holy Cross faculty on a show-of-hands vote approved the ad hoc committee's recommendation to admit women. In April 1969, after additional study by the faculty, the college decided officially to become coed. The first women entered Holy Cross in the fall of 1971. Williams College also began its study of coeducation in 1967. The findings of the study and its recommendation to admit women as undergraduates were endorsed by the faculty and approved by the board of trustees in June 1969. The first women enrolled at Williams in 1971.

The fourth college, Amherst, did not accept upper-class women until

1975 and first-year women until 1976. In 1972, after extensive analysis and discussion, President Ward recommended that Amherst expand by admitting women. The board of trustees, however, rejected the recommendation, requesting further study. It was only in 1974 that the trustees endorsed coeducation. By then Amherst was one of the last elite men's colleges to remain single sex.

A combination of reasons convinced the men's colleges in our study, and across the country, to become coeducational. The reasons generally fell into four categories: financial, competitive, social, and educational. The catalyst for change at each college differed. For some colleges, a decline in the quality and number of applicants prompted discussions about coeducation. Other colleges realized that they were experiencing financial difficulty or heading there and that expansion was the best way to avoid further financial problems. For most of the colleges that became coed, however, no one set of reasons convinced all the constituents that the college should become coed; rather many factors taken together indicated that the best path for the future of the institution was to admit women. Underlying all the discussions was a recognition of the profound social changes that had taken place in American society since the women's and civil rights movements had gained momentum.

Financial Pressures

Financial considerations played an important role in the decision of three of the four men's colleges in our study to become coeducational. When the tidal wave waned in the late 1960s, many colleges were left with underutilized facilities and unsustainable student/faculty ratios. Even those colleges that had not expanded much in the 1960s faced pressures to grow in order to offer more classes, build better facilities, and attract students. In 1968 Joseph Kershaw, the provost at Williams, wrote an influential report that argued that expanding the student body could help colleges deal with their financial difficulties.[17]

Many of the men's colleges in our study took Kershaw's advice to heart. As described in Chapter 1, three of the four formerly men's colleges in our study used coeducation as a way to expand their enrollments. At Kenyon the creation of a coordinate college for women enabled the college to expand its enrollment and improve its financial position through increased tuition revenues and greater economies of scale. Even at Amherst, which was in a strong financial position, the Long Range Planning Committee "calculated that some expansion of the student body would enhance Amherst's long-range financial operations and that the addition of women would be the best way to accomplish this expansion."[18]

Williams's final report on coeducation described at great length why the marginal costs of additional students in general and additional women students in particular would be lower than the average cost of current students and, therefore, why increasing the size of the college by admitting women would have a favorable impact on the college's operating budget:

> There are a number of expenses which are fixed within a fairly wide range of size and which must be carried on for any good educational community. A full range of course offerings for a liberal arts college is one such fixed cost. In addition, general administrative services and general institutional and plant expenses can handle fairly substantial additional workloads with rather minimal increases in staff capacity or equipment. Most of the expenses of the library operation are involved with acquiring the basic collection and with general operation rather than with book circulation per se. There is a substantial possibility of increased utilization of our physical plant, including classroom facilities, . . . infirmary space, heating plant, athletic fields, and scientific laboratories.

> One of the principal reasons for the lower marginal cost of women students is that the projections assumed that the student/faculty ratio would rise from its present level (less than 10/1) to approximately 12/1. . . . In principle, this kind of economy could be obtained whether one added male or female students. In fact, according to expected departmental registrations for men and women, it will be much easier to reach an overall student/faculty ratio of 12/1 by adding women than it would by adding men. This is because of the fact that women will tend to 'fill in' more of the under-enrolled departments than would additional men. . . .[19]

For all three colleges, the long-term financial benefit of larger classes outweighed the short-term costs of converting facilities, dormitories, and the curricula to accommodate coeducation.

Competitive Pressures

The men's colleges also worried that they could not continue to be competitive in admissions if they remained single sex. Toward the end of the 1960s admissions officers realized that not only had the number of high scoring applicants leveled off, but students also preferred coeducational schools. In January 1968, Smith and Princeton surveyed seniors at 19 "superior private and public secondary schools throughout the country." Of the 4,680 students who replied, 81 percent of the males and 79 percent of the females in the upper two-fifths of their class felt that a college enrolling both men and women, as compared with students only of one's own sex, would "increase its attractiveness."[20] Princeton's Patterson Report noted, "too many of the students who apply, whom we admit and whom we would most like to have at Princeton, go elsewhere,"[21] principally because of the lack of women students. The Patterson Report concluded:

> The evidence is clear that an overwhelming majority of the most able persons in the age group 18–22 strongly prefers to share the undergraduate educational experience with members of the opposite sex. This desire on the part of Princeton's prospective students is so great that it cast serious doubts on the ability of an all-male Princeton to attract students in anything like the numbers and quality characteristic of present and recent classes.[22]

The men's schools in our study confronted similar problems. In 1965, Kenyon debated whether to expand by enrolling more men or by admitting women. Kenyon recognized: "that the small men's college no longer has the broad appeal that it once had. We cannot ignore the fact that the number of applications to Kenyon has not risen as sharply as have the numbers at neighboring coed institutions. Nor can we ignore what seems to be a national movement towards coeducation."[23] Although administrators at Kenyon worried that trying to enroll more men would compromise the college's quality, they reasoned that admitting women would potentially improve their admission situation: "Coeducation then, seems to be an attractive and reasonable alternative. Women pose no problems so far as recruiting is concerned; indeed, most institutions set higher admissions standards for women because of the press of applicants."[24] The Committee on Coordinate Education at Williams also realized that "it would not be wise for Williams to limit its potential applicants to a small and diminishing percentage of college bound male students if it wishes to continue to attract the high quality student it has in the past."[25]

A 1969 Holy Cross report cited estimates that there were no more than 14,000 male secondary school seniors in the country able to score above 600 on the SAT verbal tests, and whose families' total annual income was over $16,000.[26] Such a small pool was particularly worrisome for Holy Cross since it was apparent that even graduates of Catholic high schools preferred nondenominational, coeducational colleges. Becoming coeducational, Holy Cross hoped, "would tend to upgrade the quality and increase the number of male applicants seeking admission to the College, as well as give us a large number of bright female students to consider for admission."[27]

Although Amherst went coed after the other colleges, Dean of Admissions Wall also noted the consequences of the declining interest among high school students in single-sex colleges. A survey released by the Educational Testing Service in December 1972, found that 92 percent of seniors scoring above 600 on the verbal SAT preferred a coeducational college. Only 4 percent listed a men's college as their first choice.[28] In 1973, after the trustees rejected the president's first recommendation to become coed, Wall expressed his concern for Amherst's future: "There is no doubt in my mind that we will continue to attract *good* students even if we remain a men's college . . . but I fear that in the future we may not be able to attract our share of the *best* students available."[29] Around the same time, a prominent women's studies professor at another institution remarked: "Women can get along perfectly well without Amherst. Can Amherst get along without women?"[30] Since most secondary schools were already coeducational, people increasingly viewed separate education as anomalous. Wall conceded: "I worry more and more that the emphasis at Amherst will not be on a quality education, but that candidates will seek out the school for its unique peculiarity it has chosen for itself—this artificial maleness in a day when humanness has to be stressed, taught, and practiced in every facet of living."[31]

Educational and Social Pressures

Wall's quote underlines not only the admissions concerns but also the larger educational and social concerns that prompted the men's colleges to become coed. The coeducation reports of the men's colleges devoted considerable space to discussing the positive effects that women would have on their institutions both intellectually and socially. At Williams, for example, the final recommendation on coeducation stressed that the "present growth of range and diversity in the college community would be reinforced by the inclusion of women [since] men and women together form a community which is stronger in its variousness, and more fully human in the play of its attitudes and responses, than is a community made up solely of men or solely of women."[32]

Most colleges believed the addition of women would enhance the educational experience. The Patterson Report asserted, "The ability of women fully to participate in the intellectual life of the university cannot be contested."[33] Women tended to perform better academically than their male counterparts, both in secondary school and in college. Additionally, "Men and women bring different approaches, different angles of vision, different viewpoints to many subject matters; bringing them together in the classroom improves the education of both. A not unimportant benefit is that unsupportable biases based on sex differences are more quickly exposed and abandoned."[34] Faculty members who had taught both coeducational and all-male classes preferred the coeducational classes and found that the presence of the women students enlivened and broadened the discussions. According to the Williams report, "women tend to be less vocational than men in their expectations of the liberal arts, and their perspectives thus

provide an important reinforcement of the fundamental liberal arts character of our program."[35] Men's colleges also expected the presence of women
to even out enrollment distributions, because women preferred different
disciplines than men.[36]

Opponents of coeducation asserted that the presence of women would
detract from the purposefulness of the men's intellectual activity. To the
contrary, the Patterson Report responded, "We have found little support
for the view that in the highly selective colleges, women seriously distract
men's attention in the classroom or library."[37] Instead, one report argued,
the presence of women would have a "calming effect . . . on the otherwise
obstreperous male."[38] Since in a coed environment women would be on
campus on a day-to-day basis, many colleges believed that male students
would concentrate more on their schoolwork and less on arranging their
weekend plans. Holy Cross, for example, stressed the social benefits of
having men and women together on campus:

> From the broad social point of view, undergraduate education in an all-male
> environment is undesirable. According to Dr. James J. Gill, a Jesuit psychia-
> trist, isolation of the sexes generates fantasizing about the opposite sex. Bring-
> ing them together makes the views of each more realistic. Life at Holy Cross
> tends to confirm this analysis. Although it is not now as unusual to see a
> college-age girl on the campus during the week as was the case in the past,
> nevertheless the only significant contact with young women for the typical
> Holy Cross student takes place on weekends when he either leaves the
> campus or attends a Holy Cross mixer. Mixers customarily involve bringing
> busloads of girls from women's colleges. That the mixers are dubbed "cattle
> calls" by our students testifies to their undesirability for establishing normal
> contacts between the sexes. Indeed, the picture of college students chasing all
> over New England in search of normal heterosexual relationships is, if not
> bizarre, at least an inefficient use of the weekend.[39]

Kenyon also recognized the social desirability of having women on
campus: "While much speaks for the retention of Kenyon's traditional all-
male character, there is much also that speaks against it. Whenever the
problems of social life at Kenyon are discussed, the absence of women is a
chief topic. . . ."[40] The combination of educational and social benefits led
Princeton to conclude, "The notion that a coeducational Princeton would
be simply a husband-hunting ground for many of the women, and a source
of social and sexual convenience for the men, simply does not stand up
under examination."[41]

The many strong reasons given for coeducation did not mean that everyone at these colleges favored admitting women. Most of the arguments
were not against coeducation *per se* but rather against a particular institution becoming coed. At Holy Cross, Patrick Shanahan, a faculty member,

wrote an impassioned essay in which he outlined why Holy Cross should remain all male: "Coeducation is not something new. It has been an established form of education for almost three quarters of a century. The arguments in support of it given now are not much different from the arguments given in its favor one hundred years ago. There does not seem to be any college of even modest renown which faded away primarily as a result of a determination to remain all-male."[42] Although Shanahan recognized the merits of coeducation, he argued that Holy Cross would be a stronger institution if it remained all male. He wrote, "one cannot discount the possibility that the recent changeovers to coeducation have made more room at the top for the well-regarded men's colleges."[43] Other arguments against coeducation included a fear that some alumni would cease to support the college, or that the conversion costs were too high.

A Changed Environment

Shanahan's and others' arguments might have prevailed in a different period. But fundamental changes in how men and women related and the position of women in society in the mid- to late 1960s made coeducation almost inevitable for men's colleges. The Patterson Report summarized:

> We believe that for Princeton to remain an all-male institution in the face of today's evolving social system would be out of keeping with her past willingness to change with the times. . . . Princeton is confronted with the challenge of adapting herself to fundamental changes in secondary education and in the nation's values and mores. For familiar reasons, women are rapidly assuming all the rights and obligations that their many talents—including powerful intellectual ones—warrant. . . . Segregation of the sexes was fully consistent with our social institutions only a generation ago; but now in the late 1960s it is, quite simply, seen as anachronistic by most college students.[44]

Edward Lund, president of Kenyon, echoed the Patterson Report: "Separate education is an anachronism in an age that admits less and less distinction between sexes in both professional and social life."[45] An article in the *Williams Alumni Magazine* also recognized "the fact that today most of our students come from co-educational schools and will go from us into a world in which women play increasingly important roles outside the home."[46]

By the time Amherst decided to admit women, the issue had changed subtly. No longer was the question whether admitting women would make the college stronger; rather the question was whether the institution could survive otherwise. The Report of the Amherst Visiting Committee on Coeducation questioned the meaning of Amherst's position as almost the "sole surviving example" of its type of single-sex education: "What Amherst's leaders must decide," it posited, "is whether this position within the changed context of American education and American society will provide the basis for educational leadership or educational obsolescence?"[47] The report concluded, "The fundamental reason for change at Amherst is a change in the world which the College motto dedicates us to 'illumine.' Amherst needs to admit women because women are now entering all the significant areas of our society. . . . Any institution which sets itself aside from this process will risk relegating itself to relative insignificance in the development of our communal culture."[48] By the time Amherst became coeducational, the decision to admit women had shifted from a concern about becoming anachronistic to worries about survival and even moral arguments. Indeed, the preliminary report of the Committee on Educational Policy at Amherst centered its argument upon the "moral imperative for justice in ending the arbitrary exclusion of women from Amherst."[49]

All of the discussions about whether the men's colleges should become coed stressed why it would be advantageous for them to admit women. The men's colleges never seriously considered what the advantages to women would be in attending their institutions. Less than one page of the 55-page Patterson Report addressed whether Princeton could "do justice to women students."[50] At the beginning of its report, Holy Cross stated: "This report will not discuss the advantages that the College has to offer female applicants. We are of the opinion that a girl coming here would not be short changed."[51] Aside from discussions of how the dorms and other facilities would need to be spruced up, none of the men's colleges considered what other changes could be made in their overall programs and environments to welcome women.[52] This oversight, and the underlying assumption that women would fit comfortably into the men's college world, were indicative of an attitude that made the decision whether women's colleges would become coed less simple and straightforward than it was for men's colleges.

THE WOMEN'S COLLEGES REAFFIRM THEIR COMMITMENTS

Reasons to Become Coed

The adoption of coeducation by the most selective and prestigious men's colleges prompted women's colleges to consider their options. In October 1967, Clara Ludwig, admissions director at Mount Holyoke, reflected:

> No report on admissions in 1967 for a college for women can fail to mention the issue of coeducation. . . . Miss Newcomer's book *A Century of Higher Education for American Women* was published in 1959. The events of the past year lead one again to consider her prediction that women's colleges would be

converted to coeducational institutions or die in another twenty years. One wonders now whether even she may be surprised by the speed of events in the men's colleges only eight years later. It is hard to find a college for men that does not talk about the possibility of admitting women. Separate education is under attack in a way it has never been before. How can we argue our case and not be constantly on the defensive?[53]

In the first years of coeducation, women's colleges reacted to the actions of their male counterparts. Fearful of losing both students and future applicants to the newly coed Ivy League, many women's colleges, including Vassar, Bennington, Skidmore, Sarah Lawrence, and Connecticut, decided to admit men. The presidents of the women's colleges that went coed were among coeducation's strongest and most vocal supporters, arguing as Al Simpson, the president of Vassar, did: "Nowhere in the world is anyone really making a powerful argument for separate education anymore."[54] Connecticut College President Charles E. Shain agreed: "In this age a young American's education, when it is shared with the opposite sex, is superior in its basic learning conditions to an education in a single-sex environment."[55]

Simpson's and Shain's view of single-sex education fit well with the burgeoning women's movement of the late 1960s. During the 1960s there was considerable tension between the women's movement and women's colleges.[56] The feminist movement that emerged in the 1960s was dominated by liberal feminists who rejected the notion that there were essential differences between men and women. To many of these feminists, single-sex education was unnatural and anachronistic.

Popular attitudes regarding women's colleges were also generally unfavorable. A 1968 admissions report from Mount Holyoke described two national magazine articles that "caused . . . great concern"—one in *Seventeen* and one in *Mademoiselle*. The articles presented negative images of women's colleges and argued that such schools were no longer effective. Ludwig worried, "Both of these magazines are widely read by all teenage girls and they can not help but have had some effect upon attitudes."[57] These types of articles also could not help but have an effect on the women's colleges themselves. Faced with a lack of support for their mission by some of the leading feminist thinkers and a concomitant decline in interest among young women in single-sex education, many of the women's colleges believed that their very survival depended on becoming coeducational.

The decision by Vassar to become coeducational is illustrative of the pressures felt by women's colleges, particularly at the beginning of the coeducation movement. Vassar was one of the most elite and selective colleges in the nation. In 1967, Vassar and Yale announced that discussions were underway on the feasibility of Vassar moving from Poughkeepsie to

New Haven to become a coordinate college for Yale. For Vassar, which was particularly isolated, the discussion was prompted by a concern for the future survival of liberal arts colleges together with Yale's announcement that it had decided to admit women. Administrators and trustees at Vassar knew that Yale would potentially be a fierce competitor for Vassar's brightest students. Moreover, they assumed that the trend toward coeducation was permanent and that the original mission of the college, to provide "one sex all the advantages too long monopolized by the other,"[58] was no longer relevant. The option of whether Vassar could or should remain a women's college was never really considered as an acceptable alternative. The assumption was that Vassar needed to incorporate men; the only question was how. After the trustees decided that a relocation to New Haven was not in the college's best interests, they moved quickly to propose that Vassar admit men as undergraduate degree candidates.[59] Vassar's decision was not surprising considering the tenor of the times and the prevailing attitudes toward separate education.

The women's colleges in our study also carefully examined the question of coeducation—yet all decided to remain women's colleges. At Wellesley, despite the recommendation by the Commission on the Future of the College to admit men, the board of trustees reaffirmed Wellesley's mission as a women's college in 1971. Also in 1971, the faculty and trustees at Smith and Mount Holyoke voted overwhelmingly to remain women's colleges. Wheaton College similarly decided to retain its all-women character, in spite of President Prentice's reservations about single-sex education and a 4:1 faculty vote in 1970 to become coed.

Why did the women's colleges in our study decide to remain single sex when all the men's colleges in our study as well as many of the other women's colleges in the country chose to become coed? The answer to that question lies not only in the missions and cultures of the individual colleges but also in the particular timing of their decisions. The early 1970s were a time of considerable and rapid change in the women's movement and in how separate education was viewed. Whereas in the late 1960s many people believed that separate women's colleges were no longer relevant, the experiences of some of the women's colleges that went coed at the end of the 1960s suggested that there was still a need for women's colleges. The decisions by Wellesley and Smith to remain single sex are instructive.

Wellesley Rejects Coeducation

In 1969, the trustees at Wellesley suggested that the college form a special commission to study its future, including the question of educational opportunities for women and prospects for remaining a women's college. As President Ruth Adams explained, "The question of the future of the College, and particularly the question of coeducation, has to be faced. If we refuse to do any thinking about coeducation, we would be the greatest female ostrich in the educational zoo."[60]

The Commission on the Future of the College at Wellesley recommended that the college begin to admit men as transfer students and degree candidates. Many of the faculty and students at Wellesley had begun to view a women's college as outdated and even contrary to the original purpose of its founders. In its 1971 report to the trustees, the commission wrote:

> Mr. Durant's [the founder of Wellesley] ideal of equal educational opportunities for women today requires reinterpretation. Dedication to his ideal in the 1970s implies the introduction of men onto the campus where they will work together with women in the classroom and in related campus activities. . . . By educating students of both sexes in a context that recognizes and consciously focuses on the complex but as yet not clearly perceived role of women in society of the future, Wellesley can provide distinguished leadership.[61]

Like the men's colleges that were concerned with maintaining the quality of their applicant pools, Wellesley believed that the presence of men would enable the college to continue to attract strong women, the majority of whom preferred coed colleges. The commission reported that in a 1969 survey of high schools from which top-ranked women applied to Wellesley, the percentage who entered women's colleges declined from 35 percent to 23 percent between 1965 and 1969. A 1970 survey of high school guidance counselors also showed that coeducation was the single most important factor for young women in choosing a college.[62]

Although the commission was clear in its recommendation to increase the number of men on campus through the expansion of exchange programs and the admission of men as transfer students and degree candidates, President Ruth Adams dissented from the report's recommendation. Adams argued:

> Wellesley has an historical commitment to the education of women, a commitment that, in these times of heightened consciousness on the part of women, is perhaps more consequential than for many prior years. . . . I believe that the climate of thought concerning the translation of women's institutions to coeducational colleges has changed in the past year, due in some part to the better elements of the women's liberation program and due to the serious reviews given their identification by such colleges as Bryn Mawr, Goucher and Chatham. The value for women of colleges devoted particularly to their needs receives today wider support. . . . I believe that we should devote our energies

and our resources to building from within, to keeping Wellesley the best of the
women's colleges in America, indeed in the world.[63]

The board of trustees concurred with Adams and voted to accept all of
the commission's recommendations except the admission of men as degree
candidates. The importance of timing in the Wellesley decision should not
be underestimated. The commission's report was finished and presented to
the board of trustees two years after the study commenced. The chair of
the commission described "the sea of change in the national attitude towards women's colleges" as a significant factor in the board's decision not
to become coeducational.[64] By 1971, the recognition of the educational
importance of women's colleges was strong and played a decisive role in
the decision regarding coeducation.

Smith Follows Suit

The effect of the shifting attitudes toward women's education can also be
seen in Smith's deliberations. Discussions about coeducation began as early
as 1964 when an ad hoc committee recommended that a study be undertaken to determine the feasibility of coeducation at Smith. A Faculty Planning Committee was set up in 1965 to explore the issue. In 1968 this
committee surveyed alumnae as to their views and charged Professor Ely
Chinoy with conducting a study of the viability of coeducation in terms of
finances, buildings, and the recruitment and retention of faculty and students. Chinoy recommended that Smith move toward coeducation by
gradually expanding.

In 1970, Smith convened another committee to evaluate the question of
coeducation. The final report of the Planning Committee on the Question
of Coeducation at Smith College, issued in April 1971, considered various
aspects of the coeducation decision. At the core of the discussion was
Smith's continued commitment to its historical mission to provide women
with an education "equal to those which are afforded in our Colleges to
young men" and the question whether single-sex education was still the
means to achieve that goal. After careful examination, the committee reaffirmed Smith's position as a women's college:

> It is the conclusion of the Committee that at the present time, when the status
> and roles of women in American society are being reexamined with a view to
> their improvement, an important option that should remain open to women is
> attendance at a college of the highest caliber in which women are unques-
> tionably first-class citizens. Such a college can provide for many women a
> place for intellectual and personal growth that they would not attain as easily,
> if at all, in an undergraduate student body dominated by men.[65]

Although the commitment to women's education dominated the discussion of coeducation at the women's colleges in our study, administrators also carefully considered the financial implications. For many of the men's colleges, coeducation clearly offered an opportunity to expand enrollments and, therefore, to increase tuition revenues. Smith also recognized that "a factor to be considered . . . is the financial position of all private colleges as they face the inexorable pressures of inflation and the real danger of becoming prohibitively expensive if they try to increase their income from students too rapidly. . . ."[66] For Smith, however, unlike for Williams, Amherst, and Kenyon, coeducation was not an attractive way to solve financial problems. Smith did not want to reduce the number of women it educated. Yet adding men in any sensible ratio would have meant greatly enlarging the size of the college, an option that was not favored since the college was already one of the largest liberal arts colleges in the country.[67] Smith worried that an expansion of the college would require substantial capital outlays for construction costs as well as put pressure on financial aid dollars. In short, because Smith was already significantly larger than most of the men's liberal arts colleges, it would not recognize the benefits of marginal cost improvements to the same extent as the other schools.

Another concern related to increasing the size of the college was the uncertainty of attracting men of the same quality as the women. Smith noted: ". . . it is not at all clear that substantial numbers of highly qualified men students could be found who would choose to come to Smith College. . . . Nor is it clear that any increase in the size of the student body could be accomplished at this time without a lowering of the average quality of those admitted."[68] For the men's colleges, becoming coed provided the opportunity to attract top-quality women to their programs in the midst of a declining market. The projected declines in the number of top-quality students was a concern shared by all of the colleges. The women's colleges in our study, however, doubted that admitting men would solve their recruitment problems. At Mount Holyoke, Clara Ludwig asked:

> How then to maintain the drawing power of the past few years? Become coeducational? That might increase our appeal for girls but a women's college which attempts this has a stupendous problem for several decades at least. Some few colleges have done it—Rockford and MacMurray—but not without great pain. Even top-flight coeducational colleges today have different admissions standards for boys and for girls for admission to the honors program, for instance. Hampshire is concerned not about finding able girls for admission but about finding comparable boys. Becoming coed is drastic action that hardly seems necessary until other possibilities have been exhausted.[69]

Looking back at the period, Sally Montgomery, dean of the college and longtime faculty member at Mount Holyoke, recalled that in the early

1970s a men's college becoming coed was seen as a sign of strength, whereas a women's college becoming coed was seen as a sign of weakness. Men's colleges, even after they became coed, still represented the dominant culture. Consequently, formerly men's colleges were able to attract the highest quality men and women, while women's colleges that became coed had much more trouble enrolling the most sought after students.

First Experiments with Coeducation

This situation is somewhat ironic given the early experiences of students at newly coeducational colleges. Women at formerly men's colleges did not always feel comfortable in their new environments. One woman student at Yale, for example, remarked, "We are treated as special gifts to the classroom, but not as intellectual equals."[70] At women's colleges that became coeducational, however, men students began to dominate classroom discussions and leadership positions. At Bennington College, a man in the first coed class was elected president of his first-year class. Women students expressed strong objections to the new students. "If there are one or two boys in a class they do all the talking. And frankly, it's goddamn annoying,"[71] complained a senior at Bennington. Her complaint was borne out by the observations of Thomas Meehan, a reporter for the New York Times who spent time on campus in the fall of 1969, immediately after the school went coed. In one class Meehan attended, the one boy out of 16 students in the class did 85 percent of the talking.[72]

Similar problems were experienced at Vassar. Like Bennington and other women's schools that went coed in the late 1960s, Vassar went to great lengths to "alter her ladylike image."[73] These efforts sometimes irritated the female students. At an open hearing by the trustees, one Vassar woman testified, "The first men weren't a problem, we could absorb them into the female scene, and we stood a good chance of sensitizing them to the needs of women. But now there are so many of them, they're taking over."[74] Taking over they were, and not just at the student level. In 1967/68, 43 percent of the full-time faculty were women; by 1973/74, only 38 percent of the full-time faculty were women. During this same period, women department chairs fell from 38 percent to 19 percent while the percentage of women instructors, lecturers, and nontenured appointments increased from 50 percent to 70 percent.[75]

The experiences of the newly coed colleges, among other things, led feminists to alter their assumptions; it became acceptable, even expected, to point out differences in the actions and treatment of men and women. As a result, proponents of women's education had new ammunition to fuel their arguments that single-sex education had a place in American higher education. The decisions by the women's colleges in our study to remain single sex were in line with the current thinking regarding women's education in the 1970s. Mariam Chamberlain summarized:

> Beginning in the 1970s . . . women's colleges took on a new lease on life. After years of acting like sleeping beauties, they saw themselves once again as leaders in articulating the educational needs of women just as they had in the pioneer period. If we look at women's colleges and their institutional responses to the pressure for coeducation between 1960 and 1985, we find that the early years were characterized by a "flight" pattern that later changed to a "fight" pattern. After losing some of the brightest women students to the newly coeducational Ivy League schools such as Yale and Princeton, the women's colleges rebounded, recruited students more aggressively, and strengthened their commitment to the production of high achieving women.[76]

One reason that the women's colleges began to "fight" was the growing evidence that coeducation was not always advantageous to women. Educators acknowledged, "Perhaps the strongest argument for the college for women is its potential for providing women with educational advantages more nearly comparable to those afforded men in coeducational institutions. For the fact is that equality of educational opportunity is not the same as equal education."[77]

This distinction between equal opportunities and equal education was made over and over throughout the 1970s to explain the different experiences of men and women at newly coeducational colleges and in response to critics who felt that women's colleges were a relic of the past. After Mount Holyoke announced its decision to stay a women's college, President David Truman asserted that coeducation, "whatever else it may be, is not itself a solution for the problems of women's education. As some recent converts to coeducation are discovering, you don't meet the needs of today's young woman merely by treating her as another of the boys."[78] Jill Ker Conway, president of Smith College, stressed, "Although the same persons may be teaching the same male and female students, who have access to the same library and laboratories and meet in the same classrooms, these men and women are not necessarily having the same educational experience."[79] Supporters of women's education based their claims on both anecdotal information and the growing number of studies on the effect of women's colleges on career achievement, self-esteem, performance, and so on.[80]

In general, people cited four distinguishing features of women's schools. Conway described three of these features in a 1977 *New York Times* editorial:

First, women students in such an environment are free to choose their area of academic specialization without reference to sex stereotyping. . . . Secondly, undergraduates have always been thought to learn more when exposed to a civilized and humane environment. . . . Finally women in a single-sex—and thus self governing—student body take on managerial and leadership roles in greater numbers and on different terms than is possible in society at large.[81]

The fourth advantage was the greater number of women faculty members and administrators available to serve as role models at women's colleges.

The arguments for women's colleges were upheld throughout the 1980s by the different experiences of women at coed colleges versus single-sex colleges. Studies found, for example, that even the brightest women often kept silent in mixed-gender classes, and that female students at women's colleges were more likely to pursue careers in science, math, and engineering than were female students at coed institutions. In 1987, Wellesley President Nan Keohane stressed that at women's colleges, students "enjoy not only equal opportunity but every opportunity." Keohane added, "Maybe there will come a day when women and men will be able to work equally and professionally across the board. Perhaps when that day comes, our mission of educating women alone will be accomplished. I don't think it's going to happen soon."[82]

During the 1980s and first half of the 1990s, no more than a couple of women's colleges went coed in any given year, and each year a few schools, after studying the coeducational alternative, renewed their commitment to single-sex education. The Women's College Coalition reported that despite competition from the newly coed colleges, enrollment at women's colleges increased by 25 percent between 1970 and 1980. Two factors contributed to these increases. The first was the continuing increase in college enrollment rates for women. In 1960 only 38 percent of female high school graduates enrolled in college. By 1970 this number had reached 49 percent and continued to rise so that in the early 1980s 53 percent of women high school graduates enrolled in college. The second factor was the increasing participation of nontraditional-age women in higher education—a market which many women's colleges courted and accommodated.

The 1980s did see a number of the stronger women's colleges admit men, including Goucher, Chatham, and Wheaton colleges. During the 1980s whether a school became coed or not depended at least as much on the financial and admissions situations of a college as on its ideological principles. The 1980s were a difficult decade for all liberal arts colleges, due to the shrinking number of college-aged students and the declining economy in the late 1970s. Because only 2 percent of senior high school girls preferred single-sex colleges, by opening up admissions to men, women's colleges were able to greatly expand their applicant pools. As

Billy O. Wineman, president of Queens College, explained when asked why Queens went coed, "It wasn't a question of whether it was going to be a college for women, it was a question of whether it was going to be a college at all."[83]

Gender-Balanced Coeducation at Wheaton

Wheaton confronted the question of survival in the 1980s as its enrollment situation continuously worsened. Wheaton's 1989 Institutional Self-Study reported steady applicant and enrollment declines beginning in 1982.[84] For the class entering in 1986, Wheaton admitted over 90 percent of its applicants, up from 76 percent in 1980, yet full-time undergraduate enrollment was only 1,043, down from 1,163 in 1980.

Alice Emerson, president of Wheaton, described how she and the other college officers recognized the necessity of coeducation at an off-campus officers' planning retreat in August 1986. At the retreat they did a series of planning exercises and realized that if Wheaton continued to become smaller, they would be forced to make major changes in the character and content of the school that would limit academic opportunities and render Wheaton less attractive to prospective students. The officers concluded that "there was no possibility that Wheaton would be able to continue its current size and quality as a liberal arts residential college for women."[85] Emerson recalled that they were all so struck by the realization that no one even wanted to say the word "coeducational." Emerson gave the material from the retreat to the board of trustees, which came to the same conclusion regarding Wheaton's future:

> Demographic projections and recent trends and the patterns of college choice by women high school graduates coupled with Wheaton's admission experience of the past few years led trustees to the conclusion that Wheaton must significantly expand its potential pool of applicants. The committee also concluded that even the most intensive effort to enroll women of non-traditional age or more women from two-year institutions could not yield enough students or tuition revenue to sustain Wheaton's current educational program. Becoming a coeducational institution held by far the most promise in terms of enrollment and would enable the college to continue its liberal arts mission.[86]

In January 1987, Wheaton's trustees announced their decision in principle for Wheaton to become a coeducational college. According to the self-study, "The trustee announcement came as a shock and engendered immediate anger and criticism. Both the process and the substance of the trustee action were deplored, and faculty members in particular expressed great anger at not having been consulted in advance of the trustee tentative decision."[87] Students at the college were extremely upset by the decision to admit men. *Newsweek* reported that "a new ritual has entered Wheaton lore: 'Black Thursday' named for the day two months ago when the board of trustees announced plans to admit men in the fall of 1988. Distraught undergrads . . . have donned black armbands and draped black banners from their dorm windows every Thursday in protest."[88] Some alumnae were also very angry since Wheaton had recently completed its sesquicentennial campaign, the slogan of which, "Women into the 21st Century," was seen as misleading, considering the coeducation decision. Nine people who donated money to the college sued Wheaton to keep the college from using the money once it became coeducational. Although Wheaton offered to return any of the $16 million that it had raised during the campaign, ultimately only 56 donors, whose contributions amounted to less than $200,000, requested that their money be given back. The reaction to Wheaton's decision was an indication of how divided were opinions concerning women's colleges. Students and alumnae who had chosen and firmly believed in the importance and value of a separate education for women felt betrayed.

The president and trustees at Wheaton saw coeducation as an opportunity not only to attract more and better students but also to enable Wheaton's mission to "evolve and expand"[89] and to experiment with a new kind of education:

> The changing focus of the national women's movement over the last decade and an examination of likely future life patterns for women both made clear that women's roles and responsibilities as well as the factors which would enable women to enjoy a full range of life's possibilities, would be increasingly different from those of prior generations. Whereas access and an education which would prepare and encourage women to enter fields of endeavor not previously open to them had been a major focus only a decade or two ago, now the mainstream for women was achieving successful partnerships with men in the work place, the family and the community—partnerships based on modes of interaction reflecting new levels of gender understanding and sensitivity. Trustees and College officers believed that these societal changes called for new educational approaches which sought to prepare young women and men for the kind of interactions their futures would require and, that Wheaton was uniquely positioned to expand its mission toward this end.[90]

According to Emerson, "Not only must coeducation involve the education of men and women together, but it also must involve the development of a frame of reference, a set of underlying assumptions, which go beyond conventional or stereotypic views of the roles and interrelationships of men and women."[91] Because of Wheaton's history as a women's college, Emerson hoped that sensitivity to gender issues, together with the gender-balanced curriculum and faculty that were already in place, would transform the educational experiences for both women and men.

The other women's colleges in our study also revisited the issue of coeducation during the late 1980s and early 1990s. All reaffirmed their commitments to women's education. The Report of the Committee for Wellesley in the Nineties summarized the college's mission: "Wellesley seeks to educate women who will make a difference in the world."[92] Wellesley recognized the need to get the message out to high school girls that "women's colleges, and particularly Wellesley, provide exceptionally strong environments for educating women ... and offer unique opportunities for talented and ambitious women at this stage in history."[93]

Both Smith and Mount Holyoke have also remained women's colleges. However, because they are not in as strong a position as Wellesley, the coeducation discussions there seem to be more frequent and pressing. The Planning for 2000 Committee at Smith deliberated on the value of women's education and on the consequences of the college abandoning its market niche. Although the committee concluded that "we should affirm our intention to remain a college for women for the immediate future," the first goal of their strategic agenda was, "We should improve our understanding of the kind of environment and variety of experiences that together provide the best education for women of high aspiration and ability." To that end, the committee recommended that the college revisit the issue of coeducation every five years, and that "we should conduct a comparative study of women's education both in single-sex and in coeducational colleges, a study which will provide the material for the next decision."[94]

At Mount Holyoke, where the admissions situation in the late 1980s was discouraging, coeducation has been a particularly touchy issue. According to administrators, there have been a few active and vocal proponents of coeducation who have brought the issue to the fore through inflammatory articles in the college newspaper. Although Mount Holyoke's admissions situation had improved by the mid-1990s, administrators developed optimistic and pessimistic models for the college both as a women's college and as a coeducational college, projecting admissions and financial trends under various scenarios. In 1996, Mount Holyoke decided to remain all-female, but, as at Smith, the issue of coeducation is likely to resurface periodically.

THE ROUTE TOWARD FULL COEDUCATION

Just as the timing of the decision and the particular circumstances of a college influenced whether it became coed, so too those factors affected *how* a college became coed. There was no uniform conception of what coeducation meant. Rather, coeducation entailed a range of possibilities including numerically equal proportions of men and women, admissions policies based on equal access, predefined quotas, coordinate colleges, and even exchange programs for those women's colleges that decided not to admit men as degree candidates.

Coordinate Colleges

One of the earliest ways that some men's colleges became coed was through the establishment of a coordinate college on or near the campus. Two years after Mary Low enrolled at Colby in 1871, the second woman, Louise Helen Coburn, entered. In an article in Colby's alumni magazine commemorating the 125th anniversary of coeducation at the college, J. Kevin Cool explained why Colby decided to establish a coordinate college for women:

> This trickle became a flow and the flow became a flood. By the turn of the century the worst fears of the men who had originally opposed coeducation had come true—female students not only outnumbered men but were out-performing them in the classroom. In 1890 to end the "undesirable competition between young men and women," the all-male Board of Trustees voted to split the college into separate men's and women's divisions. The result was a system of "coordinate education" that persisted until the 1960s.[95]

Coordinate arrangements still existed at many colleges, including Brown/Pembroke and Harvard/Radcliffe, when Kenyon was debating first whether and then how to become coed in the mid-1960s. As described above, financial expediency dictated that Kenyon expand its enrollment. Bruce Haywood, academic dean, summarized the three options the college considered in 1965 to bolster its class size: "We have carefully weighed the advantages and disadvantages of three ways of expansion open to us. We have considered the obvious step of adding 500 men, the possibility of Kenyon's becoming a coeducational college, and of creating a college for 500 women which would have its separate name and campus but which would share Kenyon's program and facilities."[96] Noting the difficulties the college had been experiencing with recruitment and retention of men and recognizing that men's colleges no longer had a broad appeal, Kenyon decided that adding men was not a feasible alternative. Nonetheless, Kenyon was not prepared to become a fully coeducational college:

> One of Kenyon's claims to uniqueness in its area is that it is a college for men when coeducation is the rule. So much of its tradition argues in favor of keep-

ing the Hill essentially what it has been. Certainly too, we value the dialogue between men that has been part of our tradition. To put women's dormitories on the Hill or to have women dining in Pierce Hall would violate much that we have valued. We have turned then to the coordinate college for women as a way of gaining the advantages we seek while preserving the best features of Kenyon. . . . We propose a scheme which would leave the Hill as it is, with a separate campus for women sufficiently close so that joint instruction is practicable but separated by its site and architecture from Kenyon sufficiently as to propose separate identities for the two colleges.[97]

Kenyon began coeducation in 1969 as a coordinate college, but this structure was quickly replaced by a more fully coeducational arrangement in 1972. William R. Chadeayne, secretary of the board of trustees, explained some of the reasons behind the change:

In reality, the shift in thinking resulted from experience, for even during the first year when women came to Gambier, it began to be apparent that the women themselves generally preferred coeducation to coordinate education or, in other words, that they preferred to participate in and share Kenyon traditions rather than create their own. This manifested itself in various ways, as for example protests over being excluded from the matriculation oath and not sharing fully in student government. In short, it developed that the concept of coordinate education was becoming a divisive influence on campus rather than a unifying one, with the result that an unhealthy polarization began to emerge.[98]

Some of the other men's colleges in our study subsequently considered establishing a coordinate college or merging with a women's college but rejected both ideas. Holy Cross, for example, felt that a coordinate college was impractical:

We do not feel that the question of a coordinate college is a practical one for the following reasons: a) the financial expense of founding such a college is beyond the means of Holy Cross. . . ; b) talking with administrators of girls' schools has made it clear that they see no great advantage in exchanging their present geographic locations for ours. . . ; c) the present trend, e.g., the many recent decisions of colleges for males and colleges for females to become coeducational, and of coordinated colleges like Radcliffe to seek union with their partners, appears to indicate some dissatisfaction with the coordinate college situation.[99]

In 1967, Williams, which earlier had explored the possibility of creating a women's college at nearby Mt. Hope Farm, also concluded that "it would be inappropriate and unwise to recreate a coordinate pattern that emerged in the late 19th century, and that is now being rapidly outgrown at other institutions."[100] Princeton also questioned the practicality and expense of creating a separate "Princeton" to educate women. The Patterson Report noted:

> The cost of enlarging Firestone Library to accommodate 1,000 more Princeton students would be much less than the cost of a new library for a separate college of 1,000 women even if the number of volumes was far smaller than Firestone's. So too with the infirmary and the gymnasium. . . . The mind boggles at the cost per student of reproducing a curriculum for a coordinate college of 1,000 women which would be as rich as Princeton's present one.[101]

Instead of coordinate education, most men's colleges, including three in our study, resolved to move fully into coeducation by admitting women as degree candidates.

Numerical Quotas

Despite their commitment to full coeducation, many men's colleges hesitated to reduce the number of male students, because they were wary of offending alumni by changing the character of the college too drastically. The authors of Princeton's Patterson Report "were asked to assume that any women admitted at the undergraduate level would be in addition to—not in place of—the present number of men."[102] Similarly at Yale, administrators assured the trustees that Yale would continue to produce "1,000 Yale men to be leaders each year." Williams also reported that "no reduction in the number of men is contemplated."[103] Dartmouth even added a semester and went to year-round operations to assure that there would always be 1,000 "Dartmouth men." Many women's colleges that considered coeducation were similarly reluctant to admit fewer women. Wellesley's Commission on Coeducation, which recommended to the board of trustees that Wellesley admit men, nevertheless insisted, "Wellesley should make every effort to continue to educate approximately the same number of women as at present, either as degree candidates or as exchange students, for opportunities for women's education at Wellesley should not be reduced."[104]

Two of the men's colleges in our study did reduce the number of entering male students when they became coed. Holy Cross's projections were based on the assumption that the college would not grow since the faculty felt that at 2,400 students the college was already too large. Instead, Father Brooks, former president at Holy Cross, recalled: "Coeducation offered the college the opportunity to lop off the bottom 200 men of the class (later the bottom 300) and replace them with more qualified women."[105] By 1975, Holy Cross had established a 60:40 ratio of men to women, and by 1980 the college was enrolling as many women as men. Amherst also purposefully scaled back the number of men in order to achieve a student body of 1,500 and a male/female ratio of 2:1. In 1976, the first year that Amherst admitted women as first-year students, the committee decreased the number of men in the first-year class from approximately 320 to 250 and enrolled 125 women as first-year students.

Although some men's colleges reduced the number of male students when they became coed, and others didn't, most of the colleges in both groups initially established male/female targets. Pledges to enroll the same number of men after as before coeducation sometimes hampered colleges' attempts to establish viable ratios. When Princeton was considering what would be an appropriate ratio of men to women, the Patterson Committee found that most coeducational colleges had undergraduate ratios of approximately 60 men to 40 women. Princeton did not even explore that possibility, because "it did not seem reasonable to assume that Princeton's undergraduate body could be increased so rapidly in the foreseeable future."[106] The Yale/Vassar Joint Study Committee recommended a ratio of two men for each woman but even that option was not acceptable to Princeton since it would require a 50 percent increase in the college, which also "seemed of doubtful feasibility." Instead, the Patterson Committee's "approach has, consequently, not been a search for the 'optimal' ratio from an educational point of view. Rather, we have attempted to determine the minimum number of women necessary to reap most, if not all, of the benefits of having both sexes in the student body."[107] The committee finally recommended that there should be no fewer than three men for each woman enrolled. Based on budgetary projections, Williams determined that enrolling 650 women would be desirable. Since Williams, like Princeton, planned to maintain its male enrollment, which stood at 1,200, there would be an overall male/female ratio of 2:1.

Equal Access

In 1974, the board of trustees at Princeton decided to begin to admit women on an equal access basis instead of according to numerical quotas. Equal access is a policy by which students are admitted regardless of their sex based on their individual abilities and potential to contribute to the class. William G. Bowen, president of Princeton, described the policy: "Equal access means simply that no applicant to Princeton, male or female, is denied admission simply because a previously established quota for men or women has already been filled."[108] The purpose of an equal access policy is to achieve representation of each gender in the class approximately proportional to their numbers in the applicant pool. Princeton switched policies with the full understanding that it could not maintain both the same male enrollment and a policy of equal access without a significant expansion in the size of the college. "When it came down to the point of decision, the strong feeling, broadly shared, was that limiting the growth of the college was more important than insisting that male enroll- ment be maintained at 800 per class,"[109] Bowen wrote in his 1975 presi- dent's report. Four main considerations were responsible for the move to equal access at Princeton. First, Princeton was committed to enrolling the best students possible regardless of their sex. Second, administrators real- ized that it was neither educationally sound nor socially healthy to have such a limited number of women on campus. Moral considerations and the issue of fairness toward the women who applied was a third concern. The fourth issue was a legal question of whether the quotas were discrimina- tory and violated the law.[110]

In 1975, Williams College also reevaluated its policy of admitting women based on established quotas. The president set up the Committee on College Expansion to evaluate the experience of Williams as it made the transition to a college of 1,200 men and 650 women. The committee found that overall the experience had been positive and successful but stressed "the committee's strongest view that the present sex ratio at the College is not satisfactory."[111] Although the entering class of 1975 consisted of 36 percent women, in the previous three years, women had constituted less than 30 percent of each class, leaving the overall percent of women on campus at 33 percent. The committee reported that both men and women are "conscious of the fact that the overall ratio does relegate women to minority status."[112] Williams's decision to abandon its quota was motivated by many of the same factors that prompted Princeton to adopt an equal access policy:

> The pool of qualified women applicants has grown somewhat more rapidly than the pool of qualified men, and the Admissions Office has responded to these pressures. In our view, this has been a move in the right direction and we would like to see it continued. . . . Indeed in our view, the ideal circum- stances would be for the Admissions Office to accept what it feels is the "best possible class" regardless of sex if in fact that will bring a class that is roughly balanced between men and women. In doing this, the Admissions Office would be admitting "sex-blind" which, we should like to emphasize, is not synonymous with 50:50. If this institution goes to a sex-blind admissions policy, we are not confident where the ultimate ratios would settle down.[113]

Despite the recommendation of the committee, Williams did not move immediately to a policy of equal access. Philip Smith, dean of admissions at Williams, recalled that in the early years of coeducation, he got "chewed out" one year when there was an unexpectedly high yield on the women so that there were significantly more women in the entering class than ever before. It was not until 1990, in fact, that the number of women in Williams's entering first-year class exceeded the number of men.

Although by the time Amherst decided to become coed in the mid-1970s, many of the previously men's colleges had moved toward, or were at least considering, equal access policies, Amherst initially targeted a fairly conservative male/female ratio of 2:1. Like Williams, which had begun coeducation by admitting women as upper-class transfers and exchange students, Amherst admitted 50 women as junior transfers in 1975. These women were expected to serve as mentors and advisers to ease the transition for the first 125 freshmen women who would enroll in 1976. Even though Amherst knew that many of the formerly men's colleges had already moved toward policies of equal access, the college decided that targeting a male/female ratio was still an advisable means of admitting the first groups of women. Without previous years of admissions statistics to serve as a guide, Amherst worried that it would be difficult to predict the number and quality of female applications, or what the yield would be on the admitted women. As might be expected, Amherst abandoned its quota after a short period. By the class of 1983, Amherst was admitting women on an equal access basis, a policy administrators figured would lead to a 60:40 ratio of men to women. In fact, since the early 1980s, Amherst has enrolled approximately 55 percent men and 45 percent women.

Exchange Programs

In 1968, immediately before the first wave of coeducation, 12 leading liberal arts colleges established the Twelve College Exchange to allow their students to spend a semester or two at another college.[114] Shortly thereafter, Five Colleges, Inc., which consisted of Amherst, Smith, Mount Holyoke, Hampshire, and the University of Massachusetts, was established in part to allow students to register for classes at any of the other institutions and to provide free shuttle service between the campuses. At their inception, such exchange programs were not necessarily seen to be wholly advantageous to the women's colleges. In 1968, Mount Holyoke College considered various ways to remain competitive as a women's college. Clara Ludwig understood the limitations of exchange programs: "Exchange programs with men's colleges have been suggested, although it should be noted that so far most of these have been proposals for only one-way traffic. Especially irksome has been the arguments for this plan by some of its proponents. Rarely does it include any advantage for the girls, but only how the presence of girls will help to increase motivation of boys, reduce drinking and strengthen weak departments."[115] Nonetheless, Ludwig recognized:

> It seems clear that the women's colleges which have joint arrangements with men's colleges are pushing this fact with applicants more than ever. Bryn Mawr, for instance, which has had extensive exchange with Haverford for some years has never given this program particular play in its admissions publications, but this fall they will have a pamphlet devoted to just this subject. . . . It does seem as if for the present at least, closer cooperation with our neighbors is the best and most obvious answer to the problem. We cannot become urban but at least we can reduce the feeling of isolation we hear so much about from students; we cannot admit boys but at least we can increase opportunities for mixed classes and other kinds of exchanges.[116]

A few years later, when the women's colleges recommitted themselves to the education of women, they again acknowledged that there were social and educational benefits to having a modest number of men on campus and that many women wanted the option of a coeducational environment. The best way for the women's colleges to accomplish these aims without becoming coed was to take advantage of exchange programs. Wellesley's Committee on the Future of the College administered questionnaires and found that faculty and students supported bringing more men to campus, particularly through the continuation and expansion of exchange programs. After the board of trustees rejected the recommendation to go coed, Wellesley expanded its already extensive exchange programs with both Dartmouth and MIT. At Smith College, the Augmented College Planning Committee recommended that resident and course exchange programs "should continue to be encouraged as ways of obtaining for Smith students many of the advantages of coeducation without impairing the basic character of the College."[117]

The first group of men at Wheaton constituted 20 percent of the entering class. Wheaton hoped to achieve eventual numerical parity among the men and women. But, seven years after coeducation, men constitute approximately 30 percent of the class. Wheaton's inability to achieve a 50:50 ratio is not atypical for women's colleges that became coed or even for liberal arts colleges more generally. Just four of the thirteen coed colleges in our study enrolled more first-year men than women in 1994, and the percentage of men at those schools ranged only from 51 to 54 percent of the entering class. Male first-year enrollments at the rest of our coed colleges ranged from 26 to 48 percent. With their focus on liberal arts subjects, general lack of business and engineering curricula, and relatively modest athletic programs, liberal arts colleges have struggled to attract men throughout their histories, particularly during periods of declining college enrollments, such as the period from which we are now emerging.

FULFILLING MISSIONS

The coeducation decisions reached by the men's and women's colleges in the late 1960s and early 1970s differed in large part because of differences in both their circumstances and historical missions. Men's colleges could no longer justify denying an education to women simply because that was what they had been doing for two centuries. Women's colleges, on the other hand, still arguably provided women with an education they could not receive elsewhere; thus, they had less of a moral imperative to allow men to enroll.

The founding mission of many women's colleges, including all those in our study, was to provide a high-quality education for women since most of the other elite colleges and universities denied them access. Their self-definitions and, thus, their success were integrally related to their emphasis on women. The founding missions of the men's colleges focused on providing a quality liberal arts education. The fulfillment of their purpose was dependent on the quality of education provided, not on the gender composition of their student body; it was irrelevant whether they were educating men or women. As President Ward at Amherst argued in his first recommendation for coeducation in 1972, "The simple reason [to admit women] is that the fundamental purpose of the College has nothing to do with the difference between the sexes. A place of learning is built upon qualities of mind and imagination. Sex, religion, ethnic origin and race do not enter into it."[118] For the men's colleges, extending the education they offered to women was another way of fulfilling their original purpose. For the women's colleges, opening admission to men could be seen as tantamount to abandoning their traditional missions. The decision by Wheaton to become coed in 1987 makes sense in this light. By the late 1980s, President Emerson did not see coeducation as an abandonment of Wheaton's traditional values. Instead, Wheaton committed itself to providing the same type of gender-balanced education it had provided to its women students to its men students.

Although the men's colleges and universities debated the merits of coeducation, ultimately there was no real choice if they wanted to be viable in the changed world. Coeducation at the men's colleges was inevitable. There was almost no room in America in the late 1960s and 1970s for a leading college that denied access to women on the basis of their gender. As Christopher Jencks and David Riesman eloquently stated in 1968, "The pluralistic argument for preserving all-male colleges is uncomfortably similar to the pluralistic argument for preserving all-white colleges, and we are far from enthusiastic about it. The all-male college would be relatively easy to defend if it emerged from a world in which women were established as fully equal to men. But it does not."[119] Since women, unfortunately, had

not yet achieved equality in society, colleges dedicated to the equal education of women were still deemed necessary.

In the 1980s and 1990s, the question of viability has been at the core of
women's colleges' decisions about their own futures. Although most of the
women's colleges still believe that separate education for women is an important option to preserve, some have been confronted with enrollment
declines and admissions problems and now worry about their health and
viability. For those women's colleges like Wellesley that still command the
highest share of the market for women who want to attend women's colleges, the future looks bright. The other women's colleges, however, face
the same plight as other liberal arts colleges in the country that are strug-
gling for students. A decision about their future is not a simple one and
will depend in large part on how the entire liberal arts college sector fares.

CHAPTER 5

Minority Recruitment

In 1955, most of the colleges we studied enrolled a handful, if any, minority students.[1] In the 1960s, in response to the civil rights movement and the commitment to equal access and opportunity that its supporters espoused, our colleges began to recruit black students aggressively. Despite concerted efforts, few of the colleges were able to achieve or maintain black enrollments above 6 percent. More recently, the colleges have expanded their conception of a diverse student body to include other nonwhite students, most notably Hispanic American and Asian American students. Over the decades, initiatives to increase minority enrollments have stemmed from both idealistic and pragmatic concerns and have met with varying degrees of success.

EARLY EFFORTS (PRE-1965)

Although the major push to attract more minority students had its beginnings in the 1960s, a few of the colleges had longer standing commitments to enrolling black students. In 1835 Oberlin's board of trustees declared, "The education of the people of color is a matter of great interest and should be encouraged and sustained in this Institution."[2] Similarly, in 1863, the trustees of Antioch College resolved, "Antioch College cannot according to Charter reject persons on account of their color."[3]

Despite such commitments, few of the colleges in our study or in the country enrolled many, if any, minority students before the mid-1900s. Up until the Civil War only 28 black Americans had graduated from college in the United States. Eight black students enrolled at Antioch before 1900, none attended between 1900 and 1929, and two enrolled in the early 1930s, one for only one year. In the spring of 1940, student and faculty members of Antioch's Civil Liberties Committee investigated why the college had no black students. The committee identified three primary reasons: (1) Antioch's reputation for being all white; (2) limited funds with which to engage in the type of specialized recruiting necessary to enroll black students; and (3) Antioch's high tuition, which was prohibitively expensive for low-income black students. Although a few national organizations provided scholarships in the 1940s, most of them were limited (if not in print then in practice) to white students or to black students attending historically black institutions.[4] The committee recommended that Antioch begin an active recruitment policy to attract more minority students and raise money for an interracial scholarship fund. Between 1941 and 1954, Antioch enrolled 123 black students. The college discontinued the scholarship fund in 1955 because "Antioch had proved its intentions to maintain an interracial student body and ... Negro incomes were up sufficiently (because of Fair Employment Practice acts in many states) so that no special scholarship funds for Negro students were needed."[5]

The mid-1950s began a period of significant change nationwide in the enrollment of black students in college, particularly at predominantly white northern institutions. Between 1954 and 1968, the number of black students attending northern colleges more than doubled from 45,000 to 95,000. Part of this increase is related to the migration of black Americans from the South to the North. By 1960, five of the six cities in the country with the largest black populations were located in the North and the West.[6] Independent organizations were also committed to increasing black enrollments. The National Scholarship Service and Fund for Negro Students (NSSFNS) was begun in 1948 to counsel and refer high-achieving black students to primarily interracial colleges across the country. The NSSFNS also provided supplementary financial assistance. By 1966, the service had counseled 9,000 students. In 1963, with support from the Ford Foundation, the National Merit Scholarship Program established the National Achievement Program, which identified and awarded college scholarships to 200 black students based on their high school records.[7]

During the early 1960s, private colleges "began publicly to recruit Negro students,"[8] and the Ivy League and the Seven Sisters developed a cooperative visiting program to selected segregated schools in the South. The Cooperative Program for Educational Opportunity, as it came to be known, was officially launched in February 1964. By working with black alumni in targeted communities, the colleges hoped to expand their minority applicant pools. The participating colleges realized that not all the recruited students would be able to meet their high admissions standards, so with support from the Carnegie Corporation, they partnered with the Association of College Admissions Counselors to place all the recruited students at higher education institutions of the appropriate level.[9]

Many of the colleges in our study not only participated in the national programs described above but also developed their own programs to attract more black applicants. The admissions director at Mount Holyoke College, for example, began visiting "schools which might provide promising Negro applicants"[10] in 1959; and in 1963/64, some Williams's students, who were active in the civil rights movement, visited predominantly black high schools in the South during their vacations.[11] Both programs met with limited success. In 1964, Williams received 14 applications from black students, twice as many as ever before, and Mount Holyoke enrolled 10 black students, more than double the two to three the college had been averaging. Wellesley also visited predominantly black high schools in large cities and the South during the early 1960s. In addition, in 1963, the college introduced a new program to supplement its modest black enrollments—"Junior Year in the North." For three years, beginning in 1963, Wellesley recruited outstanding juniors from as many as 10 United Negro College Fund institutions to spend a year at Wellesley with support from the college.

At the same time that colleges were trying to identify talented minority students, they were also working to enhance the preparation of such students. In the early 1960s, many institutions, including Dartmouth, Princeton, and Yale, developed summer enrichment programs to prepare talented students from disadvantaged backgrounds for the rigors of college. Private high schools also sponsored programs. In 1965, for example, Hotchkiss received foundation support to offer 100 high school students supplemental instruction for three consecutive summers as well as follow-up activities during the school year.[12] Nationally, the Office of Economic Opportunity provided funds for colleges and universities to establish Upward Bound programs. By 1966, the office was supporting projects at 200 institutions.

Ohio Wesleyan was one of those institutions. In 1966/67, Ohio Wesleyan received support to work with "100 eleventh- and twelfth-grade students of average or above-average intelligence, who came from backgrounds that are likely to interfere with entrance or success in college." The purpose of Ohio Wesleyan's Upward Bound program was to encourage participating students to attend college and to provide them with the academic skills necessary to be successful there. To that end, Ohio Wesleyan organized an intense, seven-week summer program on campus and extensive follow-up activities during the school year, including ongoing tutoring, monthly events on campus, and college counseling.[13]

Both the summer enrichment and minority recruitment policies operated within the traditional framework of selective college admissions; colleges judged black applicants by the same standards as their white peers and gave them comparable aid packages. The programs were at best modestly successful. A 1965 article by S. A. Kendrick, executive associate of the College Board, reported that in 1965/66 there were only 2,216 black students enrolled at New England colleges and that at the private, four-year colleges, such as those in our study, blacks generally represented about 1 percent of total enrollment. In the same article, Kendrick postulated why selective colleges in New England and other College Board members elsewhere had been less successful than their public counterparts, particularly in the South, at increasing their minority representation:

It appears that the selective schools which have been trying to recruit Negro students have often failed to do so, while "open-door" public colleges have added more and more Negro students, at least at the freshman level. The difference is that the selective colleges would rather be selective than integrated and the others would rather be "open-door" than segregated. . . . This is an ironic fact, for it is also true that Board-member colleges have been among the first in pointing out the need for special and preferential treatment of Negro candidates, in supporting compensatory-education programs in both school and college, and in supporting and cooperating with agencies that assist Negro youths in attending college. . . . It is not, then, a lack of awareness of or interest in selective colleges that has created this pattern of Negro college attendance. No doubt financial considerations have had much to do with it. . . . But a second basic problem seems to be that the Negro high school graduate seldom presents the intellectual credentials selective colleges are accustomed to demanding.[14]

Kendrick did not believe that "tinkering" with admissions tests and providing short-term remedial programs would solve the segregation of selective colleges. As the 1960s progressed, our colleges seemed to reach similar conclusions.

MORE RADICAL APPROACHES (1965–1975)

By the late 1960s, the colleges were taking much more extensive and radical steps to attract and retain minority students. The civil rights movement and the riots and protests that accompanied it during the 1960s brought national attention to the plight of black Americans. In the wake of these tensions, the Kerner Commission issued a report that predicted a nation, "moving toward two societies, one black and one white—separate and unequal." In order to prevent this result, the commission urged action to "end racism and eliminate the economic and social disparities that victimize minority citizens."[15] In addition, the social and political revolution that was taking place on campuses left students with little tolerance for discrimination, whether based on sex or race. The assassination of Dr. Martin Luther King, Jr., in 1968 catalyzed blacks and whites, students and administrators, to press for change.

Influenced by this climate, in the second half of the 1960s and the first half of the 1970s, most of the colleges we studied implemented comprehensive strategies to attract, enroll, and retain minority students. Although the specific features of these programs were shaped by the particular institutional cultures and histories of the institutions, in general, the new programs shared philosophies and characteristics distinct from those of the earlier period.

The minority recruitment policies of the early 1960s were motivated by a desire to enroll students from disadvantaged backgrounds. By the mid-1960s this desire had become almost an obsession. As the director of admissions at Amherst commented in 1966, "It is interesting to note the change in status symbols over the years in the fraternity of admissions officers. Twenty years ago 'status' depended on the average CEEB scores of an entering class; ten years ago the key was the number of National Merit Winners in an entering class; today it is the number of Negroes in a freshman class."[16]

One reason that the number of black students in an entering class came to be viewed as a status symbol was that the competition for the best black students was intense. In 1965, Williams cited "the keen competition that exists for the outstanding Negro candidate." That year, only nine of the 16 students from disadvantaged and nonwhite backgrounds whom the college accepted decided to enroll. The seven students who declined Williams's admissions offers enrolled at Yale (2), Harvard, Brown, Oberlin, Haverford, and Georgetown. Three years later, the competition was even fiercer. In 1968, only seven of the nineteen black students Wellesley accepted enrolled. According to Ruth Adams, Wellesley's president, "The chief reason that so few black students who are accepted actually enter is that the number of adequately-trained black girls is insufficient to fill the places offered to them by institutions with Wellesley's standards."[17]

In the early and mid-1960s, the primary motivation for enrolling black students had been to provide them with the same opportunities and education as their white peers. Oberlin was one of many colleges in the mid-1960s to receive support from the Rockefeller Foundation to diversify its student body. Oberlin emphasized the effect the program would have on minority students and their communities:

> The major aim of this educational program is to increase the numbers of educated and responsive leaders within selected minority populations through the special recruitment and education of students with high potential for academic excellence and general leadership. A major premise of this special effort at increasing the leadership base is that little improvement will occur in the general quality of life within minority populations without such special efforts.[18]

By the second half of the 1960s, many of the colleges realized that the presence of minority students would benefit majority as well as minority students. Dixon Bush, head of the Antioch Program for Interracial Education (APIE) stated, "Our non-deprived students need these other students we are seeking. And we believe they can teach us something."[19] Similarly, when it decided in 1971 to extend and expand the program that it had begun in the mid-1960s with Rockefeller funds, Oberlin stressed, "Students from minority backgrounds have much to give to majority students with regard to questions of values, life-styles and commitments."[20]

Whereas in the early 1960s the colleges made general commitments to increase the number of minority students who enrolled, in the late 1960s and early 1970s, most of the colleges set specific, and ambitious, enrollment targets. In 1969, the Williams College faculty approved a resolution "to increase the number of academically qualified black students and students of other racial minorities" and set a goal of "about 10 percent black students in future freshmen classes."[21] Oberlin also enumerated specific objectives of 100 black students and 10 Spanish American students by the class entering in 1972,[22] and in 1970 Amherst's Faculty Committee on Admissions and Financial Aid voted "to increase the representation of qualified minority students to at least 20 percent of a class of which per cent three-fourths shall be black."[23] That same year, Antioch proposed, "That in 1971, 1972 and 1973 the College should have a minimum of 10 percent of its entering classes composed of students from low-income and working class and ethnic backgrounds."[24] Antioch further recommended that "approximately half of that number be considered as 'high risk' when measured by traditional academic criteria." Robert Davis, associate director of admissions, described some of the factors the admissions office considered when evaluating "high risk" candidates in a report to Antioch's administrative council in June 1970: "Instead we look to other factors such as maturity and self-reliance, and we would look favorably upon people who had been actively involved in their communities and in effecting social change."[25]

"Uniquely Qualified" Students

By the end of the decade, Antioch had "become increasingly less doctrinaire in [its] consideration of standardized test results, and secondary school course and diploma requirements."[26] Antioch was by no means the only college in our study to expand its admissions criteria in the late 1960s to attract minority and low-income students. Other colleges also targeted minority students with nontraditional credentials.

In the spring of 1968, in response to student protests, Wellesley unsuccessfully tried to recruit an additional 25 black students to the class entering in the fall. Wellesley's efforts failed in large part because the college established unrealistic guidelines for recruiting additional students: "No student who had been on our wait list could now be admitted, no student who did not meet objective standards equal to those of the black students who had already been admitted would qualify, and no student who had already been admitted to another college could be recruited for Wellesley."[27] The next year, Wellesley accepted 66 minority students under regular admissions standards and another 39 "uniquely qualified" students. A 1969 article in the *Wellesley Alumnae Magazine* compared the so-called uniquely qualified students to the "conventionally qualified" students:

> The "uniquely qualified" student in contrast to the "conventionally qualified" student is the high school graduate whose potential for academic success cannot necessarily be identified or established by her secondary school record and test scores. The "uniquely qualified" applicant ... is the person who presents evidence of academic potential to survive academically and to benefit from an education at Wellesley College. This potential can be measured by evidence of a strong desire to be useful to society as a result of that education. These students may reflect unusual talents or skills, frequently of nonacademic nature.[28]

Gordon College also arranged to admit students from educationally disadvantaged backgrounds who showed promise of achievement even though their grades and/or test scores were below the college's usual standards. Specifically, the faculty agreed to admit such students for one year and then evaluate their performance to determine whether they should continue. Gordon's 1971 Self-Study reported, "To date, no minority group students admitted under this provision have been discontinued for academic reasons."[29]

At the recommendation of the Ad Hoc Minority Enrollment Committee, the Oberlin faculty adopted alternative criteria for high-potential students from minority and less advantaged backgrounds. In its initial report, the committee characterized such students:

> By one reliable indicator or another, the student is defined as capable of high achievement at the college level and beyond. However, by reason of membership in selected racial/ethnic/religious populations and residential settings, these students are "educationally disadvantaged." Societal discrimination and prejudice may limit exposure and benefits of exposure to continuous, rigorous preparatory work for college, of access to information necessary for coping with institutional/residential arrangements in college, and of access to information and detail regarding vocational and career-planning information for upward social mobility.[30]

Although as an institution Oberlin embraced alternative admissions standards, some people at the college worried about the effects of such policies. In a minority opinion concerning Oberlin's plan to recruit 100 black students, one faculty member asked, "In what way will we be helping minority students if we institute this program?" He continued, "I think we have held implicit assumptions about the worth of Oberlin for black and other minority students which must be carefully scrutinized."[31] Dean Whitla, director of institutional research at Harvard, was also troubled by what he feared would be the likely effect of enrolling students with lower admissions qualifications on the campus environment. "Two standards of admissions can cause real second-class citizenship in the university setting and there just have to be explosions because of this,"[32] Whitla wrote in February 1970, to Van Halsey, director of admissions at Hampshire College. Julian Stanley, professor of education and psychology at Johns Hopkins University, expressed a related concern at a Wingspread colloquium in June 1970: "Recently many selective institutions have decided to waive test scores (and sometimes high school grades too) in admitting disadvantaged applicants. . . . I would urge the reversal of the current trend. The more disadvantaged a college applicant seems to be socioeconomically, the more objective information one needs about him. . . . It is well to consider non-cognitive measure also, but not in lieu of the cognitive ones."[33]

Why, given such concerns, did so many institutions aggressively recruit underprepared minority students? The tendency of the colleges we studied, and other institutions with high standards, to recruit minority students with relatively marginal academic records reflected in part the small number of high-scoring minority applicants. In his article on the segregation of selective colleges, Kendrick estimated that "Not more than 15 percent and perhaps as few as 10 percent of these Negro high school seniors would score 400 or more on the verbal section of the SAT. Only 1 or 2 percent would be likely to score 500 or more."[34] In comparison, in 1970, the median combined SAT score at our colleges was about 1200. As important, however, the tenor of the times dictated that colleges focus not just on minority students, but on disadvantaged minority students. As Whitla also wrote to Halsey, "Even if one could attract into the applicant pool a large number of able, well-trained black candidates, one would be accused of paying too much homage to middle class mores; so as compensation, students are admitted whose credentials are marginal."[35]

The pressure to establish different admissions criteria for minority students also reflected national civil rights aims. President Johnson's civil rights initiatives were designed to compensate blacks for the nation's history of slavery and to redress past wrongs—as he explained in an oft-quoted passage, "You do not take a person who, for years, has been hobbled by chains and liberate him, bring him to the starting line of a race and then say, you are free to compete with all the others."[36] Some of our colleges expressed the same sentiment:

There has evolved in America a rich pluralism stemming from forced racial and economic isolation. This pluralistic isolation is reflected in the geographical patterns of every major city in the United States. . . . The evidence supporting this pluralism stands in direct contradiction of the traditional concept on which our nation was built and our educational process designed to achieve—the "melting pot concept"—cultural unity among American people despite race, color, creed or origin. It is with this aim in mind that present admissions procedures have tacitly been designed. As a result, many talented and intelligent individuals are being required to meet criteria which by design were not intended to be universal, but rather to mold conformity of an American personality, character, style, ethos. Logically, such criteria are totally inappropriate for measuring the wide variety of talent and intellectual ability found among culturally and economically diverse populations. The charge of cultural bias increasingly being levied at present admissions criteria speaks directly to this point.[37]

In short, because of their past histories and underpreparedness, poor black students were not expected to meet the same criteria as more advantaged students.

New and Improved Strategies

In order to reach their ambitious targets and identify black students from lower socioeconomic backgrounds, the colleges in our study intensified their visiting programs. In a recent interview, Father Brooks, who was a dean at Holy Cross in the late 1960s before becoming president, described a visit he and an admissions counselor took to a few religious schools in Philadelphia in 1968 to recruit minority students: "In one day we interviewed between 50 and 60 Black students and made scholarship offers totaling $80,000."[38] Although Holy Cross's method might seem risky, it apparently worked. Between 1967 and 1968 the number of entering minority students almost tripled from 11 to 28. Moreover, Father Brooks and others characterized that first large class of minority students, whose ranks include a Supreme Court justice, as among the strongest in the college's history. Many other colleges employed similar tactics in the late 1960s. In a 1967 article, Bush at Antioch, described how he and his colleagues recruited minority students in the mid-1960s:

> We found these students by going into the big-city ghettoes and asking social workers, teachers and ministers to help us. We said we wanted young people of high native intelligence and savvy who had not done well in school, perhaps high school dropouts who would not get any post–high school education. We suggested that such people might have used their potential to become gang leaders or in other such a-social or antisocial areas. . . . We then met with the individual students recommended to us and made our selection. We had au-

thority to admit the students without further consultation, and we could offer full expenses.[39]

Though not to the same extent as Antioch, most of the other colleges also expanded their visitation programs to predominantly black high schools and sent students, alumni, and other representatives to inner-city schools to identify potential candidates.

In order to support such expanded visitation programs, many colleges hired additional admissions officers whose primary jobs were to recruit minority students. In 1968, for example, Wellesley added four new members to its admissions staff—three black students and a full-time black field representative. A letter from the president in the *Wellesley Alumnae Magazine* outlined the responsibilities of these new positions:

> Three of these positions are to be summer jobs for present black undergraduates at Wellesley who will visit appropriate secondary schools, organizations and programs both to identify promising candidates and to identify Wellesley as a college that welcomes black students. ... The fourth position will be a year round full-time staff member in the Admissions Office whose responsibilities will be the recruiting of minority students and the supervision of the summer recruiting program.[40]

In that same year, the year-end report of the Admissions Committee at Ohio Wesleyan looked forward to the addition of a black graduate to the admissions staff and a black undergraduate to the Admissions Committee to help identify and encourage qualified minority applicants.[41] Two years later, the Committee on Admissions and Relations to Secondary Schools at Oberlin recommended that the Admissions Office hire a full-time staff member "to work as a specialist in the area of minority student recruitment."[42]

Brooks's and Bush's descriptions of their early minority recruitment visits highlighted not only the need for additional admissions personnel but also the importance of financial aid to minority recruitment. As described in greater detail in Chapter 6, during the late 1950s and early 1960s, all of the colleges in our study gradually adopted need-based financial aid policies. Some of our colleges were initially unhappy with such policies, in part because sometimes they dissuaded well-qualified minority students whose parents "had saving ways" from enrolling. An article from the mid-1960s in the Amherst College archives entitled "No Room for the Winner?" described the plight of Mary Jones—valedictorian, cheerleader, member of the church choir, secretary of her high school class, and area finalist for the Ford Foundation minority achievement program. Mary was denied aid, because her parents had saved too much money:

Both parents were school teachers who had worked hard, saved money instead of spending themselves into debt and finally reached financial stability. Their honest report on the "Parent's Confidential Financial Statement," which almost all scholarship committees require, showed them solvent. Though they had too little for tuition at Mary's chosen school, they had too much for a scholarship there. Parental success had disqualified a child's winning record.[43]

Although most of the colleges in our study maintained need-based aid policies, as the 1960s progressed they increased their scholarship funds substantially in order to meet the needs of admitted students such as Mary Jones. In 1969, the director of financial aid at Wellesley reported, "The substantial increase in awards granted and College funds committed to an entering class reflects the College's new commitment to 'uniquely-qualified' students and heightened concern for representation from among minority groups."[44] The next year, the trustees at Smith College allocated another $300,000 to financial aid,[45] and beginning with the class of 1975 Amherst increased its aid budget by $100,000 to ensure that the financial needs of all accepted applicants were met, because "for the future it seems imperative that Amherst devote more of its resources to two of America's greatest problems—poverty and racism."[46]

Many of the other colleges also modified their financial aid practices to attract minority students. The various decisions made by Mount Holyoke during the 1960s and early 1970s are representative of the types of changes the colleges made to attract and retain minority students. In the spring of 1963, Mount Holyoke's Scholarship Committee ruled "that special treatment would be granted to [black students]." Whereas white students needed to attain a certain level GPA to qualify for financial aid after the first year, black students had to maintain just a passing average.[47] Six years later, Mount Holyoke further liberalized its aid procedure for returning minority students, this time renewing scholarships "in March to the disadvantaged on the assumption that they will return in the fall," and developing a committee to help black students with financial aid questions.[48] At the same time, Mount Holyoke altered its aid policy to increase its yield on entering minority students: "The Committee voted in April 1969 to offer aid to all black applicants to the Class of 1973 needing assistance."[49]

In addition to increasing high school visits and making financial aid more available, colleges also tried to find alternative and innovative ways to locate and enroll students from diverse backgrounds. In 1971, for example, Oberlin started the Congressional Black Caucus program. The program, which lasted for a decade, permitted black members of Congress to nominate between 10 and 15 qualified black students from their congressional districts to Oberlin. Oberlin would then admit at least four of those nominated by each caucus member and provide financial aid as needed.

Despite the commitment by predominantly white colleges and universities to increased representation of black students, the transition for the students was often difficult. As Alan Pifer explained in a 1973 lecture, "The prevailing expectation of white administrators and faculty was that the new black students would simply conform to the mores, standards and outlook of the majority white culture on campus, much as the few middle-class black students had done in the past. This however was not to be the case."[50] Audrey Smith-Whitaker, a member of Wellesley's class of 1974, recounted what it was like to be a black student at a selective liberal arts college in the early 1970s: "I remember and experienced during my four years at Wellesley tension, enlightenment, anger, sharing, fear, joy; a mixture of emotions which in many cases transcended the Wellesley campus but nevertheless always came back to my existence at a college which was experiencing its first substantial number of minority students."[51]

Some of the colleges tried to counter this isolation. In 1967, Dixon Bush, outlined a program to ensure that Antioch retain those disadvantaged students who enrolled. Bush proposed that the college sponsor a pre-matriculation session and create a faculty resource group to provide ongoing support. Working with the students in Antioch's APIE program, Bush had discovered that "students very often begin with considerable enthusiasm, fall a little behind, and failing to ask for help get further and further behind until they become discouraged and stop attending class."[52] The next year, in a report examining separatism at Antioch, Lois Sparks suggested among other things that the college "make a deliberate effort to recruit minority faculty members" and include specifically race-related and vocational offerings in its curriculum.[53] Oberlin's 1971 Proposal to Increase Recruitment of Minority Students included similar recommendations. Specifically, Oberlin's proposal recommended that the college provide educational and support services "to improve the academic competence of black and other minority, less advantaged students," develop Afro-American Studies and related program efforts, and accelerate the recruitment of black administrators and faculty members to achieve a goal of 10 to 15 percent blacks and other minorities in both the faculty and the administration.[54]

Campus Protests

These programs were not enough. The isolation that many black students felt on predominantly white campuses led them to actively petition and demonstrate against the administration. The demands of Ethos, Wellesley's black student organization, typified those of black students at other colleges and universities across the country during this period. On April 26, 1968, the 24 members of Ethos asked President Adams to enroll more black undergraduates, hire additional black faculty and staff, include material relevant to the Afro-American culture in the curriculum, and establish a fund to memorialize Dr. King. On May 7, unsatisfied with the president's response, Ethos students issued demands and threatened a hunger strike if their demands were not met within 24 hours. After meeting with other administrators, the president met first alone with the students and then with the students and two professors to draft an agreement to avert the strike. The new admissions positions and the uniquely qualified recruitment program described above were direct results of the protest.

Almost a year to the day after Wellesley's protest, on May 5, 1969, black students at Mount Holyoke petitioned the college to change its financial aid renewal policies. The anxiety of eight black freshmen who received letters from the Committee on Financial Aid indicating that their scholarships would not be renewed until their entire year's records could be reviewed prompted the petition.[55] In a letter to Mrs. Groverman B. Payne, director of financial aid, the Afro-American Society demanded that "No student's scholarships should be taken away or decreased because of academic standing, unless her academic standing falls below that which is required for return the next academic year" and that "Mount Holyoke offer financial aid to all black students who are accepted and need such aid."[56] The college eventually agreed to implement both demands.

Protests about minority issues reached their height in the Connecticut Valley of Massachusetts early on the morning of February 18, 1970, when 250 black students from Amherst, Mount Holyoke, Smith, and the University of Massachusetts occupied four Amherst buildings. Students presented both Five College and institution-specific demands. The president of Smith was sympathetic. In his 1969/70 annual report, he wrote that the protest "showed the commitment of black students to achieve more self-determination and, self-definition and a better sense of identity in a predominantly white community. . . . What is the significance of the demands of the black student community and the College's response to them. . . . Their appearance and reappearance illustrate the genuine, heart-felt, and long-ignored concerns that lie beneath which all whites, at Smith and throughout the country, must try to understand, appreciate and respond to."[57]

Campus protests were not limited to our Massachusetts colleges. During the early part of 1968, the U.S. Office of Civil Rights informed Denison that it had the lowest percentage of minority students enrolled in the Great Lakes Colleges Association—0.7 percent. In response to pressure from students and faculty, both white and black, the college committed to increasing the representation of blacks on campus to 100 students and 5 new faculty by the end of 1970/71 through more intensive recruitment and allotment of financial aid. The next year, Denison enrolled 24 black students. When Joel Smith became president in 1969, however, he criticized the demands as unrealistic. A crisis developed in which classes were canceled and an "alternate college" was set up to discuss the issues. The crisis was eventually resolved and classes resumed.[58]

The colleges we studied were not the only campuses on which students protested. In a 1970 letter to Van Halsey, Dean Whitla alluded to "occurrences" at Wesleyan, Brandeis, Cornell, and to a lesser degree Harvard, once critical masses of black students had been enrolled. Trinity College in Hartford also experienced protests. On April 24, 1968, more than 150 students at Trinity barricaded the trustees' room, demanding a large increase in scholarship aid to black students. The trustees responded, almost tripling the aid budget for minority scholarships from $75,000 to $200,000. Less than a year later in January 1969, the Coalition of Black Students issued a 12-point ultimatum demanding that blacks comprise at least 11 percent of subsequent freshmen classes and that a black professor be hired in every department.[59]

No college in our study and arguably few colleges in the country were as racked by protest in the late 1960s and early 1970s as Antioch was. Antioch's very success in enrolling black students led to the tensions. Among our colleges, Antioch had the largest number of black students; during the late 1960s and early 1970s, there were between 200 and 300 enrolled. Michael Meyers, a black student who entered Antioch in 1968, wrote an article for *Youth and Society* in which he described the virulent racial tension that had developed on campus. According to Meyers, the most vocal blacks on campus were separatists who coerced other black students through threats of violence to live in the black only dormitory and dominated the Afro-American Studies Institute (AASI), which offered courses only to blacks. He recalled, "The effects of racial apartheid on the campus were predictable. Blacks formed rigid stereotypes of whites and made farfetched generalities about the 'white culture.' ... Whites, living in their own islands of fantasy, especially those who have never known a black person in their lives, stereotyped Blacks' life style, notoriety, rage, and (inferior) mentality. ... Amidst an atmosphere of racial hostility, Antioch became two armed camps."[60] Violence ensued as did a legal battle to desegregate the AASI.

In 1970, Antioch announced its New Directions plan, which was in essence a new version of the APIE program designed to enroll even more high-risk black students. These New Directions students required extensive financial aid—90 of the 140 New Directions students admitted in 1970 were full-need—which necessitated cutbacks in other areas of the college. In 1973, according to the proposed Nixon administration budget, only two-thirds of the maximum Basic Educational Opportunity Grant (BEOG) would be funded, and the National Direct Student Loan program would be replaced by a Guaranteed Loan Program with higher interest rates.[61] The proposed budget cuts would have meant a loss of close to $1 million in funds for Antioch's financial aid students. Students in the New Directions program demanded that the board of trustees "honor its commitment" and guarantee to replace the threatened federal funds. When the administration refused to supply a written contract guaranteeing students the same financial aid package they had received the year before, students engaged in a full general strike, which closed down all facilities and classes on the campus for seven weeks until a court injunction was enforced against the strikers.[62] The strike, which had closely followed a disruptive month-long strike by union workers in January and February, gained national publicity and had tremendous financial and admissions implications for the college.[63] A year after the strike, the number of applications was less than half what it had been the year before, and by 1975, the entering enrollment had plummeted 65 percent from its 1970 level.

Clearly, Antioch's efforts to recruit disadvantaged black students, and ironically its success, had drastic consequences. What were the effects of the minority recruitment programs at the other schools we studied? In the short term, the programs devised by the colleges in our study were very successful at increasing the percentage of entering black students. In 1965, the maximum percentage of black students in the entering class for the colleges for which we have data was 3 percent; by 1970, all except one of the nine colleges for which we have data enrolled a freshmen class that was at least 7 percent black. This growth mirrored national trends. Total enrollments of blacks in higher education more than doubled from 4.3 percent in 1960 to 9.8 percent in 1975. According to David Karen, a sociologist at Bryn Mawr, between 1967 and 1976 black representation at the elite selective institutions improved markedly—from 2.3 percent to 6.3 percent of the Ivy League enrollments and from 1.7 percent to 4.8 percent at a group of other prestigious colleges. In 1966, 8.5 percent of blacks attended a high-ranked college versus 23.4 percent of whites—a ratio of 0.36. Just six years later, 11.8 percent of blacks and 17.3 percent of whites were at these institutions—a ratio of 0.68. Karen concluded: "During this period then, blacks seem to have become much more likely to be represented in prestigious colleges relative to whites than they had been before."[64]

RETRENCHMENT (1975–1985)

Unfortunately, the gains of the late 1960s and early 1970s were short-lived. In 1976, 42 percent of black high school graduates were enrolled in college, but by 1986 this percentage had declined to 37 percent. Not only did black enrollments fall but the gap between white and black enrollment rates that had narrowed to 7 percentage points in 1976 widened to 19 points by 1986. During this period too, the number of blacks enrolled in four-year colleges and universities nationwide declined from 5.5 percent of the total enrollment to 4.4 percent. After reaching their peak in the early 1970s, black enrollments at all but two of our colleges for which we have data fell; in 1986, the median percentage of blacks enrolled at the colleges was less than 5 percent.

Niara Sudarkasa, president of Lincoln University, attributed the drop in black enrollments during the late 1970s and early 1980s to many factors:

> By now, it is well known that the reduction and redirection of federal financial aid dollars was a major factor in the decline of minority enrollment, particularly of black enrollment. In the context of back-to-back recessions in the late seventies and early eighties, shifting national priorities meant that financial aid appropriations did not keep up with inflation. Aid in the form of grants had been increasingly cut back since the mid-seventies, and loans were considered too great an economic burden by many low income students and their families. . . . Cutbacks affected minority enrollment in less direct ways. . . . Many universities made substantial cuts in . . . [support] programs, thereby lessening the chances of many minority students to complete their education successfully. . . . Add the cutbacks . . . to the exponential rise in tuition and the skyrocketing of black unemployment in the late 70's and early 80's, and it is no wonder that, for many black high school graduates, a college education at other than a low-cost community college became an unaffordable option.[65]

In addition, national economic problems, declines in the overall college-going rate, and a leveling off of enrollments during the 1970s superseded colleges' concerns with minority recruitment. In the late 1960s, minority recruitment strategies had dominated the admissions and financial aid reports of our colleges. Between 1975 and 1985, however, minority policies became just one other aspect of an admissions picture that, as described in Chapter 2, was becoming increasingly complicated.

The second half of the 1970s was very different from the late 1960s and early 1970s, when colleges, fired up with the ideology of access and the goals of the civil rights movement, devised aggressive programs to increase their minority enrollments. Although the colleges in our study continued to send minority recruiters and students to inner-city and majority black high schools and to work with alumni groups to identify potential black applicants, few of the colleges devised new programs, and most discontinued their initiatives aimed at enrolling high-risk or underprepared blacks. According to Sudarkasa, at many colleges the cessation of minority recruitment programs was due to "the increasing conservatism of the national political climate. Vocal opposition to special recruitment and retention programs for minority students and to affirmative action in the hiring of minority faculty led to a curtailment of these efforts on many campuses."[66]

As described in Part I, competition for all students became more intense during the 1970s. Minority students were no exception. In 1973, Fred Copeland, admissions director at Williams remarked, "It is clear that the recruitment of Blacks has become an intensely competitive and highly specific task."[67] According to John Kushan, admissions director at Kenyon, the college's lack of success in recruiting black students "boils down to two things. One, many places have over-awarded in trying to recruit those students, and two, the students who apply to Kenyon and were awarded aid by us are also very heavily recruited by other schools."[68] The heightened competition seemed to affect application numbers as well as yields. In 1979 Admissions Director Carl Bewig noted that Oberlin was unable to meet its targeted minority enrollments. Bewig "pointed to the difficulty in persuading preliminary applicants to become final applicants." "To meet our goal we need 400–500 applicants. Part of our problem is that other institutions have followed our lead in recruiting minorities; there is more competition," Bewig explained.[69] Even Ivy League institutions had low minority yields. Clara Ludwig of Mount Holyoke reported:

> A member of ABAFAOILSS (Association of Black Admissions and Financial Aid Officers of the Ivy League and Seven Sisters) did an "overlap" study of all minority applicants at seven of the Ivies (excluding Dartmouth) and MIT and Barnard in 1978. The yield of those entering any one of these colleges was less than 50 percent. This is surprising since it seems to us as if we lose a high proportion of our admitted students to those very places. The ABAFAOILSS group is deeply concerned by the figures which underscore how very difficult it is to recruit minority students.[70]

One reason for the falling minority yields was the introduction of minority searches by the College Board. Beginning in 1974, as part of its Student Search Service, the College Board offered colleges the opportunity to contact students who had identified themselves as minorities. The colleges in our study embraced this new option. Indeed, four of the five searches that Oberlin used in 1980/81 were targeted at specific ethnic groups. Although the College Board searches made it easier for our colleges to reach talented minority students, it made it easier for everyone else to recruit them too. Top-caliber black students, who in the past might have been approached by one or two private colleges, became the focus of attention of many institutions vying for them. Ludwig described the pros and cons of the Student Search: "Despite the depressing results (10 students out of 3,700 letters), this program [minority Student Search] probably continues as the best way to reach potential candidates. The problem is that hundreds of colleges use these same means to find minority candidates and it is clearly a buyer's market."[71]

In the late 1970s, there was a subtle change in how race was used in the admissions process. As described above, some programs initiated in the late 1960s actively sought black and disadvantaged candidates of high potential regardless of whether their academic qualifications were in line with the credentials offered by other applicants. Commitments to equal opportunity and redressing the past wrongs of society led many colleges to pursue "ghetto youth" or severely underprepared students, a policy which led to tensions among students and protests on campus. During the late 1970s, possibly as a result of the tensions experienced in the earlier decade, and possibly due to what was perceived by some as unfair advantages given to less qualified students, colleges began to look for minority students who more closely fit the profile of their class. Race became just one of many, rather than a primary, criteria in admissions.

The 1977 *Bakke* case before the Supreme Court, in which Alan Bakke challenged the affirmative action plan of the U.C. Davis medical school, caused colleges to worry that they would no longer be able to consider race at all in admissions. In his annual admissions report, when the case was still pending before the Court, Edward Wall at Amherst discussed the case and its possible outcomes for college admissions: "*Amicus curiae* briefs in the *Bakke* case ... have shown that [those medical and law] schools would have few if any minority students in their student bodies if the factor of race were removed as a 'scale tipper' in an admission decision. The same would hold true for highly selective colleges such as Amherst." Wall described Amherst's policy regarding the admission of minority students: "In effect we look for a reason to admit, not for a reason to reject. In short we discriminate. In fact, we discriminate every time we offer admission to an applicant. One of the reasons to admit is membership in a minority group just as we take into account, for purposes of diversity, working class or blue collar background."[72]

In a 1977 essay, William Bowen, president of Princeton, expressed his thoughts on the *Bakke* case and why he believed that race was a relevant factor in admissions decisions:

> I am persuaded that, at this juncture in our history, race *is* relevant. It is relevant because ... 'wearing blindfolds' would make it harder for us to do three important things in admission: 1) to understand as fully as possible what the record of each applicant really represents in the way of past achievement and future promise as a student; 2) to attain a diversity within the student body that can affect significantly both the quality of the immediate educational experience on the campus and the long-term ability of people of different races to work well with each other; and 3) to assess as thoughtfully as possible every applicant's potential long-run contributions to the society.[73]

The *Bakke* decision in 1977 allowed colleges and universities to consider race as a factor in their admissions decisions. In 1996, the Supreme Court declined to rule on a lower-court decision that declared the University of Texas Law School's affirmative action admission program unconstitutional. Once again, colleges and universities are concerned that their own admissions policies, which take race into consideration, may be in jeopardy.

Of primary importance to Bowen at the end of the 1970s were the needs of the institution to enroll a diverse student body and the requirement that society have well-educated black leaders. Bowen's concerns were representative of the shift away from the belief that higher education for black Americans was necessary mainly to "redress historical inequities and to open society to those who have been kept out because of race," which continued to characterize some of our colleges' policies even through the 1970s. The idea that selective colleges and universities should enroll minority students because "it is good for the institution and good for the nation" has distinguished minority recruitment policies since the 1980s.

A RESURGENCE IN RECRUITMENT (1985–1994)

In the mid-1980s, educators and policy makers became increasingly concerned about the growing disparity in educational achievement among the country's various ethnic groups. The introduction of *One Third of a Nation*, a major report released by the Commission on Minority Participation in Education and American Life in 1988, stated:

> America is moving backward—not forward—in its efforts to achieve the full participation of minority citizens in the life and prosperity of the nation. . . . The goal we suggest is simple but essential: That in 20 years, a similar examination will reveal that America's minority population has attained a quality of life as high as that of the white majority. No less a goal is acceptable. For if we fail, all Americans—not just minorities—will be the victims. But if we succeed, all Americans will reap the benefits.[74]

To accomplish these goals, the first challenge set by the commission was for "America's institutions of higher learning to renew and strengthen their efforts to increase minority recruitment, retention and graduation."[75] In response to *One Third of a Nation* and other reports, the colleges stepped up their minority recruitment activities.

The colleges in our study were also well aware that minority students would make up an increasingly large part of the college-age population as the twentieth century ended and the twenty-first century began. A 1987 article in the Kenyon alumni magazine described minority recruitment as being in the college's "enlightened self-interest." The article explained,

"Kenyon is making a concerted effort to recruit minority students who, statistics show, will make up 18 percent of all eighteen-year-olds by the turn of the century."[76] Stephanie Chapko Kinard at Antioch was more blunt: "Given current demographic information, those colleges expecting to survive the 21st century must effectively recruit and serve minority populations."[77]

The missions of liberal arts colleges inspired them to strive to become more diverse too. In his 1994/95 report, William Cotter, the president of Colby, wrote:

> Diversity of every sort—not just of race but of religion, geography, socio-economic background, nationality, beliefs and talents—is essential in any academic community, because we know that students learn as much from one another as they do in the classroom. Liberal arts without curricular diversity is an oxymoron, and a diverse student body reinforces the liberal arts philosophy. Diversity is at the heart of liberal learning, which insists upon a broad exposure to a wide array of subject areas.[78]

Such a broad exposure became especially important as the makeup of American society changed. Hiram President G. Benjamin Oliver explained, "We must enroll meaningful numbers of minority students, not only to provide educational opportunities to these students, but to be responsible in preparing all our students to be part of the emerging multicultural society which will be America."[79] Peter Pouncy, the president of Amherst from 1984 to 1994, would undoubtedly have agreed with Oliver. In her 1993 admissions report, Dean of Admissions Jane Reynolds described the pivotal role Pouncy played in diversifying Amherst: "At the time of his arrival, he saw incoming classes which did not fully represent the demographics of a changing American society; he puzzled over why the College was returning unspent resources to the financial aid budget year after year; and most significantly he argued that to be a truly great institution of national prominence, the College must bring 'a full sample of the nation's talent' to the campus."[80]

It was not just college presidents who articulated the need to attract more minority students to liberal arts college campuses. In the late 1980s, many parents and prospective students did too. John Anderson, dean of admissions at Kenyon, recalled that one factor that encouraged Kenyon to augment its minority recruitment activities was comments from parents that Kenyon was "too sheltered" and that their kids needed to be exposed to people from different backgrounds.[81]

Our colleges' efforts to recruit minority students in the late 1980s had a much broader focus than their earlier endeavors. Almost all the minority recruitment programs in the 1960s targeted primarily, if not exclusively, black students. At that time, Hispanic and Asian students comprised a small proportion of high school graduates. Perhaps as important, the colleges were relatively inexperienced in recruiting nontraditional students and, thus, could not realistically mount broader recruitment initiatives. Even Antioch doubted that it was up to the challenge. The 1971 summary report on the Antioch Program for Interracial Education concluded: "The Antioch Program for Interracial Education is really a class-centered program, not a race one. . . . It has been the intent of the Program to include poor whites, Indians, and people of Spanish speaking ancestry, but the black imperatives have overshadowed the rest. . . . It may be beyond our financial and maybe emotional capabilities to adapt to too much multiculturalism."[82] By the 1980s, the Hispanic and Asian populations had grown rapidly and were more visible percentages of high school students. Moreover, after their experiences of the late 1960s and 1970s, the colleges had larger admissions staffs and a more sophisticated admissions machinery with which to implement comprehensive recruitment programs.

On the one hand, the colleges intensified their traditional methods of recruiting minority students in the 1980s and early 1990s. They visited more predominantly minority high schools, extended their minority alumni networks, dedicated additional admissions counselors to minority recruitment, and produced more targeted mailings and publications. A few of the colleges also expanded or introduced summer enrichment programs for minority high school students. Since the late 1980s, Smith College, for example, has run a six-week summer science program on its campus for 8th to 11th grade girls. Ann Wright, enrollment manager at Smith, estimates that the college enrolls five to ten minority students from this group each year.[83]

On the other hand, the colleges experimented with new recruitment techniques. In particular, during the 1980s many of the colleges in our study provided travel subsidies to enable minority students to visit campus. In addition, some of the colleges developed ongoing relationships with specific minority communities. According to Admissions Director Gary Craig, in the late 1980s Hiram adopted six or seven Cleveland public high schools both as a community service to get students to think about college and as a recruitment tool to attract and recruit students.[84] More recently, Gordon began both a degree and a nondegree program in Boston in cooperation with a few Boston African American churches.[85]

Once again financial aid played an important role. During the 1980s the use of merit aid expanded considerably (see Chapter 7). All of the colleges we studied that established merit programs targeted some of their merit scholarships to outstanding minority students. One of the first merit scholarships that Oberlin instituted, for instance, was a $4,000 grant for high-achieving black and Latino students.[86] Hiram used not only its own money but also funds from the Lilly Endowment, the Knight Foundation, and the

Howard Hughes Medical Institute, to attract and retain minority and international students.[87] Even those colleges in our study that did not give merit awards often packaged their need-based awards to minority students more generously, giving them fewer loans and more scholarships.

Some colleges apparently learned from their earlier efforts that one key to recruiting more minority students was to ensure that the minority students on campus were well integrated into the campus community. To that end, the 1988 Smith Design for Institutional Diversity included not only strategies to recruit more minority students but also plans to diversify the college's staff and administration and to sponsor campus programs to reduce stereotypes and encourage inclusivity.[88]

Many colleges were also careful not to oversell their campuses. One recommendation of Kenyon's 1987 Task Force on Diversity, for example, was: "Present to counselors and teachers an accurate picture of the college."[89] Some colleges, however, learned the hard way not to promote their campuses too aggressively. One admissions director recounted how she learned this important lesson.

> The sudden jump in Black students in the late 1980s and early 1990s was the result of, in retrospect, too aggressive recruiting by a new staff member who stressed the "one big happy family" part of the school without preparing the Black students for an environment which was overwhelmingly White. Unfortunately, the retention rate for minorities plummeted during that period, because the college was a bad match for many of the students who expected one experience and found another without much support. The situation was also bad for bringing in new minority students, because when prospective students would visit campus, the Black students who were already there would discourage them from applying.

Although the college's efforts may in hindsight have been misguided, they provide evidence of the importance the college attached to minority recruitment. The resources devoted specifically to minority recruitment in the late 1980s and early 1990s and more generally to altering elitist reputations also testify to just how serious colleges were about diversifying their student bodies. According to Dean of Admissions Janet Lavin, Wellesley's admissions office probably spends more time and money on minority recruitment than on anything else.[90]

The Affirmative Action Record (1980–1994)

To some extent efforts to recruit more minority students worked. Figure 5.1 indicates the degree to which whites have become less dominant at the campuses in our study since 1980. The median minority enrollment in-

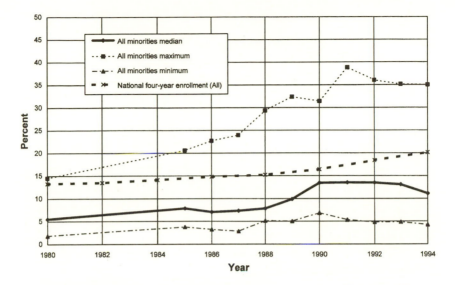

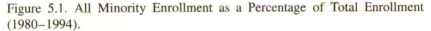

Figure 5.1. All Minority Enrollment as a Percentage of Total Enrollment (1980–1994).

Source: U.S. Department of Education, National Center for Education Statistics, *Digest of Education Statistics, 1995* (Washington, DC: U.S. Government Printing Office, 1995).

creased from just over 5 percent in 1980 to more than 13 percent between 1990 and 1993, before declining to 11 percent in 1994. Those colleges with relatively high minority enrollments experienced even more dramatic growth in minority representation. Whereas the maximum minority enrollment was about 15 percent in 1980, by 1991 the maximum exceeded 35 percent. Nationally, the percentage of Asian, black, and Hispanic students enrolled at four-year institutions increased from 13 percent in 1980 to 20 percent in 1994. In order to understand why some of the colleges were doing well relative to the national norms, even though the medians generally fell below the national enrollments throughout the period, it's necessary to look beyond the aggregate data to experiences recruiting specific minority groups.

Figure 5.2 depicts the median, maximum, and minimum percentage of black students at the colleges in our study, as well as the national enrollment at four-year institutions during the 1980s and early 1990s. Both the college median and the national norm are essentially flat. Despite the many initiatives described above, the colleges we studied consistently had black enrollments below the national level for four-year colleges. A number of factors may be responsible, including the small sizes of these colleges, their predominantly white cultures, their rural locations, and their

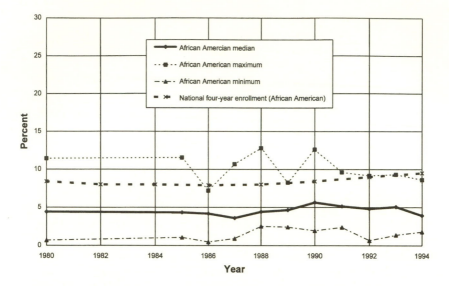

Figure 5.2. African American Enrollment as a Percentage of Total Enrollment (1980–1994).

Source: U.S. Department of Education, National Center for Education Statistics, *Digest of Education Statistics, 1995* (Washington, DC: U.S. Government Printing Office, 1995).

high costs. All but three had lower black enrollments in 1994 than in 1980, and all of the colleges for which we have data had lower black enrollments in 1994 than in 1970. Lavin at Wellesley attributed these declines to the broadened competition for the most qualified black students: "Top students have a huge choice, since all the schools are competing for the best students and some are offering large financial incentives to Blacks to attend. . . . It is hard to compete."[91]

A comparison of black enrollments by state supports Lavin's conclusion. In 1994, the median black enrollment at the Ohio colleges in our study was 5.3 percent, while the median at the Massachusetts colleges was only 3.9 percent, despite the greater selectivity of the Massachusetts schools. Part of this difference undoubtedly reflects statewide differences in minority enrollment. In 1994, 9 percent of the higher education students in Ohio were black; in Massachusetts the comparable figure was only 6 percent.[92] As Lavin suggested, however, some of the difference may also be due to the success of merit aid programs targeted at minorities. As described at length in Chapter 7, merit programs, including those targeted at minorities, are much more prevalent in Ohio than in Massachusetts.

Very few of the colleges even kept data on Hispanic enrollments before the 1980s, which is understandable given the tiny numbers. In 1980, only two colleges—Amherst and Mount Holyoke—had Hispanic enrollments of more than 3 percent, and the median was 1 percent. Since then, the median percentage of Hispanic students has climbed to between 3 and 4 percent, approaching the national enrollment at four-year institutions (see Figure 5.3). These increased percentages reflect the overall increases in Hispanic participation in higher education that has occurred in the last two decades. Between 1978 and 1988, Hispanic enrollment jumped 63 percent from 417,000 to 680,000 students.

Some colleges were much more successful than others in recruiting Hispanic students. In 1994, only three colleges—Amherst, Williams, and Wellesley—had Hispanic enrollments greater than 5 percent. At the other extreme, the peak enrollments at the four Ohio colleges with the smallest Hispanic representation were less than 2 percent. Again, one reason for this discrepancy was the relative number of Hispanic students enrolled in each state. In 1994, only 1 percent of the students attending college in Ohio were Hispanic; in Massachusetts, Hispanics comprised 4 percent of the state's college students. At least one of our Ohio colleges has decided not to aggressively recruit Hispanic students. Even though there is a large Spanish-speaking population nearby, this college has focused on African Americans, because it doesn't have the resources to support more than one

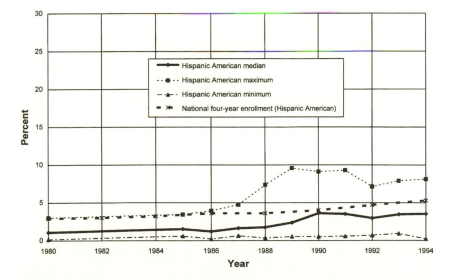

Figure 5.3. Hispanic American Enrollment as a Percentage of Total Enrollment (1980–1994).

Source: U.S. Department of Education, National Center for Education Statistics, *Digest of Education Statistics, 1995* (Washington, DC: U.S. Government Printing Office, 1995).

minority group. Interestingly, in 1994, all the women's schools in our study had higher Hispanic than black enrollments. As the number of Hispanic students has exceeded the number of black students, administrators have begun to wonder whether, and if so how, the dynamics and relationships on campus will change.

Although we have more data from our colleges on Asian American than Hispanic enrollments, the picture is still very incomplete before 1980, probably because before this time Asian enrollments were minimal. Asian immigration to the United States increased rapidly beginning in the early 1970s. Between 1971 and 1980 alone, 1.6 million Asian immigrants arrived in the United States, and this immigration continued to rise during the 1980s and 1990s. The Asian population in the United States doubled between 1976 and 1986, and Asian enrollment in postsecondary education tripled as the children of the immigrants reached college age.[93] As shown in Figure 5.4, between 1980 and the early 1990s, the median Asian American enrollment at our colleges increased from 1 percent to about 5 percent, thereby coinciding with the national enrollment at four-year institutions. By 1994, 6 percent of all college students in Massachusetts and 2 percent of those in Ohio were Asian.

Asian American enrollments peaked at all but one of our colleges be-

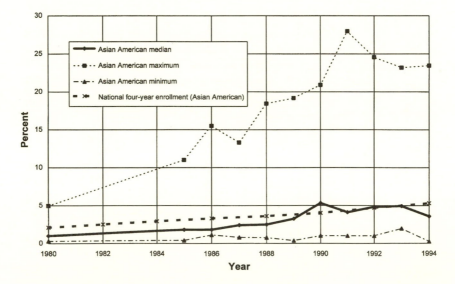

Figure 5.4. Asian American Enrollment as a Percentage of Total Enrollment (1980–1994).

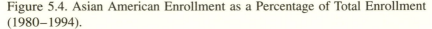

Source: U.S. Department of Education, National Center for Education Statistics, *Digest of Education Statistics, 1995* (Washington, DC: U.S. Government Printing Office, 1995).

tween 1991 and 1993, a period marked by controversies in the California system. California has one of the highest concentrations of Asian Americans in the country. Admission to colleges and universities in the California system is based on a composite of SAT score and high school grades. Prior to 1988, to be accepted at Berkeley, all applicants had to rank among the top 12.5 percent of the state's high school graduates. Relatively few Hispanic and black students met this criteria. In 1988, officials relaxed the criteria for Hispanic Americans and blacks so that these groups would have a representation at Berkeley more comparable to their representation in the population. Asian American students faced a very different situation. Although only 9 percent of high school graduates were Asian, 33 percent of Asians were eligible for Berkeley based on their high school class ranks. After the 1988 change, Asians received 28 percent of the places in the freshmen class. The new California admissions criteria forced many highly qualified Asian American students to seek admission outside California, which unquestionably has benefited elite and selective institutions nationwide, including many in our study.

Perhaps the most striking feature of Figure 5.4 is the considerable difference between the maximum Asian American enrollment line and all the other lines in the figure. This difference seems to be the result of two phenomena: the tendency of immigrant Asian, particularly Korean, families to send their daughters to women's colleges and the emphasis on educational quality in many Asian communities.

Since 1990, Wellesley's Asian American enrollments have exceeded 20 percent, reaching 28 percent one year. According to Admissions Director Janet Lavin, the increasing number of Asian American students at Wellesley has not been deliberate. Lavin believes that Wellesley has become the personal school of choice for many Asian American women who immigrated to America as young children in the early 1970s, because their parents value both education and prestige, and they don't want their daughters in a large city. Koreans, who account for nearly 12 percent of Wellesley's enrollment, are the single largest Asian group. Lavin conjectured that the strong presence of Koreans could be attributed to the striking resemblance between Wellesley and Ewha Woman's University, the largest women's institution in the world, which is located in Seoul, Korea. Lavin explained that when Korean families visit Wellesley, it reminds them of the school where their wife or sister or mother attended.[94] Asian American enrollments at Smith and Mount Holyoke have also been consistently high.

Amherst, Williams, and Oberlin are the other three colleges that have enrolled large numbers of Asian students. Their percentage of Asian Americans more closely mirrors the proportion of Asian Americans at Ivy League universities than at other small colleges. According to Lavin, Asian

American communities are small and close-knit, so the reputations of schools spread quickly.[95] Reynolds at Amherst would concur. She believes that the major reason that the number of Asian American applicants and enrolled students have risen at Amherst is that *U.S. News and World Report* has repeatedly ranked the college first or second. Because for many Asian families it's important that their children attend a top-quality school, Amherst began to matter. Particularly at a time when more and more students were being turned away from Harvard, Yale, Princeton, Stanford, and Brown, top liberal arts colleges, like Amherst, became attractive alternatives.[96]

One final group of students that many of our colleges now recruit aggressively is international students. Indeed, just as in the late 1960s colleges first appointed admissions counselors to deal exclusively with minority recruitment, many colleges are beginning to create dedicated positions for international recruitment. Enrolling all but wealthy international students can be costly, because international students do not qualify for federal financial aid. Nonetheless, some of our colleges have decided that such students are worth the investment, not only because they increase diversity on the campus but also because they raise academic standards and enhance the educational climate of the colleges. Despite the attractiveness of international students, most of our colleges cannot afford either to be need blind in the admission of international students or to meet their full financial needs. Although our colleges have generally tried to establish relationships with specific secondary schools overseas, they have admitted students from all over the world. In 1994, for example, Mount Holyoke enrolled students from 56 countries across four classes, and international students have constituted between 13 and 15 percent of matriculants. At Ohio Wesleyan, international students have recently accounted for a greater percentage of the class than have American minority students.

If history repeats itself, efforts to recruit more minority students will proceed in fits and starts.

During the last 3½ decades, the colleges we studied expended considerable time and resources to enroll and retain minority students in general and black students in particular. Despite their Herculean efforts, black and Hispanic enrollments have remained essentially flat. Some might argue that the efforts have been a waste of time and money since the outcomes have been numerically insignificant. Others, however, would submit that the recruitment of minority students has made an important difference to both the colleges and the students who have enrolled. The impetus to recruit black students in the late 1960s was the civil rights movement and the emphasis given at that time to the ideals of equality and opportunity. The federal government, minority students, majority white students, and college administrators—all believed that first-rate institutions must include black students. It would have been unimaginable for a top college not to recruit black students aggressively. The recent push to enroll minority students has been prompted by a second, more pragmatic concern, namely recognition that in the coming decades, nonwhite students will comprise an increasing proportion of the college-age population.

All in all, the very experience of recruiting minority students has been, we suspect, highly educational for the colleges and their students. Both the student participants in the recruitment process and the college officials have had opportunities to test idealistic convictions, and many have no doubt emerged from the process with a more nuanced sense of race in America. Moreover, both the individuals and the institutions have seen that good intentions do not guarantee desired results, and that it is necessary to be realistic about what is possible, as well as hard-working in the service of one's ideals.

Part III

THE EVOLUTION OF FINANCIAL AID

CHAPTER 6

The Development of Need-Based Aid

IN 1955, there was no federal aid program; institutions awarded modest scholarships on mostly *ad hoc* bases, and John Monro of Harvard had just developed the needs-based formula that would become the cornerstone of financial aid allocations. By 1994, federal aid totaled more than $35 billion; our 16 institutions were spending on average $10.3 million annually on financial aid, and allocating awards had become a complex process involving teams of people and complicated statistical models. At the same time that the scope of aid increased and the financial aid machinery grew, the goals of awarding aid evolved to reflect not only national and institutional values but also changes in underlying admissions and financial realities. In this chapter, we trace the development of financial aid at both the federal and institutional levels from 1955 to 1994. Then, in the next chapter we explore the growth of merit aid during the 1980s and early 1990s.

AID AS A REWARD (1950s)

The first major federal program of student aid in this country was the 1944 GI Bill, which provided tuition and stipends for returning World War II servicemen who enrolled in colleges and universities. Although the many veterans who took advantage of this bill were responsible for the significant enrollment growth at colleges and universities across the country during the late 1940s and early 1950s, the GI Bill did not actually represent a new federal commitment to student aid. Rather, it was a practical and efficient way to reward men for their service during the war and to reintegrate them into the national economy.

The real beginning of a federal student aid system in this country dates to the passage in 1958 of the National Defense Education Act (NDEA). This act, which established a federal loan program for academically superior science and foreign language students, was specifically a reaction to the launching of *Sputnik I* in the then USSR, but more generally a response to the growing awareness among both academics and policy makers that many able but poor students, whose talents the nation needed, could not afford to attend college. Such "talent loss" was thought to undermine not only the nation's national defense but also its economic strength.

Although the effects of the NDEA program were to some extent distri-butional—in that the NDEA loans enabled some lower-income students to attend college—the dominant motivation was not. As Martin Kramer, for-merly director of higher education planning at the U.S. Department of Health, Education and Welfare, explained, "The rationale behind the Na-tional Defense Education Act . . . was not that the nation owed a special group an opportunity for education but that the nation needed a special group—the talented—whose education could help in scientific and tech-nological competition with the Soviet Union."[1] This emphasis was clearly stated in the act's enabling legislation: "The security of the Nation requires the fullest development of the mental resources and technical skills of its young men and women. . . . We must increase our efforts to identify and educate more of the talent of our Nation. This requires programs that will give assurance that no students of ability will be denied an opportunity for higher education because of financial need."[2]

The NDEA was symbolically very significant for it established a federal commitment to higher education. However, most liberal arts colleges, includ-ing those in our study, were at best marginally affected by it. Many, in fact, opted not to take part. The Committee on Student Aid at Williams College, for example, studied the loan program in 1958 but voted not to participate, because it felt that it could not "justifiably ask for more loan funds" until Williams established a "broader scholarship-combined-with-loan program."[3]

Williams was by no means alone in not having enough resources to cover scholarship needs. During the 1950s, most institutions had only lim-ited scholarship funds. Thus, even very rich institutions, such as Princeton, were not able to meet the full need of all admitted students. The increase in enrollments and broadening of applicant pools at most schools after the GI Bill had simply outpaced scholarship budgets.

In the early part of the 1950s, colleges gave set awards to strong appli-cants who met threshold need criteria. At Williams, for example, in 1952 there were only two aid options. If his family's income were below $7,500, a student received full tuition, and if his family's income were between $7,500 and $15,000, a student received half tuition.[4] Although, like Wil-liams, most schools limited their grants to "needy" students, it is important to remember that until the late 1950s there was no standard method of determining need. Thus, a student deemed needy at one school might not be considered needy by another school, even if the two institutions consid-ered the same information, which often they did not.

Early Bidding Wars

The lack of a uniform method for determining need led to bidding wars in the early and mid-1950s. In 1952, Fred Copeland, director of admissions

at Williams, reported that "the rapidly fluctuating policies among our competitive colleges in regard to the basis for granting financial assistance to
freshmen" was one of the most troublesome admissions problems that
year. Copeland elaborated:

> [The] problem is created by the inflationary trend in the country resulting in
> higher cost of education, as well as by our broader search for capable boys
> from high schools and consequently from moderate income brackets. The
> number of our scholarship applicants increased again this year and it soon
> became apparent that other colleges had recognized better the inflationary
> effect on family budgets by liberalizing their base figure on family income for
> scholarship. . . . Our Scholarship Committee was hesitant, and, I feel short
> sighted, to revise our policy due to the fear of overstretching the scholarship
> funds available. It is my opinion that this hesitancy cost us a good many boys
> who really wanted to come to Williams but accepted better awards elsewhere.[5]

Reports at other colleges in our study also described the increasing use
of scholarship funds to attract and enroll students. Benjamin Fletcher
Wright, president of Smith, wrote in his 1955/56 report to the board of
trustees:

> One of the somewhat surprising aspects of the current admissions situation is
> the strong competition among colleges and universities for the applicants who,
> on the basis of school record, College Board scores and other data, give prom-
> ise of being top-ranking students. The number and value of scholarships of-
> fered to this relatively small group has increased markedly during the last
> several years. There is some danger that this competition, like that for fast half
> backs in the athletic colleges, and for outstanding students in graduate school,
> may get out of hand.[6]

The situation was surprising because there were more talented students
enrolling at colleges and universities than at any time before then in American history. John Monro, dean of admissions at Harvard College, believed
that the new emphasis on recruiting was responsible for the heightened
competition:

> In the past 25 years most of us have moved from a laissez-faire program of
> college admissions, where we took what came, to a program of planned re-
> cruiting. We use scholarships actively in our new plans. We want students of
> particular abilities or background, and we award scholarships to get them. . . .
> So we find ourselves competing and sometimes of course, bidding against one
> another. . . . We are helping good students, most of whom need scholarship
> help to go to college. And to a degree it is fun, a good sharp contest. But . . .
> most of us appear to be fishing in the same suburban pools for the same young
> men. We must certainly ask ourselves if we are, individually or as a group,
> putting scholarship money where it will do the most good for the country.[7]

The Beginning of Needs Analysis

In 1954, the College Board, under the leadership of Monro, established the College Scholarship Service (CSS) in an attempt to alleviate the bidding wars by bringing both a greater amount of and more consistent information to scholarship committees about the financial status of the families of scholarship applicants. An Oberlin report explained the significance of the CSS: "The Service provided for the first time a uniform, precise and logical approach to assessing need, replacing a wide variety of very informal estimating techniques."[8] Many of the basic needs principles advocated by Monro and adopted by the CSS are still the basis of needs analysis today. In particular, Monro insisted that colleges look at both income and assets, consider the family situation as it is (not as it ought to be), and expect parents to be the first provider (to the extent they were able). Monro also believed that students should help finance their education through summer employment, work during the semester, and past savings. In looking at family income, the CSS method made allowances for taxes, basic family support, and other expenses over which families had only limited discretion.

Although established in 1954, it was not until the 1960s that the CSS system of needs analysis became generally accepted and widely used. When the Service first advanced its need formula, fewer than 200 colleges belonged to the College Board. Some of those colleges, including a few of the schools in our study, began using the CSS formula soon after it was established. Williams, for one, embraced the new methodology:

> The Scholarship Committee continued to use the CSS as a clearing house for obtaining financial information on our candidates. They also used the CSS computation methods in determining the all important "need factor" which is the base for deciding about the graduated scholarship award. We try to calculate [the] "base" exactly the same as other colleges in an attempt to prevent "undercutting" or "overbidding" on financial grounds. We go even further in this respect by sharing information on dovetail candidates with the Amherst, Bowdoin, Dartmouth, Harvard and Wesleyan scholarship officers. The CSS has been in operation for four years now and I believe schools and parents are beginning to appreciate the fact that scholarship awards are granted basically to enable a worthy boy to continue his education and not as an enticement.[9]

Other colleges used the methodology to calculate need, but they also continued to consider a student's academic qualifications when awarding aid. A 1959 report entitled "Student Aid" described Wheaton's experience with the CSS methodology, as well as the college's method and philosophy of distributing aid:

Our intention has been to use the student aid funds to attract to the college freshmen who can be pace setters intellectually for the entire class. . . . No awards have been given unless need were established, and the size of the scholarship reflects the calculated need, however, the higher awards have gone only to students whose academic performance was outstanding. . . . We now offer to a freshman no less than the full amount calculated under the College Scholarship Service formula. If her performance and promise do not warrant so much, we admit her without financial aid, knowing she may not come . . . we are disappointed with the academic performance of students admitted with student aid since the College Scholarship Service form was introduced.[10]

Like Wheaton, many institutions which were used to targeting their limited funds to reward performance took a while to adjust to a system based on need. They may never have made the adjustment had their admissions situations not improved when the first baby boom students began to reach college age. As described in Part I, the tidal wave increased substantially the number of qualified applicants, causing admissions standards to rise everywhere. According to William G. Bowen, president of Princeton University, when admissions standards rose, "admissions itself (rather than any additional criteria) began to be regarded as evidence of sufficient academic accomplishment to merit scholarship aid if need could be demonstrated."[11]

AID TO ENSURE ACCESS (1960s)

Need-based aid also might not have taken hold had the Kennedy and Johnson administrations' "War on Poverty" not ushered in a concern for equity and access and had the federal government not developed substantial student aid programs. Although through most of the 1960s federal aid remained a relatively unimportant source of aid for the students attending the liberal arts colleges in our study, the change in approach toward aid at the federal level nevertheless influenced how institutions distributed their own aid. Moreover, by the end of the decade, federal aid was beginning to become an important source of revenue for even well-endowed colleges.

The 1965 Higher Education Act

The 1965 Higher Education Act was the federal government's first attempt to develop a need-based student aid program. The act had three major components. First, it established a small program of grants for low-income students (originally named Educational Opportunity Grants [EOGs], they later became known as Supplemental Educational Opportunity Grants [SEOGs] when the Pell grants program was established in the early 1970s). The 1965 Higher Education Act also created a guaranteed student-loan program, which leveraged bank loans by guaranteeing them against default and by subsidizing interest rates both while students were in school and even as they paid back their loans. Finally, the act transferred the College Work Study (CWS) program, which had begun as an experiment under the Economic Opportunity Act of 1964, from the Office of Economic Opportunity to the Office of Education.[12] All three components were intended to ensure that "every young American [could] be educated, not according to his race or his means, but according to his capacity."[13] Thus, the basis of eligibility for all the programs was financial need. Although the government required institutions to "make 'vigorous' efforts to identify and recruit students with exceptional financial need,"[14] it did not legislate a particular formula.

The year 1965 also saw the expansion of benefits under the Social Security program. Of most relevance to higher education was the new provision that allowed children of deceased, disabled, or retired parents eligible for Social Security to receive benefits as dependents while they attended college. The 1965 Higher Education Act and the expansion of Social Security substantially increased the federal government's commitment to student aid. More important, these programs represented an important philosophical shift. Earlier federal aid programs, such as the NDEA and the GI Bill, were created primarily to promote national defense interests or to reward national service. By the mid-1960s, the government understood well the many ways that the society would benefit from having well-educated citizens. The focus of the 1965 legislation turned to ensuring that the benefits of economic growth generally, and education more specifically, be fairly and equitably distributed to all members of society.

This change in emphasis was evident in the titles of many of the major reports on higher education issued during the mid- to late 1960s, such as the 1966 Coleman report, "Equality of Education," and the 1968 Carnegie Commission report, "Quality and Equality: New Levels of Federal Responsibility for Higher Education." The new focus on access was also reflected in the evolving language of the federal acts. The 1965 act, although targeted to students from poor families, had a provision that applicants "show evidence of academic or creative promise." By 1967, when the legislation was amended, this provision had been eliminated and replaced with a recommendation that a study be conducted to determine the means of "making available a post-secondary education to all young Americans who qualify and seek it."[15] Access to higher education had became a right rather than a reward.

The Emergence of Financial Aid Offices

An almost immediate consequence of the passage of the 1965 Higher Education Act was the establishment across the country of financial aid offices to administer the new grant, loan, and work-study programs and the concomitant development of a new type of professional—the financial aid officer. To support this new field, the National Association of Student Financial Aid Officers was founded in 1966. By 1969, it had become the largest higher education association in the country—larger even than the National Association of College Admissions Counselors.[16]

The financial aid offices at the liberal arts colleges in our study were no exception to these national trends; they changed profoundly during this period. In a recent article on financial aid, Robert Massa, director of admissions at Trinity University in Texas, wrote, "The image of the dean sitting by himself in a dark room awarding $100 scholarships to 'fine young men' is probably not too far from a true picture of how aid was awarded before the federal government identified the concept of 'need' as a priority."[17] Add "fine young women" to Massa's description, and you have a fairly accurate account of how aid was awarded at most liberal arts colleges until the 1960s. At many of these colleges, financial aid was the responsibility of the admissions office and/or the dean of students' office until the mid- to late 1960s. A look at one college's decision to separate and expand its financial aid office is illustrative.

Until 1968/69, the dean of students at Wheaton College handled financial aid for returning students, and the dean of admissions awarded aid to first-year students. The fact that aid was overseen by two offices complicated the distribution of aid. Because both offices had other primary responsibilities, neither office fully understood the evolving CSS formula. Consequently, the two offices often awarded aid inconsistently. Such inconsistencies led to competition between the two offices for Wheaton's limited aid funds and precluded the coordination of aid distribution in a way that made most sense for the college. Moreover, as students became aware of discrepancies in aid packages that could not be attributed to different need levels, they began to lose confidence in the program and to believe that personal considerations played a role in aid allocation.

Wheaton's system also frustrated the disbursement of federal student aid funds. The EOG program and the college work-study program were college based. Colleges requested and were awarded allocations based on the number of students expected to be enrolled and needing financial assistance for the following year. Any request that did not bear close relationship to the number of currently enrolled financial aid recipients had to be thoroughly and painstakingly documented, an undertaking that was difficult for a well-coordinated office and all but impossible for decentralized offices. Given this allocation procedure, Wheaton rightly worried that "responsibility for seeking outside funds is hazy."[18] Prompted by concerns about both the distribution and the acquisition of aid, in 1968/69 Wheaton decided to consolidate financial aid responsibilities into a single financial aid office.

Even those colleges in our study that had established financial aid offices relatively early were affected by the changing nature of financial aid. Smith, for example, has had a separate financial aid office since 1933. In 1967, the college changed the title of its director from "Director of Scholarships" to "Director of Financial Aid." The President's Report of 1966/67 explained that the change in name was warranted because financial aid was no longer reserved for the best students: "Some students are given more financial aid than others, because after careful review of their financial situation, it seems clear that they could not come without the additional help. . . . They are no longer necessarily among the ablest applicants for Smith; one hopes they will be the best motivated."[19] Smith changed the title of its director, and other colleges separated offices, to reflect a new reality—instead of being a reward for achievement, aid had become a means to ensure that students of all economic backgrounds could attend college.

During this period, Smith and many other colleges made another significant change in how aid was administered. When Ann Keppler became Smith's director of financial aid in the early 1970s, she eliminated the faculty financial aid committee. The decision to remove faculty from the financial aid policy and appeals loop was an acknowledgment of the growing complexity of aid administration—what the director of financial aid at Mount Holyoke in 1974 described as "a bewildering array of technical legal language, confusing interpretations of the law by the Office of Education, endless new regulations, incredible amounts of paper work, and financial responsibility for the accuracy of hundreds of thousands of dollars."[20]

Although many colleges established separate financial aid offices, for the most part financial aid was still seen as an auxiliary responsibility of the college, of little strategic importance. It would not be until the 1980s that financial aid moved into the center of a college's concerns. Nevertheless, hints of what was to come can be found in many financial aid reports from the 1960s. For example, in 1966, Harriet Sullivan, the first financial aid officer at Wellesley, reflected on the responsibilities of her new position:

Financial aid is by the nature of the work a many headed monster. A Financial Aid Officer must work with students, with faculty, with alumnae, with scholarship donors, with Town, State, and Federal governments, with other colleges, with many administrative offices within this College (Deans, Controller,

Students' Aid, Development Fund, Admission, Placement, Recorder, Public-
ity, Personnel). . . . The establishment of a separate office to handle financial
aid matters this year has resulted in clearer lines of public communication,
more adequate work space, easier inter-office relationships, increasing central-
ization and better coordination of financial aid procedures. . . . I believe a
significant function of a Financial Aid Officer in the future will be to assist in
the formulation of institutional policies and procedures . . . the Financial Aid
Officer . . . should, I believe, be a member of the Academic Council . . . and
should report directly to the President or to an administrative official concerned with both academic and fiscal College policy and appointed to act as a
deputy for the President."[21]

It is remarkable how closely Sullivan's description reflects today's reality.

Despite the increase in federal funds and growth of financial aid offices,
institutional aid still provided the vast majority of funds at the liberal arts
colleges in our universe through the 1960s. In order to qualify under the
EOG program, a student's gross annual family income had to be less than
$6,000, a level that the families of most students who attended the colleges
exceeded. Many of the colleges in our study were also hesitant to burden
their graduates with large debts. Coed and women's colleges avoided sad-
dling their female graduates with heavy loan burdens, because "they felt
that a woman couldn't repay a loan the way a man could."[22] Of course,
some of the colleges feared that their male students wouldn't be able to
service large debts either. In 1964, for example, Flynt expressed concern
over Williams's increasing dependence on loans: "Working close to the
pressure points of students facing the problems of financing higher education . . . one grows more concerned about the magnitude of loan repay-
ment that will confront some of these students. Too often are overlooked
the many other economic demands made upon the moderate income of
the young graduate and the new family. Quite obviously, too heavy or
exclusive reliance on loan financing of higher education is not the answer."[23]
Finally, although the college work-study program was promising, it was
difficult to increase federal funding levels substantially from one year to
the next. One director of financial aid described how the federal government was very conservative in its allocations:

> . . . any increase must be with exactness and proof positive and in spite of such
> documentation is often discounted unless there is documented a similar in-
> crease in total student population. An appeal for increased money on the basis
> of freshman students whom one might expect to enter if funds now insuffi-
> cient to cover the needs of all applicants could be expanded considerably, is
> tough to justify to the Office of Education's satisfaction. . . . The only way to
> break out of the mold of so rigid an application form is to present anticipated
> needs colored by an exuberant imaginative flair and with fervent hope that the

request will pass the scrutiny of the panel review board and will not lead to jail (the stated penalty for inaccuracies)![24]

This statement underscores not only the difficulty of increasing federal allocations but also the inability of most colleges to provide sufficient funds to meet the full financial need of applicants. Before colleges adopted need-based aid methods, they had often limited their financial aid awards to tuition or a portion of tuition, even when that amount did not meet the full need of a student. As needs analysis became more widespread and enabled colleges to calculate a family's financial need more exactly, colleges tried to offer admitted students the full amount of their need. The federal loan programs provided a portion of the funds needed, but colleges also began to give larger awards from institutional sources. Between 1960 and 1965, the median total institutional aid awarded by the colleges in our study increased from $207,500 to $391,000, and by 1970, the median reached $638,000 (see Figure 6.1).[25] Despite this threefold growth, financial aid expenditures still represented only about 10 percent of our colleges' median net tuition revenues (see Figure 6.2), and many colleges still could not meet the full financial need of all of their students.

Admit/Deny Policies

Throughout the 1960s, the favored method of dealing with insufficient funds was a practice known as "admit/deny." Under this policy, students

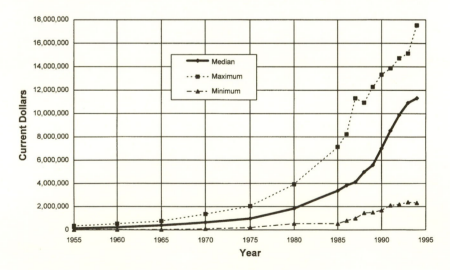

Figure 6.1. Total Institutional Scholarships (1955–1994).

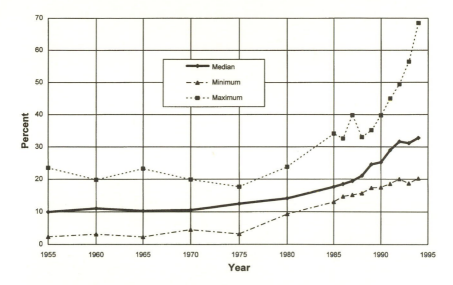

Figure 6.2. Institutional Scholarships as a Percentage of Net Tuition Revenue (1955–1994).

were accepted to the institution regardless of their family's financial situation; the admitted students were then ranked by the admissions office, and aid was distributed to meet the full need of students until financial aid funds were depleted or a predetermined limit was met. If the college's funds were not adequate, students at the bottom of the distribution would be accepted without aid; that is, they would be admitted to the college but denied aid. This practice enabled colleges to separate admissions and financial aid decisions.

The use of admit/deny policies varied considerably across colleges, depending mostly on the magnitude of a college's financial aid funds. Among the Seven Sisters, for example, Radcliffe had sufficient funds to meet the needs of every student to whom it offered admission, and Wellesley, Vassar, and Bryn Mawr could almost meet all admitted students' needs. Smith, Barnard, and Mount Holyoke, on the other hand, were forced to deny aid to growing numbers of students as the 1960s progressed. In 1969, for example, Mount Holyoke denied aid to 280 of the 405 entering students whom it had accepted and who qualified for aid, including even a handful of presumably well-qualified early decision candidates.[26]

Admit/deny was certainly not limited to the women's colleges. As the 1960s unfolded, the Ohio liberal arts colleges found themselves denying aid to an increasing number of students. So did the eastern men's colleges. In 1969 Eugene Wilson, dean of admissions at Amherst, expressed regret that "For the first time we were not able to award financial aid to all accepted candidates. We shall probably have to continue to accept some students and grant no aid. Whether or not a student applies for financial aid will not influence the final action of his acceptance or rejection."[27] That same year Flynt reported that Williams and Dartmouth also could not meet the full need of all accepted students.[28]

As the number of admit/denials grew, colleges became concerned about "what it means to the student to be beckoned with one hand and pushed away with the other."[29] Nonetheless, there were both philosophical and practical reasons that many colleges favored admit/deny policies rather than refusing admission to those students it could not fund.

Philosophically, admit/deny policies enabled colleges, even those with limited financial aid resources, to maintain at least a one-way separation between admissions and financial aid by ensuring that financial need would not be a factor in admissions. Such a need-blind stance was strongly favored by the CSS and other national organizations, including the National Association of College Admissions Counselors. In fact, colleges that created financial aid wait lists or considered financial need as a factor in admitting the last group of candidates risked being censured by these organizations.[30]

Some colleges continued their admit/deny policies for practical reasons—in this decade of robust enrollments and competitive admissions, they worked. Indeed, many students who were accepted but denied aid pieced together outside funds to enroll at the college of their choice. At Mount Holyoke College, for example, typically over one-fourth of the admit/deny candidates chose to come despite not being awarded aid. At Denison, 61 of the 237 students (25 percent) who were admitted without aid between 1966 and 1970 enrolled at the college.[31]

One danger of enrolling students with unmet need was that they would seek support in their sophomore, junior, and/or senior years. The difficulty of denying aid to such students in subsequent years, especially if they had outperformed students on aid, made some colleges wary of adopting admit/deny policies and was at least in part the reason that admit/deny policies eventually fell out of favor at many colleges. Another reason that admit/deny policies began to unravel in the late 1960s was that they conflicted with a priority of growing institutional importance—the increased recruitment and enrollment of minority and economically disadvantaged students.

Minority Aid Programs

As described in detail in Chapter 5, most of the colleges adopted formal programs to attract more minority students in the mid- to late 1960s. Although these programs initially focused on recruitment, the colleges soon realized that, without additional financial aid support, enhanced recruitment efforts were fruitless. Thus, during the late 1960s and early 1970s, the financial aid budgets at many of the colleges grew substantially to ensure that minority students who were admitted received whatever aid they needed. Although for the most part black students still comprised only a small percentage of liberal arts college enrollments, they often received a much larger percentage of financial aid funds. For example, at Wellesley, in 1969, 37 percent of the financial aid recipients were black even though black students comprised only about 10 percent of the entering class.[32]

Part of what drove colleges to focus more aid on minority students was a genuine commitment to increased access and diversity. The founders of Hampshire noted in 1966, "Diversity of student population has become one of the ten commandments of the admission policy of most private colleges, and adherence to that commandment is assured, in turn, by the existence of endowed scholarship funds."[33]

The intense competition for qualified minority students also led colleges to commit more money to financial aid. In April 1969, for example, the Committee on Financial Aid to Students at Mount Holyoke voted to offer aid to all accepted black applicants to the class of 1973 who needed assistance, because, "with increased sophistication in matters of application and college attendance students no longer accept our offers at almost 100% as was true 4 years ago. We are anticipating that only one-third would accept our offer. ... Comparative statistics with the other Six Sisters on black acceptances are of interest. They show a far different picture from last year when the money spent on black students was far less for all colleges and Mount Holyoke's relative standing was much higher."[34]

Such increased competition for minority students undermined many colleges' admit/deny policies. Wellesley, for example, ended its admit/deny practice for minority applicants in 1972 when some students from an East Boston High School with whom Wellesley had worked as part of a program to upgrade the quality of local Boston high schools got into Wellesley but were denied aid and could not come.[35] The tension between, on the one hand, efforts to increase minority student enrollment and, on the other hand, financial aid principles that in just one decade had become widely accepted, was articulated in the 1971 annual report of Mount Holyoke's board of admissions:

The awarding of financial aid to incoming students seems to present more problems each year. Originally great care was taken to be sure that the decision on admission was completely separate from the financial aid status of an applicant. Any stray reference to financial need in the Admissions Committee would immediately bring censure. This policy was based on the theory that each student had paid an application fee and she deserved to know the decision on her application without regard to her family's income and economic situation. With the increase of minority applicants, it became clear that the theory no longer stood up so well. Minority students as well as talent-searching agencies looked upon an "admit but deny aid" decision as hypocritical—a kind of giving with the right and taking with the left. After some unhappy experiences with the policy in the spring of 1966, we decided beginning in 1967 that for all black students if aid could not be granted, admission would not be granted. This policy has gradually been applied to other minority groups as well. . . . Probably the hardest thing about this whole issue is how to phrase current policy and practice so that our procedures can be understood. We have now eliminated the statements that the two decisions are independent of each other but what to put in its place?[36]

Ironically, the policies in conflict—need-blind aid and increased minority recruitment—shared a common goal, namely to increase access. What created the tension was the fact that few schools had the resources necessary to pursue either policy fully.

Perhaps nowhere was the tension between access and diversity in a climate of finite aid resources so evident as it was in the early history of financial aid at Hampshire College. Hampshire College was established in 1969 to offer an alternative liberal arts education. Because it was founded without an endowment, Hampshire did not have adequate resources to provide full financial assistance. In order to keep financial aid costs under control, the founders decided "to give full scholarships only, and then only to students of great promise and profound need."[37] To this end, the college planned to identify 14 boys and girls in the fifth grade each year and provide them with full scholarships when they reached college age. This policy of early identification and encouragement was intended to enhance access but control financial aid expenditures. Since the early identification plan would take at least seven years before it could be implemented at the college level, administrators decided that in the interim, as a way to provide education to poorer students, they would offer full scholarships to those applicants who demonstrated 100 percent financial need. Students who qualified for partial need, based on the CSS formula, would not be eligible for Hampshire scholarships.

Not surprisingly, Hampshire's plan to award scholarships only to those who had full need quickly came into conflict with its desire to enroll a diverse class. In its first year, the Scholarship and Financial Aid Committee recommended that "the financial aid resources of the class be directed over the range of need levels represented by the incoming class." Aid allocations should be made to meet the need of all types of students applying for admission, not just those with full need. In making this recommendation, the committee expressed concern that Hampshire not be viewed as an institution primarily for upper-middle-class students. Critics of the full-need policy were particularly worried that the college would be unable to attract minority applicants, because "a policy of providing financial aid to only full-need students would mean that it would be the rare case where Hampshire would attract a minority student who could afford to pay part but not all the cost of Hampshire College."[38] In addition, they feared that maintaining a full-need-only policy would "contribute to the alienation of blue collar families" who also would be able to pay partial tuition but not the entire costs.[39] Although its lack of endowment and full-need-only policy exacerbated Hampshire's situation, the dilemma it faced—how to promote access and diversity without exceeding its resources or alienating middle-class applicants—was in fact the same one that confronted not only the other liberal arts colleges in our study but also most private institutions in this country as the 1970s began.

AID TO ENABLE CHOICE (1970s)

If the 1960s was the decade of access, then the 1970s was the decade of choice. Whereas the 1960s were marked by a commitment at both the federal and institutional level to ensure that minority and low-income students could afford college, the 1970s witnessed growing concern for middle-class students and their ability to afford not just any college but relatively high-priced private ones. According to Ronald G. Ehrenberg and Susan H. Murphy, "Historically, qualified high school graduates in the United States were guaranteed access to higher education through the provision of state-supported low- or zero-tuition public institutions. Beginning in the 1970s, however, the federal government sought to provide students with the opportunity for choice as well as access."[40] As the decade progressed, the concept that poor but qualified students should not be prevented from attending college because of cost was supplanted by the more far-reaching idea that cost differentials among institutions should not influence which college a student chose to attend.

Middle-Income Squeeze

The phrase "middle-class squeeze" dominated not only the financial aid reports of our colleges in the early and mid-1970s but also the national press.[41] This phrase referred to two related perceptions—that middle-income families were increasingly sending their children to lower-cost public institutions and that there was a "polarization of the rich and the poor"[42] at private institutions.[43]

In 1975, Howard R. Bowen and W. John Minter published their first annual report on private education in the United States. One of the many trends that Bowen and Minter examined was the "tuition gap" between selected groups of private and public institutions between 1927/28 and 1974/75. Until the early 1950s, the ratio of private to public tuition at medium-sized schools was about 2.5:1. During the 1950s and 1960s, tuition increases at private colleges and universities outpaced those at public institutions, so that by 1967/68, the ratio had climbed to 4.2:1. From the late 1960s through the mid-1970s, student charges at both private and public institutions rose, but the price ratio remained constant.[44]

What accounts then for the perceived middle-income squeeze in the 1970s? Although the tuition gap was not new, changes in enrollment patterns and financial aid policies combined to bring it to the fore. Before the baby boom, the majority of college students, particularly at private colleges, came from upper-income families. Subsequently, when enrollments exploded, colleges began to admit students from more varied socioeconomic backgrounds. Between 1960 and 1975, the cost of attending college rose in both nominal and real terms (see Figures 6.3A and 6.3B), making tuition a relatively greater burden for all parents. Lower-income students qualified for need-based aid, so that for them the net cost at private institutions was not much more than tuition at public colleges and universities, and was sometimes even less. However, the higher tuition levels strained the resources of middle-income parents whose incomes just exceeded the need-based eligibility requirements.[45] Although the ratio of private to pub-

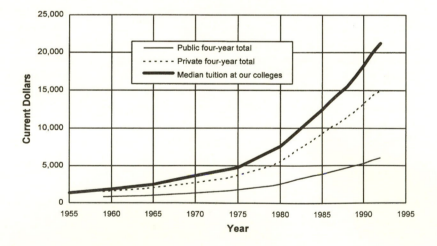

Figure 6.3A. Tuition, Fees, Room and Board (1955–1992), Current Dollars.
Source: U.S. Department of Education, National Center for Education Statistics, *Digest of Education Statistics, 1995* (Washington, DC: U.S. Government Printing Office, 1995).

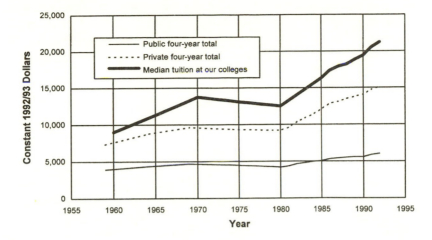

Figure 6.3B. Tuition, Fees, Room and Board (1959–1992), Constant 1992/93 Dollars.

Source: U.S. Department of Education, National Center for Education Statistics, *Digest of Education Statistics* (Washington, DC: U.S. Government Printing Office, 1995).

lic tuition remained constant during this period, the absolute levels of tuition increased. As Bowen and Minter pointed out, "People do not pay ratios; they pay dollars. And so the critical gap is the dollar difference in annual outlay between attending a private and a public institution."[46] Earl Cheit also noted in his 1971 report, *The New Depression in Higher Education,* that "increases in student fees [at private institutions] are reaching a 'saturation point,' that is, they are driving students from middle-income families away and creating conditions on some campuses such that only the very rich and the very poor can afford to attend."[47]

The *New York Times* reported the sentiments of one mother who had just finished paying tuition for two students in the Kenyon class of 1974: "I feel broke." The *Times* continued, "The feeling is shared by many middle-income parents and some upper income ones, too, according to a recent cost study by the College Entrance Examination Board. With college bills jumping by better than one third in four years, many families, especially those with more than one student attending the generally high-priced private institutions—suddenly find themselves, in a matter of a few years, owing tens of thousands of dollars."[48]

Both the federal government and the institutions moved to address the concerns of middle-income students as the decade progressed. According to Martin Kramer, the federal government acted because "liberal Democrats had achieved a working control over both the House and the Senate and there was the tendency, often noted in other areas of public policy, of middle-class constituencies to capture for themselves benefits originally intended for the deprived."[49] Private institutions responded because, for the first time since before the enactment of the GI Bill, they worried about their enrollments.

1972 Higher Education Act

The 1972 Higher Education Act was one attempt by the federal government to deal with the growing need for financial aid. The act established Basic Educational Opportunity Grants (BEOGs, now known as Pell grants) and State Student Incentive Grants. In addition, it reauthorized the college work-study program, guaranteed student loans and national direct student loans, and converted the Educational Opportunity Grants into Supplemental Educational Opportunity Grants (SEOGs). These programs increased substantially the amount of money available for needy students to attend college. In 1970, federally supported student aid programs totaled $1.6 billion. By 1975, the addition of the BEOG grants and the expansion of existing programs had increased the amount of federal aid to $3.1 billion. Allocations grew rapidly, because the 1972 act restricted neither the number of beneficiaries nor the amount paid to each beneficiary—a quasi-entitlement program had been created.[50]

The increased federal funds were augmented by additional state funds allocated in response to the State Student Incentive Grants. Within five years of the 1972 act, all the states had established state scholarship programs totaling $60 million. As at the federal level, most of the state grant programs were need based. By 1976, 39 states had established tuition-offset grants to help reduce the tuition gap between public and private colleges and universities.[51]

The structure of the BEOG grants further minimized the public/private tuition differential. Unlike their predecessors, BEOG grants were not campus based. Rather, these portable grants were made directly to students whose families' estimated financial resources were less than an established "ceiling." Students were entitled to a grant equal to the difference between the amount their family could contribute and the ceiling. Using means tests to determine not only eligibility but also the amount of the benefits, had two major effects. First, it meant that "the means tests, and only the means tests, were to be the keys to the treasury vaults."[52] Second, it meant that the BEOG grants had at least a weak choice emphasis, because a student attending a higher-priced institution received more aid than if she attended a lower cost one.[53]

The new federal student aid programs confirmed the centrality of the need tests for determining both who was eligible for financial aid and how much support each person would receive. The need-analysis test continued, however, to leave many middle-class families ineligible for aid. Michael Behnke, assistant director of admissions at Amherst, recognized the dilemma faced by middle-income students and their families:

> The sons of white-collar middle-class families pose a problem. . . . Many want to come and are qualified but few feel they can afford it. If we want more students from this group we need to give them more money. In order to do so we will either have to violate the College Scholarship Service guidelines on ability to pay, which would involve a return to the anarchy of bidding for students, or wait for our competitors to join us in changing the guidelines.[54]

Robert Huff, director of financial aid at Stanford, also acknowledged the burden that the CSS formula placed on the parents of middle-income students and called for the CSS to revise its guidelines. "In the past," he wrote, "as I have attempted to regale the particular advantages of an institution such as mine, I have talked in terms of the financial sacrifice which we have always asked of middle-income families at higher cost institutions. The amounts, however, which I have had to talk about in the last year or so have seemed to me to border on the ridiculous and to have gone beyond reasonable sacrifice."[55] Huff surveyed 50 leading independent colleges and universities and found that almost 58 percent of those that responded "are deviating from the straight computation of financial need in accordance with CSS tables."[56]

A Liberalized CSS Formula

In response to pressure from middle-class parents and private institutions to lessen the financial burden on middle-income families, the CSS substantially liberalized its formula during the early 1970s. The first major change to the formula actually occurred in 1969. A number of the colleges we studied immediately felt the 1969 adjustment, which lowered the expected contribution from both middle-income families and families with more than one child in college. At Amherst, for example, financial aid applicants jumped from 33 percent to 45 percent of the entering class in 1969, forcing the college for the first time to deny financial assistance to 23 students with demonstrated need.

In 1974 the CSS made even more significant changes to its formula. In addition to adjusting the formula for inflation, the CSS included Social Security taxes on the list of acceptable deductions, reduced the tax on discretionary income from 25 to 22 percent, and removed housing from the list of expenses that a family was expected to forego once a child was at college. The effect of all these changes was to reduce the expected parental contribution substantially.

Many applauded the changes, including administrators at some of the colleges in our study. In 1974, Edward Wall, dean of admissions at Amherst, reported:

> Financial aid officers all over the country have been concerned during the past few years, that the CSS tables have placed an inordinately heavy burden upon middle income families. We are, therefore, especially pleased that the CSS has completed a thorough review of its need analysis system with the result that middle income families, in particular, will find substantial relief in the expected parental contribution in 1975/76.[57]

Not everyone, however, was as pleased as Wall was with the changes in the CSS formula. Some schools that were already having difficulties providing aid to all the students they admitted worried that the new need formula would exacerbate that problem, as more students became eligible for more aid. As a result some colleges, including Oberlin, modified the way that they determined need or distributed their funds:

> Students applying for financial aid this year were required to fill out both the financial aid form provided by the College Scholarship Service and a separate Oberlin application. . . . Mr. White explained that in the past most educational institutions have followed the guidelines established by the College Scholarship Service (CSS) for packaging their scholarship and aid money. However, with the change in federal policy toward providing students with financial aid, no college will be able to meet the CSS guidelines. Some schools may cut aid across the board on a percentage basis; some schools may admit needy students but will not provide any support for some of these students.[58]

Another very important change was made to the needs system during this period. The passage of the 1965 Higher Education Act and subsequent need-based aid legislation had led to an increase in organizations that provided needs analysis. By the 1970s the proliferation of competing needs formulas had become problematic. The director of financial aid at Mount Holyoke College described why:

> A student from Vermont applies to Mount Holyoke for admission and financial aid. We require her family to complete a Parent's Confidential Statement through the College Scholarship Service. We expect her to apply also for a state of Vermont scholarship. Vermont no longer accepts the Parent's Confidential Statement form the College Scholarship Service. It deals now only with American College Testing. . . . Assuming she is eligible for the federal Basic Grant, she makes application for it, finding that it requires a different financial

form again. If she is enterprising she may find another scholarship source but alas that requires financial information also. . . . Her financial need can differ as much as $1000 between these varying types of need analysis.[59]

Because of such discrepancies and dissatisfaction with various revisions to the two most commonly used needs formulas—those of the CSS and the American College Testing program (ACT)—the federal government had often threatened to establish a federal needs system. In the fall of 1975, the government took the first step in that direction when it issued need-analysis regulations, which resulted in a series of 80 benchmark cases used to approve need-analysis formulas.

At the same time, the ACT and the CSS moved to reconcile their formulas. In 1975 the College Board Committee on Financial Aid, under the leadership of Frances Kepel, issued a report recommending a common formula and form. The CSS and the ACT then worked to develop a uniform form and methodology through the Committee of Need Assessment and Development (CONAD), which had been set up by the National Association of Student Financial Aid Officers.

Pressure to address the middle-income squeeze peaked at the federal level with the enactment of the 1978 Middle Income Student Assistance Act. This legislation broadened the base of eligibility for student aid by loosening the income requirements for Pell grants and making subsidized loans available to all students regardless of income or need. Again the colleges we studied immediately felt these changes. At Amherst, for example, the percentage of students borrowing under the GSL program rose from 40 percent to over 66 percent in the final years of the 1970s. The 1980 Education Amendments further loosened need analysis and income requirements, but most of these changes were repealed when the Reagan administration took office in 1981 and, thus, were never implemented.[60]

While the federal government expanded eligibility and increased allocations and the need-analysis services liberalized their formulas, institutions themselves also tried to accommodate the increasing financial needs of their students. Changes in the formulas together with increased college costs contributed to making more students eligible for more financial aid. As shown in Figures 6.1, 6.2, and 6.4, institutional aid increased rapidly during the 1970s, both in terms of the amount of money spent on aid and the percentage of students receiving aid. Between 1970 and 1980, the median institutional aid at the colleges in our study rose from $638,000 to $1.8 million—from 11 percent of median net tuition revenue to 14 percent of median net tuition revenue. At the same time, the average percentage of students receiving need-based aid expanded from 26 to 36 percent.[61]

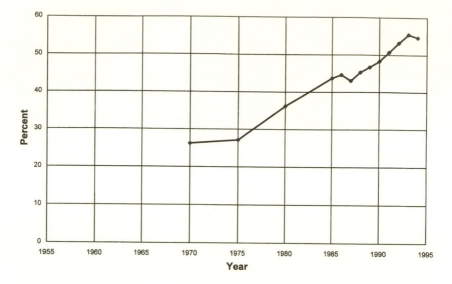

Figure 6.4. Average Percentage of Students Receiving Need-Based Aid (1970–1994).

Pressure to Meet Full Need

The 1970s were also the decade that "meeting full need" became a stated institutional ideal. Faced with the middle-income squeeze and growing competition for the most academically talented students, and committed to enrolling students from diverse economic backgrounds, private colleges sought to reassure students and their parents that they could afford private tuition by guaranteeing that their full need would be met.

Despite the general acceptance of the full-need ideal and the growth in both federal and institutional support, few institutions succeeded in meeting the full need of all accepted students. Indeed, of the 16 liberal arts colleges in our study, only Amherst, Wellesley, and Williams were able to support all accepted students during most of the 1970s. Smith was able to meet the full need of its students beginning in 1976, and the rest of our schools did not begin to meet full need until the early 1980s, if at all.[62]

The inability of a school to meet full need had significant consequences for its ability to enroll the high-quality students it desired. The increasing competition for students that characterized most of this decade was felt especially for highly qualified financial aid students since they often represented the diversity colleges sought. At Mount Holyoke College, for example, by 1974 less than 50 percent of financial aid offers were accepted "since these applications are beckoned by various colleges." Ironically, at Mount Holyoke "those applicants over whom our money will not stretch have academic qualifications perhaps somewhat less sturdy . . . [but] more often Mount Holyoke is their first academic choice."[63] This situation, which was by no means unique to Mount Holyoke, prompted colleges to institute financial aid wait lists as a way of controlling their financial aid expenditures while directing aid at the students they most wanted to enroll.

Many of our colleges that could not meet the full need of all accepted students had to attract a high percentage of full-pay students in order to cover institutional costs. This need had a dramatic impact on their recruitment and admissions policies. As the director of admissions at Oberlin in 1972 succinctly explained, "Selectivity of a freshman class is severely limited when one out of two non-financial aid applicants MUST be admitted, and only one out of three financial aid applicants CAN be admitted."[64] In order to attract full-paying candidates, colleges targeted their recruitment activities toward geographic areas and schools with proportionally large numbers of full-pay students. For example, the Kenyon Admissions Office directed its recruitment efforts toward "the sort of schools who have students who want a private education, who are willing and able to pay for a private education, and who have a high percentage of students going on to college."[65]

Interestingly, even those colleges that could afford to support most of their students suffered from the perception that only low-income students could qualify for financial assistance. In 1972, for example, the Wellesley Admissions Office, after noticing a decline in the number of applications from middle-income families, urged its alumnae to "spread the word that we distribute our funds as far as they will go, to applicants with justified need from low and middle-income families equally, but we cannot distribute this aid to the middle-income group unless they are present in numbers in the applicant group."[66] This problem continued even after the CSS revised the need-analysis formula and was so grave at Amherst in 1974 that the financial aid director commented, "The major concern at this point . . . is the declining number of financial aid applicants, *period!*"[67] He too went on to try to dispel the myths that only poor and minority students get aid and that middle-class students never qualify.

More Loans

The 1970s was also the decade that loans came to be accepted as an integral part of student assistance packages. Many studies have documented this shift in aid from grants to loans. For example, Lawrence E. Gladieux and Gwendolyn L. Lewis of the Washington office of the College Board found that while loans accounted for 17 percent of aid in 1975/76, by 1980/81 they had reached 41 percent.[68] A number of factors were responsible for this increasing emphasis on loans.

During the late 1950s and early 1960s, economists developed the "human capital" model, which stressed that investment in people, for example, through education, has returns just as does investment in physical capital. Initially, economists stressed the social returns to higher education—that is, the benefits to society of having more educated citizens. By the end of the 1970s, attention had shifted to the private return to higher education—in particular, the higher incomes earned by college-educated people.[69] Whereas the social benefits of higher education were used to justify increased federal expenditures, the private benefits of higher education were cited to justify increased loan burdens.

Broader career opportunities for women also helped to make loans more palatable. In the early 1960s, colleges had not awarded large loans to their female graduates for fear of burdening them with too much debt. As one admission director asked, "Who would marry a girl with debt? . . . A girl's dowry shouldn't be a mortgage."[70] However, as expectations of what a woman would do with a college degree changed, attitudes toward loans changed too. Consequently, as the 1970s progressed, loans—both federal and institutional—comprised a growing percentage of student aid.

Finally, the desire in the 1970s to ensure not just access but also choice made loans more popular. Whereas in the 1960s, loans were seen as a way to spread limited resources among many needy students, in the early 1970s, loans became yet another way to address public/private tuition differentials. A popular College Board slogan from that period perfectly describes this shift: "grants for access, loans for choice."[71]

AID AS AN INSTITUTIONAL TOOL (1980s AND 1990s)

Although "choice" was the buzzword of the 1970s, it quickly fell out favor in the early 1980s when the Reagan administration took office. Since that time, the real value of federal financial aid has declined, forcing institutions, such as those in our study, to spend more of their own resources on student aid. As institutions have assumed greater responsibility for financial aid, the focus of aid programs has shifted away from the national goals of expanding access and ensuring choice to institutional priorities such as building and enrolling a quality class. As early as 1981, James White, financial aid director at Oberlin, noted this shift: "In the period of the sixties and early seventies, most institutions undertook programs to expand educational opportunities for all segments of our society . . . one does not hear very much about those programs anymore. Now the emphasis seems to be on improving quality in education, whatever that means, even if that excludes many who could richly profit by the educational experience."[72] Barbara Tornow, financial aid director at Boston University, was more sympathetic to the change. In a 1995 interview, she asked, "Why do I have an obligation to educate poor students? The federal government has that obligation and isn't fulfilling it. The university's first obligation is to survive and thrive and create a positive educational environment. I wish it were different, but if I try to spread my money over the most needy students, I can help fewer students."[73] Because of the very large sums being spent on aid, institutional policies have also become increasingly budget driven. As Francis Delaney, director of financial aid at the College of the Holy Cross, admitted resignedly, "the ethics have shifted from egalitarian principles to budget strategies as the survival of the institution becomes more important than the students."[74]

The reduction in real terms of federal financial aid resources has been one of the most problematic developments in the 1980s and 1990s for institutions of higher education, including the liberal arts colleges in our study. Ronald Reagan took office in 1981 with a mandate to reduce domestic spending. That same year, Congress passed the 1981 Consolidated Omnibus Reconciliation Act, which repealed many of the liberalizing provisions of the 1980 Education Amendments, tightened GSL eligibility, and phased out Social Security benefits. These changes have not only reduced the purchasing power of federal aid allocations but also shifted the emphasis of federal funding from grants to loans.[75] Since the early 1980s, the federal government has gone from being the major provider of scholarship funds to just one of many providers.

Rising Tuition

At the same time that federal funding leveled off, tuition at private colleges and universities began to rise substantially. Figures 6.3a and 6.3b show the average tuition, fees, room and board (from here on referred to just as "tuition") in both current and constant dollars for four-year private institutions, four-year public institutions, and the colleges in our study. During the 1960s tuition at all three groups rose slightly more than inflation, and during the 1970s tuition generally just kept pace with inflation. In 1980, however, tuition began to increase in real terms at private institutions, especially at the liberal arts colleges we studied. Since 1985, the sticker price of the colleges has exceeded per capita disposable income by a growing amount (see Figure 6.5).

Many factors led to the real rise in tuition in the 1980s and early 1990s, including lagged responses to cost pressure. External economic forces con-

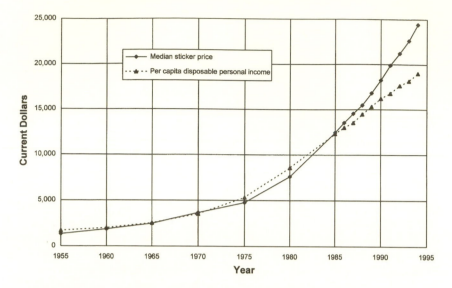

Figure 6.5. Sticker Price and Disposable Income (1955–1994).

Source: U.S. Department of Commerce, *Statistical Abstract of the United States, 1995* (Washington, DC: U.S. Government Printing Office, 1995).

spired in the late 1970s and early 1980s to raise costs substantially. Runaway energy prices, a tightened market for faculty, unfavorable exchange rates—all contributed to the increase in college costs. Internal decisions by the colleges—to maintain high-quality programs and facilities—exacerbated these pressures. Finally, the feedback loop between tuition and financial aid led to both rising tuition and increased institutional spending on aid. As tuition rises, more students qualify for more aid. Increased spending on aid in turn necessitates further tuition increases, except at institutions with very large endowment incomes. As Ehrenberg and Murphy explained, "Part of every dollar of tuition revenue generated by a tuition increase is used to provide increased grant assistance for those students whose need is increased by the tuition increase."[76] Robert Atwell, president of the American Council on Education, described the feedback loop more graphically. "Some schools resemble dogs eating their own tails," said Atwell in a 1995 *Barron's* article, referring to those institutions who spend nearly every extra dollar of tuition income on student aid.[77] Although this feedback loop has always operated, it became particularly important in the 1980s when real federal funding for student aid declined and tuition increases regularly exceeded inflation. In fact, even if tuition and disposable income had gone up at the same rate, calculated financial need would still have increased, because only part of a family's income counts in the need-analysis formula. In other words, family income would have had to rise more than tuition in order for families not to qualify for additional aid, a pattern which has not been seen since the late 1950s.

Chivas Regal Phenomenon

Another reason that institutions, particularly prestigious colleges and universities, were able to raise tuition so sharply in the 1980s was that parents and students began to view the price of a college as an indication of its quality.[78] This so-called "Chivas Regal phenomenon"[79] emerged as colleges adopted marketing strategies and practices from business in order to compete for the shrinking number of college-age students. Just as companies tried to position their products as either low cost or high quality, so too did colleges and universities in the early 1980s. In such an environment, as David Breneman has noted, "Some presidents of private colleges saw little incentive to keep prices down, particularly if that had the effect of lowering the institution's actual or perceived quality. . . . Business officers followed tuition levels closely to ensure that the college's price accurately reflected its place in the academic pecking order. The worst sin was to underprice a college relative to schools deemed weaker."[80]

The consequences of "underpricing" a college are suggested by the experience of one of our colleges in the early 1980s. Elizabeth Kennan became president of Mount Holyoke College in 1978. Convinced that "a high price was vital to maintaining a competitive position," between 1980 and 1983 she and her board aggressively raised Mount Holyoke's tuition to bring it more in line with the fees of its competitors. Despite tuition increases that averaged more than 15 percent and reached as high as 17.5 percent, Mount Holyoke's SAT scores rose slightly in the early 1980s. In 1984, Kennan took a sabbatical. By then, many people at Mount Holyoke had become concerned with the tuition increases. With the blessings of Kennan and the board, Acting President Joseph Ellis "tested the Chivas Regal argument by contradicting it." In 1985, Mount Holyoke increased tuition by only 6.4 percent, while other select schools' tuition rose by 7.8 percent. Whether due to coincidence or causality, both Mount Holyoke's applications and yield dropped. Interestingly, and suggestively, when Mount Holyoke raised its tuition by 8.8 percent the next year to bring it again more in line with its competitors, its applications rebounded.[81]

Perhaps it's not surprising that in a state like Massachusetts with a very strong private college tradition and a relatively weak state system, price was so closely associated with quality. In the early 1980s, however, the price/quality dynamic also seemed to be at work in Ohio, a state with many high-quality, low-priced public institutions. In fact, writing in 1983,

Thomas Wenzlau, president of Ohio Wesleyan, suggested that there may have been even more pressure in Ohio for liberal arts colleges to maintain their high tuition:

> . . . a lower tuition at a liberal-arts college will not be absolutely low enough to affect many decisions about whether to attend college . . . for most liberal-arts colleges the magnitude of the tuition reduction necessary to compete with public universities is too great. In Ohio, for example, the average independent tuition is 200 percent higher than the tuition at the state universities. In most states the difference is even greater. . . . A realistic tuition cut could improve the competitive position of a liberal arts college vis-à-vis other private colleges and universities but would raise image questions. The major selling points for liberal arts colleges are quality education and attention to the individual needs of students, privileges that students and their families expect to pay for when they choose such a college. Many colleges are openly concerned about the message they convey to a quality-conscious public by cutting tuition.[82]

The Chivas Regal phenomenon continued to operate throughout the 1980s. A 1988 Gallup poll of 1,000 students between the ages of 13 and 21 found that 38 percent of them agreed that "the higher the tuition costs of a college, the better the quality of education a student will receive."[83]

This attitude began to change, however, in the early 1990s. As tuition at the most selective private colleges approached the $20,000 mark, parents began to shop around for the best college "buy." In a recent article in *Change*, David Smith, dean of admissions and financial aid at Syracuse University, described the new attitude of parents:

> "Who took me? What's their price? Are they *worth* it?" the admitted family now chants. . . . Colleges have encountered the same level of marketplace as durable goods, with the consumer asking, "Am I getting what I'm paying for?" We used to hear about education as a good investment; now we hear about higher education as just one more necessary expenditure; so people "shop"— and aggressively—for price comparisons among colleges of similar perceived quality.[84]

Many administrators at the schools we visited would concur with Smith's assessment. Thomas Hayden, vice president for admissions and financial aid at Oberlin, believes that, "A number of colleges and universities have priced themselves out of the market. They have misjudged the ability and willingness, particularly of the middle class, to pay."[85] Similarly, Sandra Tarbox, Antioch's financial aid director, speculated, ". . . $20,000 seems to be a wall for many people. No one knows how many people don't apply because of the price tag."[86] David Caldwell, director of administrative information services at Wheaton, went so far as to predict, "You may end up seeing colleges acting like Saturn [the car]—setting a lower fixed price the same for everyone without any bargaining or discounting."[87] Caldwell's prediction has in fact already come true at some colleges. Muskingum College in Ohio recently announced plans to drop its tuition for the 1996/97 school year by $4,000, or 29 percent of its current tuition, after a study indicated that the college could bring in more money by charging less. President Samuel W. Speck explained, "Families who may have felt they could not afford it will look at Muskingum."[88] Muskingum's experiment notwithstanding, most colleges, including those in our study, continued to increase their tuition at rates in excess of inflation in the early 1990s.

A Greater Institutional Burden

Federal student aid funding did not keep pace with the tuition increases during the 1980s and early 1990s, so institutions were forced to pick up the slack. Between 1980 and 1985, the median institutional aid expenditure among our colleges nearly doubled, approaching $3.4 million (Figure 6.1). Since 1985, total aid expenditures have increased an average of 13 percent each year, and in 1994, the median liberal arts colleges spent over $11 million on aid. As described in the next chapter, during the 1980s many of the colleges increased their commitments to merit aid. At the same time the percent of students on need-based aid at our schools expanded from 36 percent in 1980 to 55 percent in 1994 (Figure 6.4).

As these colleges spent more institutional funds on financial aid, aid became a larger part of their budgets. In 1980, institutional aid represented 14 percent of net tuition revenue at the median college. This proportion had increased to 18 percent by 1985, to 25 percent by 1990, and to 33 percent by 1994. Even more alarming were the high discount rates at particular schools. In 1994, five of the colleges in our study were discounting their tuition revenue by more than 40 percent, and at one college, the tuition discount had reached 68 percent. At the other end of the spectrum, the minimum discount rate in the early 1990s—about 20 percent—was comparable to the maximum discount rate at the schools through the mid-1970s.

It is also instructive to compare a college's endowment income to its aid expenditures. As long as its endowment income exceeds its financial aid expenditures, a college can argue that theoretically no student is subsidizing another student.[89] Such an argument is much harder to make once a college's aid allocations exceed its endowment income. In 1970 and 1980, six of the fourteen colleges for which we have information were spending less on financial aid than they were generating from endowment income, and three others were spending almost the same amount of money on aid as their endowments were producing. By 1994 only four colleges' endowment incomes were sufficient to cover their aid expenses, and six colleges were spending more than double their endowment income on aid. This trend is particularly worrisome, given that colleges are allocating an increasing amount of their aid monies to merit scholarships. While well-to-do families may be willing to subsidize the tuitions of students from low-income families, they have understandably been more reluctant to subsidize the tuition of smart students from upper-income families.

Despite increased institutional aid expenditures, the 1980s and in particular the 1990s have seen an erosion in the ability of colleges and universities to pursue financial aid policies that ensure access and choice. In a 1994 survey conducted by the National Association of College Admission Counselors (NACAC), 91 percent of the respondents indicated that they maintained a need-blind admissions policy until May 1, or, in other words, that they admitted candidates on the basis of academic and personal criteria without regard to students' financial need.[90] Fourteen of the 16 colleges in our study also still claim to be need blind in admissions. The other two are need conscious; that is, at the margin they consider an applicant's ability to pay. One of the colleges became need conscious because it was uncomfortable with the alternative, which was an admit/deny policy. Since it became need conscious, this college has been able to fund all its admitted students with need.

While need-blind admissions resonates ideologically with the ideals of access, practically it means very little for securing access, since being need blind does not mean that an institution will meet the full need of all admitted students. In fact, only 20 percent of the institutions in the NACAC survey indicated that they met 100 percent of demonstrated need. Among the colleges in our study, only four have consistently been able to meet the full need of all their students since the early 1980s, and even those four have expressed serious concerns about their abilities to continue full need policies. Another handful of our colleges have been able to meet full-need sporadically and for varying lengths of time. Kaye Hanson, director of the Consortium for Funding Higher Education, recently estimated that there are perhaps a dozen colleges and universities in the country that are need blind and meet the full need of all admitted students.

Since most of our colleges have not been able to meet the full need of all accepted students, they have had to decide how to allocate their limited financial aid resources. Typically, these colleges rank candidates by academic qualifications or other desired traits, such as ethnicity or athletic ability. The colleges then either allocate institutional aid down the list until it is gone (admit/denying the remaining candidates) or more often "gap" students toward the bottom of their admit lists (giving them some, but not all of the aid that they need) and/or preferentially package their awards (meeting full need, but giving less attractive packages to students lower on the list). Among the NACAC respondents, gapping and preferential packaging were considerably more popular than admit/deny policies. While 65 percent practiced gapping and 54 percent preferentially packaged their awards, only 21 percent of the respondents employed admit/deny policies. As the competition for students has increased at colleges and universities across the country, it is perhaps not surprising that admit/deny policies have declined in popularity and given way to gapping and preferential packaging strategies. (The latter strategies are described more fully in the next chapter on merit aid.)

Some of the colleges have also tried to continue to meet the full needs of all admitted students by modifying their need-blind admissions policies slightly. Conventionally, need-blind admissions means that applicants should not be denied admission because they require financial aid; a corollary is that applicants should not be admitted to the college simply because they don't need financial aid. It is this second understanding of the policy that some of our colleges have modified, in order to increase the proportion of full-pay students in their classes. Recognizing that meeting the full need of all students was prohibitively costly but also aware that the college's applicant pool was too shallow and needy to abandon that goal, a faculty committee at Mount Holyoke recently concluded that "it may be possible to move away from need-blind admissions to a small degree, while still fully funding the financial needs of all accepted students. For example, admitting an additional 30 full-paying applicants could yield about 10 additional full-paying students. Ten additional full-paying students in each class would raise net tuition revenue by $1 million dollars."[91]

At Oberlin, a five-year financial aid plan proposed to the trustees in 1989 included a reduction in the percentage of students who would receive scholarship aid. However, administrators also wanted the college to continue its need-blind admissions policy and its policy of meeting evaluated need to the extent that funds were available. In order to achieve all three goals simultaneously, officials sought to attract more full-pay students:

> To achieve an increase in applicants who can pay the full tuition, members of the admissions staff will visit a few more of the affluent high schools in the country, and the office will do special mailings to students in affluent areas. Since there will be no increase in the total number of high school visits, there will be "a slight change in the mix of the high schools visited to reflect the new institutional direction," Hayden says. He adds, "scholarship money does not come from the sky." With Oberlin's relatively low endowment per student, it comes from full-paying students.[92]

It is ironic that just a decade after colleges sought to ensure access and choice by expanding their applicant pools to include more low-income students, colleges are now trying to increase the number of full-paying applicants in order to maintain, to the extent they can, need-blind policies that meet the full need of all admitted students.

The Politicization of Aid

Another development that has contributed to the increasing use of aid as an enrollment tool is the gradual politicization of the needs formula. From the mid-1970s until the mid-1980s, student eligibility for financial aid was based mostly on the uniform methodology. Each year a group of financial aid directors, government officials, and representatives from such organizations as the College Board and the American Council of Education, met to review and update the formula. In 1986, responsibility for the needs formula was removed from this private, consensus-making body and given to Congress. The new congressional methodology, as it came to be known, was similar to the uniform methodology except in its treatment of independent students. The 1992 Education Amendments merged the Pell and congressional methodologies to create the federal methodology, which eliminated home and farm equity contributions.

These changes in the federal methodology lowered family contributions so much that many institutions felt compelled to abandon the federal methodology. Today most of the colleges in our study use a separate methodology developed by the College Board to evaluate need. This so-called institutional methodology considers among other things the value of a family's house, thus lowering students' calculated need. Those few colleges in our study that employ the federal methodology use it primarily as a recruitment tool since it enables them to offer larger need-based awards.

The lack of a uniform methodology for calculating need and the varied institutional policies concerning need mark an important philosophical shift in the thinking regarding financial aid. When the goals of financial aid were access and choice, financial aid directors wanted the award packages received by students from different colleges to be the same so that a student could choose the best place for her on educational grounds alone, regardless of cost. In many ways, as alluded to here and described in detail in the next chapter on merit aid, there has been a return to the days prior to the CSS when there was no uniform method for determining need and aid packages were used as bidding chips for desired students.

Nowhere were the ideals of access and choice better represented than in the Overlap Group. The Overlap Group consisted of the eight Ivy League universities and fourteen other private, selective colleges and universities located in the Northeast. The financial aid directors at these schools met each year from 1958 to 1991 to compare the financial aid packages awarded to students who had been admitted to more than one of the institutions. The goal of the group was to ensure that all of the colleges had the same family financial information, so that the expected family contribution for each student was the same at all institutions. In 1991, a Justice Department investigation found that their cooperation represented price-fixing and was, thus, a violation of antitrust laws. Ultimately, MIT was the only institution that challenged the Justice Department and pursued the issue through the courts. The terms of the settlement that MIT and the Justice Department reached allowed the Overlap Group to resume cooperation on overall financial aid policies and principles but not to discuss individual students or prospective tuition rates or faculty salaries. Colleges were also allowed to submit student information to a third party, after the awards were made, to evaluate whether the participating colleges had arrived at similar award amounts. Unfortunately, the settlement also required that participating institutions be need blind in admissions and promise to meet the full financial need of all admitted students, a financial burden that none of the institutions could promise to undertake and continue for any length of time.[93]

Although the needs formula has become increasingly politicized, its content has actually changed little since it was developed in the 1950s despite the fact that the nature of students and the structures of families have changed a great deal. At many schools, including a few of the colleges in our study, older students comprise a significant part of each entering class. Since one of the fundamental assumptions of the needs formula as it was originally constructed is that parents will bear the primary burden for a child's education, independent students complicate needs analysis. Similarly, most federal and institutional aid policies were developed for nuclear families with one primary wage earner. The proliferation of single-parent, divorced-parent, and two-career families means that such traditional families are no longer the norm, even at small liberal arts colleges.

Changes in the tax code have also made it difficult to determine accurately family income for all types of families. One financial aid director, for example, told us of a student who qualified for full support according to the federal methodology. The college suspected that something was amiss, because she lived in a wealthy suburb and her father was the president of a private company, so they offered her only loans. Not only did the student attend the college without taking out any loans, but while she was still an undergraduate her parents donated money in addition to and well in excess of tuition costs.

Bargaining for the Best Buy

Few of the "financial aid" war stories we heard had such happy endings for the colleges. More typical is the story of a divorced, and supposedly missing, father who showed up at the college to watch his son play football, or the story of the child of an assistant pastor whose calculated need was less than that of his classmate, the child of the pastor, despite similar lifestyles. Barbara Boles, the financial aid director at Gordon College, succinctly described the change in approach to financing college illustrated by these stories: "Parents used to prepare for college by saving. Now they prepare for college by moving assets around."[94]

These stories underline not only the increasing sophistication of some parents and their accountants but also a more troubling attitude toward financial aid. Perhaps not surprisingly, as the use of financial aid has evolved, parents' attitudes toward financial aid have changed. Parents and students are no longer grateful to receive financial aid; instead, they view financial aid more as a negotiating tool. As David Miller, financial aid director at the College of Wooster, explained, "There has been a loss of the concept of a family's ability to pay. Now we have moved to a family's willingness to pay."[95] Articles in *Money* magazine and other publications that describe how to "beat the system" or depict financial aid officers as "bad guys trying to gouge families" have created an adversarial and suspicious atmosphere.

One result has been an increase in bartering and bickering about aid packages. Every school we visited told of parents calling to complain that their child had received more money from another school and to negotiate a better aid package. Although it has certainly increased since merit aid has become more widespread, bartering became popular much earlier. An article in a 1981 issue of *The (Oberlin) Observer*, for example, reflected on the "gallows humor concept" called the "slave bazaar technique," which the office used internally when an aggressive parent called to "barter" his or her child for a better scholarship.[96]

Some of this change in attitude is a result of the increased competition for students. Parents know that their children are applying to college in a buyer's market and that there are many colleges eager to enroll their daughter or son. This explanation, however, is not sufficient because financial aid directors at the most selective colleges, where they admit a third or less of the applicants, also report that parents have become aggressive. Since colleges have begun to use financial aid to attract students, the size and terms of aid packages have become a much larger part of the college-making decision for students and their parents.

Moving to the Center

As the amount of money that institutions spend on financial aid has increased and parents have become more sophisticated consumers, financial

aid offices have grown in both importance and visibility. In the words of
Kathleen Methot, longtime director of financial aid at Hampshire College,
"Financial aid has moved from the back to the front of the shop; it is now,
with admissions, the door to an institution."[97] Whereas very few applicants
used to visit financial aid offices, now most applicants do.

Internally too, financial aid has become much more central. As Michael
McPherson and Morton Shapiro explained in a 1994 report for Mount
Holyoke College:

> As recently as fifteen years ago, relatively few college or university presidents
> or trustees paid a great deal of attention to these operations, especially to the
> financial aid side. Financial aid was generally thought of as a noble charitable
> effort, more or less independent of other college operations. As long as spend-
> ing was under control, administrators tended to leave well enough alone.
> Things are different today. Aid policy is increasingly viewed as a key strategic
> instrument in meeting a college's goals—for revenue, for enrollment levels,
> and for the quality of the class. This has led to a much greater understanding
> of financial aid issues among top administrators.[98]

At most of the colleges, financial aid is now discussed not just among
admissions and financial aid staff but also at faculty, staff, and trustee
meetings.

The size and responsibilities as well as the visibility of financial aid offices have increased. Until the mid-1970s, one director, perhaps with assistance from a secretary, would prepare financial aid packages. Today, financial aid staffs, usually of three or more people, not only allocate aid but
also help develop institutional policies to meet enrollment targets and even
serve as financial counselors to students and their families.

Although the level of federal funding has declined since the 1980s, federal regulations have nonetheless increased, causing nearly every financial
aid director we met to complain about the growing regulatory burden. One
director's comment succinctly captures their feelings: "The federal involvement in the regulatory process is burying us." Federal regulations have
multiplied in part because the numbers and types of federal programs
have expanded. Another financial aid director lamented, "There are different types of loans, different rates of interest and different exit and entrance requirements." The government has also tightened its regulations in
an effort to guard against fraud and abuse and to reduce defaults. Ironically, many financial aid directors feel that despite all the regulations they
have little ability to ensure against bad loans, because loans are made on
the basis not of credit ratings but rather of calculated need.

Another major change in the role of the financial aid office has been in
its relationship with admissions. In the 1960s, most colleges deliberately
separated their financial aid and admissions offices in order to indicate, at

least symbolically, the separation between admissions standards and financial need. In the last decade, however, as financial aid has become a tool with which an institution builds a class, colleges have restructured their financial aid and admissions operations in a variety of ways to emphasize the connections and facilitate coordination between them. For example, Oberlin merged two existing committees to create a new Committee on Admissions and Financial Aid, and Mount Holyoke now has a financial aid liaison in its admissions office. Also, in the mid- to late 1980s, many of the colleges in our study, including the College of Wooster and Smith, created enrollment management positions to oversee and coordinate their admissions, financial aid, and retention efforts.

Perhaps the major reason that financial aid and admissions offices have drawn closer together is the growing use of merit awards to attract and enroll top-quality students. More than anything else, the story of financial aid in the 1980s and 1990s has been the story of merit awards, a subject we examine in the next chapter.

CHAPTER 7

The Growth of Merit Aid

IN A 1995 interview, Samuel Carrier, provost of Oberlin College, ratio-nalized the college's introduction of merit aid, explaining, "The period that Oberlin is emerging from is a relatively short period in the history of the college; merit aid is a return to prior policies."[1] A 1988 article by Sandra Baum and Saul Schwartz made a similar point: "The idea of using criteria other than financial need as a basis for aid is certainly not new. In 1958, when the National Defense Education Act was passed, the proponents of need-based aid were in the minority."[2] Although true, Carrier's justification and Baum and Schwartz's assertion obscure the magnitude and character of the merit aid programs that developed in the 1980s and early 1990s at most colleges and universities in the United States, including many of the colleges in our study.

Before looking at how the use of merit aid has evolved since 1980, it's important to define what we mean by merit aid. When we sent our finan-cial aid survey to the 16 colleges in our study, we defined "need based" as "determined and awarded solely on the basis of a need analysis" and "merit" as "not determined by a need analysis, but rather awarded by some other criteria, regardless of need." These definitions may seem straightfor-ward and clear-cut, but in practice it is not always easy to distinguish be-tween merit and need-based awards. Many of the colleges offer both merit and need-based aid, which means that depending on how a school allo-cates its award money, some merit awards may go to students who would have received at least some need-based aid.[3] In addition, even those col-leges that have not instituted formal merit aid programs consider academic and other factors when they package their need-based awards.

THE NATIONAL SCENE

In 1974, Robert Huff, director of financial aid at Stanford University, con-ducted an extensive merit aid survey. Huff sent questionnaires to 1,878 four-year colleges and universities. Of the 859 usable responses that he received, 55 percent reported that they had merit aid programs and an-other 5 percent of institutions were considering them. Huff found that the use of merit aid programs varied by geographic region. Whereas almost 67 percent of the midwestern and southern schools in Huff's survey had merit programs, only 39 percent of the eastern schools in his study gave no-need awards. Most of the merit aid programs had been in existence for at least three years; 63 percent of the merit programs were more than five years old, and another 18 percent had been established three to five years earlier. Although merit aid was fairly common in 1974, Huff found that "the most selective colleges and universities, which incidentally still control the lion's share of the total institutional aid resources of the United States, have not yet chosen to go back to merit-type awards."[4]

A decade later, Betsy A. Porter and Suzanne K. McColloch of the University of Pittsburgh Office of Admissions and Financial Aid undertook another comprehensive merit aid survey. Of the 367 responses that they received from a cross-section of four-year colleges and universities, 305— or 83 percent—reported that their institutions offered no-need scholarships to academically talented students. Almost 85 percent of the programs had been in existence for four years or more and almost half had existed for more than twelve years. The share of New England institutions awarding merit aid had increased to 42 percent, but this percentage still lagged behind the other regions, especially the South, Southwest, and Midwest, where upward of 90 percent of the institutions were providing merit aid.[5]

In the early 1990s, Michael McPherson and Morton Schapiro examined merit aid trends between 1983/84 and 1991/92 at a sample of 379 non-profit, bachelor's degree granting institutions in the United States. Over the period, they found a modest increase in institutional merit aid programs at both public and private institutions. Between 1983/84 and 1991/92, the percent of institutions that reported providing non-need-based, nonathletic awards, increased from 78 to 81 percent. At the same time, the percent of institutional financial aid allocated to merit grants increased from 44 to 56 percent at public four-year institutions and from 17 to 21 percent at private colleges.[6] A 1994 study by the National Association of College Admission Counselors (NACAC) corroborated McPherson and Schapiro's findings. Among the 346 public and private institutions that responded to the merit aid question on the NACAC survey, only 18 percent had no institutional commitment to merit-based aid and 37 percent spent more than 25 percent of their institutional financial aid budgets on merit aid.[7]

At the same time that institutions were spending more money on merit aid, so too were the states. In 1988, 29 states offered no-need scholarships, and the amount of merit funds available had increased by 45 percent from just five years earlier.[8] Gale Gaines, a research associate at the Southern Regional Education Board (SREB), documented the growth of merit aid programs among the SREB states during the 1980s. In 1978, only two

SREB states offered state-funded merit scholarships. Between 1978 and 1988, 11 other SREB states created merit programs, so that by the end of the 1980s more than half of the SREB states provided merit scholarships.[9] In 1994/95, 13 percent of state student financial aid—or $407 million—was non-need based.[10]

At the federal level too, there was growing pressure to institute merit scholarships. In 1984, Gary L. Jones, undersecretary of education, proposed in a talk at the American Association for Higher Education's National Conference on Education that the federal government establish "Learning for Leadership Grants," which would provide selected students $2,500 scholarships each year for four years. Jones estimated that an endowment of $500 million would support four-year scholarships for 20,000 students annually.[11] Shortly thereafter, the Reagan administration announced that it was considering instituting competitive academic scholarships in order to promote academic excellence.[12] More recently, the White House Science Council Panel on the Health of U.S. Colleges and Universities recommended that the federal government establish a merit scholarship program that would support 1 percent of the country's best mathematics, engineering, and natural science students for four years of college at an annual level of $15,000.[13] In early 1996, President Clinton announced his plans to create a new federal merit aid program that would award $1,000 merit scholarships to the top 5 percent of graduating seniors at every American high school.[14]

Factors Favoring Merit Aid

Many factors have led to the increased use of and interest in merit aid. When the number of college students declined in the 1980s and early 1990s, competition for the best students intensified. In this environment, merit aid became an effective way to recruit students for both public and private institutions. Eighty percent of the institutions in Porter and McColloch's 1982 study, "The Use of No-Need Academic Scholarship in U.S. Universities and Colleges: A Survey," reported that they used no-need scholarships in recruiting either to a "great extent" or to "some extent."[15] In their 1984 update, 42 percent of the schools cited "to recruit the best and the brightest" as their "primary reason for awarding no-need scholarships."[16]

During the 1980s, colleges themselves began to provide the funds for an increasing proportion of students' financial aid packages. Many colleges and universities, including some in our study, discovered that they were spending a lot of money to enroll students whom they didn't really want. Alfred MacKay, the acting president of Oberlin during the 1991/92 school year, criticized need-based aid that "offers all admitted students the same financial-aid package whether or not the students are specially wanted by us or by others" for being foolishly utopian and costly: "There are two main conclusions to draw about our utopian egalitarian approach to admissions and financial aid: 1) it's not smart, and 2) it's unnecessarily expensive."[17]

As the institutional proportion of aid increased, most colleges and universities could no longer meet the full need of enrolled students, so they used their limited funds to address institutional priorities of quality and diversity. Ross Peacock, director of institutional research at Oberlin, explained why need-based aid could not be used for such purposes: "Need-based financial aid was originally developed to allow all admitted students the opportunity to pursue a higher education without regard to cost. The principles its programs and administrators follow make no other distinctions among students. This fundamental tenet makes it very difficult to use such a program in ways other than that for which it was intended."[18] The Ohio colleges used merit aid to attract high-ability students who otherwise might not have considered attending a small liberal arts college in the Midwest. In particular, in the late 1980s, most of our colleges created targeted scholarships for high-ability minority students. In general, as Robert Massa, executive director of academic services at The Johns Hopkins University, summarized, "The goal of a merit aid program ought to be to attract and enroll students who otherwise would not attend an institution."[19]

Although Massa's statement may seem like a tautology, it represented a shift in the use of and attitude toward merit aid. In the 1950s, before the development of need-based financial aid, both federal and institutional aid were awarded to needy students who also demonstrated "merit." The purpose of those early merit programs, however, was subtly different from the aim of the merit aid programs of the 1980s. Gregory A. Jackson explained the difference:

> Originally financial aid for college students served two purposes: to reward students for academic achievement or some other actions, such as military service, or to enable needy students to attend college if they wished to do so. But in recent years there has been another reason to offer financial aid to prospective students: since the traditional pool for post-secondary education will soon decline, barring special effort colleges will be unable to enroll as many students as they now enroll. This fact, along with a sudden energy-based increase in operating costs, has elicited from colleges a variety of reactions: services for non-traditional students, grantsmanship, aggressive recruiting, advertising, and surely not least programs offering students financial aid as an inducement to attend college.[20]

Kathryn Osmond, director of financial aid at Wellesley, also stressed how the use of financial aid started to change in the 1980s compared to earlier periods: "The mission of financial aid was supposed to be to give students a choice so that theoretically all of the packages should be about the same so that the student could choose the best place for her and where she really wants to be. Now, because of marketing, financial aid has become the hook to grab in the students."[21]

There is another important distinction between early merit scholarships and today's no-need awards. Although in the early period financial aid was merit-based, grants were awarded only to financially needy students. Today merit awards are often awarded to upper-middle- and high-income students with no need.

THE OHIO MERIT WARS

All of the Ohio colleges in our study have merit aid programs. In part, these programs grew in response to competition from a strong public higher education system. The Ohio colleges have used merit awards to attract students who would otherwise have attended high-quality and far less costly public universities, many of which have merit aid programs of their own. The age and scope of the colleges' merit aid programs varies according to each college's ability to enroll a first-year class of the desired size and quality.

Figure 7.1 shows the median, maximum, and minimum amounts of

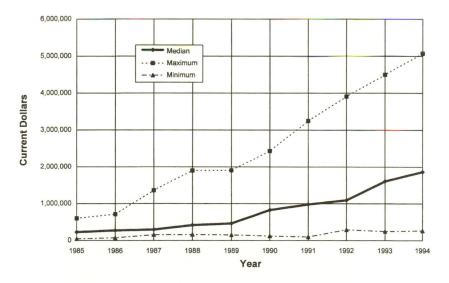

Figure 7.1. Institutional Dollars Spent on Merit Scholarships at the Ohio Colleges (1985–1994).

money spent on merit aid by the seven Ohio schools in our study from 1985 through 1994. Before 1987 no college spent more than $1 million on merit scholarships, and until 1990 still only one school had attained that level. By 1994, all but one of our Ohio colleges spent well over a million dollars on merit aid and one school had broken the $5 million mark. In 1994, half of the Ohio schools in our study spent more than $1.8 million on merit scholarships, up from medians of $227,000 in 1985 and $826,000 in 1990.

As merit aid expenditures grew, they became (not surprisingly) a larger fraction of the aid allocations at the colleges. Figure 7.2 displays merit aid as a percentage of total institutional aid at the Ohio schools. Again, the median, maximum, and minimum percentages are shown, and again there is an inexorable increase over the period, from a median of 8 percent in 1985, to 17 percent in 1990, and finally to 23 percent in 1994. The *minimum* percentage of a college's aid budget based on merit in 1994—about 10 percent—exceeded the *median* percentage in 1985—8 percent.

One reason that the Ohio colleges spent more on merit aid as the 1980s progressed, both in absolute and relative terms, is that they gave more students merit scholarships. Figure 7.3 shows the median percentage of students receiving merit awards among the Ohio colleges. Until the late 1980s, most of the colleges had modest merit aid programs targeted at the top 10 percent or less of their enrolled classes. As the competition for students heightened, some of the colleges broadened their programs to

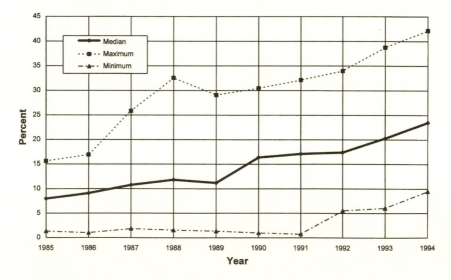

Figure 7.2. Merit Scholarships as a Percentage of Total Scholarships among the Ohio Colleges (1985–1994).

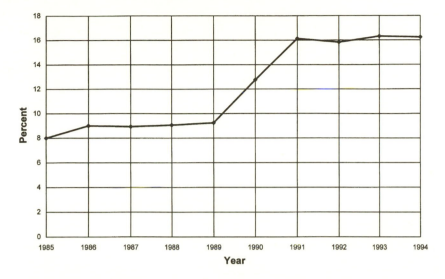

Figure 7.3. Percentage of Students Receiving Merit Scholarships (1985–1994), Median Case among the Ohio Colleges.

include good as well as excellent students. By 1991, half of the Ohio colleges awarded merit scholarships to more than 16 percent of their students. The percent of students receiving merit aid seems to have leveled off in the 1990s, but Figure 7.3 is misleading in that regard. Although the median stabilized, by 1994 all of the Ohio schools were giving merit awards to at least 14 percent of their students, and three were awarding merit scholarships to well over 25 percent of their entering classes.

At the same time that the number of students receiving merit awards increased, so too did the average size of the awards. Between 1985 and 1994, there was a steady increase in the average size of merit aid awards, from a median of $1,746 in 1985 to $4,505 in 1990 and finally to $6,981 in 1994 (see Figure 7.4). The average size of merit awards increased even faster than tuition, room, board, and fees, so that by 1993, at half of the colleges, the average merit award covered almost 40 percent of those expenses, up from 14 percent in 1985 (see Figure 7.5). At the same time, there was a convergence in the relative size of merit awards. In general, those colleges with the larger awards reduced their allocations in order to spread their money over more students, while those schools with the smaller allocations increased the size of their awards in an effort to become more competitive. In 1988, the merit awards at the colleges covered an average of between 7 and 49 percent of tuition, room, board, and fees; by 1994, the range had narrowed to between 14 and 39 percent.

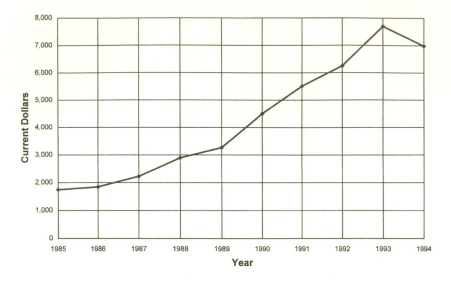

Figure 7.4. Average Size of Merit Scholarships (1985–1994), Median Case among the Ohio Colleges.

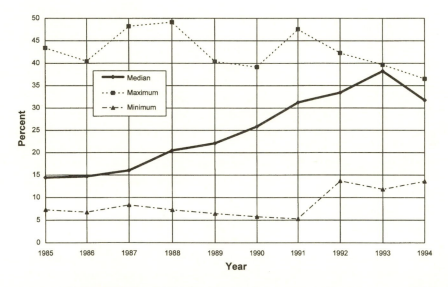

Figure 7.5. Average Merit Scholarship as a Percentage of Tuition at the Ohio Colleges (1985–1994).

The competition that developed among the Ohio colleges was foreseen by at least a few of them. In 1977, Denison decided to institute an honors program rather than grant merit aid, for fear that offering no-need scholarships would unleash a bidding war for top students:

> Presently, the majority of the council does not feel that "no-need" or merit scholarships are the answer to the problem of upgrading the academic competence of our students. We believe that using such scholarships is likely to lead us into a cut-throat competition with other schools to "buy" talent. We feel that the dynamics of this competition are unhealthy and that no one wins (except possibly certain fortunate students) when it exists. The reason is that once several schools get into a bidding war with each other, using merit scholarships as the means, the other schools with which we compete are likely to make offers which come close to matching ours. In this case, the student will ultimately choose from among a number of reasonably equal bids on the basis of what the school offers intellectually. Thus, if we want to attract—AND KEEP—better students, we can spend our resources more efficiently in enriching the academic and intellectual climate at Denison so that we can convince bright students that Denison is a place where they will be challenged and stimulated intellectually.[22]

Four years later (in 1981), Oberlin reiterated Denison's concerns: "The use of college resources for no-need awards ... can also lead to a situation of unhealthy bidding for students by colleges."[23] Oberlin also worried that "once undertaken it is difficult to pull back from such a venture."

To a large extent the fears expressed by Denison and Oberlin have proved true. In a recent interview, one administrator commented, "Merit aid is like having your first drink; it feels good but then you become addicted." Another administrator expressed regret that "We got into a game that we can't win, but we can't quit the game." Just how competitive the use of merit aid has become among the Ohio colleges in our study is also evidenced by the many war analogies that we heard when we visited them. "It's out and out warfare in the trenches every day"and "Ohio has become a big battleground" are representative comments.

McPherson and Schapiro likened merit aid wars between peer institutions of similar quality to a prisoner's dilemma:

> Each individual school tries to gain an advantage relative to its rivals by bidding down the price charged to high-quality students. But the net effect of this competitive effort is simply that all schools in the group match one another's offers, and wind up with essentially the same group of students they could have had anyway, but with less net tuition revenue. If the schools could arrive at an enforceable agreement to abstain from merit aid, the allocation of students among schools would be unaffected and the schools would have higher

net tuition revenues, and hence be better off. This is the economic logic behind efforts by groups of schools like the Ivy League to arrive at agreements
not to compete for students through merit aid awards.[24]

Although McPherson and Schapiro's analysis oversimplifies merit aid wars
by implying that colleges act in a closed environment—that there is a
small, fixed number of schools competing only with each other for a set
number of students—much of their analogy rings true when we trace the
recent merit aid histories of four of the Ohio colleges. Such an analysis also
enables us to understand better how the merit aid competition unfolded in
Ohio and how these colleges' attitudes toward merit aid evolved.

Individual Histories

Ohio Wesleyan was one of the first liberal arts I colleges in Ohio to institute a formal merit aid program. The idea behind the program when it was
begun in the early 1980s was to attract a cadre of high-quality students,
who would in turn attract a solid group of good students, who weren't
merit quality but were more qualified than the average student at the
college. "Below merit, above the profile" was the rallying cry. To that end,
between 1980 and 1985, Ohio Wesleyan increased the number of students
receiving merit awards from 25 to 127 and the average award from $841 to
$2,435. The program worked until other liberal arts I colleges in Ohio
began merit aid programs in the mid- to late 1980s, forcing the college to
spend more money to attract less qualified students. In 1987, Ohio
Wesleyan increased the number of students receiving aid to 219, and the
average award reached $6,205. Over the next few years, the college capped
the size and number of top merit awards "to make them more efficient"
and used the money saved to increase the number of smaller awards for
less qualified students. By 1994, Ohio Wesleyan was giving 620, or 39 percent, of its students merit aid.

Throughout the 1980s, Denison University gave 7 to 9 percent of its
students merit awards that amounted on average to 15 percent of the college's stated tuition, room, board, and fees. In 1989, Denison realized that
although its merit program was in line with the programs at other Great
Lakes College Association schools, "a few institutions have targeted more
funds for academic scholarships than [we have] and have drawn strong
scholar cross accepts away from us."[25] Consequently, in 1990, the college
stepped up its merit program considerably by increasing both the number
of recipients and the size of the average award. Between 1991 and 1993,
almost 20 percent of Denison's students received merit awards that cov-

ered on average 35 percent of tuition, room, board, and fees. In 1994, Denison again expanded its merit program to attract more students. Although the average merit aid award fell slightly between 1993 and 1994, the percent of students receiving merit aid climbed to 28 percent. This trend seems to be continuing. A recent newspaper article reported that in 1995 "nearly every one of the ... freshmen, rich and poor alike, got a discount thanks to scholarships that rewarded past academic success or other special talents."[26]

For a long time, Kenyon resisted merit aid. Finally, when enough families asked the college, "What can you do?" administrators asked themselves, "What can we do?" Craig Daugherty, director of financial aid, succinctly justified Kenyon's decision. "If by awarding a scholarship of a few thousand dollars to a very bright student who otherwise would not enroll, why wouldn't you?" he asked rhetorically.[27] Like many of the colleges in our study, Kenyon used merit aid to target high-quality students, particularly those who had traditionally not been attracted to the college—in Kenyon's case, minority and science students. Initially, the college expanded its merit aid program by increasing the size of the award for the top students. From 1980 to 1991, only 6 percent of Kenyon's students received merit awards, but the size of the award relative to tuition, room, board, and fees grew from 8 percent in 1980, to 26 percent in 1990, and then to 48 percent in 1991. Since 1991 Kenyon has increased the number of awards, causing the average award size to fall in both absolute and relative terms. Kenyon's merit program still involves less than 15 percent of its students.

Oberlin—the last Ohio college in our study to institute a formal merit aid policy—debated the pros and cons of merit aid throughout the 1980s. In 1984/85 the college began to sponsor National Merit scholars, and it created two small book prizes for entering students. Oberlin also began to give merit aid to students in its conservatory in order to compete with other conservatories who were "buying students out from under us."[28] It wasn't until 1992, however, that Oberlin introduced a formal merit program for its arts and science students that provided sizable grants to selected National Merit scholars and high ability black and Hispanic students. The program, which was intended to improve the yield for both groups of students, was particularly aimed at those students "who either barely qualified or barely missed qualifying for need-based aid." In many ways, Oberlin was forced into merit aid by the actions of the other liberal arts I colleges in Ohio. In 1991, one senior administrator blamed Oberlin's loss of market power on its less attractive aid offers, equating the college's reluctance to offer merit aid with a hospital's refusal to pay the market rate for surgeons:

I suspect that for many students our financial aid offers are less attractive than those of other schools—that our financial-aid policy may be a primary cause for our loss of market power. . . . In a free market, if a hospital pays all its doctors the same but the market values surgeons more than family practitioners, then other things being equal, that hospital will have better family practice and worse surgery. This will happen because, with their different market valuations, "the same salary" will be more attractive to family practitioners than to surgeons, and, over time, talent will follow reward. A college that offers all students the same financial aid will tend to get a similar free-market result—the student-body equivalent of better family practitioners and worse surgeons. The market's valuations will reflect other colleges' interests in applicants with desirable characteristics, such as intellectual ability or ethnic identity. The college's "same financial-aid offers" will be more attractive to students with less desirable characteristics and less attractive to students with more desirable characteristics.[29]

John Muffo, who studied the effect of merit aid on admissions at Virginia Tech and its competitors in 1987, reached a similar conclusion:

The primary question for the institution that grows out of this kind of market research is to what extent it is being competitive with its sister colleges or universities in recruiting the best and brightest students. . . . The danger to the university is in not keeping up with the competition, thereby enrolling only those who are good enough to be admitted, but not quite good enough to get academic scholarship aid elsewhere. Beyond all the rhetoric about need-based aid versus non-need-based aid is a simple fact of life: acting substantially different from one's peer institutions risks one's competitiveness for the most sought-after students.[30]

The ratcheting up of merit aid among our Ohio colleges certainly supports Muffo's conclusion. Interestingly, so too does the absence of merit aid until recently at the Massachusetts colleges in our study.

A DELICATE EQUILIBRIUM IN MASSACHUSETTS

If the pressure in Ohio was to give merit aid, then the pressure in Massachusetts was *not* to give merit aid. Not only was Massachusetts the home of John Monro, the architect of need analysis, but many of the financial aid directors in Massachusetts were also trained by "the founding fathers and mothers of need-based aid."[31] Just how ardent the Massachusetts colleges' commitment was to need-based aid was evidenced by the strong rebuke the financial aid directors at Smith and Mount Holyoke received from their colleagues in 1983 when they announced that they would give $300 merit awards to their top applicants. Myra Smith, financial aid director at Smith, explained, "It is my understanding that even though they were effectively book awards, they sent everyone into a tizzy. They stopped the awards quickly, because of the pressure and because they wanted to continue to participate in the overlap group."[32] One reason that people may have reacted so viscerally was that four years earlier Smith and Mount Holyoke had been among a group of 30 top northeastern institutions to sign an agreement opposing the use of merit scholarships. The 1979 Statement on No-Need (or Merit) Awards read:

> We believe that our financial aid budgets should be used to meet the demonstrated need of accepted students who could not enter our institutions without such assistance. Only with a financial aid policy based on demonstrated need can we maintain student bodies broadly representative of many different socio-economic backgrounds. We oppose the concept of no-need (or merit) scholarship. If we awarded financial aid on the basis of merit, virtually everyone enrolled in our institutions would receive financial assistance. Students are *admitted* to our institutions on merit: financial aid is given only to those with demonstrated need.[33]

The statement captures not only the attitude of most of the Massachusetts colleges we studied toward merit aid, but also some of the subtler reasons why they resisted merit aid. Most of the schools in Massachusetts had strong applicant pools, which made it both unnecessary and in some ways more difficult to award merit aid. Given the overall strength of their admitted students, the colleges hesitated to distinguish a "most meritorious" group. In their article on merit aid, McPherson and Schapiro explained why it would also be economically costly for selective colleges and universities to invest a lot in merit aid:

> These institutions face a substantial excess demand among applicants, often rejecting two, three, or more applicants for every one they accept. Given that many of these rejected applicants would be full pay students if admitted, the opportunity cost of merit awards is quite high: rather than the alternative to a merit student being an empty bed, the alternative is a student who brings respectable credentials and a substantial tuition payment.[34]

In an environment in which most schools would not benefit from giving merit aid, even weaker colleges that might profit from such programs worried what giving merit aid would do to their reputations. Alice Emerson, president of Wheaton College, recalled, "The message was that if you had to go to merit aid it was a sign of weakness. For a weak college without financial resources it was death to award merit aid."[35] Oberlin, the strongest Ohio college in our study, expressed similar sentiments in 1981 when it considered whether to implement a merit program:

The promotion of no-need scholarships can have a negative effect on the image of a college. In recent months, car manufacturers have made much of cash rebates and other gimmicks in promoting the sale of low-cost Ford, Chrysler and General Motors products. At the same time, no such rebates were advertised for the high quality cars, the Cadillacs or Rolls Royces. The promotion of no-need scholarships can lead to a type of "hucksterism" which can "turn off" the perceptive student the program is designed to attract.[36]

Oberlin was particularly concerned about the reputation effect, because it competed to a greater degree than the other Ohio colleges in our study with eastern colleges that did not award merit aid:

> A merit program might actually have a negative impact on our image in the long run. By and large, the best schools with which we compete for students either do not have such programs or have very small programs. Our program might be viewed as an expression of weakness and come to be seen for what it is: not so much an honor for the student as an enticement for them to come to Oberlin. Even recipients might become skeptical of our motives in the long run. Would we not be saying, "Oberlin isn't good enough to attract first-rate students?"[37]

Perhaps part of the reason that merit aid programs seemed to hurt reputations in the East but not in the Midwest was that attitudes toward cost and value seemed to differ between the two regions. Doug Thompson, who has worked in admissions in Pennsylvania, Rhode Island, New York, and Ohio, contrasted the attitudes of people from the Midwest and the East Coast:

> People [in the Midwest] are much less aware of the quality differences of institutions and degrees of academic prestige. People look only at the bottom line. You can't even sell quality anymore. . . . It's an eye-opener to see withdrawals to places that you've never heard of. Parents pick schools on price without realizing the difference in quality between an Ohio Wesleyan and a regional liberal arts college.[38]

Others have also noted this distinction between quality (at whatever price) and value (that is, quality for the price). In a 1994 *Change* article, David Smith, dean of admissions and financial aid at Syracuse University, described how colleges' marketing approaches had changed between the 1970s and 1990s. According to Smith, in the 1970s colleges were judged by "general reputation," in the 1980s they were preoccupied by "market position," and in the 1990s it is the "value-to-price ratio" that determines a college's success.[39]

Three Merit Traditions

Despite the myriad of forces in Massachusetts opposed to merit aid, three of the Massachusetts colleges in our study—Holy Cross, Gordon, and

Hampshire—had merit programs. Significantly, all three faced unique circumstances when they introduced their programs, which mitigated the pressures described above.

Holy Cross first introduced merit aid in 1961 when it established its presidential scholarship program. At the time, Holy Cross was still a Jesuit secondary school and college with few lay administrators and faculty. The purpose of the program, which became known as the Bean program, was "to maintain the academic excellence which has long characterized its student body and to manifest in a special way its deep appreciation to each of those Jesuit High Schools which regularly send to Holy Cross well-qualified, Crusader scholars and gentlemen."[40] The program provided a small number of four-year scholarships to outstanding seniors from selected Jesuit high schools. The scholarship usually consisted of a full-tuition stipend unless a candidate had no demonstrable need, in which case he received an honorary $200 stipend. In 1974, Holy Cross considered, but decided against, expanding the Bean program, in part because: "Strong intramural objection from peer colleges and financial aid professionals was registered during the course of our inquiry regarding financial aid policy at these other colleges."[41] By 1974, Holy Cross was a more traditional liberal arts colleges, having legally separated from the Society of Jesus in 1967 in part to ensure access to federal funding and in part to help its efforts to become a first-tier liberal arts college.

Holy Cross's athletic grant-in-aid was a much larger part of its no-need aid expenditures than the Bean scholarships. Until 1987 Holy Cross offered sizable athletic scholarships that accounted for between 25 and 40 percent of Holy Cross's financial aid budget. Francis Delaney, director of financial aid at Holy Cross, estimated that the athletic scholarships were generally twice as much as demonstrated need, which put a severe drain on the college's budget and made it impossible for the college to meet the full need of all entering students.[42] In the mid-1980s, Anthony Maruca, vice president at Princeton, approached the members of the New England Small College Athletic Conference (NESCAC) about creating a Division I football league that could compete against the Ivy League. When the NESCAC colleges declined, Colgate and Holy Cross, which already had Division I football programs, recruited four other schools to form the Patriot League. The colleges all agreed to eliminate their athletic scholarships. Holy Cross was instrumental in the formation of the Patriot League, because Father Brooks, its president, realized, "If Holy Cross was to pursue excellence we needed to abandon athletic scholarships in favor of need-based aid."[43] Forming the Patriot League provided him with a reason that the trustees and alumni could accept. Since Holy Cross stopped awarding athletic scholarships, merit scholarships have accounted for less than 2 percent of Holy Cross's total aid budget. Moreover, Holy Cross has been able to use the money saved from eliminating its athletic scholarships to reduce the self-help portion of students' aid awards and meet the full need of a larger number of students through graduation.[44]

Gordon College has by far the largest merit aid program of all the schools in Massachusetts that we studied. In 1971, Gordon established a limited number of honors scholarships to recognize "persons of outstanding ability or those with special talents in areas such as music or athletics."[45] Gordon's merit program grew substantially in the 1980s, so that by the late 1980s Gordon was awarding merit scholarships of varying sizes to between 40 and 50 percent of its students, and since 1988 merit aid has consistently accounted for 30 percent of Gordon's financial aid budget. Gordon's merit aid program is basically defensive. A Christian liberal arts college, Gordon competes almost exclusively with other Christian schools, such as Messiah College, Wheaton College in Illinois, Houghton College, Calvin College, and Taylor University, most of which award merit aid.

Hampshire is the final Massachusetts college with a merit aid program. Like Holy Cross and Gordon, Hampshire has a relatively unique mission and competes with many colleges outside of Massachusetts, some of which offer merit scholarships. Between 1985 and 1994, Oberlin, Sarah Lawrence, Bard, New York University, and Bennington consistently appeared at the top of Hampshire's list of competitors.

Hampshire's limited endowment and experimental approach also arguably made it easier for the college to institute a merit aid program. As the authors of *The Making of a College* explained in the chapter on financing, "The original 1958 New College Committee was charged with drawing a plan which would provide 'education of the highest quality at a minimum cost per student.' Much of the spirit of that statement permeates the thinking about Hampshire."[46] Lacking an endowment, Hampshire intended to operate almost exclusively on tuition revenues. Thus, Harold Johnson, one of the college's founders and its first major benefactor, insisted that financial aid account for no more than 10 percent of the budget. Over the course of the 1970s, Hampshire's scholarship program evolved into a more traditional aid program. Hampshire's merit program, which was established in the early 1980s, is very modest. At its peak in 1985, the program accounted for 9 percent of Hampshire's financial aid budget and throughout the early 1990s it represented only 3 percent of the college's aid expenses.

Signs of More to Come

Although until 1994 only Holy Cross, Gordon, and Hampshire had merit scholarship programs, when we visited the Massachusetts schools in our study during the spring and summer of 1995, a few others seemed to be on the brink of instituting merit programs, and at least one—Wheaton—

has since offered merit scholarships to students entering in the fall of 1996. Wheaton's decision to institute merit aid did not surprise us, because when we visited the college, Gail Berson, the dean of admission and financial aid, acknowledged, "Wheaton is in a position to do something bold, especially if you are looking at the return in net revenue. Also, the faculty is more willing to invest in bright students because they are well aware of the financial commitment the college has extended to weaker students."[47] Moreover, Berson noted that Wheaton had begun to see a marginal shift of more regional applicants to less costly schools and to Massachusetts colleges that had initiated merit programs, such as Clark and Brandeis.

A 1995 article in the *Boston Globe* reported that New England was becoming a "big player" in merit aid:

> Brandeis, which tries to compete for students with the Ivy League, jumped to merit scholarships in a big way this fall, awarding 240 top students grants of $7,500 to $15,000 up from about 35 in the previous class. . . . [Boston University] added 775 half-tuition merit scholarships four years ago, because "students who in the past would have gone without aid were insisting on it." . . . Merit awards were also increased substantially at UMass and Northeastern in the last few years as the schools tried to improve their academic profiles.[48] Significantly, three of those four schools appeared on the top ten list of institutions that students admitted to Wheaton in 1994 chose to attend. Boston University was Wheaton's second biggest competitor, and Brandeis and the University of Massachusetts ranked nine and ten, respectively.

While most of the other Massachusetts schools in our study lose fewer students than Wheaton does to the universities in Massachusetts listed above, they too have been hurt by other institutions' merit aid programs. Amherst, for example, has lost some students who received merit aid at institutions such as Rice and Farleigh Dickinson. In response to such competition, Mount Holyoke, Smith, and Wellesley have all considered, but for the time being resisted, merit aid programs. In 1984, Wellesley rejected merit aid "at least for the present," explaining "We would not seek an advantage over our competitors in the area of financial aid; on the other hand, we do not feel that we should operate at a competitive *disadvantage*, if indeed that is the situation we face."[49] Consultants at Mount Holyoke reached a similar conclusion in 1994: "In our view it is not a wise option for MHC to consider unilaterally introducing merit aid, although there may be cases where MHC would be prepared to respond to merit offers from competing institutions."[50]

In 1991, Mary Maples Dunn asked Smith's Planning for 2000 Committee to "analyze the potential and feasibility of acknowledging merit in financial aid by adjusting the proportion of loan and grant and creating a group of prestigious merit scholarships."[51] Like its Sister colleges, Smith decided not to institute a formal merit aid program. In 1992, Smith did, however, begin offering 150 of its applicants with the best grades and test scores the opportunity to work on a paid research project with a faculty member for their first two years of college. Many other top-tier colleges and universities, including Connecticut College, Stanford University, and Vassar College, have recently established similar research stipends. The intention and result of these programs have been to raise the yield on the best students. A year after it began offering travel funds and $1,500 research grants to 200 of its most outstanding admitted students, Stanford reported that nearly 40 percent of the students had enrolled, compared with 29 percent from a similar pool the preceding year.[52] Colleges that offer research grants carefully distinguish them from merit scholarships. Richard W. Moll, director of admissions at Vassar, explained to a reporter from *The Chronicle of Higher Education*, "We are promising Matthew Vassar Scholars a job that will pay, but it's a research job unrelated to their financial aid."[53] Ann Wright, the director of enrollment management at Smith, concurred: "In my view, this is like paying students a certain amount for work each week, assisting a professor in research work."[54] Moll's and Wright's rationales sound very much like President Philip Jordan's defense of Kenyon's first merit scholarships in 1975: "Although honored freshmen will receive a monetary award from Kenyon, Jordan said that the system would not be a 'financial aid program, properly speaking,' but 'a reward for excellence. . . . Its purpose is to recognize academic achievement in incoming students.'"[55]

SOPHISTICATED PACKAGING

Dunn's charge to her planning committee highlighted another financial aid practice that became popular during the 1980s and early 1990s—preferential packaging. Preferential packaging, which involves structuring the most desirable candidates' need-based awards with more grant monies and fewer loans and work-study dollars, is a way to recognize academic and other distinctions within a need-based framework. Originally preferential packaging was used primarily to increase the yield on the most qualified applicants, but as enrollment managers and consultants have become increasingly sophisticated, preferential packaging has evolved into a way to spread financial dollars most effectively.

In the 1984 NACAC financial aid survey, 53 percent of the respondents reported that "a student's academic performance affects the mix of gift aid and self-help financial assistance." Unlike in the merit aid case, there was no apparent regional pattern. In every region of the country, between 38 and 61 percent of the schools preferentially packaged their awards.[56] An almost identical percentage of institutions in the 1994 NACAC survey—54 percent—"employed preferential or differential aid packaging." The practice was almost twice as common among private as public institutions (67 percent versus 34 percent).[57]

Most of the colleges in our study, whether they're located in Massachusetts or Ohio, preferentially package their awards. In 1974, the financial aid committee at Holy Cross recommended that "the Admissions Department identify a nucleus of the most outstanding applicants to the Class of 1978 who have financial need for assistance. Financial aid awards meeting full need and consisting only of scholarship aid will be made to this nucleus of applicants in an attempt to enroll more significant numbers of outstanding freshmen."[58] Although it's not clear whether such a policy was implemented then, in 1986 Holy Cross's board of trustees authorized the financial aid director "to be aggressive in his packaging method and to make full use of his resources."[59] In the early 1980s, Oberlin and Wellesley also recognized that preferential packaging was the wave of the future. In 1981, David L. Davis-Van Atta, director of institutional research at Oberlin, explained:

> I am slowly coming to believe in the principle (through necessity) of awarding aid somewhat more generously to those we wish most to enroll. This is a major departure from all previous policy and from my own thinking. . . . I believe in the theory of some differential awarding of financial aid to those most qualified and desirable candidates. This may well be a necessity in order to preserve selectivity and the class qualities that we most desire given that the full financial needs of all will no longer be met.[60]

Shortly thereafter, Wellesley considered preferential packaging: "The College will probably ease into a policy (one that is already in effect to a limited degree in a number of the Ivies and Sisters) of offering the most aid to the most desirable prospective students; in other words, they will distribute scholarships on the basis of merit and need."[61]

At least one of our colleges seemed to suffer because it did not implement a preferential packaging policy until the mid-1990s. In 1994, consultants to Mount Holyoke reported, "There are a good number of high SAT and middle- and upper-income students who are not very impressed with MHC's aid offers and they vote with their feet." The consultants discovered that Mount Holyoke did less preferential packaging than its competitors. Thus the financial aid packages of its most qualified applicants were relatively unattractive, while the packages of its less qualified applicants were relatively attractive.[62] Beginning with the class of 1994, Mount Holyoke implemented a preferential packaging experiment to enhance the yield among its "strongest domestic applicants."[63]

A few of the colleges in our study, including Amherst, differentially rather than preferentially package their awards. According to Joe Paul Case, financial aid director, differential packaging entails the awarding of more attractive packages to the most needy, rather than the academically strongest students. Although intended to ensure that the most needy students do not graduate with enormous debts, differential packaging policies have also helped colleges attract minority students without explicitly favoring them. As Denison's 1989 self-study reasoned, "We have moved to reduce the loan component in financial aid packaging for needy students, and to increase the grant to needy students for personal expenses. These changes in financial aid should be of benefit to our minority students, many of whom receive substantial financial aid."[64]

In the last few years, packaging seems to have taken another twist at some institutions. A recent article in *The Wall Street Journal* reported that colleges and universities are now basing their financial aid packages on an applicant's "'price sensitivity' to college costs, calculated from dozens of factors that all add up to one thing: how anxious the student is to attend. The more eager the student ... the less aid they can expect to get ... colleges are employing the same 'yield management' techniques used to price and fill airline seats and hotel rooms."[65] Examples of such policies include Johns Hopkins's generous packages to prospective humanities majors, Carnegie Mellon's frugal packages for early decision students, and Saint Bonaventure's attractive packages to more affluent applicants. An enrollment management toolkit received by one of the colleges in our study is consistent with such practices. The toolkit presented an econometric model for calculating enrollment probabilities, based on factors such as SAT scores, GPA, ethnic background, intended major, legacy status, and whether the student applied early decision or not. One of the three primary purposes of the model was to "find the most cost-effective packaging rules to achieve your institutional policy objectives for enrollment and net revenue."[66]

THE FUTURE OF MERIT AID

So, what do the experiences of our colleges over the last decade and a half suggest for the future of merit aid? Are the merit aid programs of today really "a return to prior policies" after a short aberrant period as Carrier suggested? Or are we entering a new era in financial aid?

In some ways Carrier's analysis is correct. It is true, for example, that most colleges and universities were able to meet the full need of all admitted students for only a very short period, if ever. That period was characterized by increased enrollments, a growing economy that needed educated workers, and an expanding federal role in financial aid funding. It is

also true that merit aid in various forms has witnessed an incredible resurgence since the 1960s and 1970s. Not only have colleges started using
criteria other than need to allocate and package awards, but they have also
adopted the language of earlier periods, once again referring to their financial aid awards as "scholarships."

Nonetheless, there have been many changes since the 1950s that make
it impossible to return to the past. Between 1955 and today, colleges and
universities have gradually embraced the concepts of access and diversity,
blurring the distinction between need-based aid and merit aid. On the one
hand, as long as colleges' applicant pools were relatively homogeneous,
whether a school used need or some "merit" criteria to allocate aid, did not
really matter. Indeed, one admissions dean whom we interviewed argued,
"We are losing the pieties of language. Need-blind aid has been a sacred
cow—particularly to those architects of the system. But really we should
get over this and do what has to be done. Access was not real in 1965." On
the other hand, many of today's so-called merit awards, at least at the
colleges in our study, are targeted at minority and other students who have
not traditionally attended liberal arts colleges. Thus, these awards increase
access. Since the 1950s, the entire magnitude of the financial aid enter-
prise has also changed. Whereas, in the 1950s financial aid represented a
small fraction of a university's budget, today it is one of the largest budget
items.

Some critics are vociferously opposed to merit aid. In a 1978 article,
Barry McCarty, director of financial aid and associate director of admissions at Lafayette College, outlined eight reasons why he opposed merit
aid. He concluded:

> My view of no-need or enticement scholarships is that they are wrong—wrong
> for students, wrong for institutions and wrong for society. . . . The topic could
> be called "Buying Brains," but that tells only part of the story. Enticement
> scholarships also buy brawn, as in the case of athletic scholarships. And in still
> other instances neither brains nor brawn is important, for in many cases an
> enticement scholarship is used simply to buy a body to fill a bed. If brains or
> brawn happen to be encased in the body, that's simply a happy coincidence.[67]

Others object to merit aid programs because they believe they will ultimately be unsuccessful. In 1983, Thomas Wenzlau warned liberal arts colleges of the limits of merit aid:

> Unfortunately, no amount of merit awards can increase the number of tal-
> ented young women and men who are of college age. Merit scholarships can
> only redistribute the talent in favor of the colleges offering the largest schol-
> arships. Merit awards could be a successful technique to make the liberal arts
> colleges more competitive with state universities in the short run. However,

neither public nor private universities will allow their best students to be diverted to liberal arts colleges. They will initiate similar but more attractive awards. Historically, the scenario for this process is clearly spelled out in the somewhat sordid past of unregulated athletic scholarships.[68]

Interestingly, supporters of merit aid also use athletic analogies. Gary L. Jones, undersecretary of education, defended merit aid in a presentation at the 1984 National Conference on Higher Education sponsored by the American Association for Higher Education. Jones cited comments that Senator Richard Lugar of Indiana made at the National Forum on Excellence in Education: "We stand on our heads to stimulate athletic achievement in spectacular fashion. Underpaid or even unpaid coaches bask in community esteem. But when it comes to academic achievement, we still have not caught the spirit. This is the crisis of American education. . . . We have been a nation at risk because we have not cared enough about learning." Jones added, "It is time for us to bring to youth with other talents the same recognition we have accorded superlative athletes—the recognition that excellence matters, that it demands extraordinary effort, and that it should be honored."[69] Some students agreed with Jones's analysis. In a 1983 *Time* article, Eric Engels, then a high school senior, insisted, "It's about time they gave the same attention and money to scholars that they do to athletes."[70]

When we began our research on this book, we were opposed to merit aid. However, as we learned more about the evolution of financial aid in this country and the particular situations and practices at the colleges in our study, we adopted a more nuanced attitude toward merit scholarships.

One of the major reason we initially opposed merit aid was because we believed that merit awards reduced the amount of money available for needy students. We now understand that our initial assessment was too simplistic. Among the colleges we studied, merit aid seems to have had at most a marginal impact on need-based allocations. Although none of the colleges that award merit aid guarantee that they will meet the full need of all admitted students, all except one have continued to increase their spending on need-based aid, even as they have expanded their merit programs. Moreover, most of the schools are funding at least 90 percent of students' demonstrated need, and need-based aid expenditures are still higher than merit ones at all of the colleges we studied. It is important to remember too that the need-based numbers probably understate the colleges' commitment to needy students, since many students with demonstrated need now receive merit scholarships. It is also not clear whether and to what extent the colleges in our study would (or even could) have continued meeting the demonstrated needs of their admitted students had they not instituted merit programs.[71]

Need-based aid was developed during a period of expanding enroll-ments when most private colleges, including all of those in our study, turned away many highly qualified students. Need-based policies reached their height in the 1960s and 1970s when federal aid funding was propor-tionally very high and appropriately targeted at ensuring access. Since the early 1980s, the situation has changed in important ways. Private institu-tions now provide the majority of financial aid grants for their students, and all but a few dozen of the most selective institutions admit the vast majority of students who apply. Spending large amounts of financial aid on students who barely meet admissions cutoffs, as some of the colleges we studied were doing before they began merit and preferential packaging programs, makes little sense for either institutions or the students thus enrolled. If you believe, as we do, that the composition of a class affects the education students receive, then colleges that no longer have competi-tive admissions should be able to invest their money to attract diverse, well-qualified students from the full range of socioeconomic backgrounds. If, as supporters of merit aid imply, the existence of such programs will encourage high school scholars, like high school athletes, to excel, so much the better.

We hope that one financial aid administrator whom we interviewed was wrong when he predicted: "It won't surprise me at all if everyone gets out of need-based aid." Need, along with academic ability, ethnicity, and other factors which affect the educational environment at a college, should con-tinue to be considered in determining financial aid packages. Although we are no longer as opposed to merit aid as we once were, we do believe that beyond some point, which we acknowledge is difficult to define, merit aid becomes more harmful than helpful. McCarty is right to criticize colleges that are just buying bodies. When a college reaches the point that it is packaging awards or allocating aid "like airplane seats," not to reflect insti-tutional priorities but merely to achieve the highest yield, then it's time for that college to start reevaluating itself. A college, unlike an airline, should care who's sitting in its seats.

> People continue to debate the future of the college for women, of the college
> of liberal arts, of the college that is independent of the university, of the col-
> lege without tax support, and of the small college. At one time or another,
> each of these varieties has been declared dead or dying. Since [we are] incor-
> porated into each allegedly moribund group, we must constantly take stock of
> the evidence that we are dying and of possible manners of escape from igno-
> minious death.[1]

WILLIAM PRENTICE, president of Wheaton College, delivered this prog-
nosis in 1967. It applies not only to Wheaton in the late 1960s but also to
most liberal arts colleges during at least some part of the 40 years that our
study covers. In a June 1996 report in the *Chronicle of Higher Education*,
one college official pessimistically predicted: "There are 3,600 institutions
and I think 1,000 are going to be out of business in 10 years."[2] While we
acknowledge that financial and competitive pressures are disquieting to the
majority of colleges and universities today, this prediction is practically a
verbatim rendering of ones expressed during the 1970s and the 1980s. In
1977, for example, Donald Pyke, coordinator of academic planning at the
University of Southern California, forecast that the number of privately
supported institutions would drop 89 percent by 2007 "unless remedial
action is taken soon."[3] Six years later, experts were more sanguine but still
concerned. George Keller reported, "Experts predict that between 10 and
30 percent of America's 3,100 colleges and universities will close their
doors or merge with other institutions by 1995."[4]

In each decade since the mid-1950s, demographic, social, consumer, and
other trends have threatened the existence of the small, independent liberal arts college. Yet, despite predictions of their demise, all of the colleges
that we studied and many others like them survived the 40 years without
undergoing a radical transformation in their character. Even those single-
sex colleges that decided to become coeducational did not change the essence of the education they offered; rather, they broadened their missions
to include members of both sexes.

In his comments on an earlier version of this work presented at the
Princeton Conference on Higher Education, David Breneman, dean of the
University of Virginia's School of Education, remarked, "The overall im-
pression I received ... was one of underlying stability in this group of

colleges."[5] Concerns over admissions, responses to fluctuations in enrollments and quality, and worries about competition did begin to take on a familiar ring as we worked through material covering the four decades. Like the quotations cited above, statements from admissions reports in the later years echoed comments from previous decades; and problems that admissions and financial aid officers faced in the 1980s and 1990s, as if for the first time, had, in fact, occurred before in their colleges' histories. In 1959 Eugene Wilson, admissions director at Amherst, recounted the oft-heard criticism he received:

> According to some faculty, today's students can't read, write or think. According to some coaches, we don't get enough students whose weight exceeds their IQ; and according to some alumni, we don't get any real men in today's crop of students—men with character and personality like the men of old. A young admissions officer would probably throw back at the critics statistics showing that in the past ten years we have had more athletic victories (and against tougher opponents) than at any time in the College's history; that we have more magnas and summas than ever before; that we have produced more than our fair share of Rhodes scholars; that more graduates are going on to graduate school; and that Smith and Mount Holyoke are as eager as ever to grab our students for husbands. (This might reflect however on the kind of girls that go to Smith and Mount Holyoke today!) A veteran admissions officer, his body well scarred by the lances of critics, will probably respond to the dissatisfied, "There is some truth in what you say. We haven't mastered the mysteries of human assessment, but wait until you see next year's class."[6]

Admissions directors today, to whom Wilson's predicament is all too familiar, may wish to remind their critics that even during the period of surplus applicants their predecessors could not craft a class to everyone's satisfaction. That the admissions struggle is in many ways the same today as it was in Dean Wilson's day would not have surprised some administrators. In 1967, a Wheaton College report predicted, "If the past is any guide to the future, our fundamental problems in 1980 will differ from those today in relatively minor ways, ways that will reflect economic and population pressures of that time but will in general be comparable. We shall be concerned about attracting our share of the students most in need of our kind of education, and we shall still be competing with the same dozen or so institutions."[7]

Recognizing the recurring nature of issues and concerns, what does the history of the past 40 years suggest both for the colleges in our study and for colleges more generally? One lesson is that predictions are only that—predictions. The use of demographic projections is a case in point. Looking at the number of 18- to 24-year-olds, colleges assumed that enrollments would continue to grow during the 1970s at much the same rate as during the 1960s. In fact, however, college-going rates declined and enrollments at many colleges, particularly private ones, suffered. The opposite occurred when analysts predicted that the decline in the number of 18-year-olds throughout the 1980s would severely damage college enrollments. When college-going rates increased over the decade, the predicted enrollment declines did not materialize to the extent expected.

In the coming decades, the population of traditional college-age students is expected to rise again. Some of the liberal arts colleges have assumed that these increases will ease their enrollment problems. What they need to remember, however, is that black and Hispanic youths make up the largest proportion of the projected growth, and colleges like those in our study have traditionally had difficulty attracting and retaining those groups. A related problem is that while the number of 18- to 24-year-olds is known, the percentage of them who will graduate from high school and enroll in college is uncertain. Additionally, because high school graduates are enrolling in college at later ages, the increase in the 18- to 24-year-old population will not necessarily translate into there being more students available to enroll at liberal arts colleges. Nor are students outside the traditional-age range a certain market for liberal arts colleges since they are often financially needy and not generally attracted to rural and suburban settings.

A second lesson involves the trade-off between size and quality. Liberal arts colleges face pressure to grow because of economies of scale. At the same time, colleges are committed to excellence so they continually try to improve the quality of their classes by enrolling students with higher scores. The experiences of our colleges suggest that these aims are often difficult to pursue simultaneously. Except for the rare periods of intense growth like the tidal wave, there has always been a strong tension between size and quality. During the tidal wave, when there was a surplus of applicants, there was no apparent size/quality trade-off; that is, colleges could and did expand significantly without compromising the academic credentials of their entering classes. When college-going rates leveled off in the late 1960s and many schools went coed, we began to see a size/quality trade-off among the less selective coed schools; colleges that continued to expand experienced greater declines in their student quality than otherwise similar colleges that maintained their enrollments. Since the mid-1970s, many colleges have focused more explicitly on the size/quality trade-off, reducing their enrollments to maintain or, in some cases, even strengthen their academic profiles.

In January 1996, a news article reported that Brandeis, a small, selective, private university, had devised a restructuring plan to deal with a projected budget shortfall of $10 million. The article recognized that Brandeis confronts financial problems similar to many private colleges and universities as federal support shrinks and the need for financial aid grows. A key element of the Brandeis plan calls for the college gradually to increase the number of undergraduates while tightening its admissions standards.[5] Brandeis is by no means the only college that is planning to expand and still maintain its quality; many liberal arts colleges, including Middlebury and Bowdoin, have recently announced plans to increase their enrollments over the next decade. These expansion plans are worrisome considering the enrollment histories of the colleges in our study. Colleges have to recognize that, for all but a handful of the most selective and prestigious institutions in this country, there is an inescapable size/quality trade-off. In the decade ahead, colleges considering enrollment increases should evaluate their own admissions situations carefully to determine how great a risk to quality expansion entails.

The overall excess supply of places for top students makes expansion a particularly risky proposition today. There are more places available at highly selective liberal arts colleges than there are high-ability students who want to attend them and who can afford to do so. Moreover, liberal arts colleges compete directly against each other, so that one college's gain is another's loss. When we examined lists of our colleges' main competitors for admitted students, we found that many of them were competing for the same students. Redoubled recruitment may move high-ability students from one institution to another within the sector, but it does not enlarge the overall pool of high-scoring candidates.

A third and related lesson involves the acknowledged stratification that exists today among the liberal arts colleges in our study. This stratification, which is evidenced by differences in SAT scores, application numbers, admit rates, and even financial aid policies, is representative of the stratification that exists nationally, with the elite institutions at one end of a broad spectrum. Contrary to the popular perception that this stratification has developed only recently, we found that stratification has existed throughout the postwar years (and probably before), at least to some extent. Ironically, the first real evidence of large differences between those colleges at the very top of the academic hierarchy and the other colleges appeared in 1965 at the height of the tidal wave. Although there had been a clear hierarchy in 1955, improvements in the admissions situations at all of the colleges in our study as a result of the tidal wave masked a growing gap between those institutions at the top and those at the bottom. This gap widened in the 1970s as all of the colleges experienced declines in their selectivity. Those coed and women's colleges that were the least selective to begin with experienced the severest declines in quality. The declining college-going population and the difficult admissions situation ushered in by the 1980s heightened the competition for students, increasing stratification still more. According to Philip Smith, dean of admissions at Williams

College, the hierarchy was then set in cement by the ranking of institutions by magazines such as *U.S. News and World Report*. Although colleges at the bottom of the hierarchy have recently achieved some gains in their quality and even in their selectivity as a result of merit aid programs and more sophisticated recruitment techniques, we do not expect the stratification to narrow appreciably. When the success of the less competitive schools begins to threaten the quality and enrollments at the most prestigious colleges, the latter institutions will respond with programs of their own. Undoubtedly, the most selective colleges will win most such competitions since they are also the wealthiest and, thus, have the most resources to spend not only to improve their offerings but also to attract and retain students.

Given the size/quality trade-off, the overall excess supply problem, and stratification of institutions, what is likely to happen to our colleges going forward? Like Breneman looking backward, we, looking forward, see strong stability even as the environment continues to change in both foreseen and unforeseen ways. This is not, however, cause for complacency. The final and strongest lesson of our study is that institutional actions matter. Although they cannot negate external forces, institutional decisions and efforts—past and present—do make a difference to an institution's ability to craft a class.

Notes

Preface Notes

1. According to the Carnegie Classification System: "Baccalaureate I colleges [are] primarily undergraduate colleges with major emphasis on baccalaureate degree programs. They award 40 percent or more of their baccalaureate degrees in liberal arts fields and are restrictive in admissions" (Carnegie Foundation for the Advancement of Teaching, *A Classification of Institutions of Higher Education* [Princeton, NJ, 1994), p. xix]. We did not include Radcliffe in our study because it merged with Harvard, or Simon's Rock College of Bard because of its unusual characteristics (it accepts students after the 10th and 11th grade and has a large associate degree program).

2. The liberal arts colleges in Ohio that agreed to participate are Antioch College, College of Wooster, Denison University, Hiram College, Kenyon College, Oberlin College, and Ohio Wesleyan University. In Massachusetts, the participating colleges are Amherst College, College of the Holy Cross, Gordon College, Hampshire College, Mount Holyoke College, Smith College, Wellesley College, Wheaton College, and Williams College.

3. Throughout this book, we quote extensively from college administrators and other commentators, many of whom have held numerous positions during their careers. We have cited their titles at the time their comments were made. Thus, the same individual may be identified in more than one way in different parts of the book.

Chapter 1 Notes

1. Gardner Patterson, *The Education of Women at Princeton: A Special Report* (Princeton, NJ: Princeton University, 24 September 1968), p. 23.

2. U.S. Department of Commerce, Bureau of the Census, *Current Population Reports*, Series P-25, Population Estimates and Projections, nos. 311, 519, 917, 100, 1022, 1095. The rate of enrollment growth during the tidal wave period was impressive even considering the "century of growth: 1870–1970" documented and described by the Carnegie Foundation for the Advancement of Teaching. (See especially Chapter 3, "Past Growth," in Carnegie Foundation for the Advancement of Teaching, *More Than Survival: Prospects for Higher Education in a Period of Uncertainty* [San Francisco: Jossey-Bass, 1975].) Whereas, over the period 1870–1970 enrollments doubled approximately every 14 to 15 years, from the mid-1950s until 1970, enrollments more than doubled in 10 years.

3. See Gareth Williams, "The Economic Approach," in *Perspectives on Higher Education*, ed. Burton R. Clark, (Berkeley: University of California Press, 1984), pp. 79–83 for a good summary of the development of human capital theory.

4. Minutes of the Faculty Meeting, 14 May 1956, Ohio Wesleyan University Archives, p. 4.

5. Wheaton's Expansion Program, 1955–1957, Wheaton College Archives, pp. 1–2.

6. Wheaton's Expansion Program, 1955–1957, p. 1

7. The Size of the Student Body at Holy Cross, 1 November 1968, College of the Holy Cross Archives, p. 1.

8. Samuel Lord, "The Paramount Problem," *Kenyon Alumni Bulletin* 23 (April–June 1965): 423.

9. Throughout this chapter, we analyze percentage rather than absolute enrollment changes, because we believe that the relative changes are more meaningful. Certainly, for a college of 500 to increase its size by 250 students requires much more planning and many more investments than for a college of 2,000 or a university of 5,000 to add the same number of students.

10. Richard Pearson, "Liberal Arts Colleges and Universal Higher Education," *The College Board Review* 60 (Summer 1966): 25.

11. Frederick Rudolph, *The American College and University: A History*, 1962 reprint with Introductory Essay and Supplemental Bibliography by John R. Thelin (Athens, GA: University of Georgia Press, 1990), pp. 485, 487.

12. Wheaton's Expansion Program, 1955–1957, p. 1

13. The Size of the Student Body at Holy Cross, p. 1.

14. Summary of Russell Survey: "Meeting Ohio's Needs in Higher Education," Minutes of Faculty Meeting, 14 May 1956, Ohio Wesleyan University Archives, p. 1.

15. Staff Paper on Ohio Wesleyan's Role in the Impending Crisis in the Colleges, October 1957, Ohio Wesleyan University Archives, p. 1.

16. Letter to President Flemming from members of the Ohio Wesleyan Faculty, 1958/59, Ohio Wesleyan University Archives, p. 3.

17. Franklin Patterson and Charles R. Longsworth, *The Making of a College* (Cambridge, MA: MIT Press, 1966) pp. 35–36.

18. Michael Robinson, "Historical Analysis of Mount Holyoke" for the Planning and Budget Task Force, 1994, Mount Holyoke College, p. 2.

19. Table 178, NCES: Digest of Educational Statistics (1995)

20. Sarah E. Turner and William G. Bowen, "Flight from the Arts and Sciences: Trends in Degrees Conferred," *Science* 250 (26 October 1990): 517–21.

21. Joan Gilbert, "The Liberal Arts College—Is It Really an Endangered Species?" *Change* 27 (September–October 1995): 38.

22. The effect of the university expansion was to concentrate higher education enrollments in a relatively small number of very large institutions. "An analysis in *Science* magazine, by Jonathan A. Gallant and John W. Prothero (1972), revealed that in '. . . the fall of 1958, only ten campuses had total enrollments of more than 20,000 and these accommodated eight percent of the national student population.' One university campus with more than 30,000 students enrolled 1 percent of the national total. By 1969, 65 campuses had enrollments exceeding 20,000 and they accounted for 27 percent of all students. Twenty-six of these campuses had more than 30,000 and accounted for 15 percent of the national enrollment." As reported in *More Than Survival*, pp. 34–35.

23. *1988 Master Plan for Higher Education. Toward the Year 2000: Higher Education in Transition*, Vol. 1 (Columbus, OH: Ohio Board of Regents, 1988), p. 11.

24. McKinsey and Company, *Financial Problems of Massachusetts Private Higher Education* (1969), pp. 1–2.

25. Richard M. Freeland, *Academia's Golden Age: Universities in Massachusetts 1945–1970* (New York: Oxford University Press, 1992), p. 316.

26. McKinsey and Company, pp. 1–4.

27. Numbers taken from David Breneman, *Liberal Arts Colleges—Thriving, Surviving or Endangered?* (Washington, DC: The Brookings Institution, 1994), p. 21. Until the Carnegie classification was developed in 1970, there was no standard way to classify institutions. The 1955 and 1970 numbers cited by Breneman come from two different sources. Since the 1970 numbers are for all private colleges, not just liberal arts colleges, they may actually understate the decline in the percentage of students enrolled at liberal arts colleges.

28. Rudolph, p. 487.

29. *More Than Survival*, p. 31.

30. Stephen P. Dresch, "College Enrollment," in *The Crisis in Higher Education*, ed. Joseph Froomkin (New York: The Academy of Political Science, 1983), p. 108. Dresch explains that the exponential growth that had characterized college enrollments was replaced by logistic growth as enrollment asymptotically approached an upper limit in the 1970s.

31. Lord, p. 3.

32. Lord, p. 5.

33. Final Report of the Committee on Coordinate Education and Related Questions, May 1969, Williams College Archives, p. 5.

34. John William Ward, "The President's Recommendation on Coeducation," *Amherst College Bulletin* 62 (October 1972): 3.

35. John William Ward, A Special Report by the President: Women at Amherst, 1975, Amherst College Archives, pp. 3–4, 6.

36. For an explanation of why Amherst enrolled women, rather than more men, see Chapter 4 on coeducation.

37. The Size of the Student Body at Holy Cross, p. 1.

38. Interim Report to the Faculty on Coeducation, Faculty Meeting, 10 March 1969, College of the Holy Cross Archives.

39. Susan Nall Bales and Marcia Sharp, "Women's Colleges—Weathering a Difficult Era with Success and Stamina," *Change* 13 (October 1981): 53. A significant part of the enrollment increases at many women's colleges, including three of those in our study, was an increase in nontraditional-age and part-time students. Although those colleges that remained all female experienced enrollment increases, the women's college sector as a whole declined as a proportion of the total college system. According to Bales and Sharp, "In 1960, 13.4 percent of college-going women were enrolled in women's institutions." By 1980, that percentage had dwindled to only 2.3 percent. This dramatic drop was due to the closure of some women's colleges, the decision by others to admit men, and the dispersal of women to formerly men's institutions.

40. David Karen, "The Politics of Class, Race and Gender: Access to Higher Education in the United States, 1960–1986," *American Journal of Education* (Feb-

ruary 1991). 212, 216. See article for a further description of where women enrolled.

41. Emily Wick, "Demography, Admissions, and the Size of the College," 11 April 1982, Mount Holyoke College Archives, p. 6.

42. 1987 Smith College Self Study, Smith College Archives.

43. Mary Ellen Ames, interviewed by Idana Goldberg, 4 May 1995, Wellesley College.

44. Eleanor Rothman, interviewed by Elizabeth A. Duffy and Idana Goldberg, 27 June 1995, Smith College.

45. Thomas Mendenhall, The Report of the President, 1974/1975, Smith College Archives, p. 10.

46. "The Weekend College," Hiram College Broadcaster (Spring–Summer 1977): 4, 6.

47. It is important to note that continuing education programs were by no means panaceas. Because they were independent and could not rely on parental contributions, older students typically had higher financial needs than traditional-age students. Moreover, such students sometimes required special support programs and residential arrangements. Finally, some colleges with large continuing education programs found it difficult to maintain an image as a selective liberal arts college, particularly in those regions where they promoted their continuing education programs.

48. "Campus Scene: Now, It's 'Buyer's Choice,'" U.S. News and World Report (15 April 1974): 53.

49. Report of the National Association of College Admissions Counselors, 1972, p. 1.

50. Memo to President Joel Smith from Burton Dunfield, 10 September 1971, Denison University Archives, p. 1.

51. More Than Survival, p. 72.

52. Notice to Community, 13 November 1973, Antioch College Archives.

53. Earl Cheit, The New Depression in Higher Education: A Study of Financial Conditions at 41 Colleges and Universities, (New York: McGraw Hill, 1971), p. 138.

54. L. Edgar Prina, "The New Deprived . . . Middle Class College Students," The Cincinnati Enquirer, Sunday, 28 January 1973, p. 5-B.

55. Donald L. Pyke, "The Future of Higher Education: Will Private Institutions Disappear in the U.S.?" The Futurist (December 1977): 371–74.

56. In the first half of the 1970s, government and community support declined for the private institutions in Massachusetts, but enrollments continued to rise at the public colleges and universities. Between 1970 and 1975, enrollments at four-year public institutions alone grew 39 percent to nearly 90,000 students (37 percent of total four-year enrollment). During the second half of the decade, however, the trend reversed itself as public enrollments leveled and enrollments at private colleges increased from 145,000 students to nearly 180,000 students (U.S. Department of Education, National Center for Education Statistics, Higher Education General Information Survey, "Fall Enrollment in Higher Education"; and Integrated Postsecondary Education Data System, "Fall Enrollment").

57. Report of the Board of Admissions to the President, October 1968, Mount Holyoke College Archives, pp. 13–14.

58. Wellesley College Admissions—Past, Present and Future, Mary Ellen Ames' Presentation to the Trustees, 8 July 1976, Wellesley College Archives, p. 2.

59. The Size of the Student Body at Holy Cross, p. 3.

60. Gilbert, p. 37.

61. Turner and Bowen, p. 520.

62. Kevin Murphy and Finis Welch, "Wage Premiums for College Graduates: Recent Growth and Possible Explanations," *Educational Researcher* (May 1989): 19. There is an interesting feedback loop between college-going rates and college wage premiums. In the late 1960s and early 1970s, the number of college graduates increased and flooded the job market, depressing wages and prompting high school graduates to seek alternative career paths rather than attend college. See also Richard B. Freeman, *The Overeducated American* (New York: Academic Press, 1976) for a full discussion of this phenomenon.

63. Memo from Van Halsey to President Longsworth, Annual Year End Report on Admission, 14 June 1973, Hampshire College Archives, p. 3.

64. Mary Ellen Crawford Ames, "Answers About Admission," *Wellesley Alumnae Magazine* (Spring 1972): 21.

65. Tim Unger, "Two Faculty Meetings Face Admissions Trends," *The (Oberlin) Observer* 3 (15 October 1981): 1.

66. Academic Quality of the Oberlin Student Body: An Historical Examination, 10 October 1980, Oberlin College Archives, pp. 1–2.

67. Report of the Retention Task Force, Minutes of the Faculty Committees, 18 January 1982, Ohio Wesleyan University Archives, p. 52.

68. Report of the Retention Task Force, 31 January 1978, Hampshire College Archives, pp. 1–2.

69. Admissions Committee Report, 20 May 1969, Ohio Wesleyan University Archives, p. 3.

70. H. P. Guttmann, "Admissions: Looking to the Future," *The Kenyon Collegian* (14 February 1974).

71. Clara R. Ludwig, Report of the Board of Admissions, October 1981, Mount Holyoke College Archives, p. 36.

72. President W. C. H. Prentice, Memo to the Members of the Planning Committee, 3 January 1968, Wheaton College Archives, pp. 1–2.

73. Admission to Amherst College: Statistics on Transfer Students, 1972, Amherst College Archives, p. 1.

74. Mary Ellen Ames, "The Admission Picture: A Sobering Look Ahead," *REALIA* (June 1984): 2. One of the few commentators not to forecast massive enrollment declines was Carol Frances, chief economist at the American Council on Education. In a book entitled *College Enrollment Trends: Testing the Conventional Wisdom*, Frances argued that higher education would witness at worst a small enrollment decrease and at best a modest 3 percent increase during the 1980s. Frances based her prediction on the possibilities that the high school graduation rate would increase above 75 percent and that greater numbers of female, ethnic minority, low-income, older, and international students would enroll in college. Fred M. Hechinger, "About Education: Fervent Arguments in High Stakes Game," *New York Times*, 3 June 1980.

75. George Keller, *Academic Strategy: The Management Revolution in American*

Higher Education (Baltimore: The Johns Hopkins University Press, 1983), p. 12. In a 1988 article entitled "Whatever Happened to the College Enrollment Crisis?" Paul E. Harrington and Andrew M. Sum (*Academe* [September–October 1988]) described the difficulty of making projections at the state level. Harrington and Sum showed how differences in projection methods among the U.S. Bureau of Statistics, the National Planning Association, and the U.S. Bureau of Economic Analysis resulted in "extraordinarily large differences" in state population forecasts for the year 2000. In Massachusetts, for example, the different methods produced results that varied by more than 1.4 million people. Whereas the Census method relied exclusively on population factors—births, deaths, aging, and migration—the other two methods adjusted population projections to reflect anticipated labor-supply requirements. Of course, college enrollments are even more difficult to estimate because they depend not only on state populations but also on high school graduation and college-going rates.

76. Committee on Priorities and Resources for the 1980s: Interim Report, April 1980, Williams College Archives, pp. 3–4.

77. Letter from David L. Davis-Van Atta, director of institutional research at Oberlin, to Richard F. Boyden, director of admissions at Denison, 5 June 1987, Denison University Archives, p. 2.

78. Harrington and Sum, p. 20.

79. Murphy and Welch, p. 18.

80. Michael O'Keefe, "Private Colleges: Beating the Odds," *Change* (March–April 1989): 11–19.

81. Thomas E. Wenzlau, "The Outlook for Liberal-Arts Colleges," in *The Crisis in Higher Education*, ed. Joseph Froomkin (New York, NY: The Academy of Political Science, 1983), p. 1.

82. Report of the Committee on a Smaller College, 25 June 1982, Ohio Wesleyan University Archives, p. 2.

83. Wick, "Demography, Admissions and the Size of the College," Mount Holyoke College, p. 1.

84. Notes from Oberlin Admissions Staff Retreat, 29 May 1981, Oberlin College Archives.

85. Carl Bewig, Remarks prepared for delivery to the Plenary Session of the Oberlin Board of Trustees, 7 June 1980, Oberlin College Archives, p. 6.

86. 1987 Smith College Self-Study.

87. Letter from Michael Good, chairman of the Committee on Admissions and Financial Aid, to Provost Ken Goodrich, 1980 Freshman Class Size, 9 November 1979, Ohio Wesleyan University Archives.

88. Wenzlau, p. 12.

89. Wick, "Demography, Admissions and the Size of the College, Mount Holyoke College," p. 25.

90. Long Range Plan for Denison University 1991–1995, January 1992, Denison University Archives, p. 3.

91. Report of the Committee for Wellesley in the Nineties, February 1992, Wellesley College Archives, p. 10.

92. Christopher Hammett and Michael Matros, "Courtship and Other Admissions Rituals," *Kenyon Alumni Bulletin* (August 1994): 22–23.

93. David W. Breneman, Comment on "Riding Waves," paper presented by Elizabeth A. Duffy and Idana Goldberg at the Princeton Conference on Higher Education, 22 March 1996, Princeton University.

Chapter 2 Notes

1. Eugene Wilson, "The National Scene," *College Admission* (1959), Amherst College Archives, p. 2.

2. Noel C. Baker, "Admissions Based on a Combination of Factors," *The Hiram Broadcaster* (Fall 1964): 4.

3. The admit rate is not necessarily a reliable indicator of the quality of a college or of its student body. As John Anderson, the longtime dean of admissions at Kenyon, pointed out in a 1994 interview, "Kenyon's academic strength would be no different if the students who enrolled had been the only ones to apply." Christopher Hammett and Michael Matros, "Courtship and Other Admissions Rituals," *Kenyon Alumni Bulletin* (August 1994): 21.

4. Charlotte Weeks, Admissions Office Annual Report 1950/51, Denison University Archives, p. 1.

5. Philip Smith and Tom Parker, interviewed by Elizabeth A. Duffy and Idana Goldberg, 12 December 1995, Williams College.

6. Benjamin Fletcher Wright, Report for 1955/56 to the Board of Trustees, the Board of Counselors, and the Alumnae of the College, 1956, Smith College Archives, p. 1.

7. Frederick Rudolph, *The American College and University: A History*, 1962, reprint with Introductory Essay and Supplemental Bibliography by John R. Thelin (Athens, GA: University of Georgia Press, 1990), p. 485.

8. Memo to Members of the Alumni Admissions Committees, 1 October 1957, Kenyon College Archives.

9. Special Alumni Committee on Admissions, A Long Range Look at Amherst Admissions, c.1954–1959, Amherst College Archives, p. 1.

10. Ambrose J. De Flumere, "Admissions Office Policy," *The Hiram Broadcaster* 32 (January 1961): 2.

11. Mary E. Chase, vice president and director of admissions, "Early Decision Plan of Admission," *Wellesley Alumnae Magazine* (March 1958): 149.

12. Barbara Ziegler, director of admissions, Memo to President Meneelly, 4 November 1960, Wheaton College Archives, p. 1.

13. Eugene Wilson, director of admissions, Admission to Amherst College in 1954: Eighth Annual Report to Headmasters and Principals, 1954, Amherst College Archives, p. 1.

14. Wright, Report for 1955/56, Smith College, p. 4. Admissions directors clearly believed since their yields in the earlier period were very high that by their admissions decisions they had more control over forming their classes. In fact, however, even in that period, the decision was largely in the hands of the students who made the key choice of where to apply.

15. Miles L. Fay, Admissions Survey Report #2—Admissions Questionnaire,

Part II: Multiple Applications, 4 November 1958, College of the Holy Cross Archives, p. 1.

16. Eugene Wilson, director of admissions, Admission to Amherst College in 1955: Ninth Annual Report to Headmasters and Principals, 1955, Amherst College Archives, p. 1.

17. Daniel D. Test, Jr., headmaster of the Westtown School, Letter to College Presidents, 24 March 1960, Amherst College Archives, pp. Summary 1–2.

18. Fred Copeland, Admissions Report, 1961, Williams College Archives, pp. 34–35.

19. Fred Copeland, Admissions Report, 3 October 1953, Williams College Archives, p. 2.

20. Fred Copeland, Admissions Report, 30 September 1955, Williams College Archives, p. 1.

21. Chase, "Early Decision Plan of Admission," pp. 149, 163.

22. Mary E. Chase, Admissions 1958/59, 30 June 1959, Wellesley College Archives, p. 1.

23. Admission to Amherst College: The O'Connell Report, 1982, Amherst College Archives, pp. 1–14.

24. Memo to Members of the Alumni Admissions Committees, 1957, Kenyon College.

25. Vernon Alden, "The Expanding Role of Admissions and Financial Aid Officers," *Student Financial Aid and Institutional Purpose*, a Colloquium on Financial Aid held by the College Scholarship Service of the College Entrance Examination Board (1963), p. 3.

26. Rudolph, p. 495 quoting from *New York Times*, 21 May 1959.

27. Wright, Report for 1955/56, Smith College, pp. 7–8.

28. Fred Copeland, Admissions Report, 1962, Williams College Archives, p. 44.

29. Philip Smith, "The Ten Percenters," *Williams Alumni Review* (Winter 1976): 2–6.

30. Bruce Haywood, Letter to President Edward Lund, 23 January 1963, Kenyon College Archives, p. 2.

31. A Long Range Plan for Wheaton College, July 1963, Wheaton College Archives, p. 4.

32. Fred Copeland, Admissions Report, 3 October 1953, Williams College Archives, p. 3.

33. Walter A. Snickenberger, "Why Recruit," *Cornell Alumni Magazine* (April 1965): 7.

34. The O'Connell Report, Amherst College, pp. 1–4.

35. John Pendleton, "Visiting Secondary Schools," *College Admission* (1959), Amherst College Archives, p. 10.

36. Minutes of Admissions Committee Meeting, 17 April 1957, Oberlin College Archives, p. 1.

37. Survey Report to the President and Board of Trustees of Ohio Wesleyan University, May 1960, Ohio Wesleyan University Archives, p. 144.

38. Minutes of the Meeting of the Admissions Committee, 13 December 1961, Oberlin College Archives, p. 3.

39. The Kenyon Case (1954), Kenyon College Archives, pp. 2–3.

40. When we use the term "private" to refer to high schools, we include both independent and parochial schools.

41. Fred Copeland, Admissions Report, 1959, Williams College Archives, p. 12.

42. Ambrose J. De Flumere, director of admission, "Admissions Office Policy," *The Hiram Broadcaster*, 32 (January 1961): 2.

43. Eugene Wilson, "The National Scene," Amherst College, p. 2.

44. Eugene Wilson, Admission to Amherst College in 1966: Twentieth Annual Report to Headmasters and Principals, 1966, Amherst College Archives, p. 2.

45. Philip Smith, director of admissions, The Work of the Admissions Office for the Class of 1984, October 1980, Williams College Archives, p. 1.

46. David L. Davis-Van Atta, Academic Quality of the Oberlin Student Body: An Historical Examination, 10 October 1980, Oberlin College Archives, p. 1.

47. The yield experiences of the colleges in our study mirrored national trends. In 1973, William Jellema published a book that looked at the financial status of private colleges and universities. He found, among other things, that the yield for his national sample of 431 private institutions "tumbled downward" between 1965 and 1969. William W. Jellema, *From Red to Black: The Financial Status of Private Colleges and Universities* (San Francisco: Jossey-Bass, 1973), p. 40.

48. Carl W. Bewig, director of admissions, Remarks prepared for delivery to the Plenary Session of the Oberlin Board of Trustees, 7 June 1980, Oberlin College Archives, p. 4.

49. Edward Wall, Admission to Amherst College in 1977: Thirty-First Annual Report to Secondary Schools, 1977, Amherst College Archives, p. 3.

50. Burton Dunfield, Memo to President Joel Smith, 10 September 1971, Denison College Archives, p. 2.

51. Philip Smith, director of admissions, The Work of the Admissions Office for the Class of 1981, September 1977, Williams College Archives, p. 3.

52. Edward Wall, Admission to Amherst College in 1978: Thirty-Second Annual Report to Secondary Schools, p. 3.

53. Edward Wall, Admission to Amherst College in 1977: Thirty-First Annual Report to Secondary Schools, p. 3.

54. "New Approaches to the Campus Community," *Wellesley Alumnae Magazine* (Summer 1974): 20.

55. Philip Smith and Tom Parker interview.

56. Fred Copeland, Admissions Report, 1972, Williams College Archives.

57. Report of the Board of Admissions, October 1972, Mount Holyoke College Archives, p. 24.

58. Bewig, Remarks for the Plenary Session, Oberlin College, p. 2.

59. Mary Ellen Crawford Ames, "Answers About Admission," *Wellesley Alumnae Magazine* (Spring 1972): 17.

60. "Campus Scene: Now, It's 'Buyer's Choice,'" *U.S. News and World Report* (15 April 1974): 53.

61. Barton-Gillet Company, R.I., Report and Recommendations on Admission and Recruiting Part II, June 1971, Wheaton College Archives, pp. 17–18.

62. Mary Ellen Ames, interviewed by Idana Goldberg, 3 May 1995, Wellesley College.

63. Smith College Admission Procedures, Office of the Treasurer, 27 October 1976, Smith College Archives, pp. 1–3.

64. Mary Ellen Ames, "Admission Forecast," *Wellesley Alumnae Magazine* (Autumn 1978): 7.

65. Philip Smith, director of admissions, The Work of the Admissions Office for the Class of 1981, September 1977, Williams College Archives.

66. Philip Smith, Admissions Report to President Chandler: Work of the Admissions Office for the Class of 1987, October 1983, Williams College Archives, p. 5.

67. Smith, The Work of the Admissions Office for the Class of 1981, Williams College.

68. Edward Wall, Admission to Amherst College in 1975: Twenty-Ninth Annual Report to Secondary Schools, 1975, Amherst College Archives, p. 2.

69. Edward Wall, Admission to Amherst College in 1976: Thirtieth Annual Report to Secondary Schools, 1976, Amherst College Archives, p. 5.

70. During the late 1960s and the early 1970s, colleges began to concentrate on attracting more black students and students from lower socioeconomic backgrounds. The history of minority recruitment and enrollments at our schools is treated more fully in Chapter 5.

71. "Administration Seeks Admissions Increase to 1,000 Applicants," *The Kenyon Collegian* XCIII, no. 22 (11 May 1967): 4.

72. John D. Kushan, director of admissions, "Admissions at Kenyon: The Problem and a Solution," source unknown, mid-1970s, Kenyon College Archives, pp. 9–10.

73. Admissions Office, Memo to Committee on Admissions and Relations to Secondary Schools, Subject: A proposal for intensified recruiting in Ohio, 30 April 1970, Oberlin College Archives, p. 1.

74. Philip Smith, Admissions Report for 1975/76, 1976, Williams College Archives, p. 8.

75. Hampshire College Self-Study, February 1978, p. 85.

76. Mary Ellen Ames, director of admission, interviewed by Elizabeth Shain Green '54, *Wellesley Alumnae Magazine*, (Autumn 1978): 1.

77. Bewig, Remarks for the Plenary Session, Oberlin College, pp. 1–3.

78. William R. Mason, assistant director of admissions, "Increase in Popularity of the College Brings Era of Change to Admissions Office," *Williams Alumni Review* (Fall 1974): 1–3.

79. Peter Wells, "Applying to College: Bulldog Bibs and Potency Myths," in *Hurdles: The Admissions Dilemma in American Higher Education,* eds. Herbert S. Sacks, M.D., and Associates (New York: Atheneum, 1978), pp. 60–61.

80. Office of Admissions, Report to the President, 10 March 1972, Oberlin College Archives, pp. 8–9.

81. Jonathan Harr, "The Admissions Circus," *New England Monthly* (April 1984): 50.

82. Doermann cited in Mary Ellen Ames, "Admission Forecast," *Wellesley Alumnae Magazine* (Autumn 1978): 6.

83. Mary Ellen Ames, "The Admissions Picture: A Sobering Look Ahead," *REALIA* (June 1984): 2.

84. Dean Whitla, "The Admissions Equation," *Change* (November/December 1984): 22.

85. Hammett and Matros, "Courtship and Other Admissions Rituals," Kenyon College, p. 19.

86. Bewig, Remarks for the Plenary Session, Oberlin College, p. 2.

87. Thomas E. Wenzlau, "The Outlook for Liberal-Arts Colleges," in *The Crisis in Higher Education*, ed. Joseph Froomkin (New York: The Academy of Political Science, 1983). p. 6.

88. George Keller, *Academic Strategy: The Management Revolution in American Higher Education* (Baltimore: The Johns Hopkins University Press, 1983).

89. Summary of Admissions History, Prepared by Oberlin College Archives.

90. Samuel Carrier and David L. Davis-Van Atta, "Using the Institutional Research Office," in *Managing College Enrollments*, New Directions for Higher Education, no. 53, ed. D. Hossler, (San Francisco: Jossey-Bass, 1986), p. 73.

91. Ross Peacock, Why Some Say Yes and Most Say No: Factors Influencing Yield, 1992, Oberlin College Office of Institutional Research, p. 2.

92. Robert Zemsky, "Consumer Markets and Higher Education," *Liberal Education* (Summer 1993): 16.

93. Emily Wick, Demography, Admissions and the Size of the College, 11 April 1982, Mount Holyoke College Archives, pp. 16-23.

94. Anita Smith, interviewed by Elizabeth A. Duffy and Idana Goldberg, 21 June 1995, Mount Holyoke College.

95. Committee on Admissions and Financial Aid, Faculty Meeting: Agenda Supplement, 1 February 1995, Mount Holyoke College Archives, p. 3.

96. Wick, Demography, Admissions and the Size of the College, Mount Holyoke College, p. 13.

97. Henry Bedford, dean of admissions, Admission to Amherst College in 1983: Thirty-Seventh Annual Report to Secondary Schools, 1983, Amherst College Archives, p. 1.

98. Deena Mirow, "Colleges Being Taken by Storm," source unknown, 1987, Kenyon College Archives.

99. Dean K. Whitla, Irving L. Broudy, and Ann W. Walka, Candidate Overlap Study (Harvard College, March 1967) Antioch College Archives, p. 7.

100. Whitla, Broudy, and Walka, pp. 9-10.

101. P. F. Kluge, *Alma Mater* (Reading, MA: Addison-Wellesley, 1993), p. 121.

102. Hayden Schilling, interviewed by Elizabeth A. Duffy and Idana Goldberg, 13 July 1995, College of Wooster.

103. "A Fresh Choice for Frosh," *Stanford Observer* (Winter 1995): 3.

104. Karen W. Arenson, "Top Colleges Filling More Slots with Students Who Apply Early," *New York Times* 14 February 1996, pp. A-1, B-12.

105. Mirow.

106. Dean Whitla, "The Admissions Equation," p. 22.

107. Harr, p. 58.

108. E. Nicholas Brown, "Making Sense of the US News Rankings," *The Kenyon Observer* (November 1991): 8.

109. Harr, p. 54.

110. Brown, p. 8.

111. See, for example, Steve Stecklow, "Cheat Sheets: College Inflate SATs and Graduation Rates in Popular Guidebooks, Schools Say They Must Fib to U.S. News and Others to Compete Effectively," *Wall Street Journal*, 5 April 1995, pp. 1, A–8; and Steven Knowlton, "Hyping Numbers at Colleges," *New York Times Education Life*, 8 January 1995, pp. 48–49.

112. Brown, pp. 8–9.

113. Brown, p. 8.

114. Christopher Shea, "Rankings that Roil Also Gain Influence," *Chronicle of Higher Education* (22 September 1995): A53.

115. Mirow.

116. Henry Bedford, dean of admissions, Admission to Amherst College in 1985: Thirty-Ninth Annual Report to Secondary Schools, 1985, p. 2.

117. Kluge, p. 121.

118. "Hiram's Plan for Action," *The Hiram Broadcaster* (Winter 1986): 15.

119. R. Stanton Hales, interviewed by Elizabeth A. Duffy and Idana Goldberg, 13 July 1995, College of Wooster.

120. Richard Moll, "The Scramble to Get the New Class," *Change* (March–April 1994): 1. What "delivering bottom line net tuition revenue" means is enrolling the right size class so that after financial aid and other discounting the institution is able to achieve a positive revenue from tuition. As many colleges have discovered, it is possible to have increased enrollments yet not have a positive tuition revenue if most of the students are attracted by generous financial incentives.

121. David R. Treadwell, Jr., "If the Numbers Don't Look Good, Dump the Dean," *The Chronicle of Higher Education* (2 November 1994): A72.

Chapter 3 Notes

1. See, for example, Randall G. Chapman, "Non-Simultaneous Relative Importance-Performance Analysis: Meta Results from 80 College Choice Surveys with 55,276 Respondents," *Journal of Marketing for Higher Education* 4 (1993): 405–22; Randall G. Chapman and Rex Jackson, *College Choices of Academically Able Students: The Influence of No-Need Financial Aid and Other Factors* (New York: College Entrance Examination Board, 1987); Gregory A. Jackson, "Financial Aid and Student Enrollment," *Journal of Higher Education* 49 (1978): 548–74; Charles F. Manski and David A. Wise, *College Choice in America* (Cambridge, MA: Harvard University Press, 1983); Richard R. Spies, *The Effect of Rising Costs on College Choice: The Third in a Series of Studies on This Subject* (Princeton, NJ: Princeton University Press, 1990).

2. Committee on Admissions Annual Report, 18 May 1959, Ohio Wesleyan University Archives, p. 2.

3. See, for example, Andrew Hacker, "Affirmative Action: The New Look," review of *The Case Against the SAT* by James Crouse and Dale Trusheim, *The New York Review of Books* (12 October 1989): 64–65; Lionel S. Lewis and Paul William Kingston, "The Best, the Brightest, and the Most Affluent: Undergraduates at Elite Institutions," *Academe* (November–December 1989): 28–33.

4. Peter H. Wells, "Applying to College: Bulldog Bibs and Potency Myths," in *Hurdles: The Admissions Dilemma in American Higher Education,* eds. Herbert S. Sacks, M.D., and Associates (New York: Atheneum, 1978), p. 65. In the Epilogue to the same book, Joseph Katz also describes some of the inadequacies of standardized tests, pp. 327–29.

5. Admission to Amherst College: The O'Connell Report, 1982, Amherst College Archives, pp. 1–9.

6. Fred M. Hechinger, "About Education: Aptitude Tests Stir a Debate—But Is It Moot?" *New York Times,* 4 March 1980, p. C-4.

7. Joseph Katz, "Epilogue: The Admissions Process—Society's Stake and the Individual's Interest," p. 321 in Sacks, ed. (1978).

8. Wells, p. 66.

9. All class rank numbers in this chapter are reported as a percentage of ranked students. This method is valid only if the class distribution of the ranked students is similar to the class distribution of the unranked students, an assumption that we have been told generally holds, but which we have not independently validated.

10. Emily Wick, "Demography, Admissions, and the Size of the College," 11 April 1982, Mount Holyoke College Archives, p. 12.

11. Information in this section is drawn primarily from three sources: Christopher Jencks and David Riesman, "Admissions Requirements in the Public and Private Sectors," in The Academic Revolution (Garden City, NY: Doubleday, 1968), pp. 279–90; Richard Farnum, "Prestige in the Ivy League: Democratization and Discrimination at Penn and Columbia, 1890–1970," in *The High-Status Track: Studies of Elite Schools and Stratification,* eds. Paul William Kingston and Lionel S. Lewis (New York: State University of New York Press, 1990), pp. 75–104; David Wilmouth, "Should the SAT Be a Factor in College Admissions?" (28 March 1991), unpublished ms.

12. Jencks and Riesman, pp. 281.

13. Farnum, pp. 79–80.

14. Jencks and Riesman, p. 281.

15. Jencks and Riesman, pp. 281–82.

16. Robert J. Havighurst, *American Higher Education in the 1960s* (Columbus, OH: Ohio State University Press, 1960), p. v.

17. Havighurst, pp. v–vi.

18. Havighurst, p. 2.

19. Letter from Bruce Haywood to President Edward Lund, 23 January 1963, Kenyon College Archives.

20. Admission to Amherst College: The O'Connell Report, 1982, pp. 1–3.

21. Admissions 1958/59, 30 June 1959, Wellesley College Archives, p. 2.

22. Ambrose J. De Flumere, "Admissions Office Policy," *The Hiram Broadcaster* 32 (January 1961): v.

23. Report of the Admission Committee, Gordon College Institutional Self-Study, 1969, Gordon College Archives, p. 4.

24. David McClelland, "Encouraging Excellence," *Daedalus: Journal of the American Academy of Arts and Sciences* 90 (1961): 711, cited in Vernon Alden, "The Expanding Role of Admissions and Financial Aid Officers," *Student Financial*

Aid and Institutional Purpose (Princeton, NJ: College Entrance Examination Board, 1963), p. 1.

25. Frederick Rudolph, *The American College and University: A History*, 1962, reprint with Introductory Essay and Supplemental Bibliography by John R. Thelin (Athens, GA: University of Georgia Press, 1990), p. 492.

26. A Long Range Plan for Wheaton College, 1963, Wheaton College Archives, pp. 3–4.

27. Fred Copeland, Admissions Report 1965–1966, Fall 1966, Williams College Archives, p. 11.

28. Admissions Report to the Faculty, September 1965, Smith College Archives.

29. Havighurst, p. 43.

30. Interdepartmental memorandum from Dean Wilson to President Cole, 12 September 1956, Amherst College Archives, p. 3.

31. Fred Copeland, Admissions Report 1966/67, Fall 1967, Williams College Archives, p. 3.

32. Letter from Dean Whitla, director of institutional research at Harvard University, to Van Halsey, director of admission at Hampshire, 3 February 1970, p. 6.

33. Although Ford funding lasted for only 10 years, Williams continued the Ten Percent Program beyond the grant period. In fact, even today stretch admits are sometimes referred to in admissions deliberations as "ten percenters."

34. In 1971, the College Board changed the way it calculated the mean score for the nation. Prior to 1971, all scores from a given year were counted, even if some people had taken the test more than once. Since 1971, each test taker has been counted only once—in the cohort for her or his latest score. We do not believe that this change significantly affects the decline in reported national scores over the period we are discussing.

35. Humphrey Doermann as cited in Wellesley College Admissions—Past, Present and Future, Mary Ellen Ames' Presentation to the Trustees, 8 July 1976, Wellesley College Archives, p. 4. Doermann published numerous pieces about the shrinking pool of bright and affluent students, including *Crosscurrents in College Admissions* (New York: Teachers College Press, Columbia University, 1969).

36. Letter to the general faculty from President Robert Good, 8 April 1977, Denison University Archives.

37. Mary Ellen Ames, Annual Report to the President, Board of Admission, 1973–1974, 27 August 1974, Wellesley College Archives, p. 13.

38. Interdepartmental Memo: From Dean Wall to Professor Chickering, 26 November 1973, Amherst College Archives.

39. Report on Admissions, 1969, Amherst College Archives, p. 2.

40. Report of the Committee on Coordinate Education and Related Questions, May 1969, Williams College Archives.

41. Interim Report to Faculty on Coeducation, 10 March 1969, College of the Holy Cross Archives, pp. 2–4.

42. Patrick Shannon, "Coeducation at Holy Cross: A Dissenting Opinion," April 1969, College of the Holy Cross Archives, p. 22.

43. Edward Wall, Office of Admissions, Report to the Faculty, 6 September 1973, Amherst College Archives, p. 3.

44. Admissions at Kenyon: The Problem and a Solution, c.1974, Kenyon College Archives, p. 9.

45. Wellesley College Admissions—Past, Present and Future, p. 2.

46. Mary Ellen Ames, "Admission Forecast," *Wellesley Alumnae Magazine* (Autumn 1978): 6.

47. Carl Bewig, Remarks prepared for delivery to the Plenary Session of the Oberlin Board of Trustees, 7 June 1980, Oberlin College Archives, p. 2.

48. Note we included only 10 of the 16 colleges in Figure 3.2, because we had incomplete or incompatible information for the other six schools. We do not believe that the including the other six colleges would have changed the general trends discussed in the text.

49. The O'Connell Report, Amherst College, pp. 1–26 & 1–28.

50. David L. Davis-Van Atta, "Academic Quality of the Oberlin Student Body: An Historical Examination," 10 October 1980, Oberlin College Archives, p. 2.

51. Davis-Van Atta, "Academic Quality," Oberlin College, p. 3.

52. Profile of Denison University 1952–1972, 27 February 1962, Denison University Archives.

53. We averaged 1993 and 1994 SAT scores in order to minimize the effect of a particularly good or bad year at a college.

54. We averaged the quintile percentages for the years 1990–1994, to eliminate problems caused by idiosyncratic years. Again, a growing number of high schools have stopped ranking their students. Thus, the percentages shown in the figure and discussed in the text use "ranked students" rather than "all students" as the base.

55. Only three of our colleges appear among *Barron's* "most competitive" group: Amherst, Wellesley, and Williams. All three are in the group of high SAT colleges that also improved their SAT scores during this period.

56. Philip J. Cook and Robert H. Frank, "The Growing Concentration of Top Students at Elite Schools," in *Studies in Supply and Demand in Higher Education,* eds. Charles Clotfelter and Michael Rothschild (Chicago: University of Chicago Press, 1993), p. 130.

57. Randall G. Chapman and Rex Jackson, *College Choices of Academically Able Students: The Influence of No-Need Financial Aid and Other Factors* (New York: College Entrance Examination Board, 1987).

58. Conversation between the authors and Philip Smith at Williams College, July 1994.

59. On Sustaining Intellectual Quality; Self-Study Report of Denison University submitted to the North Central Association of Colleges and Schools for the Purpose of Evaluation and Continued Accreditation at the Bachelors Level, December 1979, Denison College Archives, pp. 15–16. We look in detail at the growth of financial aid and the recent history of merit aid in Part III.

60. The sixth school improved its score by admitting men.

61. Letter from Michele Myers to board of trustees, Denison University, May 1995.

62. Tom Parker, Report of the Director of Admissions 1992/93, October 1993, Williams College Archives.

63. George Dehne, "Thriving or Surviving?: The American Selective College," Keynote address presented to the Annapolis Group, 13 June 1993.

64. Christopher Hammett and Michael Matros, "Courtship and Other Admissions Rituals," *Kenyon Alumni Bulletin* (August 1994): 23.

65. Jeffrey Owing, Marilyn McMillen, and John Burkett, "Making the Cut: Who Meets Highly Selective College Entrance Criteria?" National Center for Education Statistics (Washington, DC: U.S. Department of Education, Office of Educational Research and Improvement, April 1995).

66. Mary Maples Dunn, Planning for 2000, 1991, Smith College Archives, p. 3.

67. Report of the Committee for Wellesley in the Nineties, February 1992, Wellesley College Archives, p. 9.

68. Strategic Planning Working Paper, October 1992, Kenyon College Archives, pp. 1, 3.

69. Strategic Planning Working Paper, Kenyon College.

70. Philip Smith, "A Time of Change," *Williams Alumni Review* (Fall 1986): 17.

71. Ben Gose, "Second Thoughts at Women's Colleges," *The Chronicle of Higher Education* (10 February 1995): A22–24.

72. John Pendleton, "Visiting Secondary Schools," *College Admission* (1959), Amherst College Archives, p. 10.

Chapter 4 Notes

1. For more information on early college building in America, see Frederick Rudolph, *The American College and University: A History*, 1962, reprint with Introductory Essay and Supplemental Bibliography by John R. Thelin (Athens, GA: University of Georgia Press, 1990), and George P. Schmidt, *The Liberal Arts College* (New Brunswick, NJ: Rutgers University Press, 1957).

2. Gail B. Griffin, "Emancipated Spirits: Women's Education and the American Midwest," *Change* (January–February 1984), p. 33.

3. Griffin, p. 34.

4. Rudolph, p. 314.

5. Rudolph, p. 314.

6. Griffin, p. 35.

7. Roberta Frankfort, *Collegiate Women* (New York: New York University Press, 1977), p. 31, as cited in Patricia Robinson, "A Study of Declining Enrollment Trends in Women's Colleges in America and the Impact on Brenau College," Ph.D. diss., Nova University, May 1990, p. 14.

8. Mount Holyoke College website: http://www.mtholyoke.edu/.

9. Carolyn Platt, "The Winds of Change: Case Studies of College Culture and Decision Making," Ph.D. diss., Stanford University, 1988), p. 105.

10. Augmented College Planning Committee, Smith College and the Question of Coeducation, A Report with Recommendations Submitted to the Faculty and the Board of Trustees, April 1971, Smith College Archives, p. 3.

11. Patrick Shanahan, "Coeducation at Holy Cross: A Dissenting Opinion," April 1969, College of the Holy Cross Archives, p. 5.

12. Shanahan, "A Dissenting Opinion," College of the Holy Cross, p. 8.

13. Griffin, p. 36.

14. J. Kevin Cool, "A Woman's Place: The Highs and Lows of 125 Years of Coeducation," *Colby Alumni Magazine* (November 1995): 7.

15. Jill Ker Conway, *True North: A Memoir* (New York: Alfred A. Knopf, 1994), p. 236.

16. Barbara Solomon, *In the Company of Educated Women* (New Haven: Yale University Press, 1985), p. 49, as cited in Robinson, p. 15.

17. Final Report of the Committee on Coordinate Education and Related Questions, 27 May 1969, Williams College Archives, p. 10.

18. Report of the Amherst Visiting Committee on Coeducation, Spring 1974, Amherst College Archives, p. 54.

19. Final Report of the Committee on Coordinate Education and Related Questions, Williams College, pp. 10–11.

20. Commission on the Future of the College, "Report to the Trustees: Composition of the Student Body," March 1971, Wellesley College Archives, p. 44.

21. Gardner Patterson, *The Education of Women at Princeton: A Special Report*, (Princeton, NJ: Princeton University Press, 24 September 1968), p. 7. Hereafter referred to as the Patterson Report.

22. Patterson Report, p. 52.

23. Bruce Haywood, "The Paramount Problem—and a Solution," *Kenyon Alumni Bulletin* 3 (July–September 1965): 4.

24. Haywood, "The Paramount Problem—and a Solution," p. 4.

25. Final Report of the Committee on Coordinate Education and Related Questions, Williams College, p. 7.

26. Interim Report to Faculty on Coeducation, 10 March 1969, College of the Holy Cross Archives, p. 4.

27. Interim Report to Faculty on Coeducation, College of the Holy Cross, p. 4.

28. Edward Wall, Report to the Faculty, 6 September 1973, Amherst College Archives, p. 2.

29. Wall, Report to the Faculty, 6 September 1973, Amherst College, p. 3.

30. Report of the Amherst Visiting Committee on Coeducation, p. 56.

31. Wall, Report to the Faculty, 6 September 1973, Amherst College, p. 2.

32. Final Report of the Committee on Coordinate Education and Related Questions, Williams College, p. 4.

33. Patterson Report, p. 10.

34. Patterson Report, p. 52.

35. Final Report of the Committee on Coordinate Education and Related Questions, Williams College, p. 4.

36. See the Patterson Report (pp. 13–14) for a discussion of the distribution of men and women in different disciplines.

37. Patterson Report, p. 11.

38. Shanahan, "A Dissenting Opinion," College of the Holy Cross, p. 10.

39. Interim Report to Faculty on Coeducation, College of the Holy Cross, Sec. 3, p. 3.

40. Haywood,"The Paramount Problem—and a Solution," p. 4.

41. Patterson Report, p. 52.

42. Shanahan, "A Dissenting Opinion," College of the Holy Cross, pp. 7, 8.

43. Shanahan, "A Dissenting Opinion," College of the Holy Cross, p. 24.

44. Patterson Report, p. 52.

45. "Better Coed Than Dead," *Time* (5 May 1967): 57.

46. John E. Lockwood, "Williams in a Changing World," *Williams Alumni Review* (August 1968): 15.

47. Report of the Amherst Visiting Committee on Coeducation, p. 13.

48. Report of the Amherst Visiting Committee on Coeducation, pp. 57–58.

49. Report of the Amherst Visiting Committee on Coeducation, p. 56.

50. Patterson Report, p. 19.

51. Interim Report to Faculty on Coeducation, College of the Holy Cross, p. 2.

52. Holy Cross, for example, described at great length what renovations in the residence halls for women would be required: "Private dressing areas next to the shower stalls, removing the urinals, providing large sinks for washing hair, a bathtub on each floor, a hair drying and laundry room, improving the ventilation system in the bathrooms of men's and women's residence halls, light kitchen facilities, full-length mirrors, additional closet space, floor lounges, one reception area in each Hall, and an office for a House Chaplain" (Interim Report to Faculty on Coeducation, College of the Holy Cross, Sec. 3, p. 1). It is ironic that planning committees remembered closet space and full-length mirrors yet overlooked the proverbial "elephant in the room."

53. Clara Ludwig, Report from the Board of Admissions to the President, October 1967, Mount Holyoke College Archives, pp. 20–21.

54. "Better Coed Than Dead," p. 57.

55. "Boys and Girls Together," *Newsweek* (27 January 1967): 68.

56. See, for example, Kate Millet, "Libbies, Smithies, Vassarites," *Change* (September–October 1970); or Marcia K. Sharp, "Women's Colleges and the Women's Movement," *The Education Digest* (February 1992).

57. Report of the Board of Admissions, October 1968, Mount Holyoke College Archives, p. 11.

58. Platt, p. 37.

59. See Platt for an extended discussion of the factors involved in Vassar's decision to become coed. Platt argued that a number of characteristics contributed to Vassar's decision to admit men including a history of trying to blend with the dominant culture and changing with historical trends; a tension in its own ideology of education whether to prepare women for service to family or for leadership in careers; and an ideal that change is necessary and welcome. In general, Platt found that institutional culture played a critical role in the coeducational decisions of institutions.

60. *Wellesley Alumnae Magazine* (Summer 1969): p. 5, as cited in Platt, p. 131.

61. "Report to the Trustees: Composition of the Student Body," Wellesley College, p. 43.

62. "Report to the Trustees: Composition of the Student Body," Wellesley College, p. 44.

63. Letter from Ruth M. Adams to the board of trustees, 3 March 1971, Wellesley College Archives, in Commission on the Future of the College, Report to the Trustees, p. 71.

64. Platt, p. 154. Platt offers a convincing analysis of the institutional characteris-

tics and external factors that contributed to the decision-making process at Wellesley and the board of trustees' surprising vote.

65. Smith College and the Question of Coeducation, p. 13.
66. Smith College and the Question of Coeducation, p. 4.
67. Smith College and the Question of Coeducation, pp. 8–9.
68. Smith College and the Question of Coeducation, p. 14.
69. Clara Ludwig, Report of the Board of Admissions to the President, October 1968, Mount Holyoke College Archives, p. 19.
70. "Girl and Boy at Yale," *Newsweek* (15 December 1969): 63.
71. Thomas Meehan, "At Bennington the Boys Are the Coeds," *New York Times Magazine*, 21 December 1969.
72. Meehan.
73. Joy K. Rice and Annette Hemmings, "Women's Colleges and Women Achievers: An Update," in *Reconstructing the Academy: Women's Education and Women's Studies*, eds. Elizabeth Minnich et al. (Chicago: University of Chicago Press, 1988), p. 222.
74. Caroline Bird, "Women's Colleges and Women's Lib," *Change* (April 1972): 65.
75. Rice and Hemmings, p. 222.
76. Mariam K. Chamberlain, ed. *Women in Academe: Progress and Prospects* (New York, NY: Russell Sage Foundation, 1988), p. 115.
77. Pauline Tompkins, "What Future for the Women's College?" *Liberal Education* 58 (May 1972): 300.
78. Charles C. Cole, Jr., "A Case for the Women's College," *College Board Review* 83 (Spring 1972): 20.
79. Jill Ker Conway, "Women's Place," *Change* (March 1978): 9.
80. See Robinson for a good summary of these many studies.
81. Jill Ker Conway, "Are Women's Colleges Necessary Today? Yes: They Teach Self-Confidence," *New York Times*, 13 November 1977, Sec. 12, p. 13.
82. "Why Can't a Woman Be More?" *Time* (5 October 1987): 75–76.
83. Douglas Lederman, "To Survive, Queens College Switched to Coeducation and Revamped Its Curriculum—and Now It's Added a Full-Scale Sports Program," *The Chronicle of Higher Education* (21 February 1990): A43.
84. Wheaton College Institutional Self-Study, 1 February 1989, Wheaton College Archives, pp. 1–13.
85. Wheaton College Institutional Self-Study, pp. 1–14.
86. Wheaton College Institutional Self-Study, pp. 1–14.
87. Wheaton College Institutional Self-Study, pp. 1–17.
88. "A Sisterhood Under Siege: Will Wheaton Go Coed?" *Newsweek* (30 March 1987): 77.
89. Wheaton College Institutional Self-Study, pp. 1–15.
90. Wheaton College Institutional Self-Study, pp. 1–16.
91. Wheaton College Institutional Self-Study, pp. 1–17.
92. Report of the Committee for Wellesley in the Nineties, February 1992, Wellesley College, p. 6.
93. Report of the Committee for Wellesley in the Nineties, p. 8.

94. Mary Maples Dunn, Planning for 2000, 1991, Smith College, p. 5.

95. Cool, p. 7.

96. Haywood, "The Paramount Problem—and a Solution," p. 4.

97. Haywood, "The Paramount Problem—and a Solution," p. 4.

98. "Letters" by William R. Chadeayne, secretary of the board of trustees, in *Kenyon Alumni Bulletin* (November 1972), reproduced in the *Kenyon Alumni Bulletin* (March 1995), p. 3.

99. Interim Report to Faculty on Coeducation, College of the Holy Cross, p. 1.

100. Final Report of the Committee on Coordinate Education and Related Questions, Williams College, p. 8.

101. Patterson Report, p. 28.

102. Patterson Report, p. 21.

103. Final Report of the Committee on Coordinate Education and Related Questions, Williams College, p. 9.

104. "Report to the Trustees: Composition of the Student Body," Wellesley College, p. 45.

105. Father John E. Brooks, interviewed by Elizabeth A. Duffy, 28 April 1995, College of the Holy Cross.

106. Patterson Report, p. 24.

107. Patterson Report, p. 21.

108. William G. Bowen, Report of the President, Princeton University, January 1975, p. 16.

109. William G. Bowen, Report of the President, Princeton University, p. 18.

110. William G. Bowen, Report of the President, Princeton University, pp. 17–18.

111. Report of the Committee on College Expansion, July 1975, Williams College Archives, p. 8.

112. Report of the Committee on College Expansion, Williams College, pp. 9–10.

113. Report of the Committee on College Expansion, Williams College, pp. 11–12.

114. The 12 original members of the Twelve College Exchange were Amherst, Bowdoin, Connecticut, Dartmouth, Mount Holyoke, Smith, Trinity, Vassar, Wellesley, Wesleyan, Wheaton, and Williams.

115. Clara Ludwig, Report of the Board of Admissions to the President, October 1968, Mount Holyoke College Archives, p. 19.

116. Clara Ludwig, Report of the Board of Admissions to the President, October 1968, Mount Holyoke College Archives, p. 20.

117. Smith College and the Question of Coeducation, p. 13.

118. John William Ward, "The President's Recommendation on Coeducation," *Amherst College Bulletin* 62 (October 1972): 4.

119. Christopher Jencks and David Riesman, *The Academic Revolution* (Garden City, New York: Doubleday, 1968), pp. 297–98.

Chapter 5 Notes

1. We include African American, Asian American, and Hispanic American students when we refer to "minority enrollment." Throughout the chapter, except

when we are quoting directly from sources, we use the term "black" to refer to students of African American or Caribbean American descent. Before the late 1960s, "Negro" seemed to be the term of choice.

2. Administrative History of the Admissions Office, 1902–1988, Oberlin College Archives, p. 1.

3. Appendix I—Historical Statement about the Education of Negro Students at Antioch College in Supplementary Program for Negro Students, 11 February 1964, Antioch College Archives, p. 1.

4. Historical Statement about the Education of Negro Students at Antioch College, p. 1.

5. Historical Statement about the Education of Negro Students at Antioch College, p. 2.

6. Frank Bowles and Frank A. DeCosta, *Between Two Worlds: A Profile of Negro Higher Education* (New York: McGraw-Hill, 1971), pp. 77–78.

7. Bowles and DeCosta, pp. 78–79.

8. Clara Ludwig, director of admissions, Report from the Board of Admissions to the President, 31 July 1964, Mount Holyoke College Archives, p. 14.

9. See Clara Ludwig, director of admissions, Report from the Board of Admissions to the President, 31 July 1964, Mount Holyoke College Archives, pp. 13–15 for a fuller description of the program.

10. Ludwig, Report from the Board of Admissions to the President, Mount Holyoke College, p. 14.

11. Philip Wick, "Admissions Assistant Reveals Marked Rise in Negro Candidates," *Williams Record* (20 March 1964): 1.

12. Disadvantaged Students, 1964/65, Williams College Archives, p. 32.

13. See Report of the Upward Bound Project, May 1967, Ohio Wesleyan University Archives, p. 1 for a fuller description of the program.

14. S. A. Kendrick, "The Coming Segregation of Our Selective Colleges," *College Board Review* 66 (Winter 1967/68): 6.

15. Report of the National Advisory Commission on Civil Disorders, Otto Kerner, Chairman (Washington, DC: Government Printing Office, 1968), p. 1, cited in *One Third of a Nation, A Report of the Commission on Minority Participation in Education and American Life* (American Council on Education, Education Commission of the States, May 1988), p. 17.

16. Class of 1970: Report of Admissions in 1966, Amherst College Archives, p. 3.

17. Ruth M. Adams, "From the College President," *Wellesley Alumnae Magazine* (Autumn 1968): 8.

18. A Proposal for Increased Recruitment of Minority Students, 1971, Oberlin College Archives, p. 1.

19. Frampton Davis, "David vs. Goliath," *Kenyon Alumni Bulletin* XXIII (April–June 1966): 13.

20. A Proposal for Increased Recruitment of Minority Students, Oberlin College, p. 2.

21. "Faculty Approves Expanded Effort to Attract More Qualified Blacks," *Williams Record* (14 January 1969).

22. A Proposal for Increased Recruitment of Minority Students, Oberlin College, p. 3.

23. Minutes of the Faculty Committee on Admission and Financial Aid, 18 March 1970, Amherst College Archives.

24. The Antioch New Directions Program, 1970, Antioch College Archives, p. 68.

25. Robert Davis, associate director of admissions, Report on the Recruitment and Selection of "New Directions" Students for the 1970 Entering Class, 2 June 1970, Antioch College Archives, p. 2.

26. Memo from the 1968/69 Admissions Committee to the Administrative Council Re: Proposed Addendum to the Admissions Policy Statement, 28 January 1969, Antioch College Archives, p. 6.

27. Annual Report of the Board of Admission, Attachment #3, Summary Statement, 4 May 1973, Wellesley College Archives.

28. Barbara Clough, "Admission: Wellesley's Response to a Changing World," *Wellesley Alumnae Magazine* (Spring 1969): 8.

29. Gordon College Self-Study, 1971, Gordon College Archives, p. 109.

30. A Proposal for Increased Recruitment of Minority Students, Oberlin College, p. 8.

31. Randy Bongarten, Minority Opinion, 1971, Oberlin College Archives, p. 2.

32. Letter from Dean Whitla, director of institutional research at Harvard University, to Van Halsey, director of admissions at Hampshire, 3 February 1970, Hampshire College Archives, p. 3.

33. Julian C. Stanley, "Predicting College Success of the Educationally Disadvantaged," *Science* 171 (19 February 1971): 642.

34. Kendrick, p. 8.

35. Letter from Dean Whitla to Van Halsey, 3 February 1970, Hampshire College, p. 2.

36. William Cotter, The President's Report, 1994/95, Colby College, p. 3.

37. Minority Recruitment, Early 1970s, Oberlin College Archives, pp. 2–3.

38. Father John E. Brooks, interviewed by Elizabeth A. Duffy, 28 April 1995, College of the Holy Cross.

39. Dixon Bush, "Disadvantaged Students at College: A New Dimension," *College and University Bulletin* (March 1967): 1.

40. Adams, "From the College President," pp. 7–8.

41. Admissions Committee Year-End Report, 1967–1968, Ohio Wesleyan University Archives, p. 2.

42. Recruitment of Minority Students, Memo from the Chairman of the Admissions Committee to Dean Donald Reich, 11 May 1971, Oberlin College Archives, p. 1.

43. "No Room for the Winner?" date unknown, Amherst College Archives.

44. Report to the President, Financial Aid 1968/69, Wellesley College Archives, p. 2.

45. Thomas Mendenhall, President's Report, 1969/70, Smith College Archives, p. 10.

46. Minutes of the Faculty Committee on Admission and Financial Aid, 18 March 1970, Amherst College Archives, p. 1.

47. Clara Ludwig, director of admissions, Report from the Board of Admissions to the President, 31 July 1964, Mount Holyoke College Archives, p. 14.

48. Mrs. Groverman B. Payne, Report of the Director of Financial Aid to Students and the Committee on Financial Aid to Students to the Acting President, 30 June 1969, Mount Holyoke College Archives, p. 5.

49. Payne, Report of the Director of Financial Aid, 1969, Mount Holyoke College, p. 2.

50. Alan Pifer, *The Higher Education of Blacks in the United States: Reprint of the Alfred and Winifred Hoernlé Memorial Lecture for 1973* (New York: Carnegie Corporation, 1973), p. 41.

51. Audrey N. Smith-Whitaker '74, admission counselor, "Admission of Minority Students," *Wellesley Alumnae Magazine* (Autumn 1978): 12.

52. Dixon Bush, Appendix B: Sustaining a New Student Mix at Antioch, December 1967, Antioch College Archives, p. 2.

53. Lois Sparks, "Separatism at Antioch: Some Causes and Suggestions," Program Development and Research in Education (June 1968), p. 21.

54. A Proposal for Increased Recruitment of Minority Students, Oberlin College, pp. 5–6.

55. Payne, Report of the Director of Financial Aid, 1969, Mount Holyoke College, p. 3.

56. Letter to Mrs. Groverman B. Payne, director of financial aid, from the Afro-American Society, 5 May 1969, Mount Holyoke College Archives.

57. President's Report, 1969/70, Smith College, pp. 9, 11.

58. G. Wallace Chessman and Wyndham M. Southgate, *Heritage and Promise: Denison 1831–1981* (Granville, OH: Denison University, 1981), pp. 183, 185.

59. "Highlights of the Times at Trinity: Years of Drama and Decision," *Trinity Reporter* (September 1995): 5.

60. Michael Meyers, "Black Education at Antioch College," *Youth and Society* 5 (June 1974): 383, 385.

61. See Chapter 6 for a history of federal financial aid programs.

62. See *The Antioch Record* between January 1973 and June 1973 for a full account of the strike.

63. Richard Philofsky, "Cost of the 1973 Spring Strike," paper for Economics of Higher Education, 21 March 1974, Antioch College Archives.

64. David Karen, "The Politics of Class, Race, and Gender: Access to Higher Education in the United States, 1960–1986," *American Journal of Education* (February 1991), pp. 215, 217.

65. Niara Sudarkasa, "Can We Afford Equity and Excellence? Can We Afford Less?" *Academe* (September–October 1988): 23–24.

66. Sudarkasa, p. 24.

67. Fred Copeland, Admissions Report, 1973, Williams College Archives, p. 39.

68. "Senate Grapples with Black, Minority Recruiting; Kushan Cites 'Financial Problems' for Disadvantaged," *The Kenyon Collegian* CIII (4 December 1975).

69. Minutes of the Meeting of the College Committee on Admissions and Relations to Secondary Schools, 16 October 1979, Oberlin College Archives, p. 1.

70. Clara R. Ludwig, Report of the Board of Admissions: Minority Applications, September 1980, Mount Holyoke College Archives, pp. 2–3.

71. Ludwig, Report of the Board of Admissions: Minority Applications, Mount Holyoke College, p. 1.

72. Edward Wall, Admission to Amherst College in 1977: Thirty-First Annual Report to Secondary Schools, 1977, Amherst College Archives, p. 2.

73. William G. Bowen, "Admissions and the Relevance of Race," in *Ever the Teacher* (Princeton, NJ: Princeton University Press, 1987), p. 433. This essay was published in the Summer 1977 issue of *University* magazine and in the *Princeton Alumni Weekly* of September 26, 1977.

74. *One Third of a Nation*, p. 1.

75. *One Third of a Nation*, p. 21

76. "Kenyon Admissions: Shall We Overcome Uniformity?" *Kenyon Alumni Bulletin* (March 1987): 10.

77. Stephanie Chapko Kinard, "Some Thoughts on Diversification," Memo to Recruitment Task Force, 1 December 1986, Antioch College Archives, p. 2.

78. Cotter, The President's Report, 1994/95, Colby College, p. 2.

79. "Planning for a Multicultural Future," *Hiram College Magazine* (Spring 1992): 18.

80. Jane Reynolds, Amherst Annual Admission Report, 1993, Amherst College Archives.

81. John Anderson, dean of admissions, and Beverly Morse, director of admissions, interviewed by Elizabeth A. Duffy and Idana Goldberg, 11 July 1995, Kenyon College. Unfortunately, according to Anderson, by the mid-1990s the frequency of "This place is too sheltered" comments had declined. Instead parents seemed to swing the other way, asking, "Why should I pay for those students?"

82. Summary and Conclusions of the Antioch Program for Interracial Education 5-Year Report, 1 July 1969, Antioch College Archives, p. 44.

83. Ann Wright, interviewed by Elizabeth A. Duffy and Idana Goldberg, 27 June 1995, Smith College.

84. Gary Craig, interviewed by Elizabeth A. Duffy and Idana Goldberg, 8 May 1995, Hiram College.

85. Pamela Lazarakis, interviewed by Elizabeth A. Duffy, 9 June 1995, Gordon College.

86. Ross Peacock, Financial Aid Packaging and Yields, Oberlin College of Arts and Sciences, Freshman Class Entering September 1992, 15 December 1992, Oberlin College, p. 2.

87. "Planning for a Multicultural Future," p. 18.

88. Smith Design for Institutional Diversity, 29 October 1988, Smith College Archives.

89. Report to the President of the Task Force on Diversity, Spring 1987, Kenyon College Archives, p. 7.

90. Janet Lavin, interviewed by Idana Goldberg, 3 May 1995, Wellesley College.

91. Janet Lavin interview.

92. As reported in *The Chronicle of Higher Education* (24 May 1996): A32.

93. Jayjia Hsia and Marsha Hirano-Nakanishi, "The Demographics of Diversity: Asian Americans and Higher Education," *Change* (November–December 1989): 22, 25.

94. Janet Lavin interview.

95. Janet Lavin interview.

96. Jane Reynolds interview.

Chapter 6 Notes

1. Martin Kramer, "A Decade of Growth in Student Assistance," in *The Crisis in Higher Education*, ed. Joseph Froomkin (New York: The Academy of Political Science, 1983), p. 62.

2. Charles B. Saunders, "Reshaping Federal Aid to Higher Education," in *The Crisis in Higher Education*, ed. Joseph Froomkin (New York: The Academy of Political Science, 1983), p. 124.

3. Admissions Report 1958/59, Williams College Archives, p. 12. In fact, Williams did not participate in the NDEA until 1965/66 when it received approximately $42,000 to support its loan program.

4. Henry Flynt, interviewed by Elizabeth A. Duffy and Idana Goldberg, 2 December 1995, Williams College.

5. Fred Copeland, Admissions Report, 1 October 1952, Williams College Archives, pp. 1–2.

6. Benjamin Fletcher Wright, Report for 1955/56 to the Board of Trustees, the Board of Counselors, and the Alumnae of the College from the President, Smith College Archives, p. 11.

7. John U. Monro, "Helping the Student Help Himself," *Journal of Student Financial Aid* 24 (1994), reprint of May 1953 article in *College Board Review*, pp. 9–10.

8. Report of No-Need Financial Grants, 20 March 1981, Oberlin College Archives, p. 2.

9. Fred Copeland, Admissions Report, 1959, Williams College Archives, p. 11.

10. Student Aid, 27 January 1959, Wheaton College Archives.

11. William G. Bowen, "Report of the President: Maintaining Opportunities: Undergraduate Financial Aid at Princeton," April 1983, Princeton University, p. 10.

12. Kramer, p. 62.

13. Editorial Projects for Education, "Life with Uncle," *Kenyon Alumni Bulletin* (April–June 1967).

14. Lawrence E. Gladieux and Gwendolyn L. Lewis, *The Federal Government and Higher Education Traditions, Trends, Stakes and Issues* (Washington, DC: The College Board, October 1987), p. 6.

15. W. Lee Hansen, "Impact of Student Financial Aid on Access," in *The Crisis in Higher Education*, ed. Joseph Froomkin (New York: The Academy of Political Science, 1983), pp. 88–89.

16. "James White's Career Spans History of Financial Aid," *The (Oberlin) Observer*, 29 March 1990, Oberlin College Archives, p. 3.

17. Robert J. Massa, "Merit Scholarships and Student Recruitment: Goals and Strategies," *The Journal of College Admission* (Spring 1991): 10.

18. Dean Kenworthy, Memo to Miss Colpitts, Miss Crandall, Mr. Anderson about Financial Aid Office, 28 July 1966, Wheaton College Archives.

19. Thomas Mendenhall, President's Report for 1966/67, Smith College Archives, pp. 19–20.

20. Report for 1974/75 of the Committee on Financial Aid to Students, Mount Holyoke College Archives, p. 3.

21. Report on Financial Aid 1965/66, Wellesley College Archives, pp. 2–3.

22. Ann O'Sullivan, "Financial Aid: Hard Times Ahead," *REALIA* (December 1985): 5.

23. Henry Flynt, Financial Aid Report 1964/65, Williams College Archives, p. 2.

24. Report for 1974/75 of the Committee on Financial Aid to Students, Mount Holyoke College, pp. 6–7.

25. The figures in this chapter are based on data from 13 of the 16 colleges in our study. The College of Wooster, Hiram, and Wheaton were unable to provide complete financial aid information. By total institutional aid, we mean grants. Institutional loans and work study contributions are not included.

26. Mrs. Groverman B. Payne, Report of the Director of Financial Aid to Students and the Committee on Financial Aid to Students to the Acting President, 30 June 1969, Mount Holyoke College Archives, p. 6.

27. Eugene Wilson, Admission to Amherst College in 1969: Twenty-third Annual Report to Secondary Schools, 1969, Amherst College Archives.

28. Henry Flynt, Financial Aid Report 1968/69, Williams College Archives, p. 8.

29. Mrs. Groverman B. Payne, Letter to the Afro-American Society, Mount Holyoke College Archives, 7 May 1969, p. 2.

30. Minutes of the Meeting of the College Committee on Admissions and Relations to Secondary Schools, 13 November 1979, Oberlin College Archives, pp. 1–2.

31. Burton W. Dunfield, Letter to President Joel P. Smith, 14 April 1971, Denison College Archives.

32. Report to the President, Financial Aid, 1968/69, Wellesley College Archives, p. 2.

33. Franklin Patterson and Charles R. Longworth, *The Making of a College* (Cambridge, MA: MIT Press, 1966), pp. 239–40.

34. Payne, Report of the Director of Financial Aid to Students and the Committee on Financial Aid to Students to the Acting President, 1969, Mount Holyoke College, p. 1.

35. Mary Ellen Ames, interviewed by Idana Goldberg, 2 May 1995, Wellesley College Archives.

36. Report of the Board of Admissions, October 1971, Mount Holyoke College Archives, pp. 18–19.

37. Patterson and Longworth, pp. 240–41.

38. Elliot Maxwell, Memorandum to Scholarship and Financial Aid Committee, 6 April 1971, Hampshire College Archives, p. 1.

39. Maxwell, Memorandum to Scholarship and Financial Aid Committee, Hampshire College, p. 1.

40. Ronald G. Ehrenberg and Susan H. Murphy, "What Price Diversity? The Death of Need-Based Financial Aid at Selective Private Colleges and Universities?" *Change* (July–August 1993): 64.

41. See, for example, L. Edgar Prina, "The New Deprived ... Middle Class College Students," *The Cincinnati Enquirer*, 28 January 1973, p. 5-B; and George Dullea, "Child Goes Off to College—And Parents Go Off to Find Money," *New York Times*, 9 April 1974.

42. Edward Wall, Admission to Amherst College in 1974: Twenty-Eight Annual Report to Secondary Schools, 1974, Amherst College Archives, p. 2.

43. Michael S. McPherson and Morton Owen Schapiro have carefully studied the so-called "middle-income melt." Using 1978, 1982, and 1989 data, they found a shift of middle-income students from COFHE schools, other private institutions and public universities to public colleges (McPherson and Schapiro, *Keeping Colleges Affordable* [Washington, DC: The Brookings Institution, 1991], pp. 75–89). More recently, however, they have documented not a middle-income melt, but rather an upper-income melt, as full-pay students have left private four-year colleges (unpublished paper for the Princeton Higher Education Conference, 22 March 1996).

44. Howard R. Bowen and W. John Minter, *Private Higher Education, First Annual Report on Financial and Educational Trends in the Private Sector of American Higher Education* (Washington, DC: Association of American Colleges, 1975), pp. 87–88.

45. For an extended discussion of pricing and the demand for higher education related to income levels, see Michael S. McPherson, "The Demand for Higher Education," in *Public Policy and Private Higher Education*, eds. David Breneman and Chester E. Finn, Jr. (Washington, DC: The Brookings Institution, 1978), pp. 143–96.

46. Bowen and Minter, p. 87.

47. Earl Cheit, *The New Depression in Higher Education: A Study of Financial Conditions at 41 Colleges and Universities* (New York: McGraw-Hill, 1971), p. 13.

48. Dullea, "Child Goes Off to College," *New York Times.*

49. Kramer, p. 63.

50. The BEOG program is technically not a full entitlement program because outlays are subject to annual appropriation limits.

51. David W. Breneman, *Liberal Arts Colleges—Thriving, Surviving or Endangered?* (Washington, DC: The Brookings Institution, 1994), pp. 27–28.

52. Kramer, p. 65.

53. BEOG grants had only a weak impact on choice because they were only loosely linked to differences in college costs. In many cases, a student would receive the same grant at any school in her choice set.

54. Michael Behnke, Interdepartmental Memo, 13 September 1972, Amherst College Archives, p. 4.

55. Robert P. Huff, "Need Assessment of Upper-Middle Income Families—Are They Being Excluded?" *College Board Review* 86 (Winter 1972/73): 25.

56. Huff, p. 26.

57. Wall, Admission to Amherst College in 1974, p. 2.

58. Minutes of the College Admissions Committee, 16 April 1981, Oberlin College Archives, p. 2.

59. Report for 1974/75 of the Committee on Financial Aid to Students, Mount Holyoke College Archives, p. 4.

60. Lawrence E. Gladieux. "The Issue of Equity in College Finance," in *The Crisis in Higher Education*, ed. Joseph Froomkin (New York: The Academy of Political Science, 1983), p. 74.

61. We could not determine the total percent of students receiving aid, because we do not know how many students received just need-based aid, just merit aid, or both.

62. If anything, the experience of the colleges in our study probably overstates the ability of institutions to meet full need. Even many of the wealthiest research universities in this country could not guarantee aid to all needy students until the 1970s. Princeton, for example, didn't begin to meet full need until 1970, and in 1971 it had to use funds from an Undergraduate Association drive to meet every student's need.

63. Report for 1974/75 of the Committee on Financial Aid to Students, Mount Holyoke College Archives, p. 6.

64. Report to the President by the Office of Admissions, 10 March 1972, Oberlin College Archives, p. 7.

65. "Senate Grapples with Black, Minority Recruiting; Kushan Cites 'Financial' Problems for Disadvantaged," *Kenyon Collegian* CIII (4 December 1975): 1.

66. Mary Ellen Crawford Ames, "Answers About Admission," *Wellesley Alumnae Magazine* (Spring 1972): 22.

67. Wall, Admission to Amherst College in 1974, p. 2.

68. Gladieux and Lewis, p. 8.

69. Burton Clark, *Perspectives on Higher Education* (Berkeley: University of California Press, 1984), pp. 79–103.

70. Editorial Project for Education, "The Money Behind Our Colleges," *The Hiram Broadcaster* (Winter 1964): 21.

71. Kramer, p. 70.

72. James White, "Merit Scholarships at Oberlin?" *The (Oberlin) Observer* (26 February 1981): 2–3.

73. Alice Dembner, "Schools Vying for Students Add Merit Aid," *The Boston Globe*, 12 September 1995, p. 6.

74. Francis Delaney, interviewed by Elizabeth A. Duffy and Idana Goldberg, 27 April 1995, College of the Holy Cross.

75. In 1975/76, only 21 percent of federal aid came as loans; in 1987/88, the comparable figure was 68 percent. Janet S. Hansen, "Student Assistance in Uncertain Times," *Academe* (September–October 1988): 28.

76. Ehrenberg and Murphy, p. 68.

77. Jonathan R. Laing, "Campus Unrest—Why Parents Are Up in Arms about Tuition Bills, and Colleges Will Finally Be Forced to Change Their Free-spending Ways," *Barron's* (27 November 1995): 28.

78. Of course, there is a fairly strong correlation between a private institution's tuition level and its quality, because additional tuition revenues enable a college to offer more, or better, services. Since public institutions are so heavily subsidized, their tuition levels do not accurately reflect the extent of their total resources.

79. The phrase "Chivas Regal phenomenon" was coined by Dean and Acting President (1983/84) Joseph Ellis at Mount Holyoke. See Barry Werth, "Why Is College So Expensive? Maybe America Wants It That Way," *Change* (March–April 1988): 13–25.

80. Breneman, 1994, pp. 32–33.

81. Werth, pp. 13–25.

82. Thomas Wenzlau, "The Outlook for Liberal-Arts College," in *The Crisis in Higher Education*, ed. Joseph Froomkin (New York: Academy of Political Science, 1983), pp. 8–9.

83. As reported in Jeffrey Gilmore, *Price and Quality in Higher Education* (Washington, DC: Office of Educational Research and Improvement, 1990), p. 3.

84. Richard W. Moll, "The Scramble to Get the New Class," *Change* (March–April 1994): 14.

85. Thomas Hayden, interviewed by Elizabeth A. Duffy and Idana Goldberg, 9 May 1995, Oberlin College.

86. Sandra Tarbox, interviewed by Elizabeth A. Duffy and Idana Goldberg, 19 July 1995, Antioch College.

87. David Caldwell, interviewed by Elizabeth A. Duffy and Idana Goldberg, 1 June 1995, Wheaton College.

88. Laura Meckler, "To Lure Students, College Cuts Tuition," *Sunday Lawrence Eagle Tribune*, 26 September 1995, p. A-6. Price-cutting strategies are becoming popular in many consumer industries. See, for example, Bruce Horovitz, "Value-minded Consumers Call the Shots," *USA Today*, 10 September 1996, p. B-1.

89. Such a comparison is admittedly rough. A more precise test, for which we don't have sufficient data, would compare a college's financial aid expenditures to its *unrestricted* endowment income, current *unrestricted* gifts, *restricted* endowment income for financial aid, and *restricted* current gifts for financial aid.

90. The National Association of College Admission Counselors (NACAC), *Executive Summary: 1994 Survey of Admissions Practices* (Alexandria, VA: NACAC, September 1994), p. 6. Many colleges consider the financial needs of students that they admit off of the wait list, after May 1.

91. Faculty Planning and Budget Committee, Subcommittee on Admissions and the Financial State of the College, May 1995, Mount Holyoke College Archives.

92. "More Full-paying Students?" *The (Oberlin) Observer* 11 (12 October 1989): 1.

93. Scott Jaschik, "Antitrust Case Closed," *Chronicle of Higher Education* (3 January 1994): A24.

94. Barbara Boles, interviewed by Elizabeth A. Duffy, 9 June 1995, Gordon College.

95. David Miller, interviewed by Elizabeth A. Duffy and Idana Goldberg, 13 July 1995, College of Wooster.

96. "Merit Scholarships at Oberlin?" *The (Oberlin) Observer* (26 February 1981): 2.

97. Kathleen Methot, interviewed by Elizabeth A. Duffy and Idana Goldberg, 23 June 1995, Hampshire College.

98. Michael S. McPherson and Morton Owen Schapiro, "Admissions and Financial Aid at Mount Holyoke: An Assessment with Recommendations," 4 May 1994, Mount Holyoke College Archives, p. 1.

Chapter 7 Notes

1. Samuel Carrier, interviewed by Elizabeth A. Duffy and Idana Goldberg, 9 May 1995, Oberlin College.

2. Sandra R. Baum and Saul S. Schwartz, "Merit Aid to College Students," *Economics of Education Review* 7 (1988): 127.

3. We tried to get around the problem of distinguishing "merit aid in excess need" from "merit aid within need" by asking the colleges to report "need within merit," but most of them could not provide those numbers, and the data that we did receive were neither complete nor consistent across institutions. Michael McPherson and Morton Schapiro confronted the same problem in their study of merit aid: "How should we cope with the relation between need and merit? In our central case, a merit scholar comes from a family that is well enough off not to qualify for need-based aid. At many institutions, some recipients of need-based financial aid are designated as meritorious, and receive part of all of their aid in the form of a merit grant. Their total award may in some cases exceed the amount of aid they would qualify for on the basis of a financial need calculation. . . . In other cases, the 'meritorious' student will receive a richer mix of ingredients in the aid package, with more grants and less loan for the same total package that a less well qualified student would receive. In still other cases, the needy student may get exactly the same award package she would have gotten anyway, with some of the dollars carrying a special label. We must be aware of these distinctions, but as we shall see, available data allow us to deal with them only imperfectly." Michael S. McPherson and Morton Owen Schapiro, "Merit Aid: Students, Institutions and Society: Who Wins? Who Loses?" (June 1993 draft), pp. 2–3.

4. Robert Huff, "No Need Scholarships," *The College Board Review* 95 (Spring 1975): 15.

5. Betsy A. Porter and Suzanne K. McColloch, "The Use of No-Need Academic Scholarships: An Update" (Submitted to the National Association of College Admission Counselors, 1 December 1984).

6. McPherson and Schapiro (June 1993 draft), pp. 5–6.

7. The National Association of College Admission Counselors (NACAC), *Executive Summary: 1994 Survey of Admissions Practices* (Alexandria, VA: NACAC, September 1994), p. 14.

8. Irvin W. Cockriel and Steven Graham, "Sources of Financial Aid and College Selection," *The Journal of Student Financial Aid* 18 (Fall 1988): 19.

9. Gale F. Gaines, "Merit Scholarships for Star Students: Keeping the Brightest at In-State Colleges," *Southern Regional Education Board* (May 1989), p. 2.

10. Linda Kopp, "States Increase Amount of Student Financial Aid Awarded," *Higher Education and National Affairs, ACE* (25 March 1996): 3.

11. Gary L. Jones, "Merit Aid Is an Investment for American Leadership," *Change* (September 1984): 26.

12. Lawrence E. Gladieux, "The Issue of Equity in College Finance," in *The Crisis in Higher Education*, ed. Joseph Froomkin (New York: The Academy of Political Science, 1983) p. 77.

13. Lawrence E. Gladieux and Gwendolyn L. Lewis, *The Federal Government and Higher Education Traditions, Trends, Stakes and Issues* (Washington Office, DC: The College Board, October 1987), p. 9.

14. Douglas Lederman, "Aid for Whom?" *The Chronicle of Higher Education* (2 February 1996): A23.

15. Betsy A. Porter and Suzanne K. McColloch, "The Use of No-Need Academic Scholarship in U.S. Universities and Colleges: A Survey" (Submitted to the National Association of College Admission Counselors, 22 November 1982), p. 10.

16. Porter and McColloch (1984), p. 18.

17. Alfred MacKay, "The College May Need to Change Its Strategy," *The (Oberlin) Observer* (19 September 1991): 5.

18. Ross Peacock, "Financial Aid Packaging and Yields, Oberlin College of Arts and Sciences, Freshman Class Entering September 1992," 15 December 1992, Office of Institutional Research, p. 6.

19. Robert J. Massa, "Merit Scholarships and Student Recruitment: Goals and Strategies," *The Journal of College Admission* (Spring 1991): 11.

20. Gregory A. Jackson, "Financial Aid and Student Enrollment," *Journal of Higher Education* 49 (1978): 548–49.

21. Kathryn Osmond, interviewed by Idana Goldberg, 3 May 1995, Wellesley College.

22. Preliminary Evaluation for CCUMG from Admissions and Financial Aid Council, 25 March 1977, Denison University Archives.

23. Dennison Smith, Minutes of the College Admissions Committee, 16 April 1981, Oberlin College Archives, p. 3.

24. McPherson and Schapiro (June 1993 draft), p. 35.

25. Reflecting on the 1980's Anticipating the 1990's: Self-Study, 1989, Denison University Archives, p. 95.

26. Alice Dembner, "Schools Vying for Students Add Merit Aid," *The Boston Globe*, 12 September 1995, p. 1. See also Ben Gose, "Colleges Turn to 'Leveraging' to Attract Well-Off Students," *The Chronicle of Higher Education* (13 September 1996): A45–46.

27. Craig Daugherty, interviewed by Elizabeth A. Duffy and Idana Goldberg, 11 July 1995, Kenyon College.

28. Carl W. Bewig, Remarks prepared for delivery to the Plenary Session of the Oberlin Board of Trustees, 7 June 1980, Oberlin College Archives, p. 6.

29. MacKay, p. 8.

30. John A. Muffo, "Market Segmentation in Higher Education: A Case Study," *The Journal of Student Financial Aid* 17 (1987): 39.

31. Gary Allen, interviewed by Elizabeth A. Duffy and Idana Goldberg, 1 June 1995, Wheaton College.

32. Myra Smith, interviewed by Elizabeth A. Duffy and Idana Goldberg, 22 June 1995, Smith College.

33. Addendum to Report on No-Need Financial Grants, 20 March 1981, Oberlin College Archives. Six of our Massachusetts colleges signed the statement.

34. McPherson and Schapiro (June 1993 draft), p. 17. McPherson and Schapiro refer to financial aid in excess of what is required to get a student to matriculate as "economic rent" (p. 13). In a 1993 article, William G. Bowen and David Breneman make a related distinction between aid as a price discount and aid as an educational investment: "A simple (conceptually at least) test allows us to tell whether student aid is a price discount or an educational investment. The key question: Does providing student aid increase or decrease the net resources available to the college to spend on other purposes? When student aid functions as a price discount, because it is needed to enroll enough students to achieve a financial objective, it increases the net resources available for other purposes by providing some incremental tuition revenue above marginal costs ... when the college could meet its enrollment

target without providing student aid, 'gross' tuition revenue is a fixed amount, and the aid provided by the college represents a discretionary educational investment that has been chosen over other claims on the revenues of the institution . . . many colleges and universities occupy intermediate positions along what is a continuum." William G. Bowen and David Breneman, "Student Aid: Price Discount or Educational Investment?" *The Brookings Review* (Winter 1993): 29.

35. Alice Emerson, interviewed by Elizabeth A. Duffy and Idana Goldberg, 13 June 1995, New York, New York.

36. James White,"Merit Scholarships at Oberlin?" *The (Oberlin) Observer* (26 February 1981): 3.

37. Committee on Admissions and Relations to Secondary Schools, Report on No-Need Financial Grants, 20 March 1981, Oberlin College Archives, p. 11.

38. Doug Thompson, interviewed by Elizabeth A. Duffy and Idana Goldberg, 10 July 1995, Ohio Wesleyan University.

39. Richard W. Moll, "The Scramble to Get the New Class," *Change* (March–April 1994): 14.

40. Holy Cross Presidential Scholarships to Jesuit High School graduates, 1960, College of the Holy Cross Archives, p. 1.

41. Working Paper of Financial Aid Committee, 16 January 1974, College of the Holy Cross Archives, p. 15.

42. Francis Delaney, interviewed by Elizabeth A. Duffy and Idana Goldberg, 27 April 1995, College of the Holy Cross.

43. Father John E. Brooks, interviewed by Elizabeth A. Duffy, 28 April 1995, College of the Holy Cross.

44. The Decade Ahead: Committee Report for Future Holy Cross Student Financial Aid, 29 April 1986, College of the Holy Cross Archives.

45. Gordon College Self-Study, 1971, Gordon College Archives. p. 112.

46. Franklin Patterson and Charles R. Longsworth, *The Making of a College* (Cambridge, MA: MIT Press, 1966), p. 236.

47. Gail Berson, interviewed by Elizabeth A. Duffy and Idana Goldberg, May 31, 1995, Wheaton College.

48. Dembner, "Schools Vying for Students," p. 6.

49. Gerald W. Patrick, "Enrollment Planning: The Art and the Gamble," *REALIA* (June 1984): 2.

50. Michael S. McPherson and Morton Owen Schapiro, Admissions and Financial Aid at Mount Holyoke: An Assessment with Recommendations, 4 May 1994, Mount Holyoke College Archives, p. 8.

51. Mary Maples Dunn, Planning for 2000, 1991, Smith College Archives, p. 6.

52. Theresa Johnson, "Here They Come: The New Student Entrepreneurs," *Stanford Observer* (Fall 1995): 4.

53. Christopher Shea, "Sweetening the Pot for the Best Students," *The Chronicle of Higher Education* (17 May 1996): A40.

54. Shea, p. A40.

55. David McDonough, "Jordan Announces 'Twin Programs' to Boost College's Caliber," *Kenyon Collegian* CIII (20 November 1975).

56. 1984 NACAC Survey, pp. 16–17.

57. Executive Summary of the 1994 NACAC Survey, pp. 10–11.

58. Working Paper of Financial Aid Committee, 16 January 1974, College of the Holy Cross Archives, p. 16.

59. The Decade Ahead: Committee Report for Future Holy Cross Student Financial Aid, 29 April 1986, College of the Holy Cross Archives, p. 3.

60. David L. Davis-Van Atta, Comments on a Proposed Administration of Limited Scholarship Funds, 1981, Oberlin College Archives, p. 2.

61. Beth Umland, "On and Off Campus: The College and Aid-blind Admissions," *Wellesley Alumni Magazine* (Spring 1982): 38.

62. McPherson and Schapiro, Admissions and Financial Aid at Mount Holyoke, pp. 4–5.

63. Committee on Admissions and Financial Aid, Faculty Meeting: Agenda Supplement, 1 February 1995, Mount Holyoke College Archives, p. 4.

64. Reflecting on the 1980's Anticipating the 1990's: Self-Study 1989, Denison University, p. 193.

65. Steve Stecklow, "Colleges Manipulate Financial-Aid Offers, Shortchanging Many," *Wall Street Journal*, 1 April 1996, pp. A–1, A–6.

66. S. H. Brooks Co., Inc. *The Enrollment Management Toolkit*, 1996.

67. Barry McCarty, "No-Need Scholarships," *The College Board Review* (Spring 1978): 38.

68. Thomas Wenzlau, "The Outlook for Liberal-Arts Colleges" in *The Crisis in Higher Education*, ed. Joseph Froomkin (New York: The Academy of Political Science, 1983), pp. 10–11.

69. Jones, p. 24.

70. Ellie McGrath, "Top Dollars for Top Students," *Time* (2 May 1983): 72.

71. Obviously, the effect that merit aid has had on need-based aid is only part of a much larger question, namely, "Has merit aid been successful?" In the chapter on quality we describe some of the recent improvements in SAT scores and class ranks that may be attributable to merit aid. In order to assess the long-term impact of merit aid, it would be important to identify the differing objectives of (a) individuals, (b) institutions, and (c) society at large and then determine if and how these goals have been met. Such an analysis, however, is beyond the scope of this book.

Conclusion Notes

1. Presidential Report to the Board of Trustees Planning Committee, 1967, Wheaton College Archives, Chapter III, p. 1.

2. "Private Colleges Fight for Financial Health; Public Institutions Find State Support Unreliable," *Chronicle of Higher Education* (14 June 1996): A15.

3. Donald L. Pyke, "The Future of Higher Education: Will Private Institutions Disappear in the U.S.?" *The Futurist* (December 1977): 373.

4. George Keller, *Academic Strategy: The Management Revolution in American Higher Education* (Baltimore: The Johns Hopkins University Press, 1983), p. 3.

5. David N. Breneman, Comment on "Riding Waves," a paper by Elizabeth A. Duffy and Idana Goldberg presented at the Princeton Conference on Higher Education, Princeton University, 22 March 1996, p. 1.

6. Eugene Wilson, "The Amherst Scene," *College Admission* (1959), p. 3.

7. Agenda Item #6: Planning Committee Meeting, September 1967, Wheaton College Archives.

8. Alice Dembner, "Brandeis Plan: Fewer Teachers, More Students," *The Boston Globe*, 26 January 1996, pp. 21, 28.

Appendix A: Survey Forms

Admissions and First-Year Student Profile

Name of Institution: Entering Year:
Form Filled Out By: Phone #:

		Enrolled First-Years (Only full-time.)	Admitted First-Years (Only full-time.)	Applicants (Only full-time.)
1	# of Full-Time First-Years			
2	# of First-Year Honors Students			
3	# of First-Year Early Decision/ Action			
4	# of First-Year Legacies (alumni parent)			
5	# of First-Year Males			
6	# of First-Year Females			
7	# of First-Year African Americans			
8	# of First-Year Hispanic Americans			
9	# of First-Year Asian Americans			
10	Mean Combined SAT : All First-Years	( )	( )	( )
11	Mean Combined SAT : First-Year Women	( )	( )	( )
12	Mean Combined SAT : First-Year Men	( )	( )	( )
13	# of First-Years in Top Decile of HS Class			
14	# in Top Half of High School Class			
15	# in First Quintile			
16	# in Second Quintile			
17	# in Third Quintile			
18	# in Fourth Quintile			
19	# in Fifth Quintile			
20	# Without High School Rank			
21	# of First-Years Who Attended Public HS			
22	# Who Attended NON-Public High School			
23	# of States Represented in First-Year Class			
24	# of First-Years from Instate			
25	# from New England States			
26	# from Middle Atlantic States			
27	# from Midwest States			
28	# from South States			
29	# from West States			

Financial Aid Information

Institution Name:
Form Filled Out By:
Phone #:

	1955/56	1960/61	1965/66	1970/71	1975/76	1980/81
1. Undergraduate Tuition						
2. Other Mandatory Fees for Undergraduates						
3. Undergraduate Room and Board (Average for On-Campus Housing)						
4. Total Institutional Dollars Spent on Undergraduate Need-Based Grants and Scholarships ($000)						
5. Number of Undergraduates Receiving Institutional Need-Based Grants and Scholarships						
6. Total Institutional Dollars Spent on Undergraduate Merit Grants and Scholarships ($000)						
7. Number of Undergraduates Receiving Institutional Merit Grants and Scholarships						
8. IF AVAILABLE, Total Institutional Dollars Spent on Merit Grants and Scholarships that Went to Undergraduates Who Would Have Qualified for Need-Based Aid ($000)						
9. IF AVAILABLE, Number of Needy Undergraduates Receiving Institutional Merit Grants or Scholarships						

Financial Aid Information

Institution Name:
Form Filled Out By:
Phone #:

	1985/86	1986/87	1987/88	1988/89	1989/90	1990/91
1. Undergraduate Tuition						
2. Other Mandatory Fees for Undergraduates						
3. Undergraduate Room and Board (Average for On-Campus Housing)						
4. Total Institutional Dollars Spent on Undergraduate Need-Based Grants and Scholarships ($000)						
5. Number of Undergraduates Receiving Institutional Need-Based Grants and Scholarships						
6. Total Institutional Dollars Spent on Undergraduate Merit Grants and Scholarships ($000)						
7. Number of Undergraduates Receiving Institutional Merit Grants and Scholarships						
8. IF AVAILABLE, Total Institutional Dollars Spent on Merit Grants and Scholarships that Went to Undergraduates Who Would Have Qualifed for Need-Based Aid ($000)						
9. IF AVAILABLE, Number of Needy Undergraduates Receiving Institutional Merit Grants or Scholarships						

Financial Aid Information

Institution Name:
Form Filled Out By:
Phone #:

	1991/92	1992/93	1993/94	Est. 1994/95
1. Undergraduate Tuition				
2. Other Mandatory Fees for Undergraduates				
3. Undergraduate Room and Board (Average for On-Campus Housing)				
4. Total Institutional Dollars Spent on Undergraduate Need-Based Grants and Scholarships ($000)				
5. Number of Undergraduates Receiving Institutional Need-Based Grants and Scholarships				
6. Total Institutional Dollars Spent on Undergraduate Merit Grants and Scholarships ($000)				
7. Number of Undergraduates Receiving Institutional Merit Grants and Scholarships				
8. IF AVAILABLE, Total Institutional Dollars Spent on Merit Grants and Scholarships that Went to Undergraduates Who Would Have Qualified for Need-Based Aid ($000)				
9. IF AVAILABLE, Number of Needy Undergraduates Receiving Institutional Merit Grants or Scholarships				

Undergraduate Enrollment Information

Name of Institution:
Form Filled Out By:
Phone #:

	# of Full-Time Undergraduates in the Fall of:	# of Part-Time Undergraduates in the Fall of:	# of Full-Time Undergraduates 25 or More Years Old in the Fall of:
1955			
1960			
1965			
1970			
1975			
1980			
1985			
1986			
1987			
1988			
1989			
1990			
1991			
1992			
1993			
1994			

Name of Institution:

Entering Year:

Form Filled Out By:

Phone #:

The purpose of this form is to determine where students whom you admitted but who chose not to attend your institution enrolled. Please list your top 15 competitors for the year specified above, and indicate how many students you lost to each school.

Name of Competitor	# of Losses
1.	
2.	
3.	
4.	
5.	
6.	
7.	
8.	
9.	
10.	
11.	
12.	
13	
14.	
15.	

Total Number of Known Losses: _____

Appendix B: Interviews

Amherst College
Joe Paul Case, Director of Financial Aid
Robert Grose, former Registrar and Director of Institutional Research
Gerald Mager, Registrar
Jane Reynolds, Director of Admissions

Antioch College
Melva Rue, Registrar
Sandra Tarbox, Director of Financial Aid
Richard Weibl, Director of Institutional Research

College of the Holy Cross
Reverend John Brooks, President Emeritus
Francis Delaney, Director of Financial Aid
James Kee, Associate Dean of the College
Ann McDermott, Director of Admissions
Elaine Rynders, Registrar

College of Wooster
Glenn Davis, Registrar
R. Stanton Hales, President
David Miller, Director of Financial Aid
Byron Morris, former Director of Admissions
Hayden Schilling, Dean of Admissions

Denison University
G. Wallace Chessman, Historian
Gordon Condit, former Associate Director of Admissions
Lynn Gilbert, former Director of Financial Aid
Parker Lichtenstein, former Dean and Acting President
Larry Murdoch, Registrar
Virginia Putnam, former Administrative Assistant in the Office of Admissions
Charlotte Weeks, former Associate Director of Admissions

Gordon College
Barbara Boles, Director of Financial Aid
Judy Garde, Registrar
Pamela Lazarakis, Director of Admissions
Steve MacLeod, Dean of Planning

Hampshire College
Kathleen Methot, Director of Financial Aid
Karen Parker, Associate Dean of Admissions
Roberta Stuart, Registrar

Hiram College
Gary Craig, former Dean of Admissions
Alan Donley, Director of Student Financial Services
William Hoffman, Professor of History
Craig Moser, Director of Institutional Research

Kenyon College
John Anderson, Dean of Admissions
Craig Daugherty, Director of Financial Aid
Beverly Morse, Director of Admissions

Mount Holyoke College
Kim Condon, Director of Student Financial Services
Joan Davis, former Director of Institutional Research
Janice Gifford, Associate Dean of the Faculty
Mary Jo Maydew, Treasurer
Sally Montgomery, Dean of the College
Harriet Pollatsek, Professor of Math, member of Admissions Committee
Anita Smith, Director of Admissions

Oberlin College
Samuel Carrier, Provost
Thomas Hayden, former Vice President for Admissions and Financial Aid
Ross Peacock, Director of Institutional Research
Howard Thomas, Director of Financial Aid

Ohio Wesleyan University
Kim Lance, Professor of Chemistry, member of Admissions Committee
William Louthan, Provost
Nancy Sanford, Associate Director of Financial Aid
Doug Thompson, Dean of Admissions and Financial Aid

Smith College
Anne Keppler, former Director of Financial Aid
Patricia O'Neill, Registrar
Eleanor Rothman, Director, Ada Comstock Program
Myra Smith, Director of Financial Aid
Marjorie Southwork, Associate Director, Ada Comstock Program
B. Ann Wright, Dean of Enrollment Management

Wellesley College
Mary Ellen Ames, former Director of Admissions
Phyllis Kelley, Financial Aid Officer
Janet Lavin, Dean of Admissions
Kathryn Osmond, Director of Financial Aid

Wheaton College
Gary Allen, former Director of Student Financial Aid
Gail Berson, Director of Admissions and Student Financial Aid
David Caldwell, Director, Administrative Information Services
Alice F. Emerson, President Emerita
Paul Helmreich, Professor of History
Patricia Santilli, Registrar

Williams College
Fred Copeland, former Director of Admissions
Henry Flynt, former Director of Financial Aid
Michael S. MacPherson, former Dean of the Faculty
Thomas Parker, Director of Admissions
Philip Smith, Dean of Admissions
Phil Wick, Director of Financial Aid

Bibliography

Works Cited

Alden, Vernon. "The Expanding Role of Admissions and Financial Aid Officers." In *Student Financial Aid and Institutional Purpose*. A Colloquium on Financial Aid held by the College Scholarship Service of the College Entrance Examination Board, 1963, 1–5.

Bales, Susan Nall, and Marcia Sharp. "Women's Colleges—Weathering a Difficult Era with Success and Stamina." *Change* 13 (October 1981): 53–56.

Baum, Sandra R., and Saul S. Schwartz. "Merit Aid to College Students." *Economics of Education Review* 7 (1988): 127–34.

Bird, Caroline. "Women's Colleges and Women's Lib." *Change* (April 1972): 60–65.

Bowen, William G. "Report of the President: Maintaining Opportunities: Undergraduate Financial Aid at Princeton." Princeton, NJ: Princeton University Press, April 1983.

Bowen, William G. *Ever the Teacher*. Princeton, NJ: Princeton University Press, 1987.

Bowen, William G., and David W. Breneman. "Student Aid: Price Discount or Educational Investment?" *The Brookings Review* (Winter 1993): 29–31.

Bowen, Howard R., and W. John Minter. *Private Higher Education, First Annual Report on Financial and Educational Trends in the Private Sector of American Higher Education*. Washington, DC: Association of American Colleges, 1975.

Bowles, Frank, and Frank A. DeCosta. *Between Two Worlds: A Profile of Negro Higher Education*. New York: McGraw-Hill, 1971.

Breneman, David W. *Liberal Arts Colleges—Thriving, Surviving or Endangered?* Washington, DC: The Brookings Institution, 1994.

Carnegie Foundation for the Advancement of Teaching. *More Than Survival: Prospects for Higher Education in a Period of Uncertainty*. San Francisco: Jossey-Bass, 1975.

Carrier, Samuel, and David L. Davis-Van Atta. "Using the Institutional Research Office." In *Managing College Enrolllments*, ed. D. Hossler, New Directions for Higher Education, no. 53, 73–87. San Francisco: Jossey-Bass, 1986.

Chamberlain, Mariam K., ed. *Women in Academe: Progress and Prospects*. New York: Russell Sage Foundation, 1988.

Chapman, Randall G. "Non-Simultaneous Relative Importance—Performance Analysis: Meta Results from 80 College Choice Surveys with 55,276 Respondents." *Journal of Marketing for Higher Education* 4 (1993): 405–22.

Chapman, Randall G., and Rex Jackson. *College Choices of Academically Able Students: The Influence of No-Need Financial Aid and Other Factors*. New York: College Entrance Examination Board, 1987.

Cheit, Earl. *The New Depression in Higher Education: A Study of Financial Condi-*

tions at 41 Colleges and Universities. A Report for the Carnegie Commission on Higher Education and the Ford Foundation. New York: McGraw-Hill, 1971.

Chessman, G. Wallace, and Wyndham M. Southgate. *Heritage and Promise: Denison 1831–1981.* Granville, OH: Denison University, 1981.

Cockriel, Irving W., and Steven Graham. "Sources of Financial Aid and College Selection." *The Journal of Student Financial Aid* 18 (Fall 1988): 12–20.

Cole, Charles C., Jr. "A Case for the Women's College." *College Board Review* 83 (Spring 1972): 17–21.

Commission on Minority Participation in Education and American Life. *One Third of a Nation.* American Council on Education, Education Commission of the States, May 1988.

Conway, Jill Ker. "Women's Place," *Change* (March 1978): 8–9.

Conway, Jill Ker. *True North: A Memoir.* New York: Alfred A. Knopf, 1994.

Cook, Philip, and Robert H. Frank. "The Growing Concentration of Top Students at Elite Schools." In *Studies in Supply and Demand in Higher Education*, eds. Charles Clotfelter and Michael Rothschild, 121–46. Chicago: University of Chicago Press, 1993.

Doermann, Humphrey. *Crosscurrents in College Admissions.* New York: Teachers College Press, Columbia University, 1969.

Dresch, Stephen P. "College Enrollment." In *The Crisis in Higher Education,* ed. Joseph Froomkin, 108–18. New York: The Academy of Political Science, 1983.

Ehrenberg, Ronald G., and Susan H. Murphy. "What Price Diversity? The Death of Need-Based Financial Aid at Selective Private Colleges and Universities?" *Change* (July–August 1993): 64–73.

Farnum, Richard. "Prestige in the Ivy League: Democratization and Discrimination at Penn and Columbia, 1890–1970." In *The High-Status Track: Studies of Elite Schools and Stratification*, eds. Paul William Kingston and Lionel S. Lewis, 75–104. New York: State University of New York Press, 1990.

Frankfort, Roberta. *Collegiate Women.* New York: New York University Press, 1977.

Freeland, Richard M. *Academia's Golden Age: Universities in Massachusetts 1945–1970.* New York: Oxford University Press, 1992.

Freeman, Richard B. *The Overeducated American.* New York: Academic Press, 1976.

Gaines, Gale F. "Merit Scholarships for Star Students: Keeping the Brightest at In-State Colleges." *Southern Regional Education Board* (May 1989).

Gilbert, Joan. "The Liberal Arts College—Is It Really an Endangered Species?" *Change* 27 (September–October 1995): 37–43.

Gilmore, Jeffrey. *Price and Quality in Higher Education.* Washington, DC: Office of Educational Research and Improvement, 1990.

Gladieux, Lawrence E. "The Issue of Equity in College Finance." In *The Crisis in Higher Education,* ed. Joseph Froomkin, 71–83. New York: The Academy of Political Science, 1983.

Gladieux, Lawrence E., and Gwendolyn L. Lewis. *The Federal Government and Higher Education Traditions, Trends, Stakes and Issues.* Washington, DC: The College Board, October 1987.

Griffin, Gail B. "Emancipated Spirits: Women's Education and the American Midwest." *Change* (January–February 1984): 32–40.

Hacker, Andrew. "Affirmative Action: The New Look." Review of *The Case Against the SAT*, by James Crouse and Dale Trusheim. *The New York Review of Books* (12 October 1989): 63–68.

Hansen, W. Lee. "Impact of Student Financial Aid on Access." In *The Crisis in Higher Education*, ed. Joseph Froomkin, 84–96. New York: The Academy of Political Science, 1983.

Harr, Jonathan. "The Admissions Circus." *New England Monthly* (April 1984): 49–58.

Harrington, Paul E., and Andrew M. Sum. "Whatever Happened to the College Enrollment Crisis?" *Academe* (September–October 1988): 17–22.

Havighurst, Robert J. *American Higher Education in the 1960s.* Columbus, OH: Ohio State University Press, 1960.

Hsia, Jayjia, and Marsha Hirano-Nakanishi. "The Demographics of Diversity: Asian Americans and Higher Education." *Change* (November–December 1989): 20–27.

Huff, Robert P. "Need Assessment of Upper-Middle Income Families—Are They Being Excluded?" *College Board Review* 86 (Winter 1972/73): 25–27, back cover.

Jackson, Gregory A. "Financial Aid and Student Enrollment." *Journal of Higher Education* 49 (1978): 548–74.

Jellema, William W. *From Red to Black: The Financial Status of Private Colleges and Universities.* San Francisco: Jossey-Bass, 1973.

Jencks, Christopher, and David Riesman. *The Academic Revolution.* Garden City, NY: Doubleday, 1968.

Jones, Gary L. "Merit Aid Is an Investment for American Leadership." *Change* (September 1984): 24–27.

Karen, David. "The Politics of Class, Race and Gender: Access to Higher Education in the United States, 1960–1986." *American Journal of Education* (February 1991): 208–37.

Katz, Joseph. "Epilogue: The Admissions Process—Society's Stake and the Individual's Interest." In *Hurdles: The Admissions Dilemma in American Higher Education*, eds. Herbert S. Sacks, M.D., and Associates, 318–47. New York: Atheneum, 1978.

Keller, George. *Academic Strategy: The Management Revolution in American Higher Education.* Baltimore: The Johns Hopkins University Press, 1983.

Kendrick, S. A. "The Coming Segregation of Our Selective Colleges." *College Board Review* 66 (Winter 1967/68): 6.

Kluge, P. F. *Alma Mater.* Reading, MA: Addison-Wellesley, 1993.

Kopp, Linda. "States Increase Amount of Student Financial Aid Awarded." *Higher Education and National Affairs, American Council on Education* (25 March 1996).

Kramer, Martin. "A Decade of Growth in Student Assistance." In *The Crisis in Higher Education*, ed. Joseph Froomkin, 61–71. New York: The Academy of Political Science, 1983.

Lewis, Lionel S., and Paul William Kingston. "The Best, the Brightest, and the Most Affluent: Undergraduates at Elite Institutions." *Academe* (November–December 1989): 28–33.

Manski, Charles F., and David A. Wise. *College Choice in America*. Cambridge, MA: Harvard University Press, 1983.

Massa, Robert J. "Merit Scholarships and Student Recruitment: Goals and Strategies." *The Journal of College Admission* (Spring 1991): 10–14.

McCarty, Barry. "No-Need Scholarships." *The College Board Review* (Spring 1978): 38–39.

McKinsey and Company. *Financial Problems of Massachusetts Private Higher Education*, 1969. Report of the Select Committee for the Study of Financial Problems of Private Institutions of Higher Education in the Commonwealth of Massachusetts.

McPherson, Michael S. "The Demand for Higher Education." In *Public Policy and Private Higher Education*, eds. David Breneman and Chester E. Finn, Jr., 143–96. Washington, DC: The Brookings Institution, 1978.

McPherson, Michael S., and Morton Owen Schapiro. *Keeping Colleges Affordable*. Washington, DC: The Brookings Institution, 1991.

McPherson, Michael S., and Morton Owen Schapiro. "Merit Aid: Students, Institutions and Society: Who Wins? Who Loses?" June 1993 draft.

Meyers, Michael. "Black Education at Antioch College." *Youth and Society* 5 (June 1974): 379–96.

Millet, Kate. "Libbies, Smithies, Vassarites." *Change* (September–October 1970): 42–50.

Moll, Richard. "The Scramble to Get the New Class." *Change* (March–April 1994): 11–17.

Muffo, John A. "Market Segmentation in Higher Education: A Case Study." *Journal of Student Financial Aid* 17 (1987): 31–40.

Munro, John U. "Helping the Student Help Himself." *Journal of Student Financial Aid* 24 (1994): 9–16, reprint of May 1953 article in *College Board Review*.

Murphy, Kevin, and Finis Welch. "Wage Premiums for College Graduates: Recent Growth and Possible Explanations." *Educational Researcher* (May 1989): 17–26.

The National Association of College Admissions Counselors. *Executive Summary: 1994 Survey of Admissions Practices*. Alexandria, VA: NACAC, September 1994.

Ohio Board of Regents. *1988 Master Plan for Higher Education. Toward the Year 2000: Higher Education in Transition*. Vol. 1. Columbus, OH: Ohio Board of Regents, 1988.

O'Keefe, Michael. "Private Colleges: Beating the Odds." *Change* (March–April 1989): 11–19.

Owing, Jeffrey, Marilyn McMillen, and John Burkett. "Making the Cut: Who Meets Highly Selective College Entrance Criteria?" National Center for Education Statistics. Washington, DC: U.S. Department of Education, Office of Educational Research and Improvement, April 1995.

Patterson, Franklin, and Charles R. Longsworth. *The Making of a College*. Cambridge, MA: MIT Press, 1966.

Patterson, Gardner. *The Education of Women at Princeton: A Special Report*. Princeton, NJ: Princeton University Press, 24 September1968.

Pearson, Richard. "Liberal Arts Colleges and Universal Higher Education." *The College Board Review* 60 (Summer 1966): 23–26.

Philofsky, Richard. "Cost of the 1973 Spring Strike." Unpublished term paper for Economics of Higher Education, 21 March 1974, Antioch College.

Pifer, Alan. *The Higher Education of Blacks in the United States. Reprint of the Alfred and Winifred Hoernlé Memorial Lecture for 1973.* New York: Carnegie Corporation, 1973.

Platt, Carolyn. "The Winds of Change: Case Studies of College Culture and Decision Making." Ph.D. diss., Stanford University, 1988.

Porter, Betsy A., and Suzanne K. McColloch. "The Use of No-Need Academic Scholarships: A Survey." Report submitted to the National Association of College Admissions Counselors, 22 November 1982.

Porter, Betsy A., and Suzanne K. McColloch. "The Use of No-Need Academic Scholarships: An Update." Report submitted to the National Association of College Admissions Counselors, 1 December 1984.

Pyke, Donald. L. "The Future of Higher Education: Will Private Institutions Disappear in the U.S.?" *The Futurist* (December 1977): 371–74.

Rice, Joy K., and Annette Hemmings. "Women's Colleges and Women Achievers: An Update." In *Reconstructing the Academy: Women's Education and Women's Studies,* eds. Elizabeth Minnich et al., 220–33. Chicago: University of Chicago Press, 1988.

Robinson, Patricia. "A Study of Declining Enrollment Trends in Women's Colleges in America and the Impact on Brenau College." Ph.D. diss., Nova University, May 1990.

Rudolph, Frederick. *The American College and University: A History.* 1962. Reprint with Introductory Essay and Supplemental Bibliography by John R. Thelin. Athens, GA: University of Georgia Press, 1990.

Schmidt, George P. *The Liberal Arts College.* New Brunswick, NJ: Rutgers University Press, 1957.

Sharp, Marcia K. "Women's Colleges and the Women's Movement." *The Education Digest* (February 1992): 18–20.

Solomon, Barbara. *In the Company of Educated Women.* New Haven: Yale University Press, 1985.

Spies, Richard R. *The Effect of Rising Costs on College Choice: The Third in a Series of Studies on This Subject.* Princeton, NJ: Princeton University Press, 1990.

Stanley, Julian C. "Predicting College Success of the Educationally Disadvantaged." *Science* 171 (19 February 1971): 640–46.

Sudarkasa, Niara. "Can We Afford Equity and Excellence? Can We Afford Less?" *Academe* (September–October 1988): 23–26.

Tompkins, Pauline. "What Future for the Women's College?" *Liberal Education* 58 (May 1972): 298–303.

Turner, Sarah E., and William G. Bowen. "Flight from the Arts and Sciences: Trends in Degrees Conferred." *Science* 250 (26 October 1990): 517–21.

U.S. Department of Education, National Center for Education Statistics. *Digest of Education Statistics, 1995.* Washington, DC: U.S. Government Printing Office, 1995.

Wells, Peter. "Applying to College: Bulldog Bibs and Potency Myths." In *Hurdles: The Admissions Dilemma in American Higher Education,* eds. Herbert S. Sacks, M.D., and Associates, 48–75. New York: Atheneum, 1978.

Wenzlau, Thomas E. "The Outlook for Liberal-Arts Colleges." In *The Crisis in Higher Education,* ed. Joseph Froomkin, 1–13. New York: The Academy of Political Science, 1983.

Werth, Barry. "Why Is College So Expensive? Maybe America Wants It That Way." *Change* (March–April 1988): 13–25.

Whitla, Dean. "The Admissions Equation." *Change* (November–December 1984): 20–30.

Whitla, Dean, Irving L. Broudy, and Ann W. Walka. *Candidate Overlap Study.* Cambridge, MA: Harvard College, March 1967.

Williams, Gareth. "The Economic Approach." In *Perspectives on Higher Education,* ed. Burton R. Clark, 79–83. Berkeley: University of California Press, 1984.

Zemsky, Robert. "Consumer Markets and Higher Education." *Liberal Education* (Summer 1993): 14–17.

College Newspapers and Magazines

Amherst College
  Amherst College Bulletin: October 1972
Antioch College
  (Antioch) College and University Bulletin
  The Antioch Record
Hiram College
  Hiram College Magazine: Spring 1992
  The Hiram Broadcaster:
      January 1961, Fall 1964, Winter 1964, Spring–Summer 1977, Winter 1986
Kenyon College
  The Kenyon Observer: November 1991
  The Kenyon Collegian: May 11, 1967; February 14, 1974; November 20, 1975; December 4, 1975
  Kenyon Alumni Bulletin:
      April–June 1965, September 1965, April–June 1966, April–June 1967, March 1987, August 1994, March 1995
Oberlin College
  The (Oberlin) Observer: February 26, 1981; October 15, 1981; October 12, 1989, March 29, 1990
Wellesley College
  Wellesley Alumnae Magazine:
      March 1958, Autumn 1968, Spring 1969, Spring 1972, Autumn 1978, Spring 1982
  REALIA: June 1984, December 1985
Williams College
  Williams Record: March 20, 1964; January 14, 1969
  Williams Alumni Review: August 1968, Fall 1974, Winter 1976, Fall 1986
Other Colleges and Universities
  Colby Alumni Magazine: November 1995

Cornell Alumni Magazine: April 1965
Stanford Observer: Fall 1995, Winter 1995
The Trinity Reporter: September 1995

National Newspapers and Magazines

Barron's: November 27, 1995
The Boston Globe: September 12, 1995; January 26, 1996
Chronicle of Higher Education:
    Febuary 12, 1990; January 3, 1994; April 27, 1994; November 2, 1994; February
    10, 1995; September 22, 1995; May 17, 1996; September 13, 1996
The Cincinnati Enquirer: January 28, 1973
Lawrence Eagle Tribune: September 26, 1995
New York Times:
    December 21, 1969; April 9, 1974; November 13, 1977; March 4, 1980; June 3
    1980; April 25, 1982; May 4, 1982; January 8, 1995; February 14, 1996
Newsweek: January 27, 1967; December 15, 1969; March 30, 1987
Time: October 5, 1987
U.S. News and World Report:
    April 15, 1974; Annual Guide to Colleges: 1983, 1985, 1987, 1988, 1989, 1990,
    1992, 1994, 1995
USA Today: September 10, 1996
Wall Street Journal: April 5, 1995; April 1, 1996
The Washington Post: March 25, 1991

Works Consulted

Anello, Michael, et al. *The People's Colleges: The State College of Massachusetts.*
    Boston: Massachusetts Advisory Council on Education, 1971.
Butler, Robert R., and Dasha E. Little. "No Need Scholarships: Intellectual Integrity and Athletic Arrogance." *The Journal of Student Financial Aid* 18 (Fall
    1988): 21–26
Carnegie Council on Policy Studies in Higher Education. *Three Thousand Futures:
    The Next Twenty Years in Higher Education.* San Francisco: Jossey-Bass, 1980.
Chafee, Ellen Earle. *After Decline, What? Survival Strategies at Eight Private Colleges.* Boulder, CO: National Center for Higher Education Management Systems, 1984.
The College Board. *Update: Trends in Student Aid 1984–1994.* New York, The
    College Board, 1994.
Crawford, Norman C., Jr. "Effects of Offers of Financial Assistance on the College
    Going Decisions of Talented Students with Limited Financial Means." National
    Merit Scholarship Corporation, Vol. 3, 1967.
Doermann, Humphrey. *Toward Equal Access.* New York: College Entrance Examination Board, 1978.

Fuller, Winship C., Charles F. Manski, and David A. Wise. "New Evidence on the Economic Determinants of Post-Secondary Schooling Choices." *The Journal of Human Resources* 17 (1982): 478–95.

Gies, Joseph, ed. *The Liberal Arts College: The Next 25 Years.* A Symposium Sponsored by the Great Lakes Colleges Association and the Associated Colleges of the Midwest, June 1984.

Gillespie, Donald A., and Nancy Carlson. *Trends in Student Aid: 1963–1983.* Washington, DC: The College Board, 1983.

Gladieux, Lawrence E., and Arthur M. Hauptman. *The College Aid Quandary: Access, Quality, and the Federal Role.* Washington, DC: The Brookings Institution, 1995.

Hansen, Janet S. "Student Assistance in Uncertain Times." *Academe* (September–October 1988): 27–31.

Iba, Debra L., Donald E. Simpson, and David W. Stockburger. "The Effectiveness of No-Need Scholarships in Recruiting Students." *College and University* (Spring 1988): 263–72.

Jaffee, A. J., and Walter Adams. "Trends in College Enrollment." *College Board Review* 55 (Winter 1964/65): 27–32.

James, Estelle. "Student Aid and College Attendance: Where Are We Now and Where Do We Go from Here?" *Economics of Education Review* 7 (1988): 1–13.

Jenny, Hans H., and Richard G. Wynn. *The Golden Years.* Wooster, OH: Ford Foundation and College of Wooster, 1970.

Jenny, Hans H., and Richard G. Wynn. *The Turning Point.* Wooster, OH: College of Wooster, 1972.

Kealy, Mary Jo, and Mark L. Rockel. "Merit Scholarships Are No Quick Fix for College Quality." *Economics of Education Review* 7 (1988): 345–55.

Levine, Arthur, ed. *Higher Learning in America: 1980–2000.* Baltimore: The Johns Hopkins University Press, 1983, second printing 1994.

Mayhew, Lewis B. *Surviving the Eighties.* San Francisco: Jossey-Bass, 1979.

McPherson, Michael S. *How Can We Tell if Federal Student Aid Is Working?* Washington DC: The College Board, 1988.

McPherson, Michael S., Morton Owen Schapiro, and Gordon C. Winston. *Paying the Piper: Productivity, Incentives, and Financing in U.S. Higher Education.* Ann Arbor: University of Michigan Press, 1993.

Moore, Robert L., A. H. Studenmund, and Thomas Slobko. "The Effect of the Financial Aid Package on the Choice of a Selective College." *Economics of Education Review* 10 (1991): 311–21.

Oakley, Francis. *Community of Learning: The American College and the Liberal Arts Tradition.* New York: Oxford University Press, 1992.

Pfnister, Allen. "The American Liberal Arts College in the Eighties: Dinosaur or Phoenix?" In *Contexts for Learning: The Major Sectors of American Higher Education.* National Institution of Education in Cooperation with the American Association of Higher Education, 33–48. Washington, DC: U.S. Government Printing Office, 1985.

Riggs, Henry E. "Are Merit Scholarships Threatening the Future of Private Colleges?" *Journal of Student Financial Aid* 24 (1994): 41–45.

Stadtman, Verne A. *Academic Adaptations: Higher Education Prepares for the*

1980s and 1990s. A Report for the Carnegie Council on Policy Studies for Higher Education. San Francisco: Jossey-Bass, 1980.

Wynn, Richard G. *At the Crossroads: A Report on the Financial Condition of the Forty-Eight Liberal Arts Colleges Previously Studied in "The Golden Years," "The Turning Point."* Ann Arbor, MI: Center for the Study of Higher Education, 1974.

Young, Michael E., and Pedro Reyes. "Conceptualizing Enrollment Behavior: The Effect of Student Financial Aid." *The Journal of Student Financial Aid* 17 (Fall 1987): 41–49.

Index